THE ORIGINS OF
THE FEDERAL REPUBLIC

While virtue warms the gen'rous breast,
Here heaven-born Freedom shall reside;
Nor shall the voice of War molest,
  Nor Europe[']s all-aspiring pride:
Here reason shall new laws devise,
  And order from confusion rise.

> —"On the Emigration to America, and
> peopling the Western Country"
> *Kentucky Gazette*, July 19, 1788

THE · ORIGINS
OF · THE
FEDERAL
· REPUBLIC ·

Jurisdictional · Controversies
in · the · United · States
1775–1787

PETER · S. · ONUF

Philadelphia 1983
UNIVERSITY OF PENNSYLVANIA PRESS

Sources of Maps

Map 1. Lester J. Cappon, ed., *Atlas of Early American History: The Revolutionary Era, 1760–1790* (Princeton, 1976), 16–17.

Map 2. Lester J. Cappon, ed., *Atlas of Early American History: The Revolutionary Era, 1760–1790* (Princeton, 1976), 15–16.

Map 3. James Whitelaw's map of Vermont (1796), reprinted as frontispiece of vol. 2 of *State Papers of Vermont* (Bellows Falls, 1922); June 11 and October 21, 1778, and April 5 and June 16, 1781, *Journals and Proceedings of the General Assembly of the State of Vermont* (4 vols., Bellows Falls, 1924–29) (the 4 vols. constitute vol. 3 of *Vermont State Papers*), 1:24, 41–45, 213–14, 242–44.

Map 4. Lester J. Cappon, ed., *Atlas of Early American History: The Revolutionary Era, 1760–1790* (Princeton, 1976), 60; April 23, 1784, and July 13, 1787, Worthington C. Ford, ed., *Journals of the Continental Congress* (34 vols., Washington, D.C., 1904–37), 26:274–79, 32:334–43.

This work was published with the support of
Worcester Polytechnic Institute.

Design by Adrianne Onderdonk Dudden

Library of Congress Cataloging in Publication Data

Onuf, Peter S.
   The origins of the federal republic.

   Includes index.
   1. Federal government—United States—History—
18th century.   2. Political science—United States—
History—18th Century.   I. Title.
JK316.058   1983   321.02'0973   83-3649
ISBN 0-8122-7889-5

Printed in the United States of America

Dedicated to
Nicholas Greenwood Onuf
Christopher Priest Onuf
and to the memory of our sister
Stephanie Onuf

Contents

List of Maps

Acknowledgments

I first became interested in jurisdictional controversies as a graduate student at Johns Hopkins. My mentor, Jack P. Greene, had agreed to help the Atlantic states work up an historic case for their offshore claims. I was hired to investigate the western land cessions. Only through these cessions, we reasoned, could the United States have established a collective title anywhere, to anything. The courts have consistently rejected this narrow interpretation of national jurisdiction, most recently and definitively in *United States* v. *Maine* (1975). But I was persuaded that the history of jurisdictional disputes in the revolutionary era might shed some light on what the founders of the American federal system hoped to accomplish, however the system subsequently has been transformed. This book is the final product of that original question: what was the scope and character of state jurisdiction in the newly independent United States?

Many friends and colleagues have assisted me in the preparation of this manuscript. Jack Greene continues to be an ideal mentor, offering advice and inspiration at regular intervals. At Columbia, Eric McKitrick gave me crucial encouragement and my students provided a sympathetic audience for my developing ideas. Myra Sletson was a valuable research assistant in 1980–81. My good friends, Herbert Sloan and Cathy Mitten, both doctoral students at Columbia, read the entire manuscript with extraordinary care. Richard Ryerson of the William Penn Papers and Fredrika Teute of the Virginia Historical Society carefully reviewed various chapters. I am deeply indebted to James Kettner of the University of California at Berkeley who took an early interest in this project, read chapter drafts closely and critically, and encouraged me to carry on.

A generous grant from Project '87, jointly sponsored by the American Historical Association and the American Political Science Association, enabled me to devote 1979–80 to research for this book. A grant from Worcester Polytechnic Institute helped defray publication costs. Under the leadership of President Edward Cranch, Dean Ray Bolz, and Donald Johnson, head of the Humanities Department, WPI has provided an extraordinarily supportive environment for scholarly development.

Permission to reprint previously published portions of this book is gratefully acknowledged. Parts of chapter 2 appeared in *Political Science Quarterly* (vol. 97 [1982]: 447–59); a part of chapter 4 is taken from *William and Mary Quarterly* (3d ser., vol. 34 [1977]: 353–74); and chapter 6 was published in slightly different form in *Journal of American History* (vol. 67 [1981]: 797–815).

Kristin, Rachel, and Alexandra have sustained a loving interest in the book and its author over many years. I thank them.

Worcester, Massachusetts   PETER S. ONUF
March 1983

Introduction

The drafting and ratification of the Federal Constitution function as the founding myth of the American nation. Contemporaries called the Constitution a "miracle": only God's influence could explain the resolution of bitter conflicts of interest and ideology at the Philadelphia Convention. Subsequent generations have relied less on God and more on the godlike founding fathers to explain the convention's success. The myth survives. Its continuing power is apparent in the exaggerated attention historians pay to the character, ideals, and interests of the founding fathers.

Charles Beard's iconoclastic *Economic Interpretation of the Constitution* (1913) sought to show that the Constitution was "essentially an economic document" designed to promote the interests of a small class of security holders. Still, given the divergent interests of most Americans, the founders' achievement was at least astonishing, if not miraculous. This same sense of wonder at the constitutionalists' success, whether for better or worse, informs much of the historical literature on the Constitution. Beard's followers and critics have revised or overturned his conclusions, but they have continued to subject the protagonists in the constitutional drama—drafters, ratifiers, and voters—to the same scrutiny. These investigations are supposed to explain the alignments for and against the Constitution. To a surprising extent, however, they simply provide occasions for praise or blame: Antifederalists, for instance, were (or were not) de-

fenders of democracy; Federalists were superb democratic politicians, im-
bued with a sense of America's future greatness, or they were disingenuous
aristocrats who sought to reverse the outcome of the Revolution.[1] The heroic, or antiheroic, agency of these actors is assumed, an assumption reinforced by the closeness of ratification votes in key states like Massachusetts
(187–168), New York (30–27), and Virginia (89–79) and by the Federalists' dubious contention that the American people faced an all-or-nothing
choice between anarchy and union. Because voters and convention delegates held the future of America in their hands, we cannot know enough
about them.

Students of the Constitution naturally have tended to overemphasize
the role of the framers and the originality of their thought. From a broader
perspective, there was nothing particularly remarkable about the Federal
Constitution. Many years ago Andrew McLaughlin pointed to the simi-
larities between American federalism under the Constitution and the actual organization of the old British Empire.[2] More recently, Bernard Bailyn
has delineated the extraordinary development of political thought before
the Revolution.[3] The Constitution was a great achievement in practical
politics, but the revolutionary generation had already crossed the crucial
"republican" threshold. By itself, republican ideology could not equip
Americans to deal with all the dilemmas they faced after independence.
Gordon Wood's monumental *Creation of the American Republic, 1776–
1787* (Chapel Hill, N.C., 1969) has helped illuminate this neglected
period. Wood demonstrates that American political thought developed
dynamically during these troubled years. Still, because he paid little attention to the problems of interstate organization, Wood was unable to link
this ideological development and the struggle over the Constitution without lapsing into a confusing analysis of the social forces supposedly struggling for supremacy. Here again, by way of Charles Beard, was the old
myth of the founding fathers.

The present study examines the history of the American state system in
the years before the ratification of the Constitution. It is both a political
history and a history of political ideas. Wood has given us an exhaustive
and authoritative interpretation of what articulate Americans said and
meant during the preconstitutional era. But many important ideas and assumptions, particularly those relating to the organization of the union,
were not fully or coherently articulated. Republican ideology was liberat-
ing for Americans in their struggle against British "tyranny," but it was less
useful in constructing new polities. It was virtually useless in explaining

how sovereign states could be combined in a union with sovereign powers. Ignoring the problem would not make it go away. Even before the revolutionary war was successfully concluded, Americans were forced to confront the vexing issues of how to reconcile state and congressional authority and of how to provide for the interests of the states collectively and of the American people in general. These concerns reduced to two related questions: What did Americans mean by "state"? and What did Americans mean by "union"?

It is not even now clear where the boundaries of state and national authority are located, though the subject has absorbed the attention of generations of scholars and practitioners. The preconstitutional origins of the relationship and of ideas about it are still more obscure. They will not be discovered in conventional literary sources. The design of this book is to look for the meaning of statehood in the history of states actually attempting to define their jurisdictions against each other and in relation to the central government. These often implicit working understandings of the limits of state authority also suggested conceptions of the union.

All states—landed or landless, large or small, old or new—looked to the states collectively in Congress to recognize and uphold their claims. At the beginning of the Revolution, many observers lamented the prevalence of interstate conflict, fearing that it would impede cooperation in the common cause. Paradoxically, however, it was this chronic and pervasive conflict, combined with the unwillingness of Americans to go to war with each other on behalf of state claims, that provided an important impetus toward enlarging the scope of federal authority.

Part One of this book discusses the development of American concepts of statehood and union, as they were revealed in the history of jurisdictional conflict within and among the states.

Part Two examines the jurisdictional travails of three important states—Pennsylvania, Virginia, and New York—with different kinds of territorial claims and thus with different concepts of statehood. In each case, state authorities discovered that jurisdiction was vulnerable not only to other states but also to the pretensions of unruly citizens. Pennsylvania struggled to establish its jurisdiction over Connecticut settlers in the Wyoming Valley long after a Confederation court upheld its claims there; Virginia was compelled to relinquish its trans-Ohio claims and to make provisions for the independence of the Kentucky District; and the northeastern counties of New York split off to form the unauthorized state of Vermont. Even these "big" states were not truly autonomous, self-sufficient polities; they relied on each other and on a higher authority to guarantee their claims, and they all had to adapt their jurisdiction to the political ambitions and property claims of settlers whose loyalty was contingent at best. The case of Vermont (Chapter 6), an independent state outside the American union, illuminates the diminishing character of statehood claims throughout America. Vermont's leaders were unable to establish broad popular support for their regime and were driven to negotiate, openly and covertly, for the protection and recognition of the United States or of the supposed British enemy.

Part Three considers the connections between jurisdictional issues and national constitutional reform. The development of provisions for territorial government and the creation of new states best reveals the implicit notions of statehood and union that emerged full-blown in the debate over the Federal Constitution. The new states envisaged in the 1784 and 1787 ordinances were clearly subordinate to Congress; the careful demarcation of new state boundaries *before* settlement was supposed to prevent the territorial disputes that continued to embroil the original states; most public lands were to remain national property even after the attainment of statehood. These new states would not be able to make the same jurisdictional and property claims as the old states; the reconception of the union implicit in the ordinances—with a broad jurisdiction over interstate controversies, public lands, and subordinate territorial governments—also stood in striking contrast to the existing union.

The problem with American governments, on all levels, was that they did not inspire confidence or loyalty. The states were not effective polities; the union was not a polity at all. The crisis that precipitated the movement for constitutional reform was the result of a generally recognized discrepancy between conventional ideas about what made governments legitmate and the way American governments actually functioned; the discrepancy became apparent in the "critical period," when many Americans began to draw connections among various and hitherto unconnected problems confronting the states. The weakness of the United States in international politics was increasingly apparent; Americans began to fear that their states were vulnerable to British counterrevolution in discontented frontier regions. The inability of the states to maintain jurisdiction over frontier separatists and other malcontents underscored the weaknesses of the component parts of the American state system and of the system as a whole. Growing awareness of divergent state and sectional interests led pessimists to doubt the desirability as well as the durability of the union itself.

How did Americans respond to the "critical period" once, and if, they recognized its existence? The conventional political wisdom of the day was not particularly useful, except in a negative way: simply to think systematically about American politics would convince most Americans that the United States could not survive. But to reconceive the American state system, Americans had to articulate and institutionalize new ideas, ideas that had developed over the previous decade but that had remained largely implicit and unarticulated. Federalist proponents of the Constitution fashioned these strands into a coherent system that rationalized and legitimized the hitherto hidden logic of American politics.

The origins of the American federal republic are not to be discovered in the interests and ambitions of reformers alone. Federalists articulated a conception of the union which Americans were prepared to accept and embrace. The power of the Federalist persuasion was therefore not to be found in its originality. American concepts of statehood and union were the product of long and often painful experience with the problems of federal organization. The origins of American federalism are thus to be found in the history of the American state system.

PART · ONE

THE · EARLY · AMERICAN · STATE · SYSTEM

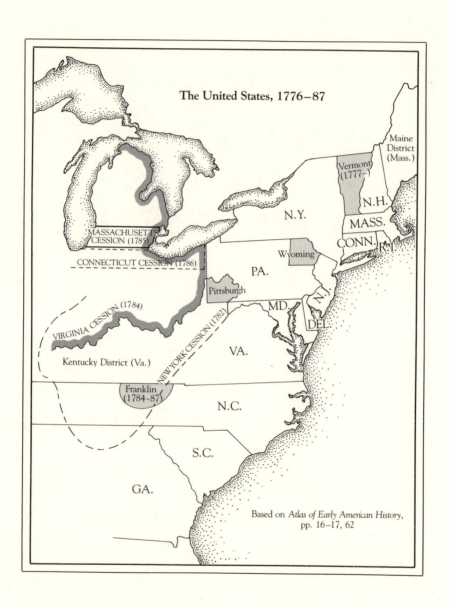

The United States, 1776–87

Maine District (Mass.)

Vermont (1777–

N.H.

MASS.

CONN.

R.I.

N.Y.

Wyoming

MASSACHUSETTS CESSION (1785)

CONNECTICUT CESSION (1786)

PA.

Pittsburgh

N.J.

MD.

DEL.

VIRGINIA CESSION (1784)

NEW YORK CESSION (1782)

VA.

Kentucky District (Va.)

Franklin (1784–87)

N.C.

S.C.

GA.

Based on *Atlas of Early American History*, pp. 16–17, 62

· 1 ·

Congress and the States: Conflict Resolution in the New Nation

The early constitutional history of the United States was shaped by jurisdictional struggles within and among the states. Territorial controversies continually threatened to undermine the war effort. Large states—and some small ones too—were beleaguered by separatists who jeopardized their contributions to the common cause. The Articles of Confederation were not adopted until 1781 because of seemingly intractable differences over control of the western lands. Despite these portents, the United States did not collapse. Indeed, the territorial controversies illuminated the limits of state power in early American thought and practice. The American states did not behave as independent sovereignties were expected to behave: they did not act like true states.

The "imbecility" of the union more than matched that of the states. But jurisdictional confusion created a mandate for a stronger central government. Large states sought recognition and guarantees for their claims; small states sought to circumscribe their large neighbors; frontiersmen sought to divide the large states and establish new states more responsive to their needs. All these pressures promoted the expansion of congressional power: to guarantee boundaries, to administer the national domain created by state land cessions, and to supervise the formation of new western states. This expansion of congressional power was possible because Americans believed that there should be a superintending authority with jurisdiction over the states—even though the Confederation Congress usually fell far short of the mark.

Pessimistic observers feared—or hoped—that intercolonial conflicts over territory would undermine resistance to Britain; independence would free each colony to pursue its particular interests at the expense of the others and at the risk of general destruction.[1] "What would be the Consequence," John Randolph asked in 1774, "if *Great Britain* had not a directive Power" over colonies with conflicting interests? "The heat of one, and obstinacy of the other, before they could have time for reflection, might precipitate them into hostilities, and end in the debility, perhaps the destruction of both."[2] The only way to forestall the calamity, short of submission to British authority, was to create a strong central government to succeed the Empire and guarantee harmony among the colonies. Proponents of national constitutional reform made the same argument. Interstate warfare and rebellions against state authority were inevitable without the institution of a more powerful national government.[3]

Nationalists naturally emphasized the defective organization of the central government. They assumed that the only effective limitations on state action were imposed by higher authority. Without such limitations, the American states would be like other states, free to use any means to secure their own interests. This latent statehood had been held in check in the Empire. Boundary disputes had been adjudicated before Privy Council.[4] Colonial Americans generally had not cared where provincial boundary lines ran, provided their own property was not affected. Up to the eve of the Revolution, the Crown's right to make new colonies out of old ones had not been challenged. But the independent American states were determined to maintain territorial integrity and control over their own public lands. This aggressive posture, combined with the weakness of the American Congress, was supposed to result in a state of war—the potential for armed conflict over controversial claims. According to this logic, peace could be maintained only by the establishment of a strong central government.

The overthrow of British authority in America did lead to pervasive interstate conflict, but this conflict did not become violent. Nor were many casualties reported in state actions against domestic insurgents, despite the fact that rebels in several states succeeded in shutting down courts—through which jurisdiction was exercised—and in some cases actually set up their own governments. These jurisdictional controversies were drawn out precisely because in most cases they could not be resolved by military means. During the war years, state leaders claimed that they would not jeopardize the common cause by taking up arms against other Americans, whatever the provocation. But the states' "usual animosities and jealousies will return with an elastic force" in the postwar period, according to a British prediction.[5] "Disputes will arise among them, quarrels, contentions, open hostilities." Postwar America would be like a tinderbox: "the flames of war breaking out in one point will stop, God knows where."[6] When the time came, however, nobody was prepared to fight in any of the many predicted wars. "The general voice reechoes against bloodshedding," a correspondent reported from New York.[7] "Talk not . . . of a *civil war*," exclaimed a Maine separatist; "the idea harrows up my soul!"[8] Congress was too notoriously impotent to impose peace on the states. The states did not go to war with each other because they could not effectively command the loyalties and resources of their citizens. Thomas Jefferson suggested, "Our citizens can never be induced, either as militia or as souldiers . . . to cut the throats of their own brothers & sons."[9] The American states could never live up to the dire predictions of their bloody demise because, however willing, they were unable to act like true states.

Fears of imminent anarchy and bloodshed were vitally important in creating a climate favorable to constitutional reform. Had the states been able to pursue their interests aggressively, there would have been no hope for the union. The very fact that such fears were unfounded demonstrated the defective and diminutive character of early American state power that permitted the institution of a stronger central government.

Interstate conflict was limited by the unwillingness and inability of the states to resort to violence to enforce their claims. The anomalous character of the American states, and disagreements about what kind of territorial jurisdiction was incidental to statehood, encouraged land companies, separatists, and Congress itself as well as other states to challenge a particular state's claims. The legal and political standing of the protagonists was therefore often as much at issue as their conflicting claims. Few jurisdictional conflicts found one state directly challenging another, even though Congress repeatedly insisted on the territorial monopoly of the thirteen states: all land in the United States was located in one state or another.[10] Even where states that recognized each other's right to make claims confronted one another in a jurisdictional dispute, settlers and speculators were potential protagonists with distinctive interests and claims.[11] Interstate conflict thus sponsored a proliferation of different kinds of claims that made it difficult to decide who was involved and on what basis, much less to determine questions of right.

The difficulty of defining jurisdictional disputes so that they could be adjudicated was compounded by the ambiguous role of Congress, the presumptive judge. Congress did not always stand above these conflicts; for instance, it had interests of its own in the western lands. While the Articles of Confederation remained unratified (because of the western lands controversy) Congress generally declined to interfere in jurisdictional disputes. Though Article IX subsequently offered a procedure for settling conflicts, it was so complicated that only one case, *Connecticut v. Pennsylvania* (1782), was ever resolved under its provisions. Well might Henry Knox, writing at the time of Shays's Rebellion, indict the American state system:

> The powers of Congress are utterly inadequate to preserve the balance between the respective states. Not only is State against State, and all against the Federal Head, but the States within themselves, possess the name only without having the essential concomitant of government, the power of preserving the peace.[12]

But it was easy to exaggerate the impact of popular discontent and to impute it to "imbecilic" government.[13] The success of the American state system—in avoiding interstate warfare and in containing popular discontent—was less conspicuous, because it defied conventional logic. Defects in state power were integral to this success. The combination of limited state power, a general acceptance of a congressional jurisdiction that was rarely invoked, and the actual resolution of disputes by continuing negotiations between or among states and between states and their citizens guaranteed the survival of the American state system.

As former British colonies accustomed to submitting their disputes to imperial arbitration, the states tended to look on their claims as legal rights, provable in the appropriate court. According to Samuel Huntington of Connecticut, "the Question of [territorial] Right must be determined by the Principles of common Law."[14] In one sense, such a formulation lifted "rights" above the level of mere assertion to a status that others (including the court, as well as counterclaimants) were bound to respect. This notion of right had been particularly useful during the Imperial Crisis, when the colonists hoped to convince the British that they were violating their own constitution and breaking their own laws. At the same time, however, this legalistic approach reinforced a diminutive concept of statehood and state rights, because it assumed that there was, or ought to be, some higher superintending authority with jurisdiction over interstate conflicts. The fact that the British government disqualified itself for this role did not mean that the role ceased to exist. Even when states insisted that their sovereign rights were nonjusticiable, because they were essential for the states' very existence, they depended on the United States to recognize and enforce them. In other words, state sovereignty was identified not with the will to make and enforce claims but with claims that could be made by right, and that should be upheld by all the states, individually and collectively.

Congress had a mandate to adjudicate interstate conflicts and to guarantee state rights that was broader than the specific charter of powers delegated by the states in the Articles of Confederation. Indeed, prior to Maryland's ratification of the Articles in 1781, Congress had no constitutional standing at all. But there were other, informal sources of congressional authority. Many Americans simply assumed that Congress had succeeded to the authority of the British Crown. This assumption was reinforced by the popular notion that the American people collectively, under the direction of Congress, had overthrown King George III when he had betrayed his trust. Therefore the states were supposed to defer to Congress and to the common revolutionary war effort.[15] Congress also accumulated powers in an ad hoc fashion, as it responded to contingencies: the goals of the Revolution legitimated the means Congress employed to achieve them.[16] This informal constitution was enough to sustain Congress through most of the war. Whatever its constitutional defects, the states behaved as if Congress had a superintending jurisdiction, even when it failed to intervene, or intervened ineffectively, in their disputes. The only alternative, aggressive diplomacy with warfare as the ultimate sanction, was unacceptable.

Constitutional reformers exploited the disjunction between Congress's formally delegated powers and what it was actually expected to do. Many Americans believed that Congress represented the American people as a whole, but congressional delegates were sent by the states, often under binding instructions, to promote state interests. The reformers asserted that the United States could not survive this fundamental failure of political logic, the failure to recognize that the United States itself was, at least for certain purposes, a state. As one commentator stated, "The people of America have mistaken the meaning of the word *sovereignty*: hence each state pretends to be sovereign. In Europe it is applied only to those states which possess the power of making war and peace."[17] The United States alone could claim such sovereignty, but exaggerated state claims rendered it ineffective at best. Yet if, according to this view, the state of the union was critical, in fact the United States under the Confederation succeeded in avoiding violent conflict among its members, without a central government with coercive powers to enforce collective security. The history of the American state system prior to the adoption of the Federal Constitution shows how constitutional reform could seem imperative, according to conventional logic, even while the system worked, ambiguities and inner contradictions notwithstanding.

Strategies for dealing with interstate conflict emerged in piecemeal fashion. Judicious procrastination was often the most effective response, as the passing years demonstrated. Given the unwillingness of the states to make war on each other, delays encouraged the protagonists to work out peaceful solutions of their own, or to agree to postponements until a more propitious time. The belief that there was an ultimate appeal to Congress predisposed states to negotiate in good faith.

But in 1776 many observers could not foresee the possibility of the peaceful adjustment of conflicts. Carter Braxton of Virginia pointed to several sources of trouble: Connecticut had sent out "eight hundred Men in Arms" to enforce its claims in the Wyoming Valley, causing "heartburning & Jealousy between these People"; "New York is not without her Fears & Apprehensions from the Temper of her Neighbors," and "even Virginia is not free from Claims on Pennsylvania nor Maryland from those on Virginia."[18] Incredible to Braxton, "some are for lugging us into independence . . . without any adjustment of their disputes." Clearly "all disputes must be healed & Harmony prevail" before the colonies declared themselves independent. To guarantee that harmony, "a grand continental league must be formed." As Braxton advised in his *Address to the Convention of Virginia*, Congress should "have power to adjust disputes between Colonies, regulate the affairs of trade, war, peace, alliances, &c."[19]

The potential for intercolonial conflict was certainly great. The aggressive western policy of Virginia's governor, Lord Dunmore, had precipitated a struggle for jurisdiction and scattered violence in the Fort Pitt region. "The uncertainty of the Boundaries between Virginia and Penn-[sylvani]a is the Cause of Great uneasiness," stated one report.[20] Meanwhile, in the Wyoming Valley, settlers and speculators from Connecticut sought to defend their titles under the Susquehannah Company against

Pennsylvania and its claimants. Both sides threatened to use force. Separatists in western Virginia and northeastern New York threatened to dismember two of the most important colonies even as they prepared to withdraw from the British Empire.[21]

According to a congressional committee on the Wyoming controversy, "the most perfect Union between all the colonies, is essentially necessary for the preservation of the just rights of North America."[22] But Congress was not prepared to intervene, even though such controversies tended "to weaken the Union of the Colonies at the present alarming Crisis."[23] Instead, the delegates called on would-be protagonists to lay aside "all animosities, which have heretofore subsisted among you as inhabitants of distinct colonies" in order to cooperate in seeking the "preservation of every thing that can make our common country dear to us."[24] The Wyoming people were to "live together in peace & Good Order," leaving the question of which state they belonged to until after the war.[25]

Americans were reluctant to acknowledge real differences among themselves. Many agreed with Silas Deane that "Artful Enemies to the general cause of America" were at work in Wyoming and elsewhere, "blowing up the Flame, in hopes of breaking the general Union."[26] Thomas Smith believed that the conflict between Virginia and Pennsylvania was "set on foot by a designing tool . . . in order to set the Colonies at variance with one another."[27] Patriotic Americans were asked to wait until the war was over to settle their differences, and these, once the British were beaten, could hardly be serious. Just as the Revolution was supposed to free American virtue from British corruption, it would enable the new states to overcome the contentiousness that afflicted their colonial predecessors in the Empire. By such logic it was possible to turn Carter Braxton on his head: intercolonial conflict was an effect of the imperial connection that could only be removed by independence.

But if Americans were able to explain away the causes of interstate conflict, they could not ignore it. Americans were predisposed, for good reason, to doubt each other's loyalty. Enemies to the common cause would soon show their true colors and take advantage of this "time of distress" to promote their own interests. Yorkers and Yankees in the New Hampshire Grants eagerly impugned one another's patriotism.[28] Pennsylvanians feared "that part of the forces [being] raised in Connecticut" would be deployed in Wyoming.[29] Pennsylvania titleholders would not lie supine in the face of repeated aggressions. Deane reported that "the most opulent inhabitants" of Philadelphia were raising a private army to march into

Wyoming.[30] There was an "immediate danger of Hostilities . . . on the Susquehannah," Richard Smith confided in his diary.[31] Pennsylvanians were also convinced that Virginia troops sent to garrison Fort Pitt represented a gross violation of the truce there. "The dispute must end in open violence," warned Arthur St. Clair.[32]

Paradoxically, these exaggerated fears helped normalize interstate relations. When it became clear that there was no immediate danger of warfare between Connecticut and Pennsylvania, or between Pennsylvania and Virginia, or between New York and its refractory citizens in the New Hampshire Grants, it became possible to reconsider Congress's role. In 1775 there was pressure for immediate intervention to resolve jurisdictional confusion: Congress should decide who belonged to which state. "We must have an umpire," said Thomas Willing of Pennsylvania.[33] Confrontation politics in Congress, backed by threats of imminent "bloodshed" and other "dangerous consequences," made congressional intervention seem imperative.[34] But every substantive proposal for congressional action aroused immediate opposition. The Connecticut delegates objected violently when their Pennsylvania counterparts asked that jurisdiction in Wyoming be awarded to their state, "she agreeing . . . that private property shall not be affected." For their part, the delegates from Pennsylvania were "very angry and discontented" at a proposed truce which they thought would strengthen Connecticut's claim.[35] The proposal sounded too much like Connecticut's call for a "temporary line" between the two states, preserving its jurisdiction until a full adjudication was possible.[36] The Pennsylvanians, however, did not hesitate to advocate a similar "temporary line" with Virginia which would strengthen its own hold on the Fort Pitt region in the same way.[37]

The Wyoming controversy demonstrated that Congress would have little freedom to act without raising suspicions of its own motives. As a result, it sought to establish its own legitimacy by following procedures that would render its ultimate decisions unexceptionable. Provisions in the Articles of Confederation for resolving disputes were the upshot of this procedural elaboration. Congress would have to depoliticize its interventions—it would have to act like a court—in order to overcome objections by protagonists. The naming of a committee on the Wyoming dispute to "hear evidence on the possession and jurisdiction of the lands in dispute" attested to an early awareness of this fact, though resolution of the conflict was still years away.[38] It was more important for Congress to arrive at the right kind of decision, according to recognized procedures, than to take quick action, as it was first pressed to do.

The need for a full adjudication reflected apparently intractable differences and mutual suspicions between the conflicting parties. But it also reduced the scope of their disagreement. While a decision was pending (and Article IX proceedings on Wyoming could not even begin until after the Articles were ratified in 1781), Connecticut and Pennsylvania had to cooperate with each other as if they had no conflict. This ability to distinguish areas of conflict from areas of common interest made it possible to think that territorial controversies were justiciable and that an adverse decision was not necessarily an assault on state sovereignty. In practical terms, this meant that territorial disputes could be protracted indefinitely without the dangerous consequences many had predicted. Indeed, if there was any doubt about how a state might react to an adverse decision, it made sense to put off the decision until after the war.

Delays helped reduce the scope and impact of interstate conflicts. Inevitably, they also had important effects on the ultimate settlement of these disputes. Temporary arrangements, such as the extension of the Mason-Dixon line to Pennsylvania's western limits as an interim boundary with Virginia, had a way of becoming permanent. The passage of time also enabled the Vermonters to strengthen their new state enough to defy Congress as well as New York.[39] The Connecticut settlers in the Wyoming Valley added new recruits and continued to manage their own affairs in defiance of Pennsylvania. Confusion about the status of the western lands encouraged settlers to defy state authority and plan their own new states. The effect in every case was to strengthen the position of the actual settlers in defending their interests. The states had limited coercive resources, and the United States collectively were unwilling and unable to deploy their might to secure state boundaries or put down new state movements, particularly when the rights of different claimants remained undetermined. Settlers therefore had leverage over states that claimed them as citizens. It was in their power to nullify state authority and, as the Connecticut River towns demonstrated, to survive unconnected with any state at all.[40] Consequently, settlers in these areas were able to bargain, more or less effectively, for confirmation of their property titles, military protection, and the benefits of civil government—all at considerable expense to the claiming states.

The interests of affected populations complicated the straightforward resolution of claims controversies between or among states. At the same time, however, frontier discontent was channeled into the same continuing processes of negotiation and adjudication that marked the limits of interstate conflict. As a revealing counterinstance, the failure of the United

States to discover some practicable mode for dealing with Vermont, toward the end of the war, showed how easily the political aspirations of frontier settlers could be deflected into outright treason. But most frontier people, including most Vermonters most of the time, considered themselves patriotic Americans, even as they defied state authority. The reluctance of Congress to interfere, except in a quasi-judicial capacity, made it possible for them to define and defend their interests and to participate directly or indirectly in jurisdictional settlements.

During its first sessions, Congress prepared the way for a more authoritative successor, capable of dealing with interstate conflict. In the meantime, it did not attempt to impose instant political solutions on hopelessly complex jurisdictional controversies. While contention itself was stigmatized as unpatriotic, no one was alienated from the revolutionary coalition by an unfavorable decision on territorial claims. Everyone was encouraged "to cultivate harmony, to consider themselves as jointly interested in the event of the American cause," regardless of animosities inherited from the colonial era.[41] Congress did not forfeit its own prestige by reaching a decision that was bound to favor one state or another (thus legitimating the aggressive pursuit of state interest) and that was unenforceable in any case. Dangerous situations were contained and defused by appeals to Congress. While pessimists doubted that the United States would survive its jurisdictional controversies, the protagonists in these disputes demonstrated that they could put aside their differences while joining in the common cause.

Early American political thought was absorbed in drafting new state constitutions. There was relatively little concern about the precise nature of congressional power. The Articles of Confederation were drafted and finally ratified long after Congress had begun meeting, and this constitutionally anomalous situation did not appear to hamper its operations. (Ratification might never have taken place, in fact, had the Americans not been compelled to prove to foreign powers that the states were capable of organizing effectively and therefore deserved assistance.) Congress was supposed to exercise whatever powers were necessary to guarantee the survival of all the states against the common enemy and to secure the legitimate claims of one state against another. There was little debate over how Congress was constituted as long as Congress was conceived in these terms. "We have heard much of the Continental Constitution," John Adams wrote, but he saw "no occasion for any But a Congress."[42] Only a few lines of his *Thoughts on Government* were devoted to this question. Congress's powers and the legitimacy of its authority would be more closely scrutinized only when the United States itself was seen as a kind of state with interests of its own, possibly opposed to the interests of particular states.

Americans were much more concerned about the relative size and strength of the confederating states than with defining the powers of Congress. The crucial question at first was the willingness of the states to recognize and guarantee each other's territorial claims. Ratification of the Articles without prior boundary negotiations would fix the existing unequal distribution of territory among the states. "It would not be safe" for the small states to confirm the large, landed states (particularly Virginia) in their extensive charter claims, said Samuel Chase of Maryland.[43] "It would be destructive to her [Virginia's] sisters and to herself." The problem, Noah Webster later argued, was that

> the boundaries of the several states were not drawn with a view to independence; and while this country was subject to Great Britain, they produced no commercial or political inconveniences. But the revolution has placed things on a different footing. The advantages of some states, and the disadvantages of others are so great—and . . . materially affect the business and interest of each.[44]

Yet since the beginning of the Imperial Crisis, colonies like Virginia had based their claims to autonomy, and then to independence, on their colonial charters; charter claims thus became associated with pretensions to sovereignty. As a result, demands for renegotiated boundaries hardened the resolve of the landed states to insist on their extended claims, as a test of state sovereignty.

Even the landed states agreed, however, that Congress would have to play a significant role in setting and securing state boundaries. As Benjamin Rush pointed out, "We are dependent on each other—not totally independent States."[45] The large states depended on the willingness of the smaller states to support their claims. Because charter claims were often mutually inconsistent, the territorial right of a particular state could not be presupposed. The large states were therefore interested in establishing a superintending authority that could determine what their rights actually were, and then enforce them.

There was little disagreement in theory about what Congress should do. John Adams's prescription was typical. He thought that Congress's authority "should sacredly be confined to . . . war, trade, disputes between Colony and Colony, the Post-Office, and the unappropriated lands of the Crown."[46] There was heated controversy over how Congress should go about acquiring a national domain, but its power to administer public lands, once they were acquired, was rarely questioned—even though the Articles made no provision for it. Congressional superintendence over the states was understood to be the sine qua non of union. Every state depended on the guarantees of state rights written into the Confederation. But landless and landed states alike resisted leaving the determination of western claims to future adjudication. The landless states sought to curtail western claims as a condition of their joining the union; the landed states were determined to preclude any claim by the landless states or the land companies, through Congress, before they submitted to having their own overlapping claims sorted out. The western lands controversy thus became inextricably bound up with the terms of union itself. The settlement of state western boundaries was a special category of interstate conflict that had to be resolved by extrajudicial means and, if the landless states could have their way, before any territorial guarantees became operative.

Congressional debates over the Articles in 1776 emphasized the connection between the prior settlement of contested boundaries and territorial guarantees. According to the first printed version of the Dickinson draft, entered in the journal on July 12, "When the Boundaries of any Colony shall be ascertained by Agreement" or by adjudication, "all the other Colonies shall guarantee to such Colony the full and peaceable Possession of, and the free and entire Jurisdiction in and over the Territory included within such Boundaries" (Art. XV). Another proposed article (XVIII in this draft) provided for "Limiting the Bounds of those Colonies, which by Charter or Proclamation, or under any Pretence, are said to extend to the South Sea, and ascertaining those Bounds of any other Colony that appear to be indeterminate."[47] In support of this proposal, Samuel Chase asserted that no "Colony has a Right, to go to the South Sea."[48] There could be no confederation among states of such unequal size, particularly since extensive claims were untenable without the support of all the states. Chase's colleague, Thomas Stone, insisted that "the small Colonies . . . would have no safety if the great Colonies were not limited." "Pennsylvania has no right to interfere in those claims," James Wilson conceded, "but she has a Right to say that she will not confederate unless those Claims are cut off."

The solution to this impasse was already at hand. Wilson hoped "the

Colonies themselves would cutt off those Claims." Speaking for Virginia, Jefferson had "no doubt that the Colonies will limit themselves." Samuel Huntington of Connecticut did not "doubt . . . the Wisdom of Virginia will limit themselves," and this intention was announced in the first state constitution.[49] Jefferson was anxious only to be assured that "Congress will not curtail the present Settlements of the States."[50] Connecticut's Roger Sherman agreed that "the Bounds ought to be settled," though he thought the Articles should explicitly provide that "no Lands [are] to be seperated from any State, which are already settled, or become private Property."[51]

This promising dialogue, anticipating the western land cessions that finally resolved the issue, was subverted by the pervasive mistrust that characterized early relations among the states in Congress. The landless states had no guarantee that the landed states would limit themselves. Therefore they withheld their approval of the Articles, offering amendments that would establish a collective American title in the West without waiting for the states to relinquish their claims. The landed states naturally interpreted such proposals as challenges to the sanctity of charter rights. "We all unite against mutilating Charters," Huntington insisted. Benjamin Harrison of Virginia wondered "how came Maryland by its Land, but by its Charter?" He warned, "Gentlemen shall not pare away the Colony of Virginia." Huntington argued, "A Mans Right does not cease to be a Right because it is large," and neither did a colony's. The landed states would not permit Congress simply to proclaim away their rights and to become a claimant itself. If Congress should claim territory on its own behalf, no state could be secure in its own claims.

While the Articles remained unratified, different states entertained varying notions of what Congress's role should be in regard to specific territorial claims. Attempts by landless states to circumscribe landed state claims through Congress raised the specter of a dangerous concentration of power in the central government. These fears showed how easily Congress's quasi-judicial superintending role could be compromised. Obviously justiciable conflicts between states shaded off into fundamental constitutional questions of what kind of claims, within what limits, the states would agree to recognize. There had to be a prior understanding about what could be adjudicated and therefore guaranteed. The question of how this agreement would be reached—the main issue in the western lands controversy—led to the broader question of the ultimate source of authority in the new nation. Who would establish the rules of the game? The logical answer, if the issue was pressed, was that the states were the constituent power. But this logic was at odds with the expectations of the American people, and of the states themselves, about the kind of authority Congress should exercise.

Americans found it difficult to conceptualize Congress, even if its necessary powers, abstractly considered, seemed self-evident. The new state constitutions preempted the parliamentary model for their own sovereign legislatures.[52] In any case, congressional powers more closely resembled the mixture of executive and judicial functions exercised by the British Crown. Proponents of expanded congressional power often made this connection explicitly, arguing, for instance, that Congress succeeded to jurisdiction over Crown lands in America.[53] Such thinking was also reflected in proposals to establish a "continental majesty" that would have the power to settle "all Disputes about Land, that is about Boundaries of Colonies."[54] The monarchical model was attractive because Americans had developed a radically diminished idea of the royal prerogative during the Imperial Crisis, reconcilable with the legislative pretensions of little colonial "parliaments." The American people were accustomed to monarchy, and it was easy to imagine Congress as successor to George III.

But there were problems with the monarchical model in a land of dedicated republicans. Even if American concepts of sovereignty derived from their interpretation of royal authority, Congress was not the only or the most likely successor. According to the American idea of kingship, the sovereign was identified with, and inseparable from, the community he governed; he was reduced to the status of a glorified public servant.[55] These colonial communities were succeeded by the new states created by the sovereign people. Congressmen represented the sovereign states. State supremacy was apparent in the equality of state votes and in the ability of a single state to veto any proposed change in the Confederation—or to prevent it from being adopted in the first place. As finally adopted, the Articles stipulated that "each state retains its sovereignty, freedom and independence, and every Power, Jurisdiction and right, which is not by this confederation expressly delegated to the United States, in Congress assembled."[56] This delegation was by the states themselves. Consequently, there was a tension between the role Congress was supposed to play and the way it was constituted, a tension that was particularly apparent in its jurisdiction over interstate conflicts.

Paradoxically, the states were most conscious of their sovereign rights, and of their supremacy over Congress, precisely when Congress was supposed to exercise the jurisdiction over interstate conflict that they all endorsed in theory. At such times, Congress was seen not as successor to the king but rather as an ad hoc combination of sovereign states with disparate interests. When Congress's judicial role was put into practice, its political character became most apparent. Congressional authority over interstate conflict was a scarce resource that easily could be squandered. Awareness of this fact resulted in different approaches, all cautious, to different kinds of conflict.

Interstate conflicts were resolved in several ways, most after long delays. First, the great controversy over state claims in the unsettled western lands was settled by their cession to Congress. Congress served as intermediary and was the ultimate beneficiary, but it did not take a leading role in what were, in fact, political transactions among the states. Second, in the sole instance of *Connecticut v. Pennsylvania*, conflicting state claims actually were adjudicated according to the Articles of Confederation. This was the only case in which Congress, through a special court set up under its auspices, fully performed its anticipated superintending role. Finally, and much more frequently, states resolved their differences through bilateral negotiations, sometimes after initiating actions under the Articles. The negotiation between Virginia and its citizens in Kentucky, leading to statehood for the district, may be included in this category. Vermont's separation from New York was the only important jurisdictional issue that was not settled by adjudication or negotiation, or, as in the case of other separatist movements, by the successful assertion of state authority.

The western lands controversy could not be adjudicated because its outcome was so crucial to the constitution of the American state system. The completion of the Virginia cession in 1784, finally breaking the claims impasse, freed Congress from having to reach controversial decisions that would have favored one state or group of states over the other. Cessions allowed suspicions to dissipate at the same time that they created a national domain, giving substance to the idea that there was a common American interest that transcended state interests.

The completion of the western land cessions constituted a substantive amendment of the Articles of Confederation and reinforced the tendency of the states to seek peaceful solutions to conflicts. By relying on state initiatives, rather than on direct congressional action, it was possible to achieve a massive renegotiation of state boundaries without jeopardizing congressional authority. The landless states had encouraged Congress to disregard state claims and assert its own title, which arguably was as "good" as state claims based on charter. But this campaign was bound to fail. By acting on its own behalf, Congress, as an interested party, would have forfeited its disinterested, superintending role; the Articles made no provision for adjudicating issues between the states collectively and an individual state. Any decision reached by a vote of the states in Congress, at the expense of one of the states, was obviously political. Such a decision would extinguish a state's claims without a hearing, thus presenting a fundamental challenge to its sovereignty. But the cessions solution preserved Congress's legitimacy as a disinterested tribunal while recognizing the standing of the ceding states: their right to maintain and then relinquish claims in the West.

The renegotiation of state boundaries through western land cessions continued long after the Articles were ratified in 1781, notwithstanding the small states' anxieties that the landed states would invoke guarantees in the Articles to secure the jurisdictional status quo. Contrary to these expectations, delays did not result in the consolidation of state claims or in an escalation of interstate conflict leading to the reduction of the small states. All the interested parties—the claiming states, the landless states, and Congress—needed a compromise solution that was beyond the scope of the Articles. The large states faced difficulties in governing their extended claims, and the small states remained insecure as long as they retained them. Collectively, the states were interested in securing a national domain, and this common interest worked to break the deadlock. State land cessions could resolve all these problems without raising fundamental constitutional issues.

The western lands controversy stalemated other, unrelated issues as long as Maryland and other landless states brought pressure on the claiming states by withholding their approval of the Articles. If anything, however, these delays promoted the peaceful resolution of conflicts. The corollary of a diminutive notion of state power—which inhibited the use of force in interstate diplomacy—was a faith in the wisdom and disinterestedness of a higher authority. It was more important to preserve this faith in Congress than to bring it to the test in a particular instance and find it wanting. The nearly disastrous attempt of Congress to intervene in the Vermont controversy was a striking demonstration of this truth.

Like the western lands dispute, with which it was related, the Vermont question was politically controversial. The admission of a new northern, and landless, state would affect the sectional balance of power in Congress as well as alignments on state western claims.[57] Recognition of a self-proclaimed new state in territory claimed by New York was bound to inspire separatists in other large states. At various times, Congress supported New York, attempted an impartial adjudication, offered to recognize Vermont, and withdrew its offer—to the infinite confusion of all concerned. But the only sensible policy, Congress learned, was to avoid the issue altogether. Congress could act effectively only where all the interested parties were states—and this was true neither in the case of Vermont nor in the western lands controversy—and when the states bound themselves to submit to its decisions. The Vermont dispute showed that Congress could enforce nothing. Its determinations had to be self-executing.

Congress was prudent to leave Vermont alone, as it finally did, until New York could come to terms with the separatists. But if such forbearance was crucial, it was also necessary for Congress to show that it had recourses other than neglect in other cases. With the ratification of the Articles, it finally became possible for formal proceedings between states to take place under congressional supervision, without undermining its authority or endangering the union. The resolution of the jurisdictional conflict between Connecticut and Pennsylvania over the Wyoming Valley by the trial at Trenton in late 1782 had an enormous impact on interstate relations—even if it did not bring peace to that troubled region. According to a contemporary account, "this celebrated cause . . . presents to the world a new and extraordinary spectacle" of "two powerful and populous States, sovereign and independent (except as members of the federal union)" submitting to "the arbitration of judges mutually chosen from indifferent states."[58] The case became a model for the way the American states were supposed to behave, simultaneously reinforcing a diminutive notion of state power and enhancing congressional prestige.

Connecticut v. Pennsylvania justified Congress's protracted efforts to fashion an article that would provide for the adjudication of interstate conflicts. Article XVIII in the July 1776 draft gave the United States "sole and exclusive Right and Power" to settle differences "between two or more Colonies concerning Boundaries, Jurisdictions, or any other Cause whatever." But the article (now number XIV) was amended in October 1777 to take on its ultimate form, as laid down in Article IX.[59] Special jurisdictional courts were isolated from Congress in order to give them a more judicial character. A proceeding would begin when one state petitioned Congress, which then would notify the other state. Congress was to set a date for the appearance of agents from each state "who shall then be directed to appoint by joint consent, commissioners or judges to constitute a court." In case such agreement was not forthcoming, the article established an elaborate procedure—including nominations by Congress, the striking of unacceptable names by each party, and a drawing by lot—that would produce a court of seven to nine judges, five of whom would make up a quorum. The trick was to conjure such a court into existence, a problem exacerbated by the distressing tendency of would-be judges to decline their nominations.

The extraordinary difficulties involved in bringing a claims controversy to court ensured that *Connecticut v. Pennsylvania* would not be replicated. The establishment of a procedure for resolving conflicts may even have sponsored new conflicts that the procedure finally proved too cumbersome to settle. But the important thing about these conflicts (for instance, between New York and Massachusetts and between South Carolina and Georgia) was that they reflected the pursuit of limited goals and that they presupposed and depended on a higher authority.[60] Because an Article IX proceeding was such an expensive and time-consuming undertaking, however, the states were encouraged to resort to more modest and direct expedients, compatible with adjudication as the ultimate recourse. Article IX defined the outer limits of interstate conflict: it was the most arduous path toward the vindication of state claims, the American equivalent of war.

Congress's record as an active agent in interstate conflict resolution was not distinguished. But the American state system itself worked remarkably well. States did not go to war with each other. Aside from the Revolution itself, most American violence was committed by discontented citizens against their own states, and by states against their citizens. The incidence of domestic violence was symptomatic of the very weakness of American state power that inhibited interstate warfare. But the American state system survived not only because of the weakness of the states and diminutive notions of state power, but also because the United States was seen as a community of states—an idea that often rested on little more than faith alone. The American states discovered various means of resolving their differences, in which Congress rarely played more than an indirect role. But these jurisdictional settlements would not have been achieved without the implicit acceptance of a common interest and of the legitimacy of a higher authority. The ability of the American states to come to terms with each other helped establish a solid foundation for the more vigorous central government established under the Federal Constitution.

• 2 •

From Colony to Territory:
Changing Concepts of Statehood

Early American concepts of statehood were drawn from several sources. States as territorial communities were inherited from the colonial period; states as governments were created by the revolutionaries; and states in a community of states existed by virtue of the recognition of other states. Each definition carried limitations with it that inhibited the exercise of state power. These limitations became manifest when one idea of statehood was invoked against another during the many jurisdictional controversies between or among the states and between the original states and separatists who sought to set up new states. The resulting confusion encouraged Americans to reexamine statehood claims, in general terms as well as in particular cases. Though the precise extent of states' rights remained controversial, a diminutive notion of statehood became predominant by the mid-1780s. The new synthesis was apparent in congressional policy for the territories, which were destined to become "states," and in the radical expansion of national power, at the expense of the states, in the Federal Constitution.

According to the doctrine of state succession, new state governments succeeded old colony governments in political communities or "states" that long antedated the Revolution. The doctrine suggested that prior acts of the colonial governments, except for the "unconstitutional" encroachments that led up to the Revolution, remained binding—an idea that was particularly attractive to the propertied classes. It also implied that the new states, like their colonial predecessors, were part of a larger community and should be subordinate to a higher authority. American experience in the Empire remained paradigmatic after independence, and state succession theory provided the link.[1]

The Revolutionary assumption of authority and creation of new governments apparently offered a much broader mandate for expanded state power. But patriotic Americans had denounced the legislative supremacy claimed by Parliament and were wary of according extensive powers to their own governments. The American idea that the people, not the government, were sovereign constituted a fundamental limitation on state power.[2] Popular sovereignty was institutionalized in the drafting of new state constitutions, which limited the powers of the new state governments. Popular sovereignty and the imperial model of interstate organization thus both reduced the scope of state power.

Finally, the identification of the American states with the common cause and membership in Congress directly worked against notions of truly independent statehood. The states naturally looked to each other for collective security, but in doing so they had to compromise their various pretensions. The states had to agree not to seek alliances or resort to coercive means as individual states; in other words, they denied themselves the means of independently extending and enforcing their claims. It also meant that the large states would have to renegotiate their boundaries, in order to bring all the states closer to that equality of size and power which many contemporaries—particularly from small states—thought was essential for their peaceful coexistence. Such negotiations, particularly over western boundaries, reduced the territorial claims of the large states. They also tended to diminish state power in general, first by establishing the primacy of mutual recognition in statehood claims, second by creating a tangible common interest in the new national domain, created by state land cessions, as a counterweight to state interests.

In the years between the Declaration of Independence and the Constitutional Convention, the relative importance of these different definitions of statehood shifted. At the outset, state succession claims and the natural rights of Americans to set up their own governments were mutually reinforcing in supporting the autonomy of the states and the legitimacy of their new governments. But neither definition, alone or in tandem, provided an adequate rationale for American statehood. The Revolution was a continental effort, and the need for cooperation among the states was obviously paramount. Thus the idea that statehood derived from membership in Congress and participation in the joint war effort became increasingly important. This formulation was also attractive to proponents of new states in frontier regions which had not been separate colonies; state succession doctrine was worse than useless to them, because it was an essential prop to the exclusive claims of the original states. At the same time, the efforts of the original states to suppress popular uprisings against their authority, as well as unauthorized separations, discredited political pretensions resting on natural rights alone. All these developments pointed to mutual recognition as the ultimate legitimating source of statehood claims. But this concept of statehood deprived the states of an autonomous basis for making claims against each other. By definition, the states could claim no more than the other states were willing to recognize, and they were necessarily subordinate to the higher authority which was supposed to enforce their mutual agreements. With statehood thus diminished, the institution of a more powerful central government logically followed. A general agreement on the limited scope of state power set the limits for controversy over ratification of the Federal Constitution.

Ambiguous and sometimes contradictory concepts of statehood reflected, and in turn contributed to, the low level of political integration actually achieved in the new American states. The establishment of legitimate authority constitutes a dilemma for any new regime. In America, state succession doctrine helped minimize the initial shock of the transition from colony to state, but it also contributed to the conceptual confusion that impeded the consolidation of state authority. The American revolutionaries lacked a doctrinal rationale for taking power into their own hands and using it to achieve collective goals, beyond independence itself.

The difficulties of establishing new governments were apparent on several levels. First, there were disagreements over the basic organization of state power, evident in the drafting and redrafting of state constitutions.[3] The earliest constitutions were simply enacted by revolutionary legislatures or conventions, without popular ratification. However they may have been subsequently constituted, state governments subject to frequent alteration lacked legitimacy. Second, there was intense partisan activity in every state, and partisanship itself was suspect.[4] Identification with particular class or sectional interests undermined claims by revolutionary state governments truly to represent their communities, reinforcing the distinction between the state as a political community and the actual state government which constitution-writing encouraged. Finally, the emergence of a "volitional" idea of citizenship undermined the ability of new state governments to command the support of the people in actions against other states.[5] If theories of popular sovereignty have sanctioned the radical expansion of state power in the modern period, they also have tended to destroy traditional bases of social and political obligation.[6] The new states did not have "the aid of habit and hereditary respect; and, being . . . the result of preceding tumult and confusion, do not immediately acquire stability or strength."[7] The new political man was, to an extent that alarmed many contemporaries, a free agent whose commitments were calculated and contingent. "People are now to be governed by clear perceptions, not blind attachments," said one writer. "Every man ought to know what he does, and do it because it is approved of by reason."[8]

Challenges to national territory are ordinarily supposed to encourage national solidarity, but this can be true only where political community already exists. Recently settled frontier areas, often including emigrants from different colonies with different ethnic and religious backgrounds, had not achieved a high level of political integration when the Revolution began. Disputes among the new states subverted state authority; they legitimated disintegration. Settlers weighed the relative advantages and disadvantages of inclusion in one state or another. They argued the merits of different state constitutions; they calculated how their private property claims would be treated and what kind of political power they would be able to exercise. Assuming that ordinary citizens were qualified to decide such questions, it was not surprising that settlers in outlying regions should so often take the next step and set up new states of their own.[9] Constitutional ferment suggested that the people could choose what kind of government they would live under; territorial controversies appeared to make membership in one state or another equally negotiable.

The American states were not highly integrated, terminal political communities that inspired popular patriotism. Indeed, the states were not supposed to enjoy such an exalted position. Limits on state power reflected the colonial origins of American concepts of statehood. Claims to local jurisdictional autonomy did not anticipate broader pretensions to sovereign power after independence. Nonetheless, state claims to succeed to colonial jurisdictions provided the most durable basis for early American concepts of state power. State succession doctrine enabled new regimes to assimilate their own claims to those of the colonial polities, or "states," that had resisted British tyranny.

During the Imperial Crisis, American radicals argued that their colonies had enjoyed and ought still to enjoy a high degree of political autonomy within the British Empire. American ideas about statehood were shaped by these claims. It is worth noting, therefore, that resistance polemics asserted that colonial autonomy was not incompatible with the imperial connection and that Americans remained loyal subjects of the British king. Tory critics thought they could discern a secret intention to break with the Empire and set up independent states; the radicals were either disingenuous conspirators or such poor political logicians that they did not see the absurdity of claims that amounted to an "*imperium in imperio.*" [10] Radical ideas of the statehood of the colonies were consequently defined against the pretensions to full sovereign authority that their opponents imputed to them.

American patriots protested that they sought only a limited jurisdiction over their own affairs. They did not seek to inspire loyalty to the colonies as such; the independence of these states was never presented as an end in itself. The very structure of the debate over the British constitution, which imperial reform was supposed to have violated, compelled Americans to suppress state particularist claims. Revolutionary congresses, conventions, and committees could be justified only as extraordinary responses to extraordinary threats to British liberties throughout America.

Resistance polemics emphasized tax and legislative exemptions and American autonomy in internal affairs. Explicitly or inferentially, Americans acquiesced in British jurisdiction over external affairs. Through general commercial legislation and a coordinated foreign policy, the British government alone could maintain balance and harmony among the component parts of the Empire. Governor Thomas Fitch of Connecticut said, "It becomes plainly expedient that there should be some supreme Director over all His Majesty's Dominions; and this Character and Authority, all men must acknowledge and allow, properly belong to the *British* Parliament." [11] When patriotic Americans could no longer acknowledge parliamentary authority in America, they looked to the king himself for a superintending authority that would connect the various parts of the Empire.

Though American claims to the privileges, immunities, and rights associated with each colony's "constitution" escalated as the Imperial Crisis progressed, no positive doctrine about colonial "state" power in external affairs emerged. Revolutionary rhetoric sought to justify violent resistance as a defensive response to ministerial tyranny; the values that were being defended were imputed to the British constitution itself. Because resistance was supposed to be a struggle for the reform of the British constitution, Americans dwelt on the violation of their individual rights as Englishmen, not as members of particular colonies.[12] Consequently, the development of doctrine about colonies as political communities and their collective rights was retarded. This conceptual poverty was reflected in the subsequent history of interstate relations.

Even when American writers argued for colonial distinctness and autonomy, they minimized the scope of positive state action. John Adams and James Wilson both saw treaties of commerce, "by which . . . distinct states are cemented together, in perpetual league and amity," as paradigmatic for imperial organization.[13] Though English publicists Malachy Postlethwayt and Thomas Pownall anticipated such proposals by several years, they saw a "commercial union" or a new imperial constitution as positive acts by consenting parties.[14] But American radicals were bound by the historicist logic of republican theory to assert that their ideal empire already existed; they merely meant to preserve the "ancient constitution" of the empire.[15] Adams said, "We have by our own express consent contracted to observe the Navigation Act, and by our implied consent, by long usage and uninterrupted acquiescence, have submitted to the other acts of trade, however grievous some of them may be."[16] Similarly, Thomas Jefferson suggested, Americans had tacitly consented to the abrogation of their charter rights when new colonies were created out of old ones.[17] But Americans would not submit to the recent outrageous encroachments on their constitutional rights. Characteristically, then, only Tory and English commentators saw the need to put the Empire on an entirely new footing and thus resolve jurisdictional confusion. Radicals were reluctant to consider an explicit formulation of the imperial relationship which would necessarily compromise their rights; a reformulation of that relationship—from which claims to rights would henceforth be derived—was unthinkable.

The radical critique of British colonial policy was premised on the idealization of the old Empire. American claims were not self-consciously revolutionary; they were authenticated by history. Any negotiation between Britain and its colonies resulting in an actual "treaty" or new imperial constitution would imply that Americans had not previously enjoyed such rights as these agreements might secure. In other words, Americans would be forced to concede that they were something less than Englishmen and that the rights of Englishmen were not their birthright.

Revolutionary Americans had a highly developed sense of their rights as individuals. But they had not thought much about what it meant to be citizens of particular colonies, except as the local settings in which those rights were actually enjoyed. The cosmopolitan premises of patriotic rhetoric—advancing from the rights of Englishmen to the rights of man—and the high premium placed on intercolonial consensus inhibited the development of political community at the state level. Rather than emerging from the resistance era with a doctrinal rationale for the exercise of power, the new American states were virtually powerless—in theory and in fact.[18]

The states declared their independence in order to prosecute a united war effort against British tyranny. But because the colonies always had been "states," according to American writers, independence did not constitute a fundamental break. Many years later, Thomas Jefferson argued that the "nation of Virginia" and the laws it had made for itself remained unchanged by the Revolution:

> Before the revolution, the nation of Virginia had, by the organs they then thought proper to constitute, established a system of laws. . . . When, by the declaration of Independence, they chose to abolish their former organs of declaring their will, the acts of will already formally & constitutionally declared, remained untouched. For the nation was not dissolved, was not annihilated; it's will, therefore, remained in full vigor; and on the establishing the new organs, first of a convention, & afterwards a more complicated legislature, the old acts of national will continued in force, until the nation should, by its new organs, declare its will changed.[19]

This doctrine was adopted by the U.S. Supreme Court and passed into international law as the law of state succession. According to Chief Justice John Marshall, "the people" may "change their allegiance . . . but their relations to each other and their rights of property remain undisturbed."[20]

Conservative revolutionaries had many reasons for endorsing the idea of colony-state succession. It provided a basis for statehood claims, a legitimating prehistory, that did not depend on other states or on mass political action. It meant that Americans had not returned to a "state of nature" when they declared their independence: they were never stateless. Nor were the American states thrown into a state of nature with each other, the natural condition of sovereign states. Interstate relations were a continuation of intercolonial relations. Boundary settlements, for instance, remained in force. Most important, the doctrine secured private property rights. A state's territorial jurisdiction, guaranteeing the private rights of its citizens, was integral and inviolable; it was the essence of state sovereignty.

Spokesmen for states with extensive charter claims naturally favored state succession doctrine. If these royal grants were not scrupulously observed, they argued, anarchy and chaos would break loose. Colonial charters, according to Edmund Pendleton of Virginia, were "the only criterion by which the territorial claims of each state can be ascertained."[21] "Landless" state leaders—and separatists in the "landed" states—agreed that it might be expedient to maintain charter lines in settled areas where they had served as intercolonial boundaries. These boundaries were effective because they were generally recognized, not because they had been specified in charters. In the unsettled western lands, where no colony had exercised jurisdiction, overlapping charter claims confused rather than clarified state territorial pretensions. Western Pennsylvania separatists suggested, "If all charter boundaries were to be strictly observed, nothing but anarchy and confusion must be the unavoidable consequence."[22] States bounded by these charter lines—if they ever could be sorted out—assumed fantastic dimensions. "No Person could pretend to think it consistent with common sense to have a Governm[ent] 60 miles wide, & 3000 miles long," Benjamin Franklin was reported to have said in 1763; but this is what Connecticut would look like if its newly revived charter claims were upheld.[23] Charter claims were mutually contradictory; they were absurdly large and, in the cases of Connecticut and Massachusetts leaping over New York, discontinuous. Consequently, though many American statesmen agreed with Pendleton and endorsed charter claims in principle, they were reluctant to recognize specific claims—advanced by other states.

The major weakness of charter claims was that they did not define the territorial limits of actual political communities. Like private land companies, states had a speculative interest in western lands as a source of public revenue and, for their politicians, private profit.[24] But the vindication of a state's distant charter pretensions was not a vital issue to most of its citizens. Indeed, the loyalties of frontier settlers, who were most affected by overlapping charter claims, did not run deep. They were inclined to believe that "the ease, happiness and convenience of the people ought to be the general rule of the limits, extent and government of human societies."[25] States that sought to uphold their jurisdiction in frontier areas rarely invoked charters in negotiations with the settlers. Instead, the states promised protection from the British or Indian enemy or argued that frontier regions could not bear the heavy expense of a new state government and lacked the necessary legal and political talent.[26] If there were any transcendent political obligation, it did not derive from a charter, but was created by membership in a state—evidenced by consent to its constitution and by representation in its legislature—and by benefits actually rendered by a state government.[27]

State succession doctrine could become more generally useful as a source of legitimacy for all the states only when large states agreed to concede particular advantages flowing from colonial precedents. It was also necessary to reconcile the apparently conservative aspects of the doctrine with emerging concepts of popular self-government. According to state succession doctrine, statehood was attributable to communities inhabiting particular territories, not to their governments. But not all the British colonies in America became independent states, in spite of a standing invitation to join the cause. Americans had to create new governments in order to preserve their individual rights and the "statehood" of their colonies. States as territorial entities might have been inherited from the colonial era—though particular claims were disputable—but states as governments were created by the revolutionaries themselves.

The revolutionary right to self-government could be set up against state succession claims. According to a Maine separatist, "the people alone have an incontestible, unalienable, and indefeasible right to institute governments, and to reform, alter, or totally change the same."[28] State succession doctrine stood in counterpoint to such radical claims, the conservative answer to popular sovereignty. It could be invoked against state legislatures that jeopardized property relations as well as against separatists who sought to establish new states within the limits of the old ones. These two sources of danger were frequently associated.[29] Legislatures that courted popularity, popular nullification of state authority—most notably by the Shaysites in Massachusetts—and the outright rebellion of new state secessionists like the Vermonters were all symptomatic of imminent "anarchy," the unwillingness of Americans to be governed by anyone, even by themselves.[30]

It would have been foolish, however, to insist on a contradiction between popular sovereignty and state succession and thus encourage radicals to attack state claims based on colonial precedent as counterrevolutionary. Even conservative patriots needed popular sovereignty as a counter to British tyranny; more or less reluctantly, all patriots agreed that the people had the right to choose at least some of their own governors. But the fixation on representation narrowly limited the revolutionary agenda.[31] The most radical expansion of electoral power could be reconciled with the fundamental premises of state succession doctrine: the "people" as a collective entity antedated the Revolution; until government made itself illegitimate, its acts had been lawful and remained binding.

The ultimate expression of popular authority was not in mere legislation but in the adoption of state constitutions designed to preserve the existing social and economic order. Property rights, for which the Revolution was being fought, depended on the maintenance of the colonial legal order, adapted to the exigencies of independence. The preservation of colonial jurisdictions, under which property rights had been created and enjoyed, was crucial. If state constitutions recognized the sovereignty of the people, they also guaranteed that popular governments—which were not sovereign—would not tamper with private rights.

Constitutionalism inhibited state power, the power of the sovereign people, in much the same way state succession doctrine did. Once a constitution had been adopted, a binding political obligation was created. No town or towns, county or counties had "a right totally to disengage itself from it's constitutional connexions, and set up a separate government," according to an opponent of Maine separatism. "The constitution is *equally binding*, in all its parts, on *every subject* . . . if one article is broke, the *whole is dissolved*—and anarchy and confusion the consequence."[32] Whether Americans were thrown briefly into a state of nature (as the logic of constitution-writing suggested to radical opponents of state succession claims) or not (according to the claim that "statehood" was continuous from colony to state), the political power of the people was carefully circumscribed. The people were not free to choose what state to join or whether to establish new states.

Revolutionary regimes vigorously denied that a revolutionary situation (or "state of nature") existed. Separatists had to be shown that the people could have nothing to say about boundaries. Once the colonies had constituted themselves as independent states, their jurisdictional limits were to remain fixed. According to Nathan Dane, "a power so capable in its nature of being abused in America as that of dividing states, counties, towns, &c ought . . . only to be exercised by those who have a right to form the society de novo," for once and for all.[33] In adopting the Massachusetts constitution, an opponent of Maine separatism argued, "The people have given up *all and every of their natural rights, except those which they have therein specially reserved to themselves*"—and these were all private rights.[34]

State succession and popular sovereignty were in complementary ways essential components of early American statehood claims; together they served to secure and legitimize the exclusive pretensions of the original states. The drafting of state constitutions represented the synthesis of these apparently contradictory concepts: the colonies as political communities cut themselves loose from the Empire and created new governments, binding their citizens to each other in perpetuity. (Strictly speaking, this was a reaffirmation of existing community that was necessary only because so many putative citizens—loyalists and separatists— were oblivious to their political obligations.) But neither doctrine, alone or in combination with the other, provided a viable basis for adjusting interstate territorial controversies. The validity of state succession claims by charter was itself the issue in the case of the western lands; and, by general agreement, it would have been an invitation to anarchy to consult the "sovereign" people on such questions. The American states never conceded that plebiscites should be held to resolve contested boundaries, even though separatists, as good revolutionaries, assumed that local preferences should be determining.[35] Peace among the states could be secured only by negotiations and compromises over particular issues. Implicit in this process was a definition of statehood that filled the vacuum left by other concepts; "statehood" was conferred on a state by other states because of its membership in the union and representation in Congress. In some sense, then, statehood derived from Congress and participation in the common cause.[36]

The American states apparently resembled sovereign states in their relations with one another, particularly in their determination to defend their own territorial claims and curb those of other states. But constitutionally limited state governments that could not command popular loyalties were incapable of enforcing those claims. A state's sovereignty—its territorial jurisdiction—could be secured only by the recognition and guarantee of the other states in Congress. "One of the great objects of the union . . . is the mutual protection and security" of states' rights, as Congress resolved in September 1779.[37] "The safety of the states" was, according to a proponent of a stronger central government, "the object of a political federal union."[38] The states collectively guaranteed each state's particular claims.

Though recognition is by definition the basis of any state's international standing, mutual recognition among the United States worked to diminish their independence. They agreed that only the thirteen original states were capable of receiving or according recognition. No American state could exist outside the union; therefore, membership in the union was an essential characteristic of statehood. The price of mutual recognition was a radical diminution of each state's sovereign independence in its relations with other states. "No individual state as such has any claim to independence," according to "Nestor" (Benjamin Rush); "she is independent only in a union with her sister states in Congress."[39] "The welfare, and even the existence of the American States depend on the federal union."[40] Not only did Congress exercise a superintending jurisdiction over the states, but recognition by Congress was crucial to any community's statehood pretensions. That this premise was universally accepted is apparent in the concern of new state movements to gain recognition from Congress and admission to the union.[41] To become a state in revolutionary America was to forgo what we consider the essential prerogatives of sovereign statehood.

Because the states had the power to confer statehood on one another—through recognition of jurisdictional claims—present political considerations could be invoked against colonial precedents. Would extensive claims jeopardize the equality of the states? Could a large state maintain its authority effectively throughout its territory? New York delegates repeatedly complained that the other states in Congress set policy before principle in deliberations on Vermont.[42] But large states like New York were in fact prepared to give up extensive claims for secure boundaries, colonial precedents notwithstanding. The land cessions to Congress—including New York's (1782), Virginia's (1784), Massachusetts' (1785), Connecticut's (1786), and North Carolina's (1790)—were political transactions. State title to western lands was offered in hopes of gaining recognition of its remaining claims (which, however, Congress would not explicitly accord), in addition to various guarantees of private and public rights beyond the cession lines.[43] Presumably, the circumscribed jurisdictions could be governed and defended. The cessions thus diminished the discontinuity between states as land claimants and states as effective polities that made state succession doctrine so vulnerable to attack. Cession offers underlined the importance of mutual recognition to statehood claims; they also demonstrated that boundaries were negotiable and were not fixed forever by colonial precedents.

Whatever the sources of state claims to territorial jurisdiction, the willingness of other states to recognize them was crucial. The cessions policy of large landed states was premised on this necessity, thus emphasizing the central role of Congress in achieving territorial security among the states. Opponents of charter claims argued explicitly for a congressional title based on its succession to Crown lands and jurisdiction, or on the joint efforts of "all Americans in the War for Independence."[44] All parties to the western lands controversy thus looked forward to congressional jurisdiction in the West (whether or not Congress had a prior title) and, in the protracted debates over cessions, they all accepted the notion that boundaries rested on mutual recognition through Congress. Thus proponents and opponents of state succession claims appeared equally willing to concede a larger role to Congress. And once the outstanding boundary differences were successfully negotiated, there would be less resistance to congressional enforcement of territorial guarantees.

Though the American states were all ultimately interested in securing territorial guarantees, their disagreements over specific boundaries jeopardized their claims and encouraged them to rely more and more on Congress for the vindication of titles. Separatist new state promoters also challenged state jurisdiction. Separatists did not hesitate to expose the weaknesses and ambiguities of statehood claims; at the same time—and as a logical consequence of their attack on state claims—they called for congressional intervention on behalf of "American" citizens in frontier areas. Like the small states and speculative land companies, separatists argued that Congress's title to unlocated western lands was superior to individual state claims based on colonial charters. This dissociation of territorial title and particular state claims pointed to a fundamental redefinition and diminution of statehood claims: new western states should be created by the higher authority possessing title; not only would that authority determine state boundaries, but it would also establish their land systems while retaining control over their public lands.

Pressure for the creation of new states and solicitude for the territorial integrity of the old states combined to produce an increasingly diminutive notion of statehood. For the large states the issue in the cessions controversy was their sovereign right to set their own boundaries by voluntarily relinquishing their western claims. By their cessions they endorsed the favorite idea of their landless state opponents that the states should be more equal in size. Paradoxically, the only way they could secure recognition of their title was by giving it away. Implicit in the cessions transactions was a reliance on collective guarantees for title claims and the expectation that settlers, speculators, and Congress would eventually be able to ignore state claims altogether if there were no boundary compromises. The renegotiation of state boundaries and the equalization of the states to approximate more closely the optimum size for republics pointed to an expanded role for Congress. Indeed, separatists often associated pleas for state division with the growth of national power. Would "not the continent of America one day . . . become one consolidated government of the United States," asked Judge David Campbell, a Franklin (western North Carolina) separatist. "Are we not, then . . . to be a separate people?"[45]

Agitation for new states revolved around the question of the proper size of self-governing republics. In fact, the interest in size superseded concern for self-government: if size was crucial, then it had to be predetermined by Congress and not left to the settlers themselves. The focus on territorial extent reflected not only a doctrinaire reading of republican sources but also the conviction of many Americans that the unequal size of the states constituted a continuing threat to the peace and survival of the union. Many observers believed that the preservation of colonial boundaries and the resulting inequalities among the states was incompatible with a powerful union as well as with republican self-government in the states. A writer in the *Falmouth Gazette* (Maine District) stated:

> If we could lay aside our local prejudices, and heave up all our lines that were fix'd by Charters when the Geography of the country was not known, and fix them upon generous principles throughout the whole of your territory, it might be a mutual advantage, and would have a tendency to enlarge our ideas, to destroy animosities, and strengthen the interest of the Union.[46]

Certainly the controversies among states over boundaries and between separatists and their state governments undermined the union. "Now is the time," Lafayette wrote Washington in 1783, "when the powers of Congress must be fixed, the boundaries determined, and articles of confederation revised."[47]

Separatists hoped to participate in a general renegotiation of American boundaries. They claimed that frontier areas were entitled to the same right to self-government that the thirteen colonies claimed against Great Britain. "Turn your eyes to the events of 1776," advised Arthur Campbell, a southwest Virginia separatist. "That memorable era produced a declaration of independence and a Confederation, which . . . ought to be the basis of all subordinate institutions."[48] State succession claims were compromised by their colonial antecedents: land grants and boundary settlements were corrupt bargains between royal government and land jobbers. Maine separatists pointed to the "evils arising from . . . large patents, grants, and Indian deeds." "Equality of property is the life of a Republican Government."[49] According to the Vermonters, New York had been Britain's "favourite government" and the same stench still emanated from New York State.[50] Dissidents in the Connecticut River Valley resisted the "Monarchical and Aristocratical tyranny" of the independent state of New Hampshire.[51] Kentucky settlers felt that they did "not at present enjoy a greater portion of liberty [under Virginia] than an American colony might have done a few years ago had she been allowed a Representation in the British Parliament."[52] The Franklin separatists (in western North Carolina) asserted that "an aristocratical spirit prevails" in the southern states and that only "Here the genuine republican! here the real whig will find a safe assylum."[53]

The separatists' most powerful argument, however, was not that they had the right to govern themselves, but that the existing states were too large to administer their own territories. Indeed, antiseparatists could argue persuasively against the right of frontiersmen to proclaim their own new states, but they could not argue that there should be no new states. Few Americans would dispute the conventional wisdom that republican states should be small in size.[54] "The best political writers" were agreed, according to a Philadelphia writer, that "Republics . . . should never desire an extended dominion, as it has always proved inconsistent with the preservation of their liberties."[55] In the opinion of another writer, "when it is for the interest and happiness of the people, for which all governments are, or ought to be formed and constituted, no good reason can be assigned why new states and empires should not arise and branch out from old ones."[56] The great distance of regions like the Kentucky District from the seat of government "precludes every idea of a connection on republican principles, and originates many grievances."[57] "High and impassable mountains . . . naturally divide[d]" Franklinites from North Carolina.[58] "Nature dictates a separation," according to a Maine separatist; "Nature has separated us," claimed a Franklinite.[59]

Secure boundaries required concessions on claims by the large states. A coalition of landless states successfully blocked congressional recognition of the western charter claims of Virginia and other landed states. Much was made of the "impracticability of governing the extensive dominion claimed by that state."[60] That the new American republics would have to be small, perhaps in some cases smaller than the colonies they succeeded, was generally agreed, even, in candid moments, by large-state politicians. According to a Virginia claims defense, it "would not be productive either of their or our happiness" for easterners and westerners to "remain under one government."[61] Reflecting on New York's unhappy experience in Vermont, John Jay asserted, "We have unquestionably more Territory than we can govern."[62] Many American statesmen would thus agree that it was "very natural," as James Lovell of Massachusetts wrote, "to seperate in extensive Jurisdiction."[63] "The unwieldiness of many of our present governments in extent of territory" meant that separations "must sooner or later take place," according to a newspaper writer.[64]

If there was a consensus that some states were too large and that new states should be created on the northern and western frontiers, it was also generally understood that frontier settlers could not be allowed to take the initiative. The "epidemic . . . Spirit of making new States" was as dangerous to the union as the exaggerated claims of the large landed states.[65] "The idea of making separate states is generally reprobated as product[ive] of ye worst evils [to] the Confederacy," Nathan Dane reported from Congress in 1785.[66] For, as a Cheshire County, New Hampshire, convention warned, "if every district so disposed, may for themselves determine that they are not within the claim of the thirteen states . . . we may soon have ten hundred states, all free and independent."[67] "If a county in the East may" declare its independence, an antiseparatist writer in Maine argued, "so may one in the West, from the South or any other quarter; and then what but anarchy can be expected to ensue?"[68] "If Congress are not firm on that head," Jefferson wrote, "our several states will crumble to atoms by the spirit of establishing every little canton into a separate state."[69] "Fix the boundaries," Joseph Jones advised, "and let the people who live within their respective limits know they are their Citizens and must submit to their Government."[70]

One of the most popular arguments against the creation of new states was that in the absence of common interests they would spin out of the American orbit and into the arms of neighboring colonial powers.[71] The argument assumed that the union of the states was powerless and that there was no countervailing national loyalty or patriotism in the West. The frontier was supposed to bring out the worst attributes of the new American citizen.[72] There was ample evidence for this view in the maneuvers of the many speculators in property and politics drawn to newly opened areas; every new state movement was at some point accused of disloyalty to the United States, and most were guilty as charged. But separatist agitation for new states contributed to the expansion of congressional power, even while its promoters flirted with America's enemies.

Separatists argued that the common cause of all Americans could and should be distinguished from the narrow "colonial" interests of particular states in frontier lands. Thus, these frontiersmen tended to be "nationalists," a tendency that was encouraged by their need for military protection and by their dealings with ineffectual state governments. Separatists usually had a vested interest in overturning state claims and in promoting a collective American claim, another source of their nationalism. Finally, because separatist new states were necessarily founded in the midst of jurisdictional confusion, the establishment of stable and legitimate authority was notoriously difficult. Disparate interests in a controversial area prevented unanimity among the settlers, and there was always a sizable minority in favor of the reassertion of the old state's jurisdiction. Even more than the original states, then, new states depended on the recognition and protection of higher authority. Separatists were well aware that militarily and politically they could not go it alone. This was the basis of their nationalism; it also explains their treasonable tendencies.

"There are a great many over the whole continent quite tired of their independence," the *London Chronicle* reported in 1785.[73] "We are daily in expectation of hearing of a coalition between the Franklinites and the Vermonters," leading to a general mandate from the disaffected throughout America for the reassertion of British authority. The outbreak of Shays's Rebellion multiplied such fears. Edward Carrington thought that there was no doubt that Britain was "in readiness to improve any advantages which our derangements may present for regaining her lost dominion."[74] But from the time of negotiations with Vermont, beginning in 1780, British agents knew that there was no authentic royalist revival in disaffected regions.[75] British or Spanish opportunities depended on the failure of Congress to extend recognition or secure the economic interests of frontiersmen. "Nothing will ever tempt us to take such a step" as "*revolting to Britain*," declared a Maine separatist, "except being detained and oppressed, under our present government [Massachusetts], contrary to our inclination or interest."[76] Disloyalty did not reflect the attenuation of patriotism so much as it did heightened expectations of Congress. Separatists believed Congress would transcend state interests and offer them succor and protection.

Separatists were reluctant to base their claims entirely on their revolutionary right to self-government. Statements such as that in the Franklin Declaration of Rights that "all political power is vested in, and derived from the people only" were conventional rhetorical flourishes.[77] While separatists in southwestern Virginia bravely asserted that "we are first occupants and aborigines of this country" and "freemen claiming natural rights," it is revealing that they also claimed the "privileges of American citizens."[78] The "indefeasible right" of American citizens "to consult and provide for their proper interests" was combined with "a sacred regard for the principles of the continental union."[79] This transcendent citizenship and higher loyalty could be invoked against states that demanded loyalty from their citizens. But there is considerable evidence that this sentiment was often sincere. Separatists from Vermont to Franklin had to deal with popular prejudice for Congress and against the independent assumption of authority.[80] New state leaders sought to convince their followers and themselves that Congress did possess the "power . . . to lay off a new state" where frontier areas clearly had "a different policy and different interest" from the rest of the state.[81] Beginning with Dr. Thomas Young's broadside to "the People of the Grants," promoters of Vermont statehood continually misrepresented congressional opinion by suggesting that congressmen endorsed the separation and would admit the new state to the union.[82] The nationalism of new state proponents was undoubtedly most often cynical and interested. But popular attachment to the union was also pervasive in frontier areas and could constitute a political liability to separatists, particularly when, ignored or rebuffed by Congress, they sought to forge new alliances with foreign imperial powers.

The logical result of separatist attacks on state claims was to devalue statehood in general and to advance a broader concept of national political community. It is significant that separatists so often justified themselves by citing congressional actions: for instance, the 1780 resolutions calling for cessions and the creation of a national domain where new states would be founded and, most often, the 1784 territorial government ordinance. The Franklinites believed that the ordinance justified their break with North Carolina. "The Continental Congress, by their resolves, invite us to [do] it," claimed the Franklin convention.[83] "Was it not a celebrated genius of yours" (that is, Jefferson), a Franklinite asked his Virginian correspondent, who "drew up the scheme last year of having new States 150 miles square?"[84] The ordinance was "a generous and beautiful compact . . . held out" to the inhabitants of southwestern Virginia to escape the "aristocratical domination" of that state, according to Arthur Campbell.[85] But Jefferson had *not* anticipated that separatists would invoke the ordinance to challenge state authority. Virginia had already ceded the northwest, and he supposed that further cessions would be forthcoming south of the Ohio River. The ordinance "extends not only to the territory ceded, but *to be ceded*," he asserted.[86] It was thus easily interpreted as an invitation to political action, particularly since Jefferson apparently did not believe (with Madison) that only uninhabited territory could be ceded.[87] Indeed, the North Carolina cession of 1784 (which was withdrawn in the same year) appeared to leave the transmontane settlers without government: self-government was therefore the only alternative to "anarchy." The territorial ordinance seemed to encourage this assumption of authority.[88]

The separatists' reliance on Congress to legitimate new state formation and the importance attached to recognition and reception into the union revealed the radical limitations of statehood claims by these most revolutionary of revolutionaries. The Franklinites "appealed to Congress, as the dernier resort and mean to act under their authority."[89] In other words, they conceded that their statehood claims were defective without Congress; the new state "wants only the paternal guardianship of Congress for a short period, to entitle it to be admitted with eclat, as a member of the federal government."

The underdevelopment of political community and legitimate authority in the original states encouraged separatists to set up their own governments. But these new states were even more desperately in need of recognition and legitimation.[90] Separatists thus agreed that Congress would have to exercise an expanded jurisdiction in the West. "The western people look up" to Congress "with reverence, as the faithful arbiters of the rights and interests of all the component parts of the empire."[91] "The western inhabitants can no longer be safe, or useful in society, without the protecting arm of the federal government and the priviledges of an independent state."[92] Westerners also suggested that the original states were "indebted to the continental establishment" for their very existence and that "an increase of states in the federal union will conduce to the strength and dignity of that union."[93] Ironically, separatists anticipated revisions of the 1784 ordinance toward a more forthrightly colonial policy by calling for "the paternal guardianship of Congress." Intrastate as well as interstate conflict thus mandated the growth of congressional power.

Pressure for the creation of new states—reflecting the new political aspirations of frontier populations—challenged state authority both directly and indirectly. Separatists helped reduce the large states to less threatening proportions: sponsored separatism in Kentucky and the western land cessions were designed to preempt the kind of involuntary dismemberment that New York suffered in Vermont. The statehood claims of the westerners were necessarily more modest than those advanced by spokesmen for the original states. Whether or not all the original states endorsed state succession doctrine in its most extensive applications, they all benefited as political communities from the continuities between colony and state. Separatists could not claim such colonial antecedents (though it is revealing that separatists in Vermont and Maine tried to invent distinctive colonial histories for their regions).[94] Instead, separatists found themselves compelled to attack particular state claims and were drawn by this logic into promoting a Crown title to vacant lands, to which Congress might succeed. New states did not claim a prescriptive right to a specific extent of territory based on colonial precedent. It followed that the territorial right was located in a higher, suprastate authority; that authority alone could grant territory to a new state.[95] The revolutionary right to create new governments was a political right. It could not, without totally upsetting property relations, bring with it a right to land or territory. Territorial jurisdiction, like property itself, rested on a title. Thus, paradoxically, separatists who sought to alter jurisdictional arrangements were compelled to subordinate particular state claims to national claims and so define statehood as an inferior status.

The states responded to the separatist challenge in different ways. Virginia sponsored the new state movement in Kentucky, and New York finally agreed to recognize Vermont. But New Hampshire, Massachusetts, Pennsylvania, Virginia, and North Carolina all acted vigorously to suppress popular insurrections against state authority, including new state movements. Massachusetts and Virginia sponsored a resolution against separatism that gained general support in Congress.[96] At the same time, the agitation for new states helped shape the development of a national territorial policy. Even before all the land cessions were completed, Congress began drafting ordinances to implement their provisions for the creation of new states. Jefferson believed that the first government ordinance, passed on April 23, 1784, precluded the creation and admission of new states on any other basis, thus guaranteeing the territorial security of the existing states.[97] Finally, the new Federal Constitution, drafted amid a nationwide scare over a counterrevolutionary conspiracy among debtors, separatists, and the British, was supposed to secure state territorial claims. The resulting political geography of the United States was a patchwork of compromises reflecting the extent of the ability of the states to govern, the belated recognition of the more durable new state movements, and the establishment of congressional jurisdiction in the northwest, where new states would be subsequently created. The states agreed to forgo extensive territorial claims as well as their independence in interstate affairs; they also agreed to a stronger national government.

The evolution of a system of territorial government did not suppress the political impulses of frontier separatists; rather, it expressed their own diminutive notions of political community in newly settled areas. Separatists were in fundamental accord with developing concepts of statehood and interstate organization. States should be reasonably small and roughly equal in size; once manageable boundaries had been ascertained, they should be guaranteed against any threat, internal or external; the United States collectively alone should be empowered to secure state boundaries. Congressional policy for the territories also reflected this conceptual development. It provided for new states without jeopardizing the territorial integrity of the old states; it established congressional supremacy over the new western states, which were to be called "territories" prior to their admission to the union; and, by fixing new state borders at the outset, it precluded the jurisdictional controversies that had been so troublesome to the original states. The most significant difference between the new states sought by separatists and the new states provided for in the ordinances was that the latter were to be established before there was any settlement. Such a "state" was an entirely artificial creation—it could not be compared to authentically self-created and self-governing new states.

Pressures for the creation of new states and for the security and financial benefit of the old states were synthesized with growing support for an enlarged congressional jurisdiction over the national domain in the territorial government ordinances. It was against this emerging standard of how new states should be created and then admitted to the union that Vermont and Kentucky both appeared anomalous.[98] Constitutional scruples were invoked against admitting an existing state or district. But the much broader constitutional innovations of a national territorial policy were much less controversial.

The immediate admission of states with well-known sectional political affinities was bound to raise misgivings.[99] Once the large states had renounced their neo-colonial pretensions, the large state–small state politi-cal paradigm began to seem less compelling. Instead, new states came to be considered in terms of congressional voting power, and sectional cal-culations became paramount. A state's power in league with other like-minded states in the union was feared more than its political power outside the union as a truly independent state. The states contemplated under the territorial ordinance would be years in the making, however, and their or-derly evolution under congressional auspices would presumably prevent the proliferation of client states for sectional blocs. Aside from sectional political concerns, there was a clear preference for a certain kind of new state, created and controlled by Congress. This preference was indicative of a deflation of the most expansive notions of state autonomy and power, fashioned in resistance to the British Empire and carried into the new na-tion under the doctrine of state succession. The pendulum swung away from a determination to defend the independent states from the encroach-ments of higher authority to a willingness to enlarge the scope and power of a higher authority in order to defend states from the more immediate and palpable threats of encroachments on one another. There was a grow-ing consensus for a more limited, less threatening definition of state power.

The territorial government ordinance of April 23, 1784, did not estab-lish an elaborate system of congressional control over new western states. The need to ensure public revenue from land sales and provide for the maintenance of law and order was recognized in an amendment empower-ing Congress to preserve "peace and good order" before settlers could act to adopt a mode of temporary government.[100] But Jefferson and his co-authors did not feel compelled to call these embryonic states by any other name. As soon as the settlers could act collectively, they could, by adopt-ing an existing state constitution for temporary use, enjoy the same degree of self-government as the original states. When their number increased to 20,000 they would be authorized by Congress to draft their own constitu-tion. Finally, at the moment the new state's population equaled that of the smallest original state, it would be admitted to the union. As political communities, these new states made themselves—this was the implicit concept of statehood. It was not surprising, then, that separatists inter-preted the ordinance as an invitation to political action.

But the focus on constitutionalism in the debate over western "state-hood" is fundamentally misleading.[101] The ordinances could apply only to national territory, notwithstanding separatist misrepresentations. The fact that states were to be established in unsettled areas or among populations not accustomed to self-government (such as the French settlements in Illinois) made this statehood all the more artificial.[102] The progression from one stage to another was to be authorized by Congress, thus resolving any lingering ambiguity about the constitutional priority of states and the union. Furthermore, if as self-governing communities these new states resembled the old states, the scope of political action was radically limited; private rights and the rights of the American public would be secured against the new legislatures. The ordinance prohibited the new states from interfering "with the primary disposal of the soil by the United States" as well as discriminatory taxation against national or nonresident property.

The republicanism of the new state governments and their putative equality with the original states legitimated an exploitative colonial administration of the western lands. In fact, these new states were nothing like the original states. The most revealing difference, reflecting changing American concepts of statehood, was that the boundaries of the ten new states were predetermined by Congress. (See map facing p. 149.) These boundaries did not describe the limits of existing political communities, nor did they represent claims based on colonial precedents or on the political compromises that the original states were still working out with one another. The new states could not be plagued by the chronic territorial disputes that characterized relations among the old states, but this also meant that they could not be the same kind of states. However free the new territories and states may have been to govern themselves, their territorial jurisdictions and land systems were fixed. But were these not essential characteristics of sovereign statehood? The states created by the territorial government ordinances had not always existed—they had no colonial antecedents—nor were they, like Vermont, truly self-created states. They were states made by Congress for the benefit of the United States.

The overriding concern in American territorial policy was public revenue. It is not surprising that, given the history of new state proposals by land speculators, a "state" came to be thought of as something altogether inert, something that could be "sold."[103] Securely "connecting" the new states "with the Union" was imperative if this public resource were not to be forfeited.[104] Revisions of territorial policy from 1784 to 1787 reflected these joint concerns. Jefferson was at his most doctrinaire not in his "liberal" notions of self-government but in his belief that republicanism depended on the size of the new states and that properly proportioned states would have a natural affinity.[105] These conclusions did not appear self-evident to later congressional committees or to westerners themselves. The proposed boundaries did not seem to make much sense.[106] It also became clear that more elaborate provisions would have to be made for the preconstitutional phase; Congress would have to govern its territories. A new ordinance "seemed necessary, for the security of property among uninformed, and perhaps licentious people."[107] Each new state would have to go through a period when, as James Monroe wrote, it would "in effect" be under "a colonial government similar to that which prevail'd in these States previous to the revolution."[108] The development of new terminology was a belated recognition of the fact that these new entities were nothing like states, even in the attenuated American sense. At the same time, the new "territorial" status reflected and anticipated a radical diminution of American statehood claims.

It would be a mistake to see the 1787 ordinance as a conservative betrayal of the earlier legislation. Later committees shared Jefferson's fundamental concern with preserving and extending the union of states, protecting private property, and securing public revenue. They likewise recognized the legitimizing function of republican self-government within constitutional limits. Congress did not abandon Jefferson's scheme; instead, Congress clarified the implications of the 1784 ordinance and provided for its implementation. If the 1784 ordinance could be interpreted as a "beautiful compact" by separatists, they soon discovered it was not being offered to them. The Northwest Ordinance of 1787 was also described as a "compact," but it was plainly not one into which any existing political community could enter; it more closely resembled the promises made by the British Crown in charter grants designed to encourage colonial development.[109] The promise of eventual statehood—now explicitly defined as the exclusive status of the members of the American union—may have distinguished the American "Empire" from others, but that "statehood" bore only a faint resemblance to that which the revolting colonies claimed for themselves.

The debasement of statehood was apparent in the emergence of the new status of territory and in the mechanical, automatic way in which one qualified for admission to the United States. While in a sense the territorial system was a kind of functional equivalent for the colonial origins of the original states, the differences between old and new states are striking. The artificiality and passivity of the new states stands in sharp contrast to the revolutionary seizure of power by the original thirteen. Statehood for the original United States involved a rejection of higher authority and an assertion of autonomy and distinctness, responses that made sense only in the context of imperial reorganization after the French and Indian War. But the new western states would come into being only by assimilation to higher authority, through recognition by the existing states and admission into the union. New state claims were premised on a rejection of particular colony-state claims and the consequent elevation of a congressional title to unlocated lands. A union that included these new political communities, as territories or states, was necessarily a kind of union different from that which bound the original states to each other.

By 1787 the need to establish effective control over the states was generally recognized. It was hoped that the Constitutional Convention would define "in the most accurate manner the limits of the States" and provide "an adequate remedy" for separatism and domestic insurrection.[110] Though the convention inspired new agitation for a renegotiation of state boundaries (including the popular suggestion that refractory Rhode Island be annexed to its neighbors),[111] the only basis for acceptable reform was the ratification of jurisdictional agreements—on general powers as well as specific boundaries—worked out over the previous decade. Thus, according to Article IV, section 3,

> New states may be admitted by the Congress into this Union; but no new State shall be formed or erected within the Jurisdiction of any other State; nor any State be formed by the Junction of two or more States, or Parts of States, without the Consent of the Legislatures of the States concerned as well as of the Congress.[112]

The same section also empowered Congress "to dispose of and make all needful Rules and Regulations respecting the Territory or other Property belonging to the United States." Section 4 guaranteed "to every State in the Union a Republican Form of Government."

These constitutional provisions confirmed the jurisdiction over new-state creation claimed by Congress in its ordinances for territorial government. There was a broad consensus for this jurisdiction—among large and small states, as well as among frontier settlers—even though it was not authorized by the Articles of Confederation. Landed states stipulated that new states be created in the West in their cessions to Congress; landless states had long agitated for the dismemberment of their large neighbors and the creation of new western states. With the creation of a national domain it became possible to respond to westerners' demands for more convenient governments. The resolution of territorial controversies pointed to a more diminutive concept of statehood: landless states and separatists had always advocated congressional supremacy; now the landed states retreated from state succession to colonial charter claims, as they ceded their distant western claims and looked to Congress to secure the remainder.[113]

It was also generally agreed that separatist movements could not be countenanced. Clearly it was much less risky to create new states or territories where there were few settlers and where the entire process of development toward statehood could be closely supervised and controlled. This preference revealed continuing insecurity over state jurisdiction and a pervasive suspicion among the states; it also revealed changing ideas of what a state should be. Territorial controversies had helped create a general agreement that Congress should exercise an effective, superintending jurisdiction; under the emerging territorial system, this jurisdiction was vastly enlarged. Subsequently, once Vermont and Kentucky were at last recognized and admitted to the union, membership in Congress would not confer American statehood on preexisting polities; new states would be created in national territory, according to steps set out in the Northwest Ordinance and adapted for other frontier areas.[114] Statehood thus became entirely artificial, the creation of a higher authority. The ideal new state was carved out of national territory within predetermined boundaries and with its public lands plighted to the United States in general. Such a new state could claim none of the jurisdictional autonomy—that is, control over its own territory—that the original states had claimed. Such a new state could never constitute the kind of threat to the union presented by the original states, with their overlapping claims and conflicting land and territorial policies. It is no accident that a new federal constitution radically enlarging congressional power and eliminating (as much as possible) traditional sources of interstate conflict should be drafted and ratified at a time when so many Americans had come to think of statehood in such modest terms.

PART · TWO

STATE-MAKING

· 3 ·

State and Citizen:
Settlers Against the
Pennsylvania Charter

Pennsylvania's charter claims were better defined and more defensible than those of any other large colony. The charter granted to William Penn in 1681 provided that his new colony should occupy the territory between forty and forty-three degrees north to a line drawn five degrees west of the Delaware River. Purchases from the Duke of York added further territory down the river as far as Cape Henlopen.[1] The uncertainty of the southern boundary, and its extension beyond the charter lines, led to a protracted dispute with Maryland that was resolved only in 1769 when the Crown confirmed the Mason-Dixon line.[2] But there were no other significant challenges to Pennsylvania's claims in its first seventy-five years, and—as litigation with Lord Baltimore demonstrated—the colony was well equipped, on legal grounds, to meet any that might subsequently develop. Pennsylvania enjoyed the luxury of reasonably well-defined boundaries, authoritatively established after those of its neighbors and apparently with their acquiescence.

The newly independent American states were drawn to the doctrine of state succession to colony claims as a barrier against political disintegration: colonial charters were seen as the prototypes of new state constitutions. Such logic should have helped secure Pennsylvania's territorial claims, particularly since, as a "landless" state, it was not jeopardized by the campaign against sea-to-sea charter claims. Nonetheless, Pennsylvania had as much trouble as any other American state in defending its jurisdiction, despite its apparently unexceptionable claims. "Perpetual encroachment and aggressions have irritated and distressed the inhabitants of this state," as the Pennsylvania council complained in 1780. "What people, State, or country, have we invaded, or insulted, or who has complained against us?"[3]

Pennsylvania found itself on the defensive because its claims covered two regions—around Pittsburgh and in the Wyoming Valley—that were frontiers for settlement and speculation originating in other colonies.[4] Early American boundary conflicts did not always result from a real confusion of territorial rights: a title controversy was often nothing more than a pretext for land-grabbing. Pennsylvania's claims were vulnerable because they were undeveloped, though well-defined and generally recognized. Colonies with vague, open-ended, and long dormant claims sought to overcome these defects by actually developing them: buying land from the Indians, sending in settlers, and exercising jurisdiction.[5] Such was the "late strange claim" set up by Virginia to the Pittsburgh region,[6] and the equally surprising extension of jurisdiction in the Wyoming Valley by the Connecticut Assembly in January 1774—reversing the colony's earlier position on the Susquehannah Company claim.[7] Virginia governor Dunmore's self-justification was particularly cynical, the interloper's classic claim: Virginia's right derived from "pre-occupancy" and the "general acquiescence of all persons," presumably including Pennsylvania authorities.[8] Connecticut settlers relied on their old charter—which they asserted, in the face of their own acquiescence in the Penn charter and in other boundary settlements, could not have been affected by any subsequent grant—and on land company purchases from the Indians (the wrong Indians, it turned out).[9]

In principle, Americans meant to respect each other's rights, as they would have their own respected, but in fact the right to jurisdiction was often difficult to distinguish from jurisdiction itself. The Revolution enhanced the prestige of charters and charter rights, descending unaltered to the present generation from a (relatively) distant past. But revolutionaries also insisted on government, or jurisdiction, by consent, and they did not hesitate to sweep aside whole categories of "rights" enjoyed under the old regime or to deprive the unpatriotic of their property. If territorial jurisdiction, like property, was based on a title—in theory sacred and inviolable—title, in both cases, could be forfeited. The way jurisdiction was exercised was thus crucial, in this era of rising political expectations; jurisdiction had to be its own justification. This was the lesson Pennsylvania came to learn in coming to terms with its reluctant citizens around Pittsburgh and in the Wyoming Valley. It was one thing to vindicate the state's rights against other states, through negotiation and litigation, but quite another actually to exercise jurisdiction amid malcontents.

The collapse of imperial authority over the colonies in the 1770s encouraged other jurisdictions to contest Pennsylvania's claims. The failure of the Empire and, in turn, of the United States to secure colony-state claims led to a proliferation of new claims, one leading to another. If Connecticut succeeded in establishing its claim, Pelatiah Webster suggested, "you may be assured Boston [the colony of Massachusetts] stands ready to extend their width to the South Sea also."[10] Because it no longer had effective recourse to higher authority, Pennsylvania's jurisdiction became more insecure than ever as the Revolution approached. "We have been attacked on three sides of the Province already," Governor John Penn complained, and "were not the Delaware too plain a boundary to be disputed we should undoubtedly be attacked on that side too."[11] (In fact, commissioners from New Jersey and Pennsylvania later had to determine the jurisdictional status of islands in the river.[12])

The strength of Pennsylvania's claims was undercut by the jurisdictional confusion of the Imperial Crisis. The advantage then lay with colonies that were creating new titles, not with those that sought to defend older but undeveloped claims. The fracturing of authority meant that supposedly subordinate colonial governments could act with greater independence (and not only under the leadership of radical patriots, as Virginia's aggressive western policy under Lord Dunmore demonstrated). The colonial governments of Connecticut and Virginia sponsored encroachments on Pennsylvania's claims, thus justifying the new state governments in continuing the attack and encouraging settlers to withhold their allegiance. Neighboring governments withdrew their recognition of Pennsylvania's boundaries just as it became virtually impossible to settle jurisdictional disputes, and just when intercolonial cooperation was crucial to the patriotic cause.

Connecticut and Virginia disingenuously claimed that they were willing to submit their differences with Pennsylvania to the determination of higher authority; the pretense of adjudication, provided that it did not actually take place, conferred legitimacy on their claims. Thus Connecticut agitated for a Privy Council hearing on the Wyoming question while

Pennsylvania denied that the two colonies had a common border and therefore anything to adjudicate.[13] When it became apparent, however, that the Wyoming settlers could not otherwise be dislodged, the Pennsylvanians were all for hurrying on a decision: "if the Matter was once determined against them before the King in Council we should then be able to manage them."[14] But Connecticut had no intention of waiting on a Privy Council decision. It was only necessary to "keep up appearances and delay," according to Pelatiah Webster. Webster predicted (in April 1774) that "the authority of Great Britain, or any other part of the earth over America, will lessen fast until it dwindles into nothing."[15] Dunmore was equally content to leave the controversy between Virginia and Pennsylvania formally unresolved; he suggested a "temporary line" that would in effect confirm his recent annexations of Pennsylvania territory.[16] The Pennsylvania Council later noted, "There is reason to believe those states who decline or delay such accommodation, have it in contemplation to introduce settlers, and otherwise strengthen themselves" while "the settlement of these disputes [is] protracted and embarrassed."[17]

The more aggressive the Virginians and the Susquehannah Company became, the more Pennsylvanians depended on authoritative interventions by the British to vindicate their claims, and the more they became aware of their own political liabilities. "Long may the Mother Country continue our *Umpire*, to prevent our dipping our hand in each other's Blood," Provost William Smith wrote to his friend William Samuel Johnson in Connecticut.[18] Confident in their growing numbers, however, the Connecticut settlers were not deterred by the possibility of violence. Governor Penn was "very fearful they will overrun a great part of the Province, & if they are left much longer in this Situation it will in all probability be impossible to remove them at all."[19] Smith acknowledged, "We cannot but consider them as restrained only by the authority of the Crown and parent State from over-running their neighbours."[20] The Pennsylvanians could not hope to muster an effective force against intrusions here or at Pittsburgh. "It will be in vain to contend with" the Virginians "in the way of Force," the governor advised Pennsylvania magistrates in Westmoreland County, and this went without saying at Wyoming, where there were no Pennsylvania magistrates and very few Pennsylvania settlers.[21]

When a punitive expedition was finally sent into Wyoming, it was a private force raised by subscription.[22] The colony's territorial claims did not concern most Pennsylvanians, despite patriotic pleas to prevent the dismemberment of "our country." William Smith believed that "it must be the Desire of every Friend to Pennsylvania, to see its Laws and Constitution extended and supported, through its utmost Limits, while its Rivers run or Mountains endure!"[23] But as the Connecticut delegates at Congress noted, when reporting on the dispute between Virginia and Pennsylvania, "Few or None save the Proprietors consider themselves interested in the Controversy, & the whole Attention of the public is taken up on more important Subjects."[24]

The vulnerability of Pennsylvania's claims reflected the discontinuity between the political community established by the revolutionaries and the claims of the Pennsylvania proprietors to unsold lands within the charter limits. Patriots in the other colonies argued that the king was a kind of trustee of their public lands and thus saw charter claims as integral to their pretensions to sovereign statehood.[25] But the new state of Pennsylvania was more clearly a negation of the old regime than most other new states, and this radical break jeopardized its claims to succeed to the colony's jurisdiction. Though Pennsylvania's charter claims were better defined than others, the relation of the new state to the old charter was much more ambiguous. By comparison, the strength of the Connecticut charter was not in its authoritative description of boundaries, but rather in its status as the organic law of the new state of Connecticut, under which local government continued to be exercised.[26] Pennsylvanians had been attacking proprietary claims and the charter government for many years before the Revolution, and that government had been an impediment to participation in continental resistance measures.[27] The result was that the Pennsylvanians who most vigorously defended the colony's territorial claims—the proprietary group and speculators holding proprietary titles—fell by the wayside, as Tories or neutrals, as resistance escalated.[28] The new state constitution of 1776, representing the most advanced republican thought of the day, underlined the importance of consent to membership in the state, and thus promoted the idea of the state as a community of like-minded individuals, dissociated from the colony's territorial claims. Continuing controversy over oaths of allegiance reinforced this notion of consensual community.

Pennsylvania's new state government was established in order to keep Pennsylvania in step with the other newly independent states. The new governors of the state were determined to put aside provincial particularism on behalf of continental cooperation. They were thus less concerned than their predecessors with maintaining its territorial claims, and they were inclined to attribute claims disputes to the selfish, unpatriotic interest groups that flourished under the old regime, or even to deliberate attempts to confound the resistance movement.[29] They were most concerned with inducing settlers in contested areas to cooperate in the common cause.

The break between the proprietary regime and the new state government weakened Pennsylvania's claims to unsettled parts of the old charter claims. The ambiguous character of the state's territorial pretensions was apparent in 1779 when the General Assembly finally confiscated proprietary lands and created a public domain. The justifications invoked in the preamble to the confiscation act reflected pervasive misgivings about the legality of what was seen as an extraordinary expedient. Penn's charter was supposed to have been designed for "the benefit of the settlers" as well as Penn's "particular emolument"; in any case, "it has been the practice and usage of states most celebrated for freedom and wisdom to controul and abolish all claims of power and interest, inconsistent with their safety and welfare." A small group of dissenters argued that the act was a blatant attack on property rights; the majority apparently agreed, at least to the extent of offering to compensate the proprietors for their losses. According to the critics, it "will appear to the world, as if they were now to be paid out of money ever heretofore . . . deemed indisputably their own."[30] Thus, even when Pennsylvania belatedly claimed full property rights within the limits of its jurisdictional pretensions, many Pennsylvanians questioned the legitimacy of those claims.

If some Pennsylvanians in the older parts of the state questioned the legitimacy of the state's succession to the proprietors' rights, or simply set little value on extending state jurisdiction, most settlers in the disputed frontier regions were openly hostile to Pennsylvania's claims. Large numbers of emigrants from other states had moved into these areas, while Pennsylvania's presence, in the form of undeveloped private property rights, was largely speculative. "The Lands whereof" the Connecticut people "have possessed themselves, are chiefly private Property, taken up or purchased by many Individuals in all Parts of the Province."[31] But because few settlements had actually been begun under these rights, it was easy for Connecticut propagandists to portray the proprietors and derivative titleholders as a parasitic landlord class. "The people of this colony [Connecticut], who know the value of freedom," would never submit to being "tenants under the proprietaries of Pennsylvania," said Roger Sherman.[32] Eliphalet Dyer, a prominent leader of the Susquehannah interests in Connecticut, believed that popular discontent could be exploited to strengthen his colony's claim. The "Common people" of Pennsylvania should be secured in their holdings and taught "how much better it will be for them to come in under our Colony."[33] "We can deal with the great land holders by & by when we have the main of the people [on] our side." The success of this strategy was apparent in the complaint of prominent Pennsylvanians who memorialized their assembly in October 1775. The Connecticut people were endeavoring "to draw off our Inhabitants to their Party by every undue Means in their Power; tempting some of the lowest of them with Offers of Commissions, Civil and Military; and others, particularly those who hold as Tennants, to become Landlords themselves, by Offers of the Lands on easier Terms than those of Pennsylvania."[34] The founders of Vermont, also emigrants from Connecticut, exploited the same popular prejudice against landlordism.[35]

Connecticut farmers had begun to exhaust their local land supply and were willing to move far afield in pursuit of freeholds. Silas Deane wrote Patrick Henry (respecting a proposal to start a colony in western Virginia), "We have no employ so natural for increasing youth, as the forming of New Settlements."[36] According to contemporary conventional wisdom, Connecticut's burgeoning population constituted a distinct threat to the security of its neighbors. Eliphalet Dyer reported that "Southern Gent[leme]n" in Congress believed that "if we prove Successful against the Ministerial Army . . . we shall after that make our way by force into any [of] the Southern Colonies we please."[37] Because of its large number of potential settlers, Connecticut's extensive charter claims could not be ignored: they might be the "foundation for an American empire."[38] One Pennsylvanian wondered if they "intend to leave Pennsylvania a name or Place at all among the Colonys."[39]

Pennsylvanians were badly outnumbered in the Pittsburgh region as well. "We few who are well affected to the Pennsylvania Government are held as aliens and disaffected," according to one report.[40] The area had long been a center of land speculation, drawing largely on rapidly developing areas in nearby Virginia. The Virginia colonial government had invested more heavily in the defense of the region than Pennsylvania; Virginia offered land on more favorable terms.[41] According to a Pennsylvania magistrate, who found himself powerless to enforce the colony's laws, "Every artifice are used to seduce the people; some by being promoted to civil or military employments, and others with the promise of grants of land on easy terms; and the giddy headed mob are so infatuated as to suffer themselves to be carried away by these insinuating delusions."[42]

The ability of the Virginians to mobilize an army of 1,500 to chastise the Indians and promote Lord Dunmore's speculative designs helped give substance to popular "delusions" about the status of the area. In response, Pennsylvanians could only issue dire warnings about the imminence of "anarchy and confusion, and total subversion of property."[43] Dunmore could not unilaterally assume jurisdiction: Virginia and Pennsylvania were both "parties to the dispute, and consequently neither can be judge."

Encroachments by other colonies and states supported by large numbers of settlers, in areas where its own claims remained relatively undeveloped, made the establishment of stable, recognized boundaries a high priority for successive Pennsylvania governments. The proprietary regime pursued a coordinated boundary policy, attempting not only to repel intrusions at Wyoming and Pittsburgh but also to preclude further difficulties by reaching settlements with other colonies as well.[44] Cadwallader Colden, acting governor of New York, agreed with Governor Penn "that the ascertaining and establishing the Boundaries between the Colonies is a Matter of great Importance."[45] But the friendly exchange between Pennsylvania and New York, made possible by the absence of conflicting interests, was exceptional, particularly as imperial relations deteriorated. The colonial governments were no longer checked from above, and common interests did not inhibit them from attacking one another. Governor Penn's embassy to Virginia was rebuffed, and talks with emissaries from Connecticut proved equally unproductive.[46]

The success of boundary negotiations depended on the existence of an effective higher authority, capable of determining and enforcing solutions to conflicts, or on a compelling need to harmonize claims in order to cooperate in a higher cause. Though the break with Britain aborted the proprietors' appeals to Privy Council—and no successor loomed in sight—Pennsylvanians found their old antagonists much more conciliatory, and even willing to compromise, as independent states. Governor Jonathan Trumbull of Connecticut suggested, before independence was formally declared, "If our Enemies prevail, which can be effected only by our disunion, no matter to any of us what becomes of all such Claims."[47] With the patriots in power, the colonies achieved a unity of purpose and began to overcome the antagonisms that different kinds of governments—royal, proprietary, and popular—had encouraged and that the British could no longer control. Patriotic Americans were determined to set the common cause above their particular interests. Disputed claims would in any case "remain to be occupied by Americans," the Virginian delegates at Congress wrote, "and whether these be counted in numbers of this or that of the United states will be thought a matter of little moment." [48] Colonial governments had not hesitated to provoke each other, even by acts of violence, but the revolutionaries believed that force should be used exclusively on the common enemy. In the words of Governor Trumbull, "the Gun and Bayonet are not the constitutional instruments to adjust and settle real Claims," recent colonial precedents notwithstanding. [49] Furthermore, despite institutional underdevelopment, Americans convinced themselves that they would be able to act collectively to resolve disputes among themselves. "It is probable as things are ripening," Silas Deane predicted in 1775, "that the Colonies will be Our Judges at last." [50]

Pennsylvanians were accustomed to thinking of territorial jurisdiction in terms of charter rights, and this tendency was reinforced by the relative ease with which they were able to gain acknowledgment of those rights through litigation with Connecticut over Wyoming and negotiations with Virginia over the southwestern boundary. But the apparent resolution of both controversies did not lead to an era of peace and harmony. It was not enough to vindicate Pennsylvania's rights against other jurisdictions; it was also necessary for the new state to govern its new citizens effectively. The "wild Yankees" at Wyoming remained a troublesome group, even as Connecticut leaders advised moderation and finally withdrew their sponsorship altogether. Zebulon Butler, one of the most influential settlers, taunted a Pennsylvania magistrate, "I am as Much Concerned of your Wetting us with your Watter as we are of Sheding our Blood." [51] Such sentiments took the form of active resistance to state authority in northeastern and southwestern Pennsylvania, including plans to form new states and rumored negotiations with the British. This unruliness was a direct legacy of the last years of the Empire, when Virginia and Connecticut sponsored emigrations into Pennsylvania territory.

In August 1779, commissioners from Virginia and Pennsylvania meeting at Baltimore agreed "to extend Mason's and Dixon's line due west five degrees of longitude, to be computed from the river Delaware" as Pennsylvania's southern boundary, and that another line running north from the western terminus of the southern line would be its western boundary. [52] The Virginia Assembly ratified the agreement in June 1780, under condition that Virginia titleholders be secured in their lands, and Pennsylvania accepted these terms in September. [53] During the next summer, after the Articles of Confederation had finally been ratified, Pennsylvania initiated proceedings under Article IX to resolve its differences with Connecticut over the Wyoming Valley.[54] By early 1782, there was "a prospect that all uncertainties concerning the extent of Pennsylvania will be removed before long," according to a newspaper item reporting an impending agreement with New Jersey over the Delaware River islands.[55] The decision of the Article IX court at Trenton in December 1782, upholding Pennsylvania's claims in Wyoming, apparently resolved the only important outstanding controversy.[56] The court's finding was hailed not only for vindicating Pennsylvania's jurisdictional rights, but also for "yielding a memorable proof" of the "political energy" of the Confederation. By the "peaceable and conclusive settlement of a dispute between two such powerful sovereign States, concerning a large and valuable territory," the United States had displayed—at least to the Pennsylvania Council—"a very singular and truly dignified example of a people who have wisdom and virtue enough not to waste in civil convulsions, the happiness and glory acquired by a successful opposition to their foreign enemies."[57]

Pennsylvania's victory at Trenton climaxed an extended campaign for stable, recognized boundaries. But settlements with other states did not automatically lead to acceptance of Pennsylvania's jurisdiction by settlers in the formerly disputed territories. The flaw in Pennsylvania's policy was to confuse jurisdiction, based on a right acknowledged by other states, with government, based on the consent of the people. Because they found neighboring states easier to deal with than their colonial predecessors, Pennsylvanians were optimistic about achieving jurisdictional stability. But the very fact that the American states were willing to compromise their disputes—evident in the large number of nonviolent boundary adjustments—meant that they had only a limited command of the loyalties of their citizens. This was nowhere more true than in contested frontier regions. As a result, there was an inverse relation between the ease with which boundaries could be altered or established, reassigning citizens from one state to another, and the ability of a state to govern effectively.

Pennsylvanians failed to appreciate the changing character of territorial controversies after independence. They continued to focus on reaching agreements with other states, while overlooking the problem of securing the allegiance of their would-be fellow citizens. This neglect was partly explained by the fact that the state was generally unable to exercise any jurisdiction at all until such agreements could be reached. Before Trenton, Pennsylvania authorities were virtually excluded from the Wyoming region, where settlers conducted their own affairs under the nominal authority of the state of Connecticut. From the beginning of the controversy Pennsylvanians believed that Connecticut's patronage was crucial to the recalcitrance of the Wyoming people, expecting that when the settlers "are no longer supported in their intrusion" they "will cool by degrees into a Just obedience to the Laws of Pennsilvania."[58] Because Connecticut governments, before and after independence, contrived to delay a decision as long as possible, Pennsylvanians developed an exaggerated idea of the significance of official sponsorship of the Wyoming settlement and exaggerated expectations of the impact of the decision when it was finally reached. After Trenton, a Pennsylvania officer reported that "the Conduct and Behaviour of the Inhabitants resembles that of a conquered Nation very much."[59] This description captured the sullen attitude of the Wyoming people, but it betrayed an assumption that, because Connecticut was now bound to withdraw its support, the settlers had no choice but to submit. Many years later, Timothy Pickering argued that had Pennsylvania "manifested any degree of generosity and magnanimity, if she had, indeed, consulted merely her own interest, she would have quieted the settlers in their old possessions."[60] The state should have entered into negotiations with the settlers at the outset; instead, it vacillated between lenient and punitive measures. In fact, Pennsylvania had no policy at all with respect to the Wyoming settlers; the issue was supposed to have been resolved at Trenton.

To the west, Pennsylvanians fixed their attention on the controversial boundary, and therefore on the state of Virginia, rather than the Virginian settlers. In order to resolve "the unhappy disputes upon our borders," President Joseph Reed told the Assembly, it was necessary "that there should be as early a decision of these points as possible."[61] The American commanders at Pittsburgh reinforced the idea that the failure to agree on a boundary, and later actually to run it, was the root of all evil in the area.[62] Thus, while waiting for Virginia to ratify the Baltimore agreement, Reed could hope that settlement of the line "will have an immediate Effect in restoring Peace & Tranquillity."[63] When news of Virginia's acquiescence reached Philadelphia, Reed "congratulate[d] the good People of . . . [Westmoreland] County on the happy Prospect of internal Peace."[64]

Pennsylvanians continued to attribute problems in the Pittsburgh area to the unsettled state of the boundary, even after the Baltimore agreement was ratified. Local citizens eagerly promoted this confusion in order to avoid onerous obligations. "The power of calling out the militia of this country, is more ideal than real," General Irvine told George Washington.

"Neither Civil nor Military law will take place" "till the lines between Virginia and Pennsylvania are determined, and actually run."[65] Yet to frame the problem in these terms was to deflect attention from the fact that many settlers resisted any government at all, and to look to further negotiations with Virginia to implement the boundary agreement as a panacea. But Governor Thomas Jefferson of Virginia believed that the Baltimore agreement was precise enough, and local geography well enough known, that there should have been no problem in deciding who belonged to which state without a survey. "I make no doubt but you can nearly Judge whereabouts the north line [of Virginia] will Run," he wrote Colonel Brodhead at Pittsburgh.[66] Ironically, Pennsylvania's determination to run a definitive boundary, encouraged by the exasperated complaints of the American commanders, led settlers to look at prior arrangements as "temporary" and contingent. Virginians cherished the hope that a final determination would return them to Virginia.[67] The announcement of Congress's intention to form new states in its prospective national domain (in September and October 1780 resolutions) added a further dimension to jurisdictional confusion in western Pennsylvania.[68] But confusion would not be resolved by further negotiations. It was only when Pennsylvania began to distinguish the problem of governing the West from the more limited boundary question that it was possible for it to take effective measures, for instance in proscribing separatism, to establish state authority.[69]

Despite their radical break with the old regime, Pennsylvania's new leaders carried on the proprietors' territorial policy. Because other colonies sponsored encroachments on its jurisdiction, Pennsylvania should appeal to the appropriate higher authority, to which they were bound to submit, in order to vindicate its rights; or, with this recourse in reserve, it should open direct negotiations with other governments to secure recognition of its claims. But Pennsylvanians did not see the necessity of dealing directly with its new citizens, and, as a result, the resolution of interstate conflicts did not bring law and order to Wyoming or the Pittsburgh region. In both cases, a dangerously narrow and legalistic conception of territorial controversies impeded the establishment of state authority.

The means by which these settlements were reached, as well as their specific provisions, created distinctive problems requiring distinctive responses. Direct negotiations with Virginia resulted in a more comprehensive agreement. In return for concessions on the boundary, the Virginia Assembly insisted "that the private property and rights of all persons acquired under, founded on, or recognized by the laws of either country" previous to the agreement should "be saved and confirmed to them."[70] The Wyoming litigation, however, was confined strictly to the question of jurisdiction. According to Congress's interpretation of the Articles, "the right of the tenants in possession" would have to be considered at another hearing.[71] The Trenton decision thus avoided the only important issue to the Connecticut settlers: security of their land titles. Furthermore, having provided for the interests of its former citizens, the state of Virginia could withdraw from the field, while Connecticut continued to press for recognition of the settlers' property rights. The Wyoming people could look forward to future interventions, from Connecticut or from Congress, and perhaps another Article IX court.[72] In the meantime, they could legitimately withhold full submission from Pennsylvania. Thus the Trenton decision, without further agreements clarifying the rights of settlers, was destined only to make things worse in Wyoming.

Though the agreement between Virginia and Pennsylvania should have created satisfactory conditions for a peaceful transfer of jurisdiction, confusion reigned in the Pittsburgh region for the next several years. There was a pervasive sense that jurisdictional arrangements were contingent and that Congress was prepared to ignore colonial charter claims altogether and establish new western states. Confusion about the jurisdictional future of the West was apparent in the groundswell of sentiment for a new state in 1782, in the first of a new generation of separatist movements premised on opposition to state tax and land policies and other sectional grievances. But the new state scheme in western Pennsylvania demonstrated the limits of popular discontent, as well as the region's attenuated loyalties to the state. Congress's pointed neglect of the separatists' petition—which "lay on the table without a single motion or remark relative to it"—punctured the popular myth that the United States would be a jurisdictional *deus ex machina*.[73] Commitment to the new state idea was even more ephemeral than loyalty to Pennsylvania, particularly when it became apparent that Pennsylvania meant to uphold its authority. Separatist agitation revealed the inadequacy of a policy focused on boundaries alone. New state activity encouraged state authorities to act vigorously and dispel the not entirely unwarranted belief that eastern Pennsylvanians would be just as happy to see the westerners cut adrift.[74] The articulation of grievances provided a reform agenda to accompany punitive measures against new state proponents.

The troubles at Wyoming were even longer-lasting, owing to the continuing conflict of fundamental interests, the open-ended decision at

Trenton, and misguided state policy. Pennsylvania land claimants were a powerful force working against recognition of Connecticut titles, with their own at risk; though most Connecticut people were willing to accede to Pennsylvania's jurisdiction, they were unwilling to jeopardize their land claims. The determination of the Wyoming settlers to fight for secure titles and local self-determination—and their ability to appeal beyond Pennsylvania for help—led them to organize and govern themselves, in defiance of state authority. But the idea of forming a new state was never generally popular (despite the sensational appearance of Ethan Allen) and only gained ground among extremists when large numbers of the original Connecticut settlers made their peace with Pennsylvania.[75] Many speculators in Wyoming (and elsewhere) were anxious to vindicate the Susquehannah Company's claim in its fullest extent—as opposed to the claims of particular settlers with company titles—and a new state was their only hope. But the interests of most Wyoming people were compatible with Pennsylvania's jurisdiction. Once Pennsylvania belatedly capitulated to the settlers' demands, by forming Luzerne County (September 1786) and passing the Confirming Act (March 1787), securing the titles of *bona fide* claimants, there was no longer a mass base for collective resistance to state authority.[76]

Pennsylvania was compelled to come to terms with settlers in areas where its jurisdiction had been acknowledged by the other states. The Rev. James Finley told westerners, on a propaganda mission in early 1783, that "the Right of Pennsylvania to all the Lands within her Charter Boundaries" was "universally confest" by the "undisputed Judgement of the United States."[77] But as Finley's mission itself suggested that right was not automatically translated into obedience to the state. It was fittingly ironic that Finley should be directed to invoke the example of the "submission of the Inhabitants settled under the Connecticut Claim" at Wyoming; Pennsylvania's political leaders, who had provided Finley with his arguments, were still convinced that the loyalties of citizens could be determined by interstate agreements. But "ye people seemed rather hushed than convinced" by his arguments, and Finley himself became an advocate for a more enlightened and responsive western policy.[78] American citizens would have something to say about the way they were governed, or their nominal rulers would suffer the consequences. By comparison, the interstate claims controversies that absorbed so much attention were easy to resolve—states would have to recognize and guarantee each other's rights. The rights of American citizens, in the midst of jurisdictional flux, were much more difficult to determine. It took many years for Pennsylvania's leaders even to recognize the problem.

Interstate boundary adjustments in the years after independence helped define the states as territorial entities. These agreements eventually eliminated the challenges to state jurisdiction that flourished where claims overlapped. But at the same time that statehood claims became better defined geographically, statehood itself was devalued, by the same processes. Settlers in controversial areas, often migrants from other states, learned to think of themselves as American citizens. Separatists in western Pennsylvania, for instance, called themselves "free men and free citizens of America," while claiming the "unalienable" right to govern themselves.[79] In conditions of jurisdictional flux, it was crucial to abstract individual rights from state pretensions, which might be overturned, particularly when counterclaimants pinned their hopes on another state's claims. Because "the rights of citizens are sacred," Connecticut was justified in its continuing interest in the fate of its former citizens in Wyoming after the Trenton decision. Of course, the argument made sense only if citizenship or a right to citizenship transcended the positive law of particular states. But "those Setlers undoubtedly are entitled to the rights of Citizens," Governor Matthew Griswold of Connecticut wrote Pennsylvania Council President Dickinson. "Any violation of their rights in these points infringes the General Rights of all."[80] The settlers themselves complained that since Trenton they had been "intirely" and unjustly "denied the Benefits of Citizens and Freeholders."[81]

The idea that some kind of general "American" citizenship transcended state borders was crucial not only to opponents of state authority, who sought to legitimate resistance, but also to the states themselves, in negotiating jurisdictional transfers. If citizens did not carry their political and property rights with them, how could a state ever sanction a jurisdictional cession without violating fundamental obligations to members of the community, obligations that did not cease—according to prevailing political logic—even when another state's right to the territory in question was acknowledged? Jurisdictional transfers were conceivable only to the extent that the rights of individuals were not affected.

The jurisdictional issue was complicated in Pennsylvania, however, because the internal revolution had led to the proscription of large numbers of loyalist or neutral nonjurors, and so to a narrow definition of citizenship, centering on oaths of allegiance. (The Constitutionalists used the oath to uphold the controversial 1776 state constitution as a partisan tactic against patriotic Republicans who sought constitutional change.[82]) Virginians might well wonder "whether the s[ai]d Inhabitants are free citizens of Penn[sylvani]a without re-taking the Oath of Allegiance."[83] The question remained ambiguous until the Assembly expressly confirmed the settlers' Pennsylvanian citizenship in April 1782, thus guaranteeing political rights as the earlier agreement with Virginia had secured property rights.[84] The Wyoming people subsequently invoked this precedent, claiming that their residence in the state and their compliance with its laws should entitle them to the privileges of citizens, without any further explicit submission or oath-taking that might be used against them in the struggle with the Pennsylvania land claimants. A committee of the Pennsylvania Assembly accepted these premises, replying that "the Legislative body look upon all persons residing within the chartered bounds of the State as citizens."[85] But this belated capitulation, implemented in legislation over the next two years, followed an extended period in which the political status, and the land claims, of these settlers had remained ambiguous, because of "the interest of those companies & persons who pretended a prior right to the lands in question from Pennsylvania."[86]

By 1785, wartime suspicions had abated enough to allow a more generous and inclusive notion of citizenship to emerge, recognizing everyone's rights, regardless of previous background, within determinate geographical limits. Just as the states accorded citizenship to "persons removing from one State to another," the citizenship of settlers from other states in hitherto contested regions was also, henceforth, automatically recognized.[87] But this was possible only because citizenship had lost its specific character, and did not necessarily flow from membership in particular state communities. Thus the definition of state boundaries and the emergence of the idea of residential citizenship devalued state citizenship: the "sacred" rights that all Americans were supposed to enjoy—to choose their own governors and to be secure in their property—were not rooted in the states themselves. In turn, this incipient sense of a transcendent American citizenship facilitated the creation of a national political community under the Federal Constitution.

The revolutionary war effort compelled states to minimize their differences in order to cooperate in the common cause. This meant that states attempted to mute state loyalties in contested frontier areas and encouraged identification with fellow Americans. Continental garrisons at Pittsburgh and Wyoming emphasized this community of interests transcending particular states. George Washington advised the commander at Pittsburgh, Daniel Brodhead, to cultivate "unanimity" among Virginians and Pennsylvanians.[88] General Edward Hand, one of Brodhead's predecessors, appealed to "Love of our Country"—meaning America in general—while dismissing "Invidious distinctions" between states.[89] Loyalty to particular states was likened to partisanship, the bane of virtuous republics. Because state rivalries weakened the common cause, they were doubtless promoted by enemies of the Revolution. It was an "infallible rule," according to General Lachlan McIntosh, "that whoever attempts to foment or revive these old Jelousys . . . have some sinister designs of their own and are no friends of their Country."[90] "Old Jelousys," dating from the colonial period, were no longer legitimate, particularly when the fate of the "country," the United States, was in jeopardy.

Patriotic propaganda thus helped undermine state loyalties in frontier areas. The Connecticut settlers told the Pennsylvania Assembly after the Trenton decision, "We care not under what State we live, if we can live Protected and happy."[91] Not caring was a result of not knowing what state they belonged to, a confusion that was compounded by the popular notion that membership in a political community was based on consent. William Hooker Smith, a Wyoming settler who finally aligned himself with Pennsylvania, outlined the possibilities there (in July 1786): "If we Disone being within The State of Pensylvania, we are Still under The State of Connecticut, or in a State of Nature."[92] Each position had its advocates. The residents of Pittsburgh complained that they were simultaneously subject to the jurisdiction of both Pennsylvania and Virginia, and protested against the establishment of martial law—yet a third jurisdiction.[93] Consent was more than an abstraction in both places. Citizens paid or withheld taxes, appeared in or avoided court, or participated or not in elections in one state or another, or no state at all. Political loyalties were thus both more narrowly and more generally defined as identification with particular states diminished in significance. Frontier people had a highly developed sense of their rights as individuals, notably to local self-government, as well as a generalized sense of their status as American citizens, as members of an inclusive national community. They believed that "it is not material . . . what jurisdiction prevails, provided the original principles of the government are equal and free."[94]

Settlers claimed that their rights did not flow from any state's jurisdiction; they saw citizenship as a voluntary exchange of allegiance for protection and other benefits of government. If civil and property rights were not protected, settlers were *"thrown into . . . a state of nature."* It was impossible *"that the human species should be under any obligation of allegiance to a government that does not and will not protect them in their property."*[95] The premises of this argument could not be gainsaid by state authorities, who acknowledged—in reference to chaotic conditions in the West (in March 1780)—that "it is the indispensable duty of every Government to extend its protection and care to all its subjects, yielding peaceable and due obedience to its laws."[96] This maxim could easily be turned against the state, particularly when it became apparent that it could not protect its partisans from the Virginians. Were these Pennsylvanians then released from their obligations to the state? Former citizens of other states also naturally hesitated to submit to Pennsylvania's authority, thus jeopardizing their rights. Acknowledging Pennsylvania's jurisdiction was to enter a "state of nature"—as far as those rights were concerned—not to escape it. Furthermore, basic security against attacks from the British or native American enemies was provided not by the state but by continental garrisons. It was thus not clear what the state was offering in exchange for obedience.

While state citizenship seemed increasingly contingent, because it could be so easily changed, as well as diminutive, when compared to a transcendent American citizenship, there was a corresponding inflation of popular expectations of the rights and privileges that citizens of particular states ought to enjoy. In Wyoming, submission to Pennsylvania depended on recognition of those rights, regardless of the Trenton decision. "The sooner we can have the priviledge of electing our own Officers, Civil and Military, agreeable to the constitution of this state [Pennsylvania], the sooner happiness, peace and good order will be restored to this settlement."[97] As Pennsylvania discovered, the "exercise of the Civil authority is altogether impracticable"; "the authority of the State, without respect, [was] Damned."[98] It was impossible to enforce Pennsylvania laws without armed force. In the west, malcontents "take hold of any thing that would offer to Screen themselves from the Law of this State."[99] But these were legitimate tactics for gaining concessions from the state: "They are now afraid of you and Dread your Power," William Judd wrote Zebulon Butler. "Keep up that Idea."[100]

One of the settlers' key demands was that a new oath of allegiance be forsworn (in the west) or that subscription to a state oath be accompanied by the full extension of political rights. The first local elections after Trenton had excluded the Connecticut people and were dominated by "those that Call'd themselves Land holders" under Pennsylvania, most of whom lived at some distance from the settlement.[101] In November 1785, a meeting of Connecticut settlers at Kingston protested that Pennsylvania "have withheld from us the rights of free citizens, and benefits of civil government, and participation of their laws."[102] According to a subsequent petition, "we now *wish to be received as good citizens of the State of Pennsylvania,*" provided that the settlement was organized into a new county and free elections were guaranteed.[103] When the Assembly responded favorably to this overture, large numbers of Connecticut settlers agreed to take the loyalty oath. Their participation in Pennsylvania elections was also supposed to create binding political obligations. Hard-line opponents of accommodation warned that the settlers should avoid elections, for otherwise "you are Compleatly saddled with the Laws of Pensylvania and your property all at Hazard."[104]

The most pressing concern of settlers in both western Pennsylvania and the Wyoming Valley was to secure their land claims. It was this issue that could lead otherwise patriotic settlers not only to resist state authority but to abandon the American cause altogether. Jefferson thus justified the activities of Virginia title commissioners who had been busily confirming Virginians' claims in the region ceded to Pennsylvania: "It is surely an object, worthy the attention of us all to provide that a tract of country, derelict by the State under which they wished to live, should not be urged into a secession from the common union, and into an assumption of independance by fears that their actual possessions may be made to give way to mere paper titles [from Pennsylvania]."[105] According to this line of reasoning—disingenuous as it may have been—Pennsylvania was being protected against a shortsighted discrimination on behalf of its own land claimants. These eleventh-hour confirmations gave Virginia settlers a clear standing as titleholders that was subsequently recognized in negotiations between the two states. "Good policy will induce" Pennsylvania to agree to Virginia's demands for its titleholders, George Mason wrote, while the question was still pending. It was necessary "to conciliate the affections of her new citizens; without which she will find herself involved in a very disagreeable business with these people."[106]

The fact that Virginia succeeded in securing its settlers' claims precluded the deep-seated opposition to state authority that characterized the Wyoming settlement throughout the 1780s. "We do not mean to become abject slaves," John Jenkins told Pennsylvania commissioners in 1783, and

"We do not think . . . the lawful defence of what we Esteem to be Our own can with any Justice be Termed a Disaffection to Government."[107] Three years later the settlers were still determined not to submit "unless we have a previous assurance that our lands and property are fully secured to us."[108] In 1787 Connecticut titleholders petitioned the Pennsylvania Assembly for a *"free and gratuitous confirmation of our titles to our lands."*[109] By this time, however, the issue had been complicated by further emigrations from Connecticut and the Susquehannah Company's sponsorship of the so-called half-share men, whose only hope was a complete break with Pennsylvania.[110] William Hooker Smith was convinced "thare will be a General Revolution as well in This State as others" and feared that "unless This Poor Distres[se]d almost Distracted people are made Easey in Thare Improvements it will Begin hear."[111]

The Pennsylvania Assembly finally offered terms to longtime settlers (but not to recent arrivals) in the Confirming Act of March 1787, perhaps moved by fears of imminent anarchy throughout the United States. The Connecticut people were now secured in their lands, they thought (this did not prove entirely true) and as Council President Benjamin Franklin wrote, they would henceforth enjoy *"the protection of one of the principal States in the Union."*[112]

Heightened political consciousness, combined with legitimate anxieties about property rights as well as less laudable impulses to speculate in lands at Pennsylvania's expense, led to the efflorescence of schemes for new states in both areas. These proposals were a good measure of jurisdictional confusion; they also constituted the ultimate, if implicit, sanction in negotiations between settlers and the state over land titles and political rights. "God and Nature seem to have designed that the Inhabitants upon these Western Waters should be divided in their internal government," according to a petition presented to Congress in January 1783.[113] But it was the disintegrating authority of the state and pervasive doubts about its determination to uphold its claims that made anything seem possible. At least some easterners were willing to cut off the transmontane region, and even native Pennsylvanians in the west were prepared to consider new state proposals—if the state did not respond to their grievances.

In these volatile circumstances, conciliatory gestures to former citizens of Virginia or Connecticut alienated the loyalties of many Pennsylvania settlers. "Seeing the manner faithful subjects of Pennsylvania are treated," began one complaint from the west, "would your Excellency wonder if they would be ready to join any party or new State faction that might offer?"[114] The Confirming Act, securing the claims of Connecticut settlers in Wyoming, was an "outrageous violation of the rights of freemen," according to disgruntled Pennsylvanians, who threatened to "proceed to extremities in the defence of their common freedom."[115] Pennsylvania was unable to build its authority on the minority factions that had been loyal to the state from the beginning; in fact, these groups proved to be political liabilities to the state by obstructing settlements with their opponents.

The redefinition of political community proceeded from and contributed to a sense of infinite possibility, reflecting at once the optimism of the revolutionary generation and an undercurrent of pessimism about the future of the American republics. Thomas Scott, a Pennsylvania magistrate, reported some of the possibilities being discussed at Pittsburgh in early 1781.[116] "Give up all" the territory west of Laurel Hill to Congress or "let us grow to be a considerable part of you is the cry of many," said Scott. Westerners would "certainly think themselves Intolerably agrieved" if Pennsylvania lands to their west were given up to Congress while the state held on to the settlements. Even those who considered themselves Pennsylvania loyalists insisted on the territorial integrity of the western country ("which appears so naturally connected"), and on more favorable terms "respecting the price of our land," failing which "perhaps not ten men on this side the mountains . . . would not lift arms against the state." The proposal to form a new state was simply a radical extension of this logic and flourished as long as the policies of Virginia and Congress as well as Pennsylvania remained undetermined or unknown. Once it was clear that Pennsylvania meant to retain its western lands (by invoking sanctions against separatists and by refusing to consider a cession to Congress) and that neither Virginia nor Congress would intervene, the outstanding issues between westerners and easterners could finally be resolved.

The new state idea was a recurrent motif in resistance to Pennsylvania authority in the Wyoming Valley. The example of Vermont was frequently held up for emulation, and the common origins of settlers in both places and their common determination to uphold their land claims encouraged this identification.[117] "You have been greatly oppressed, by the land-schemers of Pensylvania," Ethan Allen, hero of Vermont's revolution, told the Wyoming people. Drawing on Vermont's experience, Allen advised the Connecticut settlers, "Crowd your settlements, add to your numbers and strength; procure fire-arms, and ammunition, be united among yourselves." The alternatives were "Liberty & Property; or slavery and poverty."[118] An unknown writer told Allen, encouraging him to come to Wyoming, "Nothing but coercive Measures will Answer."[119] But such aggressive designs did not emerge spontaneously in Wyoming: they were sponsored by the Susquehannah Company (Allen was given shares), and the company relied on outside forces ("as many of your hardy Vermonters [as] may be Induced to Join You") to overpower Pennsylvania. And though the Wyoming people had always governed themselves, with or without state sanction, they disclaimed any intention of forming their own state. The "temporary system of policy" adopted in late 1785 was designed "to prevent as much as possible that disorder and licentiousness which are inseparable from a state of anarchy . . . until the laws of Pennsylvania can operate in these settlements, and be administered on constitutional principles."[120] These ad hoc associations aimed at unanimity and therefore tended to take moderate positions that did not preclude accommodation with Pennsylvania.

When Pennsylvania finally offered terms to the settlers, this unanimity was shattered. As long as Pennsylvania remained unbending, "not only the settlers, but the people of Connecticut and the majority of the people of Pennsylvania might excuse your opposition to government," according to Timothy Pickering, the transplanted New Englander who played a crucial role in winning over the Wyoming people.[121] But how could the settlers refuse the state's generous proposals? "Have we not told Pennsylvanians, and the whole World, that we wished to be owned by them in a constitutional way, and that then we would submit?" William Hooker Smith asked. Were not the Connecticut people now free to participate in Pennsylvania elections and choose their own officers?[122] These offers split the militant leadership from the moderates: "The People in General are Determened To adhear To Pensylvania," Smith reported, even before the Confirming Act was passed.[123]

After Pennsylvania gained supporters in Wyoming, and the settlers became divided among themselves, new state proponents began to rely on the collapse of state authority throughout America, in the wake of Shays's Rebellion and other popular disturbances. There were "*banditties* rising up against law and good order in all quarters of our country."[124] "The federal Government is upon its last Leggs," William Judd wrote Zebulon Butler in January 1787, "and you may stand an Equal Chance with the rest of mankind if you are firm Steady and United."[125] "The general commotion we are entering" would favor insurrectionists.[126] Shays's Rebellion was supposed to work to the advantage of militants in Wyoming whether it was suppressed (after which refugees would flock into the area) or successful, and a "state of anarchy" resulted. According to Timothy Hosmer, another Susquehannah speculator, anarchy would lead to a "Monarchical" government: "undoubtedly there will be an anihilation of State lines under a one Headed Government," which was expected to look more favorably on the Susquehannah claim.[127]

Timothy Pickering attributed the unsettled state of affairs at Wyoming "to the natural instability of the common people." Settlers there "have lived in anarchy" for years, and "the present generation of young men have grown up without any experience of the blessings of regular government."[128] The new state movement at Wyoming in 1786–87 was a reflection of this collapse of authority. When the settlers divided on accommodating with Pennsylvania, the militant minority was released from the constraints of consensus. Visions of anarchy throughout America inspired the same sense of contingency in Wyoming that characterized western Pennsylvania in 1782–83, when separatist sentiment was ascendant. But in neither case was there deep popular commitment to the new state idea. Though resistance to Pennsylvania in Wyoming had been nearly universal and the settlers had been willing to resort to violence to defend their rights, the new state movement did not command significant indigenous support. It was promoted by ambitious land speculators and depended on auxiliaries from Connecticut and Vermont or, by 1787, on the disintegration of state governments throughout America. By contrast with the earlier history of civil disobedience in Wyoming, the new state movement was curiously passive. The desperation of the militants was apparent in the way they embraced the hope that the American system would not survive; perhaps they were unduly influenced by nationalist propaganda and overestimated the "critical" state of the nation. The Constitutional Convention was a blow to their hopes. As Benjamin Rush exulted, the new national government "will overset our state dung cart . . . and thereby restore order and happiness to Pennsylvania."[129]

The resolution of jurisdictional confusion in western Pennsylvania and in the Wyoming Valley required not only agreements with neighboring governments, and agreements with the settlers themselves—as became clear in each area in the years after the jurisdictional question was supposedly resolved—but also a clarification of the role of the central government. The realization that Congress would not set up its own claim in western Pennsylvania, or encourage new state proponents, made it possible to implement the boundary agreement with Virginia and to establish Pennsylvania's authority among former Virginians. In the case of Wyoming, the possibility of a new Article IX court made the federal role ambiguous for some time after the Trenton decision. When this possibility was foreclosed, and the state of Connecticut disclaimed any further intention of promoting the settlers' interests—particularly after its western land cession was accepted in 1786—the settlers would come to terms with Pennsylvania.[130] Even more crucial, however, was the question of whether the union would survive and whether it could secure state claims, as it became apparent that the states lacked the means or the will to uphold their own sovereignty—"that Manly resentment Necessary to the Political Existence of Every sovereign State."[131] The adoption of the Constitution was thus critical to the completion of Pennsylvania's campaign for jurisdictional stability and recognized boundaries.

The balancing of citizens' rights, state claims, and central authority was a complicated task that absorbed the attention of American statesmen in the decade before the adoption of the Federal Constitution. State rights could be adjusted, because all were members of a new American "empire" that would enforce their legitimate claims.[132] At the same time, the "constitutional rights" that had been vindicated in the Revolution were "common to all the citizens" of America, and a due respect for these rights would prevent any injustice being done when jurisdiction was transferred from one state to another.

The fierce competition for public lands meant that boundary negotiations would be a most serious matter for state governments and for Congress. But it was imperative to fix the limits of the states in order to prevent jurisdiction from becoming a popular issue, as it did in Vermont. Given the apparently chaotic conditions in postwar America, and the natural conflicts of interests among states, the resolution of controversial state claims was a remarkable accomplishment. A writer in the *Carlisle Gazette* wrote in 1785, remarking on the completion of Pennsylvania's western boundary, "It is a Measure of great wisdom in the State, as it fixed their boundary and jurisdiction determinately and transmits it without equivocation to posterity."[133] Establishing boundaries defined the terms of subsequent and unabated sectional controversy. Once the limits of the states were known—and once their constitutions were generally ac-cepted—politics could be normalized. Abstract notions of citizenship and individual rights could be translated into the realities of day-to-day politi-cal life. Within the limits set by national constitutional reform and by American citizens' sense of their own rights, the new American states could begin to function as political communities.

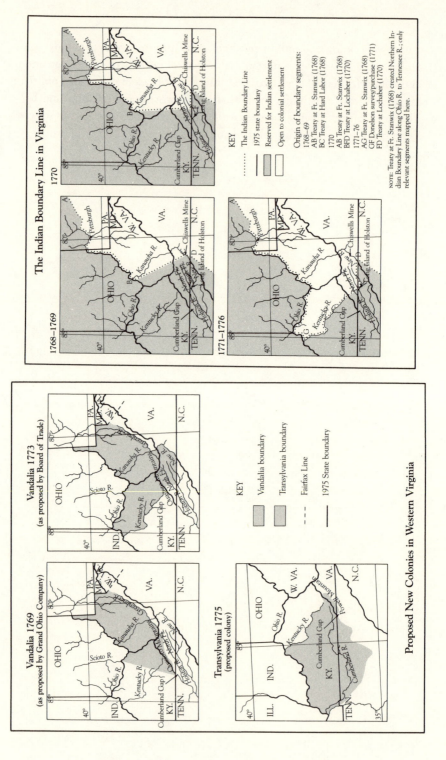

· 4 ·

Virginia and the West

On March 1, 1784, Virginia ceded its vast charter claims north of the Ohio River to the Continental Congress. This epochal transaction resolved the protracted dispute over western claims between the landed states and Congress. It secured the first strong congressional claim to a national domain and set in motion a liberal territorial policy that led to the formation of new western states.

The cession also climaxed Virginia's decade-long pursuit of policy goals in the West deemed vital to its sovereign pretensions. Virginia did not intend to retain jurisdiction across the Ohio. It did require that state claims there, based on the 1609 charter, be recognized by Congress and the other states. Though it acknowledged that abridgement of those claims was ultimately necessary, it insisted that this be done on terms the General Assembly itself should dictate. A cession of Virginia western claims to Congress, under express stipulations, was the logical culmination of this policy.

The Virginia cession vindicated the state's claims and eliminated one of the chief threats to its sovereignty. Both in a symbolic sense and a real sense, challenges to territorial jurisdiction were challenges to the existence of the new states. British tampering with colonial boundaries was seen as one of the reasons for revolution. Similarly, new state leaders had to fend off threats by domestic separatists, local and out-of-state land claimants (including loyalists), the conflicting claims of other states, and, for those states with western claims, counterclaims by Congress or other nations.

Virginia faced imperial boundary changes, implied in the Proclamation of 1763 and subsequent Indian boundaries, and explicitly in the proposed new colony of Vandalia and the Quebec Act in the 1770s. Separatists challenged colony and state jurisdiction in Transylvania (Kentucky) and in southwestern Virginia. Private land companies, including the Ohio and Loyal companies of Virginia, in addition to the the Indiana, Illinois, and Wabash companies, all dominated by out-of-staters, sought to establish property claims within Virginia's charter lines.[1] Meanwhile Pennsylvania asserted its claims in the contested Pittsburgh region. In the farther West, England, Spain, and the United States Congress promoted various title pretensions, as did Connecticut and Massachusetts on the basis of their charters, and New York State on the strength of its suzerainty over the Iroquois—all within the limits of the Virginia charter.[2]

A successful reconciliation of the states' various interests and policies was vitally important to the future health of Congress and the Union. If Virginia failed to gain guarantees from Congress and the other states for its territorial claims, it would be perpetually exposed to encroachments from its neighbors—and from Congress. Congress might assert its jurisdiction in the West on its own initiative. This would "introduce a most dangerous precedent which might hereafter be urged to deprive [any state] of territory or subvert [its] sovereignty."[3] Yet if state rights and sovereignty were secured, it would be possible to entrust Congress with larger powers, even in such ambiguous areas as commerce and taxation where it was much less certain what state rights or powers were or should be. The vindication and guarantee of state rights had to precede the enlargement of congressional powers.

The controversy over western land claims dragged on throughout the war years, despite the obvious need for harmony among the states. As early as 1776, Virginia's leaders showed a willingness to abridge the state's claims. The Virginia constitution provided for the creation of "new governments" in the West.[4] In 1778, Richard Henry Lee proposed "the Ohio as a boundary to the Westward."[5] The Northwest could be "settled for [the] common good and ma[d]e a new State." That a cession of state claims to Congress might be the best means of achieving these goals was a familiar idea by this time in Virginia and at Congress. The Virginia House of Delegates passed the state's first cession act in January 1781, in response to a congressional call for cessions in September 1780. But the cession offer aroused suspicion and hostility in other states, and Congress refused to accept it.[6]

The opposition to Virginia's claims and to its cession offer included land company speculators, chiefly from Pennsylvania, and the small, landless states, led by Maryland, another center of land speculation.[7] The small states feared that Virginia's boundary proposals would leave that state too large and powerful. Conditions attached to the cession, notably the invalidation of all private titles not recognized by Virginia in the cession region, struck directly at land company interests. Anxieties about the survival of small states in an unequal union thus combined indistinguishably with less exalted private interests.

Virginia's opponents blocked reception of the cession until 1784, hoping in the meantime to erect a congressional title on another source or to pressure Virginia into making a more generous offer. The controversy was drawn out because of confusion about the validity of overlapping state claims in the West—and the possibility that Congress might ignore them all—and also because the relation between individual states and the United States remained so ambiguous. The cession was an attempt to resolve this ambiguity and define Virginia's jurisdiction on terms most favorable to the state. The state's opponents explored every possible alternative before finally capitulating.

Virginia's interest in its western claims dated from the prerevolutionary period. As a colony, Virginia had taken the lead in the British advance into the Ohio Valley. Pennsylvania was also well situated on the Ohio frontier, and its merchants established a trade network reaching into the Illinois country soon after the British victory over the French in the French and Indian War. But Pennsylvania did not have an open-ended sea-to-sea charter. The western lands controversy began in competition between interests in these two colonies, under rapidly changing political conditions.[8] Though the colonies, and later states, confronted each other directly in the struggle for jurisdiction in the Pittsburgh region, Pennsylvania had no direct interest (as a colony or state) in the disposition of lands farther to the west. Before the American Revolution the lack of connection between Pennsylvania land speculators and the provincial government worked to their advantage. Influential English speculators could be drawn into a private venture, and the company claims were not compromised by association with American colonial claims, which the British government was beginning to view with alarm.

The Pennsylvanians turned their attention from trade to land in the wake of disappointing returns on investments in the fur trade. The Illinois and Wabash companies, which also included important members from other colonies, built their extensive claims on private transactions with Indian nations. But the most important land company, the Indiana (later Vandalia) Company, traced its claim to a public transaction, involving the colony of Virginia as well as imperial authorities. The "Suffering Traders," an alliance of Philadelphia merchants who had suffered large losses in Indian attacks in 1763, and influential politicians (including Sir William Johnson, the Indian superintendent), induced the Six Nations to make a generous compensatory land grant, "Indiana," at the Fort Stanwix Treaty of 1768. With the addition of well-placed English partners, Indiana grew into Vandalia, a new colony to be erected in what is today West Virginia. Vandalia was a land speculator's dream almost come true; it was also the culmination of a series of setbacks for landed interests in Virginia and for the colony's jurisdictional pretensions, which had begun with the establishment of Indian boundaries limiting westward expansion.

The Pennsylvania speculators and their influential allies exploited jurisdictional confusion in the West to counter the Virginians' head start in developing the region. The Vandalia plan appeared unstoppable. The Virginia Ohio Company was bought off by the Vandalians, who also agreed to secure military bounty claims and other titles originating in Virginia. At first, official Virginian reactions to the proposed new colony lacked coherence or conviction. But bad timing and the dramatic deterioration of British-American relations destroyed Vandalia almost at the point of success. In the meantime Virginians discovered new arguments in behalf of their claims and began to defend them more vigorously.

Virginian opponents of Vandalia realized that their fortunes were tied to the vindication of their colony's charter claims. The territorial integrity of the colony, within lines set down in the second (1609) charter, became one of the main concerns of revolutionary Virginians. The appeal to charter rights was buttressed by further state activity in the West, initiated by the last royal governor, Lord Dunmore, in his war against the Shawnee (and incidentally against Vandalia and Pennsylvania claims) in 1774. After the Declaration of Independence, the new state of Virginia carried on these efforts to perfect a title defense and to enforce their claims.

When the speculators lost their new colony, their American members regrouped behind the Indiana grant. The Indianans recruited important congressmen to fill the place of influential English partners, and land company claims gained sympathetic support from the small, landless states. But their failure to identify with a particular state's territorial pretensions was a handicap. At the outbreak of the war, only colonies and their successor states could make clear and unequivocal claims to rights for themselves; the role of Congress remained undefined, and private property claimants necessarily turned to the states for confirmation and protection of their titles. The position of the western land companies was anomalous. Their efforts to vindicate their stateless property claims depended on a fundamental reconception of interstate organization.

Virginia's charter claims gained new authority at the same time that political changes cut the companies adrift. Colonial charters were invoked by the new American states to define their limits and justify their pretensions to autonomy and independence. The speculators' advantageous position at the British court was a blot on their patriotism, and their attack on state authority was (the Virginians argued) counterrevolutionary. But the land companies did not submit tamely to this reversal of fortunes. Once it was clear that Virginia would not confirm their titles, they began to explore new ways to circumvent Virginia's claims. In doing so they energized the coalition of small states which feared and resented the extensive claims of large states. The land companies and their landless state allies sought to induce Congress to assert a collective American title in the West. If the United States refused to recognize particular state claims, and could effectively defend its own title, Virginia would no longer be able to block confirmation of private titles. Congress would succeed to the Crown's authority over unlocated lands, a source for a congressional jurisdiction independent of the states that could undermine the states' territorial monopoly.

The land companies hoped to dissociate private property from state jurisdictional claims. They would recognize the states' jurisdiction only if the states would recognize their property rights. But Virginians saw these efforts as a challenge to state sovereignty. They insisted not only on the vindication of colonial charter claims, but also on the state's absolute control over the distribution of property within those claims. In the contest with the landless states and land companies, Virginians had the advantage of promoting their interests as those of a revolutionary state, which had joined the war effort to redeem itself from British corruption (such as land grants to court favorites). Up until the eve of the Revolution, Virginians had little apparent choice but to capitulate to British policy changes. But revolutionary logic encouraged them to resist unconstitutional encroachments and to reinterpret their colonial past selectively, in order to promote the sovereign pretensions of their new state. At the same time, following Dunmore's lead, they were prepared to back their pretensions in the West by force, if necessary.

Virginia's position on its territorial claims was fully developed by the time of independence, and that position was maintained and defended until the successful completion of the cession in 1784. The territorial issue emerged fully only when it could be argued that colonial Virginians possessed the exclusive, preemptive right to Crown lands within their charter limits. These charter claims began to assume a new significance for the colony at the conclusion of the French and Indian War.[9] The divergent interests of Virginia settlers, land company speculators, Indians, and imperial administrators made the jurisdictional question—who would control the Ohio Valley and for what purposes?—a vitally important one. Subsequent British policy intensified the conflict of interests. White settlement was prohibited beyond the Atlantic watershed by the Proclamation of 1763; negotiations with Indians from 1768 to 1770 pushed the line considerably to the west.[10]

The clash of interests and claims in the nearby frontier region produced the first hints of Virginia's claims defense. William Nelson, president of the royal council and acting governor, defended the colony's interests against the Vandalia plan in a long letter to the colonial secretary, Lord Hillsborough, in 1770. Nelson suggested that the people of Virginia had a preemptive right to extend their own frontiers. Though he would "not presume to say to whom our Gracious Sovereign shall grant his vacant lands," he was confident the secretary would recognize that "the weight prevails" on the side of the Virginians "who have run great hazards during the course of the war, many of whom lost their lives and fortunes." If vacant lands were still Crown lands, at least the king could be expected to protect the interests of his loyal subjects in Virginia.[11]

Demands for limitations on the disposal of crown lands became more explicit as the revolutionary crisis approached. In his *Summary View*, written in 1774, Thomas Jefferson anticipated the colony's response to changes in the land grant system. "Kings are the servants, not the proprietors of the people," he wrote; changes in land policy that made "acquisition of lands . . . difficult" were unconstitutional. Jefferson did not evade the logical conclusion that the king had "no right to grant lands of himself," without the colony's approval or acquiescence.[12] In 1775 the Burgesses registered similar objections to the new land policy, announced by Governor Dunmore's proclamation of March 21. They doubted the king's "right" to make these changes but, more cautious than Jefferson, relied merely on "the established usage of granting lands."[13]

Imperial policy created a congestion of conflicting interests on the near frontier. In the midst of this confusion, audacious Virginians began to assert the rights of the colony to control the disposition of vacant lands, first against competing interests and later, while relying on a title based entirely on the royal charter, even against the Crown itself. And logically, if Virginia could control the disposition of vacant lands as they were granted, the colony's title included all the territory within its charter lines. Thus when land policy became an issue, jurisdiction likewise became an issue. Virginians were prepared not only to battle competitors for vacant lands but also to deny the right of the Crown to alter old boundaries or erect new colonies within its western claims.

Up to the outbreak of the Revolution, the Vandalia new colony proposal made progress in British government circles. In response, Virginians developed a sophisticated defense of their own claims in the same region. This defense, first outlined in 1773 by George Mason, argued that the colony's charter lines were inviolable.[14] Together with an anonymous "Vindication" of the Virginia claims—possibly also by Mason—and Jefferson's *Summary View*, this document stated the colony's mature title defense.[15] This same defense survived intact as the bulwark of the Virginia position until the successful completion of the second cession offer in 1784. Mason's "Remarks" of 1773 touched on the key points: first, that charter rights inure to the benefit of Virginians "forever, notwithstanding the dissolution of the Virginia Company"; and second, that the territory of the colony was not confined to the area "purchased from or ceded by the Indians." In other words, charter lines created the colony's jurisdiction, and Indian rights had no effect on them. The basis for Mason's claim was that Virginians "have enjoyed these Rights & privileges from Time immemorial."[16] This was an appeal to prescription; prescription also explained the creation of Maryland, North Carolina, and Pennsylvania within the charter lines. Jefferson maintained that those proprietaries had been erected "into distinct and independent governments . . . by an assumed right of the crown alone," and he warned that though Virginia had acquiesced in these changes, they would allow no others. "No exercise of such a power, of dividing and dismembering a country, has ever occurred in his majesty's realm of England . . . nor could it be justified or acquiesced under there, or in any other part of his majesty's realm." [17]

The prescriptive right applied not only to settled areas but also to undeveloped western claims. It was an exclusive preemptive right to Indian lands within the charter lines, according to the "Vindication." Indian purchases had kept pace with the expansion of settlement, first to the fall line, "then to the blue ridge of Mountains; afterwards to the Alleghany Mountains, and lately to the River Ohio." [18] It was a central point in subsequent Virginian arguments that the state's title was equally good in settled and unsettled areas anywhere within the charter lines. Kentucky was as much part of Virginia as Williamsburg, Edmund Pendleton maintained, "for she can't distinguish upon what ground she may claim the one and not the other." [19]

The outlines of independent Virginia's western policy were stated in the constitution of 1776. [20] Specific land policy and the determination of Indian and land company rights were worked out in resolutions and legislation over the next three years. The constitution appealed specifically to the charter in defining state boundaries, limited on the west at the Mississippi River by the Peace of Paris in 1763 and by the creation of new colonies to the north (Pennsylvania and Maryland) and south (the Carolinas). The constitution suggested that even these new colonies were usurpations of its charter rights but still "ceded, released, and forever confirmed" to those colonies the Virginia territory. This insistence on charter rights, however, was joined by another provision that "one or more territories shall hereafter be laid off, and governments established westward of the *Allegheny* mountains." Virginians were aware of the difficulties in administering the state's extensive territorial claims. But any separation had to be "by act of [this] legislature." It is significant that Edmund Pendleton felt such separation could be effected only after "all Land titles are Adjusted by Us, and the Several Purchases from the Crown or the Indians either confirmed or set aside." [21] The boundary question was inextricably tied up with recognition of private titles within those boundaries, and so it too was inseparable from the state's sovereignty.

Virginian concern with territorial integrity as a fundamental attribute of independent statehood reflected the persistent efforts of speculators to gain a share of the unlocated lands on the state's frontiers. The speculators' attempts to open up their own land offices and to sell land titles originating outside Virginia prompted the state to assert its absolute control over land distribution within its boundaries. Edmund Pendleton argued, "If the distribution of our Lands be not Local, there can be nothing so."[22] The Virginia Convention moved quickly to head off sales by the Indiana Company and the Transylvania Company (in what soon became the Kentucky District). Resolutions of June 24, 1776, insisted on the convention's right to decide on "the validity of the title under such Indian deeds"; in the meantime settlers should not pay for lands they occupied within the company claims.[23] No further "purchases of lands within the chartered limits of Virginia shall be made under any pretence whatever, from any Indian tribe or nation, without the approbation of the legislature." This prohibition was incorporated into the state constitution.

Territorial integrity was not simply a test of state sovereignty. As an independent state, Virginia developed a strong interest in the settlement and sale of western lands. It was generally held "that the unappropriated Lands should all be sold for the benefit of the commonwealth."[24] Thus Virginia had to have exclusive jurisdiction over land titles; it also had to have clear title to as much land as possible to pass on to purchasers. According to the first draft of the Land Office Bill, reported by Jefferson to the House of Delegates in January 1778, land sales would "increase the annual Revenue, and create a Fund for discharging the Public Debt."[25] But Jefferson also hoped to make land available cheaply and conveniently to actual settlers. This goal was compromised in the legislation that finally passed in June 1779, setting up a central land office and including other provisions favorable to large landholders and speculators.[26] Nonetheless, the state's interest in western lands was clearly established, as was its commitment to purchasers of its titles.

Policymakers in Virginia were responsive to the demands of local speculators, who did not challenge the state's authority. They were also responsive to the demands of westerners themselves, granting preemption rights to squatters and extending the benefits of state government. The strength of Virginia's western claims depended on the willingness of westerners to support them, as well as on the language of its charter. Settlers demanded an end to obstacles to westward migration, including the confusion over titles. As Jefferson wrote in 1776, emigrants to the frontiers "will settle the lands in spite of every body."[27] He later explained to Congress, which had complained strenuously about the opening of the Land Office, that "endeavours to discourage and prevent the settling our Western

Country" had been futile, and the assembly eventually found it "necessary to give way to the torrent."[28] If it had not, an "important fund for her public debt" would have been squandered.[29] But it was not only the loss of income that was critical; it was also necessary to determine the political future of the West, to establish harmonious relations between the long-settled part of the state and its frontier settlements.[30]

The question of how to govern the West, in the near future and in the distant future, was a complicated one. It was not enough to look forward to the creation of new states in Virginia's vast hinterland. It was also necessary to determine what role the westerners themselves would have in state-making, and on what terms new states would be admitted to the union. Congress appeared overeager to sponsor such state divisions, however, and Virginians were reluctant to give it a free hand in the West. These misgivings eventually gave birth to the conditional cessions policy.

The concern with western government was precipitated by the short-lived new "colony" of Transylvania, established in western Virginia and North Carolina in 1775 by Judge Richard Henderson and his land company associates. Governor Dunmore's efforts to destroy the new colony were interrupted by the sudden collapse of his administration and the establishment of a revolutionary state government. The Transylvanians claimed the "absolute right, as a political body, without giving umbrage to Great Britain, or any of the colonies, to frame rules for the government of our little society."[31] The new colony petitioned Congress to be accepted as one of the united colonies, shortly before the final break with Britain. Virginia's response to this request established a pattern for the future. Jefferson assured James Hogg, the Transylvanian emissary, "that it was his wish to see a free Government established at the back" of Virginia, "properly united" with it—and this wish was shortly thereafter repeated in the constitution. But he added that "he would not consent" that a new state "be acknowledged by the Congress, until it had the approbation" of the Virginia legislature.[32] Congress had no jurisdiction; for the time being, at least, Transylvania was part of Virginia.

Virginians recognized that Virginia would have to be divided. Pendleton, president of the convention, wrote in July 1776 that "we have it in contemplation that to keep that Countrey, when settled, united with this, will produce none of the Good Purposes of Government, and be exceedingly inconvenient to them."[33] But to recognize a new state set up by speculators, on their own authority, would be a disservice to westerners—many of whom denied Henderson's claim and turned to Virginia for protection. A division of the state must be delayed, Pendleton thought, until the confusion over land titles was resolved, in order "to prevent the affairs of the Country there in the Infancy of government from being distracted by those various claims: and until the land is settled sufficiently to support Government by taxes not too burthensome, and to afford discreet Officers of government." Most important, Virginia insisted that a division of the state could take place only at its own initiative. This crucial feature of Virginia's western policy was fully articulated in a series of resolutions adopted in October 1776 in response to Transylvania.[34] The state's congressional delegation was to remonstrate "against the dismembering this State of that or any other part of its ancient Territory, or forming any new government within its limits." The assembly warned Virginians that "proper measures" would be taken "should any person or persons . . . attempt to form themselves into a distinct or independent government, without the consent of the Legislature." But the assembly also recognized that the claims of the state were balanced by the claims of the people for its protection. Thus "for rendering the benefits of government, and administration of justice, more easy and convenient" to western settlers, three new counties would be established.

The principles set forth in these resolutions—that Congress had no authority in the West, that only Virginia could sanction its own dismemberment, and that the state's sovereignty over western settlers was coordinate with its responsibility to them—remained fixed in subsequent years. The significant omission was the title question, that is, the status of other company claims, like Indiana's, based on old grants or purchases. The assembly decided, because of the multitude of private claims to the western lands, that the problem had to be treated comprehensively in a single piece of legislation. If there were to be a public domain at all, Jefferson warned, the title bill would have to establish a just and sensible discrimination among these claims. As author of the bill, George Mason's "great object was to remove out of the way the great and numerous orders of council to the Ohio co. Loyal co. Misissipi co. Vandalia co. &c. and the thousands of entries for lands with surveyors of counties, which covered the whole Western country."[35] This discrimination was vital both to the effective operation of a land office and to the security of present and future settlers.

The original Land Title Bill, reported in January 1778, provided that good title was established only by an actual authorized survey.[36] Other surveys, "made by any other person, or upon any other pretext whatsoever [were] null and void." Except when "carried into execution . . . all orders of Council or Entries for land in the Council Books upon the Western Waters" were also voided. The assembly was not yet prepared, however, for such a categorical dismissal of so many outstanding claims. Completion of the bill was delayed until deliberations could be held on specific company claims.

The Henderson Company disavowed its separatist pretensions, being "well aware of the impropriety of erecting or suffering a separate government within the limit or verge of another," and threw itself on the mercy of the house.[37] The Virginian Loyal Company was also properly obeisant, and both groups were able to salvage a part of their original claims.[38] The Henderson Company received 200,000 acres in compensation for its investment in opening up the Transylvania region; the Loyal Company's title to another 200,000 acres surveyed and granted before the war was also confirmed. The Indiana Company proved to be considerably more troublesome. On the face of it, the company had a valid claim, sanctioned by public authority. Further, as the protracted debates in the Virginia assembly demonstrated, many Virginians supported the claim. Finally, the Indianans made it clear that they would not accept an adverse decision as final but would appeal to Congress for relief.[39]

The assembly's vote against Indiana in June 1779 was an act of "despotism in the highest degree," according to Samuel Wharton of the company. George Mason, who conducted the state's case against the claim, supposedly "insisted greatly upon political expediency and the *salus populi*." He argued strongly for Virginia's "right of pre-emption" of all lands within its chartered limits. Establishing this right, Mason reportedly explained, was "the only way to prevent other states from claiming the back lands." "Countenancing the grant to the proprietors of Indiana would exclude a fund, which might be secured to the State, by the sale" of those lands.[40]

The common element in all these decisions on company claims was the insistence on the final jurisdiction of the state legislature. The legislature did not sit as a court, and "political expediency," the interest of the sovereign state, was necessarily its overriding concern. Disallowance of the Indiana claim resolved the final ambiguity in Virginia's western land policy. When Indiana and allied land companies turned to Congress, the connection between land policy and state sovereignty became even more apparent. The landless states in Congress challenged Virginia's authority over the disposition of lands and validation of titles within its charter limits. Recourse to another jurisdiction by private interests accelerated the identification of land title and boundary questions, central to Virginia's claims defense and together constituting its territorial integrity.

Congress needed a national domain. Virginia had the best-developed claim to the trans-Ohio region that Congress coveted. Though it was willing to part with these claims, Virginia hoped to preserve its remaining claims, south of the Ohio, from challenges by speculators and separatists. A cession, in exchange for boundary guarantees, was the apparent solution. But the land companies sought to circumvent Virginia's claims altogether. Their success depended on the establishment of congressional jurisdiction over title conflicts, and its authority to protect private property from state "despotism." But a cession would be a political transaction between the ceding state and Congress, dealing with each other as equals. Such a "treaty" could not involve a close examination of title rights (private or public), because Congress would be committed to build its own title on these state claims. There would be no higher authority capable of adjudicating conflicting claims.

The companies wanted Congress to sit as a kind of court. The Indiana Company collected legal opinions on behalf of the validity of its claims, suggesting, as George Morgan told the Virginia assembly in 1777, that the company would be prepared to "submit" the question "to a proper judicatory" "in the ordinary course of justice."[41] Samuel Wharton argued that "the glorious revolution of these states was not made to destroy, but . . . to protect private property."[42] The British government had recognized the Indiana claim: "Can it be supposed, that the Congress of the United States . . . will be less sensible to the influence of justice, than the King of England was?" Congress had succeeded to the Crown's jurisdiction—who else could?—and it should thus secure justice to aggrieved private property claimants against the illegal acts of states.

The small, landless states endorsed the land companies' arguments for a broad interpretation of congressional powers, particularly as long as the Articles of Confederation remained unratified and therefore easily amendable. But they did not oppose cessions on principle, if the offers were sufficiently generous. Their interests were at least potentially distinct from those of the companies, which depended on some sort of adjudication. This disjunction was not readily apparent because so many congressmen held company shares and were interested in the confirmation of company claims. Furthermore, the threat of expanded congressional power, and parallel arguments for a congressional title to western lands independent of the states, were strategically useful while cessions remained pending. But the main purpose of such arguments was to portray large and unconditional cessions as reasonable compromises. A cession, implicitly recognizing state title to the ceded lands, was naturally unpopular with the land companies, which challenged the validity of state claims. But ultimately the small states were more interested in completing the Virginia cession, even though it invalidated private purchases from the Indians, than in saving the companies.

The Articles of Confederation that were circulated to the states for ratification guaranteed the exclusive territorial pretensions of the states. But until 1781, when Maryland finally capitulated and ratified the Articles, the extent of congressional power remained ambiguous, subject to interpretation and negotiation. Maryland refused to ratify, according to its Declaration of December 15, 1778, until "an Article or Articles be added . . . giving full power to the United States in Congress Assembled to ascertain and fix the western limits" of the states.[43] When Maryland did ratify, it insisted that it would not consider any guarantee in the Articles of the "exclusive claim of any particular State, to the soil of the . . . back lands" binding on "this or any other State."[44]

Maryland did not stand alone against Virginia and the other landed states. New Jersey and Delaware also withheld their approval of the Articles, though abandoning this strategy sooner. "Virginia has many enemies" owing to "Jealousy and envy of her wisdom, vigor, and extent of Territory," Richard Henry Lee admitted in 1777.[45] The opening of the state's land office in 1779 aroused a chorus of angry condemnations. According to Ezekiel Cornell of Rhode Island, "her whole attention is engrossed in making sale of her out lands."[46] Timothy Pickering of Massachusetts thought that "this Conduct of Virginia . . . respecting her back lands . . . which she will actually possess only in consequence of the general war with Britain" was "almost the sole bar to the completion of the Confederation."[47]

Conventional political wisdom suggested that large states could not survive as republics, and that they would jeopardize the survival of their smaller neighbors. Thus many American statesmen were convinced by Maryland's arguments that even if Virginia did not make war on its neighbors, its control over a vast reserve of public lands would enable it to "lessen her taxes," leading to the "depopulation, and consequently the impoverishment" and ruin of the smaller states. Virginia's western land policy appeared to justify such fears. Though the land companies actively stirred up opposition to Virginia's claims in Maryland and elsewhere, the ground had already been well prepared. There was a general antipathy to Virginia's extensive claims that even Virginians could not attribute entirely to the machinations of the land companies.[48]

Virginia found itself in an adversary position with the small states, and at times with Congress itself. The other states with western land claims were lukewarm allies at best. But Virginians were not convinced that they could stand alone, particularly after their poor showing in resisting the British invasion which began in late 1780. Virginia's survival depended on the willingness of other states to come to its defense. The western claims were also vulnerable without the effective guarantee of the other states. Virginians and non-Virginians agreed that the state would be hard-pressed to support its jurisdiction throughout its extensive claims. "Such is the amazing extent of that state," Timothy Pickering wrote, that "it will soon be rent in twain."[49] Richard Henry Lee conceded "the difficulty of republican laws and government piercing so far from the seat of Governmen[t]."[50] Joseph Jones told George Washington that "we are already too large for the Energy of republican Government."[51] The westerners, according to a defense of Virginia's claims, were "turbulent and unruly as befits the inhabitants of a mountainous country" and were not intended by "nature" to remain part of Virginia.[52]

The vindication of Virginia's claims thus depended not only on the demonstration of the sanctity of charter rights, but on the willingness of the other states to recognize them (valid or not), the ability of the state to maintain its jurisdiction, and the loyalty of the settlers themselves. "Much will depend upon the Disposition of the Inhabitants in the western parts," said George Mason.[53] But many of the settlers who poured into the Kentucky District were not Virginians and had little incentive to uphold the state's authority.[54] Instead, they subscribed to petitions to Congress seeking to be established as a new state. Congress was therefore in a position to offer something of value to Virginia, in exchange for a generous land cession. It could ignore pleas from speculators and separatists to recognize their respective (and often related) claims, and so help guarantee the state's shaky jurisdiction.

There was considerable pressure in Congress and in Virginia for resolving the western lands controversy. But Virginians made it clear from the outset that they would oppose any attempt by Congress to establish its authority in the West without Virginia's compliance. John Henry of Maryland reported in 1778 that the "bare mentioning" of the western lands "rouses Virginia."[55] The Virginia delegation registered strong objections when Congress received a memorial from the Indiana Company in 1779.[56] A Remonstrance drafted by George Mason and adopted by the Virginia assembly in December 1779 stated:

> Should Congress assume a jurisdiction, and arrogate to themselves a right of adjudication, not only unwarranted by, but expressly contrary to the fundamental principles of the confederation; superseding or controuling the internal policy, civil regulations, and municipal laws of this or any other State, it would be a violation of public faith, introduce a most dangerous precedent which might hereafter be urged to deprive of territory or subvert the sovereignty and government of any one or more of the United States, and establish in Congress a power which in process of time must degenerate into intolerable despotism.[57]

When George Morgan proposed to "Submit the dispute in Question between the State and the Company, to the arbitration" of an impartial court, set up according to Article IX, the Virginia delegates replied that "they could not reconcile" their state's "Sovereignty and honor" with an "appeal, from its own decisions, to a foreign tribunal."[58] George Mason thought that it was essential for the survival of the states that Congress be prevented from crossing "over the Line of the Confederation, and assume Rights not delegated to them." If this could happen "in one Instance," it could also happen "in every other that the Lust of Power may suggest."[59] Virginians were thus determined to resist "the fatal tendency of Congress thus cutting our country in pieces, at the instance of private jobbers, and land speculators."[60]

The arguments advanced by Virginia's opponents to discredit the state's western claims would have been useful had there ever been an adjudication. But their main effect was instead to encourage Virginians to see the western lands controversy as a test of state sovereignty. According to the New Jersey assembly, "the property which existed in the crown of Great Britain . . . ought now to belong to the Congress, in trust for the use and benefit of the United States."[61] Thomas Paine's *Public Good*, commissioned by the companies, included the fullest exposition of the Crown lands argument.[62] Virginia "was wholly at the disposal of the Crown of England, who might enlarge or diminish, or erect new governments to the westward." The charter was a nullity; indeed, Virginia "had no ascertained limits." The western lands were "crown residuary lands," which might be set off into new colonies, like Vandalia. The effect of such arguments on Virginians (which was considerable) was to intensify the identification between state sovereignty and territorial claims.[63] After all, if Paine's argument was correct, Virginia could never hope to persuade an impartial tribunal of its territorial rights. They could be vindicated only if they were asserted as nonjusticiable rights, pertaining to a sovereign state.

The cessions solution was suggested as early as September 1778 by a congressional committee on finance.[64] The committee recommended that "the several states having large uncultivated Territory, beyond what is in their Power to govern, be called on to cede the Same." Richard Henry Lee reported shortly thereafter that Virginia's opponents "say that if we would fix a reasonable limit" they would agree to ratify the Articles, with their territorial guarantees.[65] Virginians intimated their willingness to come to terms, even while expressing outrage at congressional solicitude for the land companies. Virginians were anxious to "remove every cause of jealousy and promote that mutual confidence and harmony between the different States so essential to their true interest and safety."[66] This "hint" was "intended to bring on offers from congress," Mason later wrote.[67] The terms of the anticipated transaction were clear enough at the time: Maryland would confederate, and the confederation would secure Virginia's remaining claims, provided that Virginia would relinquish its far western claims. John Walker reported from Philadelphia that these were the best "Terms as the Confederation could now be compleated on."[68]

The first state cession offer was laid before Congress by New York in March 1780. The offer, passed in the form of a bill for the "Completion of the Articles of Confederation," was hailed as a precedent for other state cessions.[69] A congressional committee appointed to consider Maryland's Instructions and Virginia's Remonstrance—documents defining apparently irreconcilable positions—applauded the New York cession, which had also been referred to it, as an "act . . . expressly calculated to accelerate the federal alliance, by removing, as far as it depends on that State, the impediment arising from the western country."[70] On September 6, 1780, this committee reported resolutions that committed Congress to seek a "liberal surrender" of state claims in the West. Such extended claims could not be "preserved entire without endangering the stability of the general confederacy." Congress would not "examine into the merits" of Virginia's claim or Maryland's counterclaim; this was a sure prescription for continuing paralysis. There would be no direct assault on a state's territorial pretensions. The call for cessions recognized the primacy of state titles to the western lands, as well as the states' sovereign discretion in relinquishing them.

Virginians were optimistic that a quick resolution of the controversy, on favorable terms, was now possible. "The present time" appeared to Richard Henry Lee "a favorable crisis for Congress to open a treaty with Virginia upon this subject."[71] Joseph Jones believed that "the example of New York is worthy of imitation."[72] Virginia was "more interested than any other [state] in a cession of unappropriated territory," Jones later added.[73] This interest was repeatedly stated in terms of an exchange, or "treaty," between Virginia and Congress. John Walker thought it "advisable in Virginia to give up her exclusive Claims beyond the Ohio, to be guaranteed in all her Teritory on this side."[74] George Mason, the most ardent champion of Virginia's charter rights, proposed the same terms: Virginia will "agree to fix the north-west bank of the Ohio River" as its western boundary "if congress would offer the guaranty of the United States, for our remaining territory."[75] Joseph Jones rushed home from Philadelphia, full of "hopes of promoting" such "a cession on the part of the state."[76]

The first suggestion of complications came on the same day Congress adopted its cession call. Jones had proposed additional resolutions, specifying what Congress would do with its national domain.[77] Jones's resolutions included three main provisions, and one crucial corollary: first, "the territory so ceded shall be laid out in separate and distinct States"; second, the ceding states were to be "reimbursed" for civil and military expenses in the cessions area; and finally, lands not already committed to military bounty grants "shall be considered as a common fund for the use and benefit" of the confederated states. The logical corollary to this last proposition, which Jones wanted made explicit, was that "all purchases and deeds from any Indian or Indians, or any Indian Nation for any Lands within any part of such ceded Territory, which have been or shall be made for the use of any private person or persons whatsoever, shall be deemed and taken as absolutely void." Jones explained to James Madison, who remained at Philadelphia to promote these resolutions, that they were meant to "feel the pulse" of Congress "upon these points."[78] "If Congress makes . . . [such] propositions to our ensuing Assembly," Richard Henry Lee assured Samuel Adams, "the consent of that body may be obtained to them."[79]

Subsequent debates over these resolutions revealed important areas of disagreement. The reimbursement provision was modified to exclude civil expenses, though Madison did not think these so great as "to be much worth insisting on." But "the consideration of the last resolution annulling Indian purchases was postponed" on September 18, with "an intention," Madison thought, "of not resuming it." Some congressmen supposed that such a stipulation was redundant and unnecessary, as it was by strict logic. But Madison saw "a real view of gratifying private interests at the public expense." The only recourse for the ceding states was to "annex what conditions they please to their cessions, and by that means guard them ag[ain]st misapplication."[80] The resolutions finally adopted on October 10 excluded the Indian purchases provision.[81] Congress committed itself to form new states in the national domain and also agreed to reimburse states for military expenses.

Madison claimed not to have lost faith in the good intentions of Congress. "But the best security for their virtue . . . will be to keep it out of their power" to "gratify the avidity of the land mongers."[82] Virginians were well prepared to follow Madison's advice. Once it was apparent that Congress could not be trusted, it was easy enough to translate Virginia's western policy goals into cession conditions. George Mason had already identified these conditions in a letter to Joseph Jones in July 1780.[83] The cession act passed by the Virginia Assembly on January 2, 1781, under Jones's management, faithfully repeated Mason's requirements, several of them verbatim. Some of the conditions were not controversial, such as the call for new states and for the use of the national domain as a common fund. Some were negotiable, such as the reimbursement of state expenses and provision for military bounty claimants. But two conditions, each designed to counter land company claims, drew the line between Virginia and Congress that would hold over the next three years. These were the prohibition of Indian purchases, and the requirement "that all the remaining territory of Virginia . . . should be guaranteed to the Commonwealth of Virginia, by the . . . United States." This was Virginia's main incentive to make the cession, which "shall be void and of none effect" without the ratification of the Articles of Confederation by all the states, another putative guarantee of the state's territorial integrity.[84]

The general enthusiasm for cessions concealed underlying differences that would obstruct an early settlement of the dispute. It soon became clear, for instance, that an unconditional cession was incompatible with Virginia's western policy goals. For their part, Virginia's opponents sought a much more extensive cession, and the land companies sought to save their titles.

Virginia's sanguine hopes were based on the faulty premise that its cession, combined with Maryland's ratification of the Articles, would end the dispute.[85] Conditions had to be attached to the cession because Congress was otherwise unwilling to guarantee its remaining claims (where the Indiana Company still hoped to establish its title) or to confirm the state's disallowance of private purchases from the Indians in its cession (on which were founded the hopes of the Illinois-Wabash speculators). But the Virginia delegates still flattered themselves "that the liberal spirit which dictated" the conditions "will be approved" and the cession accepted, though "not precisely conformable to the recommendations of Congress."[86] To their surprise, Congress refused the offer, invoking the letter of the September 6, 1780, resolutions and overlooking the "liberal spirit" of Virginia's cession. Congress would offer no territorial guarantees in exchange for Virginia's claims. This was a particularly troubling omission since Maryland, when ratifying, explicitly stated that it did not mean to abide by the general guarantee of state claims in the Articles.

The immediate effect of Congress's call for cessions was to emphasize the differences among the main protagonists. But once it had been articulated, the cessions policy defined the terms on which the struggle over western lands would be continued, through a lengthy impasse and to ultimate resolution. Cessions were attractive to the large states, faced with the difficulties of governing extended claims and seeking congressional guarantees for their new western boundaries. The small states also saw cessions as the best means to gain a national domain and to equalize the states.

Landless state representatives continued to propose alternatives to cessions, but their main concern was to elicit large cessions on terms most favorable to their own interests. Unilateral demands to rewrite the Articles had already failed. Once they were ratified, any amendment depended on the unanimous approval of the states; Virginia and the other landed states could not be expected to fall in with proposals to expand congressional authority in the West, while disregarding state claims. But cessions would commit the landed states to conferring equivalent powers on Congress, thus achieving through indirect means a substantive amendment of the Confederation. All states agreed that cessions were desirable, and this established a basis for unanimity. Any state offering a cession on prejudicial or unreasonable terms could be isolated from the others, and appropriate pressure could be brought to bear on it.

But there were unanticipated problems with the cessions policy. Cessions were supposed to create a national domain in the West that could be acquired in no other way and that the ceding states otherwise might exploit to their own advantage. State claims were the source of good title, though Congress would not attempt to determine the relative merits of particular claims. Paradoxically, however, the cessions call encouraged the proliferation of western claims that were worthless without congressional recognition. In a sense, then, Congress created the state titles (by recognizing them) on which it meant to build its own title. James Wilson of Pennsylvania recognized this circularity in an attack on state claims in the West in April 1783: "*If the investigation of right* was to be considered," Wilson believed, "the U[nited] S[tates] ought rather to make cessions to individual States than receive Cessions from them." [87] Connecticut, which responded immediately to the first cession request, had no prospect of ever exercising any jurisdiction within its charter claims west of Pennsylvania. But Congress's acceptance of its cession would strengthen Connecticut's position in the struggle for control of the Wyoming Valley. [88] Similarly, Massachusetts' belated cession offer was a barely concealed ploy to gain a piece of western New York State.

A western land cession offered a new means of defining state boundaries that did not depend on the actual exercise of jurisdiction, or even on their presumed legal and historical merits, which Congress carefully resolved to ignore. The crucial thing about these cession offers was what they did not include, that is, the jurisdiction the ceding states intended to maintain. It was inconsequential if the ceded claims overlapped, because they all contributed to a congressional title. At the same time, however, cessions escalated jurisdictional conflicts among the states, east of the cessions lines.

Because every cession served the ceding state's interests, at the least by proclaiming the most advantageous extension of its western boundary, each one was controversial. Even New York's unconditional offer, the model other states were supposed to emulate, was accepted only after a delay of two-and-a-half years, and only then because the landless states hoped to use it against Virginia. Many congressmen doubted that New York had a title worth ceding; in any case, the cession was a transparent attempt to gain congressional allies in New York's losing battle with the Vermont separatists.

The success of the cessions policy depended on a general agreement on where cessions should begin, and the understanding that the cessions would have no bearing on other boundary conflicts. Neither condition obtained. Ideally, the cession offers would be disinterested. But if they were disinterested, what incentive did the states have to make them? In order to avoid controversy, Congress had to accept all offers indiscriminately. But how could it accept offers that were so obviously self-interested, whether conditional or not? Yet if Congress found one offer more acceptable than another, the relative validity of the claims had to be examined. There was no point in securing an inferior title, no matter how generous the terms of its offer, if an outstanding state claim could be invoked against it.

The basic problem with the cessions policy was that the landless states sought to use it to go after Virginia's claims without dealing directly with that state or acceding to its terms. The strategy was to seek one cession at a time. After the New York cession was finally accepted, "that of Connecticut is proposed for the next object. Virginia will be postponed for the last."[89] But the apparent success of this policy in Congress was more than matched by Virginia's militant determination to maintain its claims, or cede them on its own terms. By 1783 it was apparent to congressional realists that a "treaty" would have to be negotiated between Congress and Virginia.

During the first months of 1781, cession offers from Virginia and Connecticut were placed before Congress, in addition to the New York offer. Memorials from the United Illinois and Wabash companies and from the Indiana Company were also received, and were referred with the cession proposals to a single committee.[90] The committee reported unfavorably on the cessions and recommended that Congress consider the "western limits beyond which they will not extend their guarantee to the particular states and to ascertain what vacant territory belongs to the United States in common for the general benefit." In August, the Grand Committee on the Confederation suggested that a committee be appointed to request supplementary powers from the states for "the jurisdiction of Congress in territorial questions."[91]

The landless states soon altered their strategy, however, from fruitless attempts to expand congressional power to exploiting conflicts among the various claims before Congress. A new committee on western claims was named on October 2, consisting entirely of small-state delegates.[92] This committee asked the ceding states and the land companies to prepare written briefs on their claims. The Virginia delegation protested that the committee's investigation of territorial rights was not warranted by the original request for cessions, and assumed a jurisdiction not mandated by the Articles of Confederation.[93] But the committee proceeded to consider the cession offers and land company memorials, protests notwithstanding. Its report was submitted on November 3 and became the key document in the cessions controversy during the following year. The landless states united behind the report's recommendations to accept New York's cession and to confirm the Indiana claim. (The report suggested that the Vandalia and Illinois-Wabash claims not be validated.) According to the committee, the cession transferred the state's jurisdiction, which was derived from the British protectorate over the Six Nations, "as appendant to the late government of New York." But a jurisdictional cession did not alter pre-existing property relations. The Indiana grant should therefore be confirmed, since it had been made "*bona fide* for a valuable consideration . . . with the knowledge, consent, and approbation of the Crown of Great Britain."[94]

The landless states could not muster enough votes in Congress to have the November 3 report adopted for another year. In the meantime, the Virginia delegation sought to bring on a final determination on its cession and to embarrass land speculators in Congress by requiring a "purifying declaration," revealing the extent of their holdings.[95] Back home, Virginians displayed growing hostility to Congress. The delegates counseled patience. Edmund Randolph hoped the assembly would refrain from extreme measures, but expected that it would "protest against the authority now exercised by congress" in considering territorial rights and "repeal . . . our cession."[96] Madison did not hesitate "to declare my opinion that the State will . . . find . . . ample justification for revoking or at least suspending their Act of Cession, and remonstrating against any interference with respect to cases within their jurisdiction, but that they ought in all their provisions for their security, importance & interest to presume that the present Union will but little survive the present war."[97] But neither Congress nor Virginia did anything to break the stalemate until late 1782. Calls for a final determination on the cessions were ignored. A compromise proposal by small-state delegates narrowly failed, revealing, however, that at least some of the landless states considered the company claims expendable.[98]

But by October, Virginia's opponents grew confident of success. Daniel Carroll of Maryland wrote on October 8 that "it is now intended to bring on the question on the Cession of N[ew] York, as soon as there are Seven States on the floor for it."[99] Acceptance of the cession would give Congress a title to the western lands that it could use against Virginia. Thereafter "it is probable that the States from the North of Potomac will be united on the future questions relative to the Western Territory." The anticipated event took place on October 29, with the bare minimum of seven state votes to accept the cession. Opposition was weak and scattered, however, and only Virginia cast a negative.[100]

Completion of the New York cession would be a victory for Virginia's opponents, but not a "final one," Madison had predicted, "unless Virg[ini]a means to be passive & silent under aggression on her rights."[101] Indeed, he later added, "instead of terminating all controversy" concerning western lands, it "introduces new perplexities."[102] Among the most perplexing problems was establishing public credit on such a flimsy title. Even Ezra L'Hommedieu of New York confessed misgivings on the question. "It is proposed by those Lands to establish a Fund for paying Interest of Moneys Loaned and public Debts; but whether the public Creditors will be satisfied with such security, is doubtful."[103] For, the North Carolina delegates wrote a year later, "without the Virginia cession we had nothing to give."[104]

Landless state successes in Congress precipitated a defiant attitude in Virginia. Some Virginians wondered if Congress would be trusted with a national domain, suggesting "the possibility of this fund being diverted to offensive measures" against the state.[105] According to the Instructions for the Fairfax County representatives, drafted by George Mason, a "great part of the ceded lands may be converted to private, instead of public purposes" if Virginia did not insist on the conditions attached to its cession.[106] "We desire and instruct you, strenuously to oppose all encroachments of the American Congress upon the sovereignty and jurisdiction of the separate states." Rumors reached Congress that Virginia intended to "form the western country into distinct subordinate governments."[107] Jefferson reported that Patrick Henry was "for bounding our state reasonably enough, but instead of ceding the parts lopped off he is for laying them off into small republics."[108] It seemed certain that the cession would be withdrawn. Governor Harrison did not "think the Assembly will be trifled with much longer." "It has ever appeared to me unaccountable that this Business has been so protracted."[109]

By 1783 a continuing stalemate over the western lands was increasingly unacceptable to Virginia's leaders. The state had to decide whether or not to maintain its jurisdiction in the Illinois country.[110] Unauthorized settlers swarmed across the Ohio River into the intended cessions area, jeopardizing development of those public lands, whether by Congress or Virginia.[111]

At this same time, the House of Delegates received a memorial from General George Rogers Clark's Illinois regiment, "requesting a district of Country on the Northwest of the Ohio be assigned to them."[112] The 1781 cession offer required that 150,000 acres be set aside for these men, but the cessions deadlock left them landless. The House faced a clear choice; satisfying the soldiers was "repugnant to the cession to Congress" of the lands beyond the Ohio.[113] It would signify Virginia's intention of opening up the Northwest, regardless of Congress.

Neither could Congress afford the luxury of a protracted stalemate. Throughout 1783, a coherent western policy emerged out of its various committees—on public credit, demobilization, and Indian affairs—dealing with the adjustment to peace. The implementation of this policy depended on the creation of a national domain.[114] Some beginning had to be made in satisfying public creditors through land sales. New states had to be established to facilitate settlement and defense, and a new boundary had to be negotiated with neighboring Indian nations. In the midst of these deliberations, it was more and more assumed that Congress would have to come to terms with Virginia, an assumption that was reinforced by the belligerent attitude of that state. Clear title was absolutely essential.

The shape of the ultimate compromise was suggested in April 1783 when Theodorick Bland moved that Congress "accept the cession of territory made to them" by Virginia, omitting the territorial guarantee. This would be Virginia's main concession, though it was more a symbolic concession than a real one. Between 1781 and 1783 thousands of Virginians had moved into the Kentucky District, the state's authority was solidly established, and early separatist sentiment had waned; Virginia no longer needed a guarantee of its remaining territory. Bland's motion was referred to a committee dominated by landless state delegates, which predictably reported against it.[115] But the committee was reconstituted on June 4, and within two days it submitted a new report, favorable to the Virginia cession.[116] The report contained all the significant compromises found in the completed cession, including the understanding that private purchases would not be recognized and omitting the territorial guarantee.

Congress finally adopted the report on September 13, after extended debates and a final attempt by the landless states to circumvent the Virginia cession.[117] Only New Jersey and Maryland voted against the report. Back in Virginia, Joseph Jones reported that he would be able to muster "a sufficient number to close with the terms transmitted by Congress and thereby terminate the disagreeable and dangerous controversy so warmly supported by some of the States ag[ains]t ours on the Right to that Country."[118] Madison reported that even George Mason, the architect of the original cession and champion of Virginia's charter rights, "*seemed* upon the whole to *acquiesce* in the . . . *cession*."[119] Jones successfully guided a new cession deed through the Virginia house; the Senate registered its agreement on December 20.[120]

There were still minor obstacles in Congress. In committee, David Howell of Rhode Island objected to the terms of the Virginia deed, "as extending their charter boundary, and indeed giving authenticity to their claims."[121] George Morgan laid another petition before Congress on March 1, 1784, calling for an Article IX proceeding between New Jersey, representing citizens with shares in the Indiana Company, and Virginia.[122] A motion to commit the petition failed. Finally, when the Virginia delegates pressed for a vote the same day, John Beatty of New Jersey offered a condition to congressional acceptance of the Virginia cession. According to Beatty's motion, acceptance of the cession "shall not be considered as implying any opinion or decision of Congress respecting the extent or validity of the claim of the Commonwealth of Virginia, to western territory, by charter or otherwise."[123] But "we told them we were not authorised to admit any conditions or provisoes," Jefferson reported to Governor Harrison; "their acceptance must be simple, absolute and unqualified or we could not execute."[124] The motion was soundly defeated. The stage was at last set for a vote on the Virginia deed. A first vote received support from six of nine states represented. But when John Montgomery of Pennsylvania changed his vote from no to yes, so changing his state's vote, the necessary seven state votes were assembled and the cession was completed.[125]

Virginia's land cession enabled Congress to begin implementing its plans for the sale of public lands and the establishment of new states in the West. It also removed a chronic source of friction between Virginia and the other states. Congress would never again challenge Virginia's territorial integrity. The land companies alone suffered under the terms of the cession; it had been their victory to help delay its completion for so many years.

In theory, acceptance of the cession was a vindication of Virginia's charter claims, and by implication of the state's right to its remaining territory. But Congress was pledged to accept all claims, including those in conflict with Virginia's, and it declined to offer explicit guarantees of any state's remaining claims. Thus there was no consensus on the validity of particular state titles. Congressmen continued to express their contempt for extended claims while cessions were being negotiated. According to Stephen Higginson, "Virginia and New York mean only to give them [Congress] what is of no value . . . in order to secure to themselves a valuable territory which they now have no good claim to."[126] But it was nonetheless "indispensable to obtain these cessions," Madison reminded Congress, "in order to compromise the disputes, & to derive advantage from the territory to the U[nited] S[tates]."[127]

Congress had no choice but to deal with Virginia. Recognition of this political necessity was itself a recognition that Virginia could determine its own boundaries, that its claims were "good" because they were enforceable. Virginians were convinced that their claims were valid, and they were prepared to litigate them with any other claiming state before a special court, set up according to Article IX. But submission of the state's claims in any other form to any other authority (particularly to Congress or its committees) was incompatible with its pretensions to sovereignty. As the New York delegates explained, the "Subject . . . could only be closed by Composition."[128] The Virginians insisted on a political settlement; a negotiated agreement was an acknowledgment of their state's sovereign rights.

Virginia was willing, perhaps even eager, to cede its northwestern claims. The critical point to Virginians was that the new states which must eventually be created in the West would be created with their state's consent, at its discretion and initiative. This was another test of state sovereignty and, insofar as these new states established a new western boundary, of the state's territorial integrity. The cessions agreement enabled Virginia to pursue its new state policy, through congressional trusteeship, while at the same time acting on its sovereign prerogative and defending its territorial claims.

With the disposition of the Northwest settled to its satisfaction, Virginia had no further interest in defending its relinquished claims there. It was now equally interested with the other states in opening up the region for land sales and new governments. Nor was the state interested in opposing other state claims cessions, if agreements could be reached amicably and inexpensively, through negotiation.

The completion of the Virginia cession closed the debate on the state's charter claims across the Ohio. The major issue, left in suspension by the cession, was the status of Virginia's remaining western claims, south of the

· 5 ·

An Unbounded State:
New York, Vermont, and
the Western Lands

Virginia's western land cession finally gave the United States an uncontested and usable claim to a national domain in the trans-Ohio region. In return, Congress agreed to carry out Virginia's main policy goals in the West. Congress would not extend an explicit guarantee of Virginia's remaining claims, but there were no outstanding state claims to western Virginia or the Kentucky District. The United States was committed to erecting its own western title on the basis of ceded state claims; the territorial guarantees of the Articles of Confederation were thus to be applied with equal force east and west, wherever states claimed jurisdictional rights. The Virginia cession precluded future counterclaims and effectively secured the state's territorial integrity. The substantive interest of the United States in its national domain guaranteed that the agreement which created it would not be violated with impunity.

New York was equally interested in securing its territorial integrity. Its claims, though not based on charter, were no less "good" than Virginia's. Indeed, the state's northeastern boundary, fixed at the Connecticut River by the British Privy Council in 1764, was much more authoritatively and unequivocally defined than most American boundaries, particularly in the West. New York's western claims were not so well defined, but its reliance on its "suzerainty" over the Iroquois to support them was no more dubious and farfetched than colonial charter claims which the British had disregarded, particularly after 1763, and which many Americans continued to treat with contempt after independence. Nonetheless, New York failed to gain recognition for either the Connecticut River boundary or for the boundary it proposed to the west when offering to cede its far western claims.

There were several reasons for this failure. First, New York relied too much on Congress to confirm and support its pretensions. In the case of the northeastern boundary, New York expected Congress to establish its claims against the Vermont separatists through adjudication. The undoubted validity of these claims may have made this strategy particularly attractive, but Congress was reluctant to intervene and ultimately declined to do anything at all. Congress could risk alienating New York because it discovered that the state was unable or unwilling to do anything for itself; a possible alliance between Britain and Vermont was much more threatening. New York's western land cession was supposed to gain support against Vermont, but as long as the cession remained uncompleted (as it did until October 1782 because of the resistance of other western claimants), the two controversial boundaries complicated each other and remained unresolved. Instead of being treated on their respective merits, New York's boundaries were drawn into the broader controversy between the small, landless states and the large, landed states with extensive western claims. When the western lands controversy was resolved by the completion of the Virginia cession in March 1784, the resulting confirmation of charter claims (the basis of every other ceding state's claims) discredited New York's western claims, which already had been compromised by the eagerness of the landless states to use them as the basis of a congressional title. Finally, New York's western claims were undeveloped and unenforceable. Like the state's claims in Vermont, they could be and were safely ignored.

New York's boundary problems ultimately derived from the fact that Congress was able to disregard the validity of its claims, not from any particular weakness in the claims themselves. Since boundary settlements among the states would be political transactions, not legal adjudications, it was necessary for New York to negotiate from strength, either by demonstrating that it could make good its claims by force or in some other way subvert the American war effort, or by offering to give up something of value, by ceding a jurisdictional claim that was at least possibly enforceable. But New York ceded nothing, and it gained nothing in return.

States with western charter claims promoted and defended them aggressively in order to gain favorable terms for their cession. Congressional acceptance of cession conditions and the landed states' retention of extensive territories would leave them with an advantage over their smaller, circumscribed neighbors. The ceding states would have more public lands than the small states; confirmation of their bounty grants and disallowance of private claims originating elsewhere were prejudicial to the small states and their leading men; and once these conditions were satisfied, the ceding states were still entitled to a proportional share of revenues from the national domain. Important private and public interests were thus at stake in the western lands controversy.

But New York's western claims were not based on a charter, and New York did not join the other landed states in promoting charter limits as the only legitimate basis for state boundary claims. Nor did New York have any important interests in the region it offered to cede in March 1780; its cession did not represent, as Virginia's did, an attempt to secure the goals of an aggressive western policy. The cession was not controversial in New York, and it would not have been so in Congress had not the landless states sought to make use of it. New York did not attach conditions to its offer or threaten to withdraw it in hopes of gaining further advantages in the West. New York remained a landed state from March 1780 to October 1782 because of a stalemate over cession offers and despite its interest in breaking with the charter claimants.

New York's main concern was to enlist support against Vermont. As a landed state, its virtually boundless claims aroused resentment and hostility; but as a landless state, circumscribed to the west by a reasonable boundary, it might hope to induce Congress to support its territorial integrity against the separatists. Unlike the other landed states, then, New York was always on the defensive; it depended on Congress to defend its boundaries. The other landed states generally treated boundary controversies in settled eastern areas as bilateral issues that did not concern the United States. The western lands controversy had to be mediated through Congress because a multilateral solution was necessary and Congress had an interest of its own in its outcome. But New York looked to Congress to secure all its boundaries. New Yorkers did not believe that their claims anywhere were self-evidently valid—or enforceable—without the recognition of the other states and the support of Congress. The basic premises of New York's position on boundaries were thus identical with those of the landless states, not with those of its nominal landed state allies.

New York's defensive attitude was warranted by its exposed situation. British occupation of its southern counties showed how tenuous the new state's jurisdictional pretensions were. Virginia and the other landed states never suffered the same sustained encroachments on their territories, and when they were invaded they became much more flexible on territorial issues.[1] The reestablishment of New York's authority in its southern counties depended on the successful outcome of the revolutionary war effort. The debilitated condition of the state exposed it to still further depredations from domestic insurgents. Nowhere else in America (possibly excepting Pennsylvania's Wyoming Valley) were the interests of settlers so clearly and self-consciously at odds with the nominal state government as in New York's northeastern counties, the so-called New Hampshire Grants, where separatists set up the new state of Vermont in 1777.[2] But under the vigorous leadership of Governor George Clinton (aided and abetted by fellow speculators in Vermont lands), New York was determined to regain its lost counties.[3] Congressional support was crucial.

New York's territorial policy was premised on Congress's central role in securing state claims. New York sought jurisdictional guarantees in the northeast in exchange for the cession of undeveloped claims in the west. "It is wise to conciliate our judges" in the Vermont controversy, John Morin Scott wrote in 1780; "many of the states you know are interested against our western claim."[4] As Scott later pointed out, the small states sought "large cessions" in the west, which "they expect to effect by embarrassing us with respect to the setled parts of the Country."[5] New York's statesmen recognized the distinction between different kinds of boundaries—in settled and unsettled areas—that was central to the landless state argument against western claims. "We have reason to beleive," the New York delegates reported on the eve of congressional acceptance of the state's cession, that when the western land question was resolved "few or none of the States in the union will interest themselves in favour of the Vermont Independence."[6]

New Yorkers also had reason to fear that if they did not take the initiative, Congress would assert its authority in the nearer frontier region and the state would be even more narrowly circumscribed.[7] New York would thus forfeit an important quid pro quo in its campaign for congressional support against Vermont. John Jay reported in October 1779 that Congress might be receptive to a cession offer; as long as the western claims were retained they would "always be the object of Envy and Jealousy to the other States, and perhaps the Subject of Dispute."[8] The New York Assembly passed a cession act without hesitation in February 1780; significantly it was called "An Act to facilitate the Completion of the Articles of Confederation," by conciliating landless state opponents of extensive western claims.[9]

New York had little prospect of ever being able to perfect its far western claims; they would become valuable only when given up to Congress, if, that is, the United States would then secure the state's remaining claims. A "Declaration" accompanying the proffered cession, when laid before Congress in March, testified to this overriding concern.[10] The Declaration asked that "the boundaries reserved for the future jurisdiction of the said state . . . be guaranteed by the United States, in the same manner and form as the territorial rights of the other states." But it is worth noting that even this guarantee was not a condition of the cession; New York expected to be rewarded instead by congressional goodwill. Not coincidentally, congressional hearings on Vermont were scheduled to begin immediately.

The idea of securing territorial claims by a cession had long been familiar to New Yorkers. Agent Edmund Burke had advised New York to make a cession in 1774 in order to protect its remaining claims against an extension of Quebec's boundaries. New York was vulnerable to boundary changes and the creation of new colonies at its expense. Burke felt that it was imperative for New York to meet the challenge of the Quebec Act (extending that colony's jurisdiction over the Ohio region) by an assertion of reasonable boundaries and the relinquishment of untenable distant claims. The act left New York with "a mere constructive boundary . . . and the construction, when examined, amounted to nothing more than the King's pleasure." "To define" boundaries "is to abridge them," said Burke. "Something then must be given up." "It is policy to give up handsomely what cannot be retained."[11]

Unlike the other landed states, New York could not invoke a charter against encroachments by the king or Congress, or by other colonies or states. New York's claims were associated with imperial claims and with the positive acts of the British government. Its claim to suzerainty over the Iroquois was the same claim that Britain advanced in diplomatic exchanges with the French over the Ohio Valley.[12] This was primarily a British, not a colonial, claim. Relations with the Iroquois may have been conducted through the Crown's New York government, but the British assumed direct control over Indian policy after the French and Indian War. The Proclamation of 1763, subsequent Indian boundaries (negotiated by the British), and the Quebec Act undoubtedly circumscribed New York's jurisdiction. New Yorkers had been taught to accommodate themselves to the vagaries of imperial politics; the colony's ultimate boundaries would be determined through a tortuous process of negotiation and litigation with neighboring colonies.[13] The Connecticut River boundary with New Hampshire, set by Privy Council, attested to the political skills of New

Yorkers in securing extensive boundaries. This experience predisposed New Yorkers after independence to pursue a similar course; they expected Congress—successor to the "Regalia of the late sovereign"—to ascertain and enforce the state's territorial claims. [14]

New Yorkers joined small-state politicians in their low estimation of charter claims. [15] But the logic of revolutionary ideology played into the hands of the charter claimants. Charters were supposed to be the "constitutions" of colonial communities within the limits they specified; ordinary exercise of royal authority—and jurisdictional claims that flowed from them—fell into corresponding disrepute. This meant, for instance, that the Virginia charter of 1609 (disallowed in 1624) still had constitutional force 150 years later [16] and that Vermont separatists could argue that the 1764 Privy Council decision was simply one of the many unconstitutional exercises of authority that justified Americans in taking up arms. [17]

The contrasting situations of New York and the charter-claiming states and their divergent experiences in the Empire are apparent in their expectations of Congress. Virginia's sensitivity to interference in its domestic affairs was a byword in Congress; Congress had no right to receive a petition from the Indiana Company or from dissidents in Kentucky. [18] Virginia would not submit its boundaries to congressional determination (thus jeopardizing its fundamental claim to sovereign statehood), nor would it rely on Congress to suppress domestic insurgency. Yet this is precisely what New York sought from Congress in the Vermont controversy.

New York's campaign to secure its boundaries through Congress revealed the political obstacles to implementing the guarantees of the rights of individual states found in the Articles of Confederation and in Congress's own resolutions. The landed states rallied behind New York's northeastern claims in order to establish the exclusive claims of the thirteen states and so protect their own controversial western claims. The small, landless states were reluctant to support New York in Vermont until a cession of all western claims, including New York's, should make boundary guarantees less politically controversial. The same states, however, were anxious to promote New York's western claims (once they were ceded unconditionally to Congress) as an alternative to the conditional offers of charter claimants. But the other landed states would not recognize the validity of claims derived from any source other than charters and likely to be used against their claims. Thus New York's claims were compromised by the support they received: the western lands controversy precluded an effective and unanimous response to the Vermont insurgency. In the words of Gouverneur Morris, who saw little hope for New York in Vermont, "our Delegates are very urgent with Congress to do what Congress cannot do, and what they have not the Inclination to do, if they could." [19]

It is remarkable that so many New Yorkers continued to rely so much on Congress even when they became aware that so many of the states that made up Congress were for various private and public reasons interested in Vermont's independence. [20] New York was a large, landed state, notwithstanding the proposed cession, and neighboring states were of opinion that "the less formidable she was the better." [21] As Abraham Ten Broeck complained in 1777, "Persons of great influence in some of our sister states, have fostered and fomented these divisions, in order to dismember this state." [22] But New Yorkers continued to look at the Vermont question as a claims controversy that Congress should adjudicate; they did not see it as an internal "police" problem. Impatience and disgust with Congress did not lead New Yorkers like James Duane (a notorious speculator in Vermont lands) to abandon this paradigm. [23] "It is essential," Duane argued, "in the very nature of government, that the supreme sovereignty vested with the power of peace and war [the American Congress] should be able to ascertain the Country and People which are the Objects of their high trust." [24] While attacks on Virginia's claims provoked angry threats that that sovereign state would break with the union, similar frustrations in New York led instead to more expansive arguments for congressional sovereignty. [25]

The Vermont problem was held hostage to the western lands stalemate in Congress. But this did not prompt New York to strike a direct blow against the secessionists. Offers of accommodation, accompanied by threats of reprisal, were made to New Hampshire grantees who had defied New York in order to protect their titles. But these overtures were as much for the edification of Congress as the rebels. If the Vermonters did not accept these generous terms, New York might still enhance its reputation for generosity and justice.

The goal of New York's Vermont policy was to induce Congress to adjudicate the controversy and arrive at a decision that Vermonters would be compelled to accept as legitimate. As John Jay pointed out, once Congress "interfered ever so little, they might with more ease be led to a further and more effectual interposition." [26] New Yorkers were convinced that the Vermonters would capitulate to an adverse decision; according to the delegates, Congress was "the only tribunal they fear." [27] But this meant that the

Vermonters would have to be accorded a hearing—a risky strategy at best. Governor Clinton objected to any "implied acknowledgement of their authority"; in an adjudication they necessarily would be recognized as parties to the dispute.[28]

The risk appeared to be worth taking. First, if Congress gave the separatists a fair hearing it would "take from the Inhabitants of Vermont every Pretext for Complaint."[29] They would "have nothing to say or complain of, in case the decision of Congress be against them."[30] Furthermore, Congress would have to find for New York, however much the other states might be interested in another decision, because otherwise "all their boundaries would be afloat." "So dangerous" a precedent as the recognition of Vermont "must effect every other State."[31] Vermont would be created—that is, "made a party" to the dispute—in order to be destroyed.[32] To guarantee that this policy would succeed, New York sought to interest as many other states as possible in the nonexistence of Vermont, by setting up their own claims for adjudication. The possibility of gaining territory through the partition of Vermont would counteract the sympathies of neighboring New England states for the new state. Again, the risk that New Hampshire and Massachusetts might gain territory at New York's expense was acceptable because Congress, in its judicial character, could not "be easily prevailed upon to annul" boundaries fixed with such certainty by the British government as New York's boundary with New Hampshire. As parties to the controversy, the claiming states would have to abstain from voting on the final determination; the other, disinterested states would inevitably find for New York.

There was a natural majority in Congress against any state's extensive territorial claims, and New York's situation was exacerbated by its identification as one of the landed states. The New England states were undoubtedly anxious "to gain another Voice in Congress" by the admission of Vermont.[33] Strategically the United States would have been prudent to conciliate the separatists.[34] Though none of this was lost on the New Yorkers, they still expected that Congress finally could be made to stand by the general principles on which the state's claims rested. New York sought to make Congress treat the controversy as a question of right which all the states could not avoid supporting. Certainly every American state was loath to sanction the involuntary dismemberment of any state, a precedent for unruly citizens everywhere. But a fundamental premise of New York's policy—that Congress would have to act decisively eventually, the premise of any adjudication—proved fallacious. It is ironic that New

York's unwillingness or inability to do anything for itself (in addition to well-publicized differences among the state's leaders on what course to pursue) actually made congressional inaction possible.

The obvious flaw in New York's Vermont policy was that it permitted and even encouraged delay. Inaction became the favored solution in Congress as it faced the equally unacceptable alternatives of recognizing the new state (and encouraging separatists throughout America) or attempting to destroy it by force of arms. Governor Clinton argued that it was in "the Interest of the Revolters to procrastinate, as while they continue to exercise the Powers of Govern[men]t they are gain[in]g Strength & Stability at our Expence."[35] But—provided Congress finally did decide—delays could also work to the advantage of New York; great things were anticipated, but "to precipitate might be to ruin it."[36] Vermont needed congressional recognition to legitimate its independent assumption of authority; in the first years of its independence, separatist leaders appeared to accept the New Yorkers' premise that a final adverse decision by Congress would be devastating to them. New York's attempt to get Congress to decide on Vermont statehood on its legal merits after an exhaustive adjudication was thus accurately aimed at the separatists' weakest point.[37]

Without congressional sanction, the exercise of force (had New York been able to muster one) would have been counterproductive, an admission of the legal bankruptcy of New York's position. But many observers were convinced that there would be no need for force at all once the illegitimacy of the separation was determined by Congress and announced to the world.[38] In any case, it would then "become the Cause of the United States: & we shall have a Right to call on Congress for Assistance to support *their own* authority."[39]

New York first sought to establish the "Justice" and "Generosity" of the state in regard to its wayward citizens. As Gouverneur Morris recommended, "splendid acts of justice and generosity would induce these people to submit."[40] "Give every satisfaction to the proprietors," Robert R. Livingston counseled Governor Clinton.[41] "The jurisdiction is the great point," said John Jay; "it is of no great consequence to the State, who possess and cultivate the soil."[42] Accordingly, the New York Assembly adopted resolutions in February 1778 offering pardon to the rebels and securing most New Hampshire titles, offers that were repeated and enlarged at later sessions.[43] Coercive measures would be held in abeyance until the "delinquents" had the opportunity to "do their duty."[44] But New

York's offers could be expected to produce results only if Congress decisively rejected the separatists' campaign for recognition; in the meantime, New York's "generosity" would surely influence that body.

Early in 1777, Dr. Thomas Young published a broadside letter to "the People of the Grants," advising them that Congress would welcome a statehood application and that the congressional call for new governments in the revolting colonies authorized them to make their own state.[45] This letter was supposed to have led to the Vermont declaration of independence from New York, but it also provided New York an opportunity to press Congress for a statement of principle on separatism. On June 30, at New York's behest, Congress adopted resolutions disavowing this "gross misrepresentation" of its sentiments. According to the report on which the resolutions were based, Young's recommendation was "unwarrantable in itself and highly dangerous in its Consequences; since if it should prevail, and be carried into practice, it must inevitably destroy all Order, Stability and good Government, in particular States and entail Disunion, Weakness, and Insecurity on the United States."[46] Sanguine New Yorkers may have expected these resolutions to drive the Vermonters back into the mountains, but as Clinton explained in April 1778, they had "less Effect than was expected" because of the Vermonters' effective propaganda. Indeed, New Yorkers were convinced that Vermont survived only because Vermonters were kept in the dark; perhaps a more "explicit and unequivocal Declaration" would be effective, Clinton suggested.[47] But the resolutions were more significant for their anticipated impact on future deliberations in Congress; to recognize Vermont, after passing them, would involve Congress in embarrassing contradictions.

New York's Vermont policy took its final form in 1779. Under John Jay's leadership, the New York delegation at Congress shifted its attention from producing more resolves against separatists[48] to committing Congress to resolve the Vermont controversy through adjudication, to which the interested parties would bind themselves to submit and which would commence at a fixed date. Thus, on September 24, again at New York's initiative, Congress unanimously resolved to begin hearings on February 1, 1780.[49] New Hampshire, Massachusetts, and New York were called on to "pass laws expressly authorizing Congress to hear and determine all differences between them relative to their respective boundaries," and the Vermonters were directed to appoint an "Agent or Agents" to represent them. Vermont would have a standing in these hearings, but not as a "state," equal to the others.[50] The resolutions stipulated that the "boundaries and jurisdiction" of the United States (which of course did not include Vermont as a state) were to "be ascertained and settled"; "one of the great objects of the Union of the United States of America is the mutual protection and security of their respective rights." Until a decision was reached, the Vermonters were to "abstain . . . from exercising any power" over professed citizens of any of the United States, which for their part were to forbear claiming jurisdiction over Vermonters. "Any violences committed against the tenor . . . of this resolution" would be considered "a breach of the peace of the Confederacy." Congress pledged to maintain this peace, and subsequently to "carry into execution . . . their decisions and determinations." (It could be predicted with certainty that Congress would thus have ample grounds for intervening in Vermont even if the hearings should drag on inconclusively.)

Though Jay "found it the most delicate affair to manage I ever was concerned in," the results were most gratifying.[51] The proposed adjudication clearly favored New York (the resolutions were "*hatched* up" by New York, complained Nathaniel Peabody of New Hampshire[52]); after all, the state's title had already been upheld by one authoritative tribunal (the British Privy Council), a determination that could hardly be ignored by any subsequent court. Furthermore, the other claiming states apparently had no choice but to prepare for the hearings. The New Hampshire delegation was convinced that "if the Claim of New Hampshire is not supported that Country will assuredly be annex'd to N[ew] Y[ork]," a result that "must be attended with disagreeable consequences" for the New England states.[53] Such fears were justified as long as it appeared that adjudication could not be avoided. If the hearings were held on schedule, New Hampshire and Massachusetts would find themselves joined with New York as litigants, equally interested in rejecting Vermont's claims to independent statehood.

In late 1779 there did "not appear . . . the least probability that Vermont will be allowed to be a Separate State," and such disallowance would presumably suffice to destroy the new state.[54] The question was, therefore, how was Vermont to be divided? But Massachusetts and New Hampshire were at best reluctant partners in a scheme so clearly weighted in New York's favor. Negotiations to secure each state's compliance with the September 24 resolutions and begin the hearings proceeded in an atmosphere of suspicion and antagonism. The Massachusetts General Court balked unaccountably at passing enabling legislation and preparing its admittedly dubious case; various stratagems by that state were, in Ezra L'Hommedieu's opinion, "no doubt" designed "to cause delays."[55] New Yorkers also sus-

pected New Hampshire of foot-dragging and a secret predisposition to recognize Vermont.[56] This shaky coalition was sure to disintegrate if the
hearings were delayed or aborted. Massachusetts and New Hampshire had
to be made to define their interests against the new state, rather than
against New York, as they normally were. The hearings simply had to take
place or New York's case was lost. "Delay is a Trump Card that ought not
to be permitted to remain in Hand," John Jay warned.[57]

The success of New York's Vermont policy depended on its ability to
persuade Congress that its dilatoriness would entail unacceptable risks. As
the New York House told Governor Clinton, New Yorkers had to demon-
strate "our Steadfast Purpose, to maintain the rightful Jurisdiction of this
State."[58] This amounted, in one way or another, to threatening that New
York would be compelled to reduce its contribution to, or even abandon,
the American war effort. Why should we strive "to expel a foreign
Tyranny," the assembly asked, "while we remain Subject to the domestic
Usurpation?"[59] The possibility of a "Breach betwixt the Legislature of this
State and the General Congress" was raised; in any event there would be
difficulty in "obtaining taxes from New York" until the issue was settled.[60]
New York would be forced to withdraw "the resources of the State which
ha[ve] hitherto so lavishly been afforded to the continent" in order to
make war on the Vermonters.[61] "Once we are involved in war and bloodshed, both parties will disregard Congress," Governor Clinton predicted.[62]

The incalculable dangers that might result from unnecessary delays
prompted Congress to act with (for it) extraordinary dispatch in bringing
the New Hampshire Grants controversy to the point of adjudication. But
timing was still everything. Unfortunately for New York, the backward-
ness of the litigants, the sickness of key congressmen, the belligerent attitude of the Vermonters, and the chronic problem of underrepresentation
(exacerbated by the nonvoting status of the claiming states) combined to
delay the hearings until September.[63] In the meantime nothing could be
accomplished except the passage of new resolutions warning Vermont to
cease harassing Yorkers (which, because they were unenforceable, only
demonstrated congressional impotence to the separatists).[64]

By the time hearings finally began, a critical change in sentiment was
apparent in Congress. Many congressmen now were convinced that the
New Yorkers' threats—their "breathing out . . . Death and Slaughter"—
were simply empty noises.[65] At the same time, Vermonters had made it
unmistakably clear that they would not allow their state to be adjudicated
out of existence.[66] If a "civil war" between New York and Vermont was

otherwise unavoidable, Congress might be forced to intervene; it also had to be shown that less force would be necessary if the United States, rather than New York, undertook to reduce the Vermonters. But just as they defended their state's right to exist, the separatists pledged themselves to resist any coercive intervention. Congressmen began to realize "that If the Lands are adjudged to New York the Continent must be Involved in a war to Inforce the Determination of Congress."[67] Sam Adams thought that "if there was Reason to expect that all [parties] would be satisfied with a Decision of Congress . . . the sooner [it was reached] the better."[68] But Vermont would "not submit the Question of their Existence as an independent State."[69] Therefore, many congressmen reasoned, the only responsible policy was "to prevent, what . . . we are in great danger of, a war with that people."[70] "We have business enough on our hands" already, according to Daniel of St. Thomas Jenifer.[71] In view of New York's failure to launch a campaign against the separatists (which would have been in violation of the congressional resolutions of September 24, 1779), Congress had little incentive to act. Even "those who are convinced of the Justice of our Cause wish it to yield to the pressure of our publick Affairs," James Duane reported. Some congressmen thought it prudent to leave the matter alone until the end of the war; "others wish the Discussion 10 years off."[72]

It was the Vermonters, not the New Yorkers, who most vividly demonstrated a willingness to employ violent means in open contempt of Congress's jurisdictional moratorium. Indeed, Vermont's blatant disregard of the will of Congress helped alter the way congressmen perceived the controversy. Vermont was capable of mobilizing its citizenry to support its authority. But New York could not spare the necessary manpower; New Yorkers on the de facto Vermont frontier were notably lukewarm in their loyalty to the state (and would join Vermont in 1781); the logistical problems in supporting Yorker partisans in the southeastern part of the new state were daunting.[73] In case of conflict, there was good reason to believe that New Englanders would offer at least covert assistance to the rebels. Furthermore, New York had committed itself to congressional adjudication; it eschewed violence on political as well as strategic grounds.

Because of delays in getting the hearings begun, attention shifted away from the question of right (which was properly the subject of the hearings themselves) to the political expediency of bringing the hearings on—or putting them off. The events of 1780 showed that the Vermonters could make a more powerful case for themselves on this question than the Yorkers could. They let it be known that they would "form an Alliance with Great Britain in Case Congress shall Declare them dependant on any State."[74] Persistent rumors that a truce already existed between Vermont and the British (which, ironically, the New Yorkers eagerly circulated in order to discredit the separatists) gave the Vermonters' belligerent posture a credibility that New York's blusterings could not match. "It was not a Time for America to Court New Enemies or add to the Number of the Disaffected," said John Sullivan, and most other congressmen would have agreed.[75]

Vermont's hard line toward Congress and its rumored flirtation with the British destroyed New York's adjudication campaign, the centerpiece of its Vermont policy. When the hearings finally did begin, it was debatable what form they should take and what result they could possibly achieve, given Vermont's refusal to participate. A proposal to ignore Vermont and decide between the New York and New Hampshire claims was condemned as an "unjust" and "*ex parte* hearing."[76] According to Theodorick Bland of Virginia (a maverick in that state's delegation), it would be "an indirect and unfair manner of deciding the Question" that "wou[l]d deprive the Vermonteers of all future opportunity of Vindicating their Independance."[77] Under such circumstances, Congress could not pretend to be dealing with a strictly legal issue; it is significant that some congressmen began to assert openly that the issue *had* to be decided in terms of political "expediency."[78] It was in such terms that Congress thereafter would consider Vermont.

The debates of September and October 1780 were further compromised politically by the simultaneous struggle over western land cessions. When Virginian James Madison insisted that the exclusive claims of the thirteen original states made the existence of "another Jurisdiction" in the New Hampshire Grants a logical impossibility, the principle seemed less unexceptionable than it had in June 1777.[79] The guarantee of New York's claims over Vermont would constitute a backhanded guarantee of Virginia's western charter claims. Thus drafted into the landed state coalition, New York would find the very existence of its own western claims, even as they were offered up to Congress, an acute political embarrassment. The result was that the state's Vermont claims were viewed with the same hostility and suspicion by the small states as were state claims in the West. The cession that was supposed to secure an alliance between New York and the landless states had backfired.

The success of New York's Vermont policy depended on the willingness of Congress to adjudicate at an early date, the submission of all interested parties—including Vermont—to its ultimate decision, and the preservation of the "legal" character of congressional proceedings, uncompromised by political considerations. At the beginning of 1780 New York's prospects in all these respects looked good. But once it was clear that New York had no effective sanctions to invoke in the Grants or against Congress, and that Vermont did, Congress had every incentive to procrastinate—provided this would satisfy the Vermonters. The fragile structure of adjudication fell apart; adjudication was too obviously, and too apparently, the only means by which New York could secure its jurisdiction in the New Hampshire Grants. By late 1780 Congress had more to fear from Vermont than it did from New York.

While New York's adjudication campaign was foundering in Congress, differences of opinion about Vermont began to surface in New York. As early as March 1778, Gouverneur Morris had seen the crux of New York's dilemma: "The most which can be said for us is that we have right without remedy."

> What are their claims? Occupancy settlement cultivation and the Book of Genesis. What their plea? Their mountains their arms their courage their alliances. Against all this what can we produce? Why forsooth a decision of the King in Council and a clause in the Confederacy. How ridiculous for wise men to rear any edifice upon so slender a foundation.[80]

Nor, Morris added later, could New York hope to vindicate its claims by force: "This is a Remedy which cannot at present be exhibited nor will it at any Time be agreable to see Americans embruing their Hands in the Blood of each other."[81] By the winter of 1780–81, Morris came out openly for the recognition of Vermont. He wrote to Robert R. Livingston, another pro-Vermonter, "America is now busied in teaching the great lesson, that men cannot be governed against their wills."[82] The intervening years had shown that the United States would not use force against the separatists, and nothing else could induce them to submit.

The conviction that Vermont could not be beaten became so pervasive by late 1780 that longtime Yorker partisans in Cumberland County (Windham County, Vermont) entered into negotiations with the separatists leading to an agreement to join the new state when it annexed a large number of New Hampshire towns in 1781.[83] Given the separatists' failure to respond to pardon and title guarantee offers, many New Yorkers began to argue that the state stood to gain more by a voluntary cession of its claims. "Make Vermont sovereign free and independent," Morris recommended, then get Congress to confirm the state's remaining claims and "laugh loudly at the Fools who covet extensive unwieldy Dominion."[84] Insistence on its right to Vermont undermined the larger goal of New York policy—to secure stable, recognized boundaries. Because of the western lands dispute, the small states had not supported New York in Vermont; at the same time, the Vermont imbroglio delayed settlement of the western boundary. Some New York politicians believed that these territorial controversies created artificial alliances and enmities among the states and that if the Vermont question could be laid to rest, then their state would become aligned with the eastern (northern) states. The two goals—establishing secure boundaries and forging an eastern alliance—were combined in the call for a convention of the eastern states early in 1781. According to Philip Schuyler, the convention would settle "every difference which may exist with respect to boundaries."[85] It was understood that it would be necessary "to create a new state [Vermont] in this quarter" in order to induce the New England states to come to terms.

Schuyler and his allies took the initiative when the New York Assembly convened at Albany in February 1781. On February 6, Governor Clinton forwarded an "insolent" letter from Vermont's Governor Thomas Chittenden demanding that New York relinquish its claims.[86] To Clinton's amazement, the assembly was ready to deal with the Vermonters. On February 21 the Senate adopted (by a 14 to 1 vote) resolutions to name boundary commissioners to negotiate with the Vermonters. It might yet be possible to create the impression that New York was giving something up, and thus gain for it political credit for "moderation and generosity," particularly because there was "no room to doubt the right of this government to the jurisdiction and sovereignty over the country in question."[87] When Clinton got wind of these developments, he fired off an angry message to the lower house, threatening to "prorogue you" "should you . . . agree to carry into effect these resolutions."[88] The legislature had no right to reverse its former determination to vindicate New York's claims "at every hazard"; in any case, the question "has been solemnly submitted to . . . Congress, the proper tribunal."[89]

Clinton's rationale for proroguing the house exposed the flimsiness of New York's position. Why should Congress come to the support of New York's claims when New Yorkers appeared willing to give them up? "The Conduct of our legislature at Albany last winter" helped Congress resolve any lingering scruples about recognizing the separatists; the "body of the people in N[ew] York" was said to be willing to acknowledge the new state.[90] When faced with the possibility of a British attack on their northern frontier, New Yorkers were as prone as congressmen to consult expediency. Clinton also suggested that some of New York's "monied men" had begun to speculate in Vermont land grants.[91] Though Clinton discouraged the Senate from repeating its frustrated offer to the separatists, instead repeating the timeworn call for a speedy "Decision and Determination" by Congress, this harmony was superficial at best.[92] The February confrontation has "unfortunately been the means of lessening, if not destroying, all confidence and cordiality between some of the principal characters in the State," Egbert Benson wrote John Jay late in the year.[93] Many New Yorkers continued to favor Vermont's independence. Even as evidence of the new state's contemplated treason to the American cause accumulated, Philip Schuyler "sincerely wish[ed] the controversy between the Vermonters" and New York resolved and the separatists "declared independent."[94]

When New York's delegates arrived at Congress in late July 1781, carrying instructions demanding an early adjudication of the controversy, they discovered that the "business of Vermont" was "in a manner" already settled: "A final Decision has been suspended in point of form in expectation of our Presence."[95] Wavering support for Clinton's hard line in New York, compounded by Massachusetts' voluntary relinquishment of its claims in the Grants and willingness to recognize the new state, the devastating British campaign in the south, and ominous portents of an attack from the north, strengthened the pro-Vermont bloc in Congress.[96] Meanwhile, Vermont had extended its jurisdiction to the east and west, annexing New York territory up to the Hudson River. Vermont's aggressive policy provided more evidence of its rumored alliance with the British. In the circumstances, congressmen would have been delighted to secure the separatists to the common cause; New York and New Hampshire were primarily interested in regaining their lost territory.[97] "We shall endeavour to get our remaining territorial Rights expressly guarranteed by a precise Description," the delegates wrote Clinton in early August.[98] James Duane had found that "the Doctrine that our Jurisdiction over Vermont is to be sacrifised for the publick Tranquility is pretty fully established."[99] He would make the best of a bad situation, if possible, by procuring "the establishment of our remaining limits by express bounds and under especial guarantee of the United States."

Ironically, the only explicit boundary guarantee Congress ever offered

New York was attached to its resolution of August 21 to recognize Vermont.[100] It was to "be an indispensable preliminary to the recognition of the independence" of Vermont that it "explicitly relinquish" the eastern and western unions. Congress thus agreed to defend New York's jurisdiction up to its old de facto boundary with Vermont, twenty miles east of the Hudson. The delegates sought to convince Clinton that even this guarantee could not be obtained "without Difficulty."[101] A general guarantee would have to await a more propitious moment. "The equity of our territorial rights can be so fully established that we persuade ourselves that a full Congress will conceive the Limits which we propose to establish to be moderate and the Cession to the United States liberal," said the delegates.[102] But New York's "sacrifice"—in view of its vote against recognizing Vermont and the assembly's subsequent resolves in "solemn protest" against Congress's intermeddling in the state's "territorial extent of jurisdiction"—did not inspire Congress to offer compensatory guarantees beyond fixing the Vermont–New York border.[103] At the same time, the other landed states (which most poignantly felt the sacrifice imposed on New York, even though voting to recognize Vermont) were determined to block New York's western land cession.[104]

New York's boundary policy was subverted by the state's failure to offer concessions of any value in time enough to be of good effect. The hardliners on Vermont prevented a compromise when New York still apparently had something to offer. The Vermont controversy subverted efforts to secure a favorable western boundary, and by the time the western cession was finally accepted—without reciprocal guarantees—Vermont was beyond recovery.

Vermont's agents at Congress did not agree to the boundary guarantees attached to the recognition offer. They said that they lacked authority to dissolve the unions with New Hampshire and New York towns, offering instead to submit to Article IX proceedings with each state after Vermont's admission to the union.[105] According to British intelligence, the unions were designed by the "crafty Mountaineers" to prevent congressional recognition of the new state.[106] If this was so, the usually compliant Vermont Assembly undermined the policy when it renounced the annexations in February 1782, presumably hoping to clear the way for recognition and admission.[107] But by that time congressional opinion had begun to shift once more, and the statehood offer was not repeated.

Vermont's rejection by Congress reflected the changing military situation. The southern states, no longer under the British gun, were now "much in our favor," William Floyd reported in January.[108] Discovering that nine state votes could not be obtained for admission, Vermont's supporters were for "put[t]ing it of[f]" until a more favorable moment.[109] Votes of March 1 on a committee report recommending that the Vermonters be given a month to comply with the August resolutions showed that only six states supported the new state; the southern landed states stood firmly behind New York.[110]

"The States who were with us," the New York delegates reported, "are strongly against declaring the independency of the Grants either on supposition of the want of authority in Congress" or because "the admission of the Grants . . . would be prejudicial to the United States."[111] The British alliance with Vermont had been the most powerful argument for recognizing the new state—as long as the outcome of the war appeared to hang in the balance. But many congressmen now came to share the New Yorkers' conviction that "admitting so many Serpents into our Bosom" would "poison our Councils."[112] The alleged disloyalty of the Vermonters became their biggest liability in Congress and alienated many of their former friends. But the adoption of New York's cause by the landed states was most crucial. They "utterly disclaim[e]d" Congress's "power either to decide on their [the Vermonters'] independence or to open the door of the confederacy to them."[113] Their constitutional misgivings reflected anxieties about the danger of the "precedent" of Vermont for malcontents elsewhere as well as continuing opposition to the small states' campaign to "dismember the great ones."[114] Virginians found "a disposition in the small states very dangerous to the peace and union of America," according to Arthur Lee.[115] They detected a conspiracy between the "land-mongers," land companies which sought to secure private property claims in the West, and the Vermonters.[116]

The southern states also feared that the addition of a new, small northern state would adversely "affect the balance of power."[117] The northern states "are laboring hard *to get Vermont established as an independent* State," Pierce Butler reported, "which will give them *another vote*" and enable them to "carry many measures disadvantageous to the *Southern interest.*"[118] Arthur Lee predicted that "with the admission of this little State the confederation will end; its present inequality being as much as it can bear."[119]

As James Madison correctly anticipated, the pro-Vermont bloc was vulnerable to further erosion; landless state support for Vermont was contingent on its usefulness in extorting western land cessions, which might be soon forthcoming.[120] "The general policy" of Maryland and Pennsylvania was opposed to the admission of Vermont, "and if the case of the Western territory were once removed, they would instantly divide from the Eastern States." In other words, once the Vermont problem was extricated from the western lands controversy, it would become a sectional issue, with Vermont's supporters in a distinct minority.

In the meantime, William Floyd suggested, "Nothing Effectuall will be Done."[121] Said Samuel Osgood, "We cannot make them independent: we cannot obtain a Vote to reduce them to Subjection to any of the Claiming States. The natural Inference seems to be that they must remain as they now are, If they are contented to be so."[122] Between the two parties on the Vermont question, for and against recognition, "no one proposition respecting them can be agreed on."[123] Another series of votes in April, on another committee report suggesting that Congress follow through on its statehood offer, revealed the declining strength of the pro-Vermont bloc, even though it was then known that Vermont had retreated to its old boundaries.[124]

The stalemate on Vermont was not to be broken, however, even when the completion of New York's western land cession in October removed the last obstacle to its alliance with the small, landless states. According to Madison, New York, by "*ceding a claim which was tenable* neither *by force nor by law . . . has* acquired *with Congress the merit of liberality* rendered the *title to her reservation more respectable and* at least dampt *the zeal with which Vermont has been abetted.*"[125] But the "clear alteration of Sentiment" in favor of New York had only limited value: "a wish to procrastinate still prevails," James Duane reported. Congress remained unwilling to drive the "Vermont Faction to despair." There was "no danger" that Vermont would be recognized, according to Duane;[126] moreover, New York was able to obtain pointed resolves on December 5 against Vermont's violations of the jurisdictional moratorium of September 24, 1779, acts that were "highly derogatory to the authority of the United States," requiring "the immediate and decided interposition of Congress."[127] According to Madison's notes on the congressional debates, "the proceedings . . . evinced still more the conciliating effect of the territorial cession of N[ew] York, on several States & the effect of the scheme of an ultramontane state within Penns[ylvani]a on the latter State."[128] Only "Rhode Island which is supposed to be interested in lands in Vermont and N. Jersey whose delegates were under instructions on that subject" stood by Vermont.[129] But it was also clear that Congress would not resume its aborted adjudication and that its "interposition" would not be coercive. Indeed, Vermonters had received "secret assurances that Congress will not direct any coercive Measures against them."[130] The New York delegates did not entertain any illusions about Congress's willingness to invoke punitive sanctions.[131] Instead, they interpreted Congress's actions as a tacit invitation to New York and New Hampshire to take matters into their own hands.

Throughout 1782, sentiment grew for "our State and N[ew] H[ampshire] to Come to Some Settlement between themselves."[132] New York's latest offers to the separatists and popular dissatisfaction in Vermont with the state's flirtation with the British made this a good time to intervene.[133] The New York delegates were convinced that Congress would finally do nothing, and that "this would render the States who are interested therein the more solicitous to do something for themselves."[134] When Vermont's unions were dissolved, Yorker partisans in Cumberland County returned to their old loyalties and clamored for assistance. "Conciliatory overtures . . . followed by a spirited and vigorous exertion of the civil authority of the State" would embolden its supporters "to shew themselves" against the Vermonters.[135]

Everyone agreed by now that Vermont could be destroyed only by a show of force, and New Yorkers at Congress well knew that the United States was unable and unwilling to supply it. A combination of forces with New Hampshire and a partition treaty would alone enable New York to recover "any part of the revolted territory."[136] "I do hope that our legislature will before they Rise do the needful on that subject," William Floyd wrote Clinton.[137] Surprisingly, Clinton did not bring the question up at this time.[138] Instead, he expressed "Doubts . . . whether the Legislature have Authority by any Act of theirs to consent to such a Dismemberment of the State."[139] Clinton claimed that the consensus in New York was for waiting for Congress to act, since it "has engaged to make a final Decision of the Controversy." "I am more & more convinced that on a final Decision, all Ideas of Resistance" by Vermont "would vanish—at most the putting in Motion of a very small Force would be sufficient to induce the bulk of the People to Submission."[140] It is possible that Clinton's political intelligence supported such a conclusion, but it was also true that Clinton had been told repeatedly that Congress would not complete the claims adjudication and would be unwilling to deploy even a "very small force." Again, as he "intimated before," Hamilton told Clinton that there was much reason to "doubt the perseverance of congress, if military coercion should become necessary."[141] If New York would not take independent state action, or concert measures with other claiming states, Hamilton thought the legislature should then either "relinquish their pretensions" or instruct the delegates to institute an Article IX proceeding with New Hampshire.[142]

Clinton shied away from independent initiatives, though he continued to hope that a continental force would be turned against the Vermonters.[143] The New York militia had performed abysmally in encounters with Vermont troops in December 1781; and unfortunately for New York, its partisans in Vermont were concentrated on the New Hampshire side of the Green Mountains. Even in alliance with New Hampshire, the New Yorkers would have had to attack the separatists in their stronghold, the region around Bennington. Perhaps Clinton had good reason to avoid a state campaign against the Vermonters; his lack of enthusiasm for an Article IX proceeding may have reflected a similarly realistic assessment. Such a proceeding, unlike the proposed adjudication of September 24, 1779, would not accord the Vermonters any standing at all and could hardly command their submission. The decision would still have to be enforced, and by the time it was reached Vermont would be better equipped to resist—and the United States no more enthusiastic about going to war with the Vermonters.

Whatever Clinton's reasoning, it seemed perfectly calculated to protract the stalemate. The United States would not make war on Vermont; New York would probably lose if it did. Under these circumstances the rebels had little incentive to be generous to New York land claimants like Clinton. Meanwhile, holding the line in Congress against Vermont's admission to the union, and a continuing impasse, might work to New York's advantage. In time, Vermont might value membership in the union highly enough to be willing to negotiate a settlement more favorable to New York. The premise of this policy was that Vermont could not be destroyed, a negative de facto recognition of the new state.[144]

In the related struggles among the American states over boundaries and jurisdiction, New York was the big loser. Every other ceding state had gained or retained something of value, to which it had had only a speculative, unperfected title. New York sought secure, recognized boundaries; in lieu of this, however, the state had to be content with the kind of constructive boundaries Edmund Burke had warned New Yorkers against in 1774. Vermont was allowed to exist; arguably there was no helping this. But the western boundary was left dangerously unresolved, and a greater flexibility on Vermont might have paid off here for New York. By the time the New York cession was accepted (by a narrow vote, along partisan lines), New York's western title was generally seen as worthless and contemptible; the failure of Congress to do anything with it in the next year and a half confirmed this judgment. During these months, the western lands controversy revolved around the question of which title, New York's or Virginia's, was good. Because, according to the implicit terms of the compromise between the landed and landless states, charters were upheld as the source of good title, New York's title could be dismissed—even in that area east of the cession line that it meant to retain. The acceptance of the Virginia cession in March 1784 was an invitation to the other landed states to make use of their own charter claims. Thus, for instance, Massachusetts promoted its charter claims west of the settled area in New York State with renewed vigor, and to its ultimate advantage.[145]

New York had failed to offer Congress any incentives to guarantee its boundaries. Without such guarantees and without the resources to make good its territorial claims, New York was vulnerable to further usurpations. Simply, a state's claims had to bear some reasonable relation to the jurisdiction it could effectively govern. This was a lesson that other states—including Massachusetts—would be forced to learn in the following years.

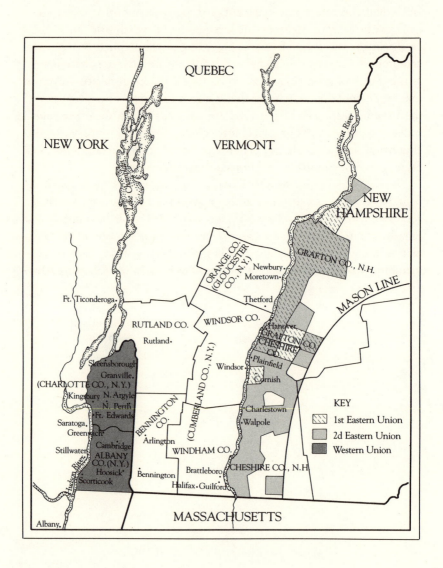

QUEBEC

NEW YORK

VERMONT

NEW
HAMPSHIRE

Connecticut River

Lake Champlain

Ft. Ticonderoga·

ORANGE CO.
(GLOUCESTER
CO., N.Y.)

Newbury·
Moretown·

·Thetford

GRAFTON CO., N.H.

MASON LINE

RUTLAND CO.

WINDSOR CO.

·Rutland

·Hanover
GRAFTON
CO.
CHESHIRE
CO.

Skeensborough·
Granville·

(CHARLOTTE CO., N.Y.)
·Kingsbury N. Argyle·
·N. Perth
Ft. Edwards·

(CUMBERLAND CO., N.Y.)

·Windsor

·Plainfield

·Cornish

KEY

Saratoga·
Greenwich·

BENNINGTON
CO.

·Arlington

·Charlestown
·Walpole

1st Eastern Union
2d Eastern Union
Western Union

Stillwater·

Cambridge
ALBANY
CO. (N.Y.)
Hoosick·
·Scorticook

WINDHAM CO.

·Brattleboro

CHESHIRE CO., N.H

·Bennington

Hudson River

Halifax· ·Guilford

Albany·

MASSACHUSETTS

· 6 ·

The New State of Vermont: Revolution Within a Revolution

Vermont was created in July 1777 when representatives of approximately twenty-eight towns in the New Hampshire Grants adopted their own constitution and declared their independence from the state of New York. New York and New Hampshire had contested for jurisdiction in the area until 1764, when the British Privy Council set New York's eastern boundary at the Connecticut River. The Vermont independence movement was the culmination of a subsequent series of challenges to the Privy Council's decision on behalf of settlers and speculators holding New Hampshire titles.[1] Vermont joined the American Revolution against British tyranny, but the revolutionary states did not embrace Vermont. Because the U.S. Congress would not sanction the involuntary division of one of its own members, Vermont was unable to gain recognition from neighboring states or protection from the British in Canada. When Vermont became independent, it became independent of all the world, and remained so until 1791, when it was finally admitted to the union.

If the United States did not welcome Vermont into their ranks, neither were they willing to tolerate it as a neutral republic. The Americans were anxious to secure their northern flank from British attack; neighboring states sought to regain or extend their territorial jurisdiction; and New York speculators hoped to establish their land titles in the Grants. The impasse over Vermont statehood—which dragged through Congress for

127

years—encouraged British overtures to the new state. The British hoped to disrupt the revolutionary cause and gain a foothold in northern New England. The threat of invasion guaranteed that the Vermonters would give the British an attentive hearing.

In the first years of the war, Vermont participated actively in the American effort, capturing Ticonderoga (May 1775) and playing an important role in thwarting Burgoyne's attack from Canada (August–October 1777).[2] In recognition of these contributions, the new state's leaders expected to be welcomed into the American union. But New York insisted that the Grants remained a part of that state, and Congress could not afford to alienate one of its most important members. Nonrecognition by Congress left Vermont in a precarious position, exposing its tenuous hold on popular loyalties. Support for the new state was strongest on the west side of the Green Mountains. But several towns in the southeast had come to terms with New York before the Revolution and continued to favor New York's jurisdictional pretensions into the 1780s. Further up the Connecticut River, townspeople agitated for a union with their counterparts on the New Hampshire side—in either Vermont or New Hampshire, should the latter's colonial claim be revived.

Factional politics in Vermont as well as the state's vulnerable strategic situation provoked the adoption of aggressive policies toward its neighbors. In June 1778, sixteen New Hampshire towns were annexed in the first Eastern Union. The Vermont Assembly dissolved the union in October under heavy pressure from the American states and the implicit suggestion that Congress would treat a statehood application favorably.[3] From this time on, New Hampshire entertained designs on the towns on the west bank of the Connecticut. More chilly responses from Congress and the threat of New Hampshire as well as New York expansionism led to new annexations; thirty-five New Hampshire towns were added in the second Eastern Union (April 1781) and twelve New York towns were added in the Western Union (June 1781).[4] Vermont's aggressive posture reflected a growing disregard for the power of the United States—particularly New York, which Vermont routed in the border "war" of December 1781—and a willingness to enter into alliance with the British. Not coincidentally, the Haldimand negotiations (so-called after General Frederick Haldimand, British commander at Quebec), beginning in May 1781, led to a cessation of hostilities in the north.[5] The talks were designed to secure Vermont neutrality during the Revolution and its eventual readmission to the British Empire as a distinct colony—including the Eastern and Western unions. News of the prospective alliance prompted Congress to offer Vermont statehood in August 1781, if it would withdraw from New Hampshire and New York.[6] But when Vermont complied with the condition by dissolving the unions (February 1782), Congress recanted.[7] Meanwhile, with American victory assured, the British lost interest in Vermont.

Vermont's tortuous foreign policy succeeded in promoting havoc and confusion among its neighbors and secured the state from invasion, but it did not establish the authority of the new state over its own citizens. Every foreign policy initiative provoked disgust and dissension in one part of the state or another. By all accounts, most Vermonters considered themselves loyal Americans; they displayed little enthusiasm for returning to the Empire when news of the Haldimand talks leaked. Westerners resented the domination of the Connecticut River towns resulting from the eastern unions; at other times, easterners resented the domination of the West. Every faction in the state suspected the motives and loyalties of the other factions. This pervasive mistrust was symptomatic of the failure of the new state government to establish stable and legitimate authority.

The founders of Vermont had to create a state where no true community had existed. They could not command the communal loyalties of former colonies with distinctive institutions and political traditions. And even though the state constitution of 1777 incorporated many of the most advanced principles of popular republicanism, Vermont's leaders were hard-pressed to convince the populace that it had a right to govern itself and that the constitution had any legal force.[8] They had to convince the rest of the world to recognize their claims, and they had to convince themselves that their self-constituted authority was legitimate. In the process, Vermonters explored and illuminated the ambiguous nature of statehood during the American Revolution.

American statehood claims rested on various potentially contradictory premises. Boundary controversies and new state movements, like Vermont's, exposed these contradictions. First, the prior status of the independent states as British colonies was invoked; new state governments simply succeeded old colony governments in political communities or "states" that long antedated the Revolution. But it was also argued that new communities came into being with the drafting of state constitutions; the sovereign people created new states. And finally, mutual recognition among the states through membership in the union and representation in

Congress was a crucial component of American statehood claims. Indeed, "one of the great objects of the union" was "the protection and security" of state rights, as Congress resolved in September 1779.[9] Thus states as territorial communities were inherited from the colonial period; states as governments were created by the revolutionaries; and states in a community of states existed by virtue of the recognition of other states.

Different definitions of statehood served different functions: to distinguish among state claims, to legitimize revolutionary governments, and to guarantee cooperation in the common cause. Ordinarily, they were compatible. The original thirteen states had all been colonies. Most adopted new state constitutions. In principle, they agreed to defend each other's claims. The American revolutionary program combined the creation of a continental union with the reassertion of each colony-state's autonomy and territorial integrity.[10] Although the Continental Congress called for the constitution of new governments in the colonies as the necessary preliminary, if not the essence, of independence, it saw itself as the creature, not the creator, of existing polities. According to a report adopted in June 1777, "Congress is composed of delegates chosen by, and representing the communities respectively inhabiting the territories" of the colony-states "as they respectively stood at the time of its first institution."[11] Therefore, as Congress explained in 1780, "the lands contained within the limits of the United States are . . . under the jurisdiction of some one or other of the thirteen states."[12]

The unanimous, if belated, ratification of the Articles of Confederation (1781) did not alter the supposition that the thirteen colony-states constituted the basic components of the American union. The Articles were supposed to guarantee the territorial integrity of the states, and they made the admission of new states exceedingly difficult, if not impossible.[13] At the end of the Revolution, moreover, the Paris Treaty of 1783 listed each American state separately, giving international recognition to the exclusive claims of the thirteen states over all the territory in the "United States."[14]

It was one thing to insist on the exclusive claims of the original states in principle, however, but quite another to establish them in practice. Unfortunately, state claims based on colonial precedents overlapped. Boundary conflicts undermined the basic premise of colony-state succession doctrine, that states as territorial communities were "given." Jurisdictional confusion encouraged separatists to advance their own claims. The Vermonters, for instance, set up one statehood claim (the right of revolutionary Americans to constitute themselves into a body politic) against another (the right of New York State to succeed to New York's colonial claims). The "epidemic . . . Spirit of making new States" strengthened the notion that old colony-state boundaries should be secured at all costs.[15] "Geographical Lines of Jurisdiction" were absolutely necessary, wrote Charles Phelps, a leader of Yorker opposition to Vermont, if there was to be government at all.[16]

American revolutionaries were thus compelled to develop a counter-revolutionary argument against the independence of frontier regions from the original thirteen states. The colonies had not been in a "state of nature" in 1776; the revolution right could be exercised only by governments that could claim to be legitimate successors to British colonial governments. In its most naked form, when applied to separatist movements, this doctrine sanctioned the exercise of state authority with the same supposedly arbitrary rationale that the British invoked against the states themselves.

Territorial controversies illuminated the difficulties that the American states faced in establishing effective authority throughout their claims. Controversial claims—and contradictory notions of statehood—encouraged separatists to set up new states. But these new states also faced serious obstacles, and most could not surmount them. The creators of Vermont, for instance, could not appeal to a colonial past, though, as we shall see, they attempted to invent one. Nor could Vermont benefit from the recognition of other states, as could the United States in Congress. It was not enough for the new state's leaders simply to claim the people's right to self-government, particularly when the people were so deeply divided on so many issues—including Vermont's independence. Thomas Chittenden, Vermont's first governor, conceded that many Vermonters were under the misapprehension "that a public Acknowledgement of the Powers of the Earth is essential to the Existence of a distinct separate *State*."[17] Indeed, few Vermonters thought Vermont could survive indefinitely without the recognition and protection of a higher authority, American or English. Thus the new state's leaders had to convince not only the "powers of the earth" but also the people of Vermont and themselves that they were entitled to statehood.

The Vermont claims defense was eclectic; it drew together apparently contradictory arguments premised on the people's natural rights, the absolute authority of the British king in Crown lands (before the Revolution), and the rights of a community derived from a spurious colonial charter. These divergent strands were synthesized in a concept of statehood which called for "independence" of the other American states and recognition by—and some kind of dependence on—a higher authority.

The "Vermont doctrine" that the people had a natural right to establish new states as well as new governments was widely perceived as the basic premise of Vermont's pretensions to independent statehood.[18] Certainly that right was routinely invoked. But Vermont propagandists—conscious of a skeptical audience in Vermont as well as elsewhere—did not dilate on natural law claims. Instead, they attempted to show that Vermont had existed as a political community long before the Revolution and so had earned a prescriptive right to self-government within determinate territorial limits. Because the other American states would not recognize these claims, Vermonters could not make the conventional argument that a colony became a state by virtue of participation in the common cause and membership in Congress. They had to demonstrate that Vermont's independence was not essentially linked with the independence of the United States.

According to Governor Chittenden, Vermont dated its political existence "from the royal adjudication of the boundary line between New-York and New-Hampshire the 20th July 1764"; therefore, they were "now [in 1783] in the eighteenth year of . . . independence [of the other states], and cannot submit to be resolved out of it" by Congress.[19] As Chittenden explained on an earlier occasion, "this important controversy" between the Vermonters and New York "subsisted many years before the late [American] revolution took place."[20] Ethan Allen, a central figure in the state's ruling group, asserted that New York "forfeited their claim of jurisdiction" after 1764 by their "illegal measures" and "oppressive acts."[21] At the same time, New Hampshire forfeited its claims (which Vermonters holding New Hampshire land titles of course considered legitimate) by acquiescing in the boundary settlement. Thus, "from the commencement of their controversy with the government of New York," Allen reported, "the inhabitants of these contested lands governed themselves, and managed their internal police under the direction of committees and conventions"—just as the colonies had when hostilities with Britain began. Roger Sherman of Connecticut, a warm supporter of the Vermont cause, argued that Vermonters "never were subjects of New York with their own consent."[22]

The people of the New Hampshire Grants participated in two revolutions. As good American patriots, they embraced the struggle against British tyranny and broke with the Empire. But beginning in 1764, they also conducted a revolution against New York (or so it was claimed), a revolution which was designed to alter, not necessarily renounce, the colonial status of the Grants. The goals of these two revolutions were not always compatible. Freedom from New York's jurisdiction and security of New Hampshire and later the new state's own land grants were most important for most Vermonters. But what if the United States ultimately upheld New York's claims? Of course, Vermont polemicists strove mightily to associate the two sources of tyranny and oppression; Congress could not support the Yorkers without betraying its fundamental ideals. New York's tyranny represented in microcosm the tyranny of the Crown; "the hatred subsisting between us, is equivalent to that which subsists between the Independent States of *America* and *Great Britain*."[23] New York had been Britain's "favourite government." Yorker partisans in Vermont were all Tories; they were in league with the "avaricious monopolizers" to reduce us to "tenants."[24] Anti-Yorker rhetoric served the interests of claimants under New Hampshire titles; it also fit perfectly with popular concepts of why the American Revolution itself was being fought. The "monopoly" that New York jurisdiction would secure to a few powerful landlords would "enslave" the people. Indeed, Ethan Allen wrote in 1779, it would be idle for Vermonters "to dispute any more about liberty, for a sovereign nod of their landlord, cannot fail to overawe them."[25] In other words, why should Vermonters be obliged to "defend the independence of the United Claiming States," Allen asked Congress in 1781, "and they at the same time [be] at full liberty to overturn and ruin the independence of *Vermont?*"[26]

When Congress seemed inclined to defend New York's claims, and Vermont's two revolutions appeared to be working at cross-purposes, manipulation of anti-Yorker sentiment made rapprochement with the British Crown less unthinkable. Furthermore, in seeking to define Vermont before the American Revolution as part of neither New York nor New Hampshire, Vermont propagandists argued that the Crown's jurisdiction had not been mediated by intervening colonial jurisdictions. After 1764, the area was "extra-provincial," "derelict" with respect to neighboring colonies. It is significant, however, that this did not mean the New Hampshire Grants were in a state of nature; they were still "crown lands" and "the King's authority . . . was therefore absolute."[27]

The argument for British imperial claims followed logically from the attempt to discredit the pretensions of the claiming states in Vermont. It also reflected the popular belief in the years before the Revolution that the British government would eventually rescind the 1764 boundary and vindicate the claims of settlers and grantees under New Hampshire against later, conflicting grants under New York.[28] The apparent contradiction between pleas for the "absolute authority" of the Crown and the notorious "Vermont doctrine" that the people had a natural right to set up their own government was resolved in their common rejection of the claims of British colonies in the region. Indeed, because Vermont was unconnected with New York or New Hampshire, "the people of Vermont legally speaking, remained under the British Government . . . from the 4th day of July 1776, to the 15th day of January next," when in convention they solemnly "disavowed the British Government."[29] A "people's declaration of independence" drafted at this session in Westminster laid the groundwork for adoption of a new constitution in July.

The attack on neighboring state claims enhanced Britain's authority in the Grants. It also encouraged Vermonters to trace their right to independent existence to authoritative British acts. This was at once reflected in the invention of a colonial charter as the putative basis of Vermont's status as a distinct community and later in the eagerness of the Vermont leadership to obtain a new colonial charter in the Haldimand negotiations.

The British government was supposed to have set up a new colony in the Grants just before the American Revolution began, with Philip Skene commissioned as its first governor.[30] (In fact, Skene was to command a garrison at Lake Champlain.) Vermonters apparently believed that a charter for the new colony actually existed; they asked Congress to postpone deliberations on the claims controversy until it could be located. In later negotiations with the British, they solicited a copy of the charter in order to support the state's claims up to the Hudson River.[31]

The Vermonters' reliance on the Skene charter was a tribute to the enormous prestige of charters in defining rights during the revolutionary era. Even when making the most radical claims to self-government, Vermonters spoke of our "charter of liberty from Heaven."[32] In the Haldimand negotiations, Vermont sought to obtain a new charter under the British Crown, modeled on Connecticut's colonial charter (still in force there as that state's "constitution"). The emphasis on charters revealed a deep-seated uneasiness about the legitimacy of a self-constituted state. With the invention of a charter, Vermont's claims became congruent with those of other American states. Paradoxically, assertions of equality with the other states were not premised on the sovereign right of the people to make themselves independent of all the world, but rather on spurious claims to have enjoyed a similar "independent" status within the Empire.

Throughout the war, military insecurity and the tenuous loyalties of its own citizens compelled the Vermont leadership to seek admission to the American union or reunion with the British Crown. Notwithstanding the brave talk of the state's propagandists, few Vermonters were ready to believe that a state could exist—in practice or in theory—without the protection or recognition of higher authority. If neutrality became a necessity as the war progressed, when it was over Vermont "*must . . .* be subject to the then ruling power."[33]

Ethan Allen claimed in June 1782 that Vermont was a "neutral Republic," but the foreign policy of the new state pointed to either incorporation in the United States or a return to the Empire.[34] According to Ethan's brother Ira, "there was a north pole" (the British in Canada) "and a south pole" (the Americans); "should a thunder-gust come from the south, they would shut the door opposite that point and open the door facing the north."[35] This ambivalent policy did not simply reflect the state's precarious situation; the vindication of Vermont independence also required the sanction of higher authority. Daniel of St. Thomas Jenifer, Maryland delegate at Congress, recognized this fundamental point: "if we do not soon make them independant" of New York and New Hampshire, "the British will endeavor to do it."[36]

International recognition was a practical necessity. It would also help Vermonters overcome their own misgivings about their right to set up a new government. It is ironic that a misrepresentation of congressional sentiment facilitated the original break from New York. According to Dr. Thomas Young's public letter to "the People of the Grants" (April 1777), Congress would be receptive to the formation of a new state.[37] The congressional call for new governments in the colonies (May 1776) applied to all "such bodies of men as looked upon themselves [as] returned to a state of nature."[38] It was necessary, then, for the people of the Grants to take the initiative, draft a plan of government, and "*become* a body politic." According to Young, "you have as good a right to choose how you will be governed and by whom" as the thirteen states already in Congress.

It did not take long for Vermont's leading men to learn from firsthand experience that little could be expected from Congress. Yet it was necessary to convince the people that the new government was committed to the American Revolution and that Congress—once it saw through the schemes of the claiming states—was bound to recognize Vermont. The state was virtually "in alliance with the States of America already," Governor Chittenden claimed in 1779.[39] In the same year, Ethan Allen asserted that a "mere formal declaration" would transform the virtual union into full confederation.[40] The popular conviction that Vermont was really part of the United States and devoted to its cause was reflected in an assembly resolution of October 1780 that it would "not consider any person born in the United States of America to be a foreigner."[41] While Vermont could not concede to Congress the right to determine whether or not it would exist (as it "does not belong to some one of the United States"), the new state's leaders repeatedly proclaimed Vermont's fidelity to the Revolution.[42] If interested parties at Congress prevented its admission to the union, Governor Chittenden was prepared to propose separate alliances with neighboring states.[43]

Popular attachment to the Revolution constituted a major limitation to Vermont's claims to independent statehood. It also severely limited the freedom of Vermont agents in negotiations with the British (the Haldimand negotiations), which began in earnest in May 1781. These talks revolved around the possibility of Vermont's returning to the British Empire as a distinct colony—with its "independence" of its neighbors finally guaranteed and the land claims of its citizens confirmed. But "nothing will induce the bulk of the people to defect from the common cause," Philip Schuyler confidently predicted in November 1780.[44] At the outset of the war, Ira Allen told the British, many Vermonters thought "Congress was next to God Almighty, in power and perfection." "It has been with great difficulty that that idea is so far erased and is at present [May 1781] in such a decline."[45] The political education of the common people thus presented the major challenge to the new state leadership. It was as necessary "the people should be prepossessed against the proceedings of congress before they" join Great Britain "as it is for a christian new light to be perfectly willing to be d[amne]d before he can become a true convert."[46]

Popular patriotism notwithstanding, the Vermont leadership became convinced that Great Britain would emerge victorious. Stephen R. Bradley believed that "American independency must fall through" and that "no solid agreement can therefore be made by Vermont except with [Britain]."[47] Neutrality was a temporary expedient: it protected Vermont from attack, and it gave the new state leaders time to prepare the common folk for a second revolution, which would return Vermont to the British

Empire.[48] Indeed, as long as Congress refused to recognize Vermont, political logic strongly suggested reunion with the Crown. The British had no designs on Vermont lands. Without their protection, Vermont faced the "great probability" of "being ruined by . . . haughty neighbors" at the end of the war. The Haldimand negotiators assured their Vermont counterparts that the Crown intended to "make you a happy and free government."[49] A proclamation was drafted, though held in reserve, announcing that Britain would consider Vermont as "a separate province, independent of and unconnected with every government in America." This independence would be secured through a new charter, identical with Connecticut's, except that the governor would be a Crown appointee. Not only would the Crown guarantee Vermont against New York and New Hampshire, it also promised to recognize the new state's claims up to the Hudson River and across the Connecticut.[50]

Declining congressional prestige and the possibility of a British alliance on generous terms helped clarify the loyalties of many Vermonters. Isaac Tichenor, a Vermont councillor who was known to be hostile to the Allens and well disposed to New York in 1780, was prepared in late 1781 to lay down "his Life and Fortune" to defend Vermont and its unions.[51] The patriotic Colonel Benjamin Fletcher was reluctantly willing to align with the Crown if "the existence of Vermont, as a separate political body, depends on it."[52] By June 1782, the usually skeptical General Haldimand thought it "probable" that the Vermonters will "close with [the British] Government, knowing how little they have to expect from Congress and their neighboring provinces if left to their mercy."[53] Vermonters were well aware of British forbearance on the northern frontier during the course of the Haldimand negotiations, and the promise of military support against Congress and the claiming states now took on an added urgency.

Ironically, the rumored progress of the Haldimand talks prompted Congress to make its only statehood offer to the Vermont separatists (August 1781).[54] But Vermont's imperialist adventures in New York and New Hampshire prevented immediate acceptance; by the time Vermont renounced its Eastern and Western unions (February 1782), the military situation was no longer critical and Congress withdrew its offer. As a result, popular support for Congress rapidly diminished. It became clear that the United States was determined to uphold the interests of New York and New Yorkers with title to Vermont lands. This identification of New York and Congress undermined congressional prestige in Vermont and strengthened the tenuous hold of the new state on popular support.

Growing popular dissatisfaction with Congress was matched by increasingly open advocacy of the British cause. One belligerent Vermonter was supposed to have sworn that "by God as long as the King and Parliament of Great Britain approved of and maintained the State of Vermont he was determined to drive it and so was its leaders."[55] It was said that Vermonters would have nothing to do with Congress, "for they had strength enough to defend their State."[56] They "damned the Congress" and "drank their confusion"—they drank to the health of George III.[57] Vermonters believed that the common folk of neighboring states would come to their aid against the Continental Army. After New Hampshire attempted to collect taxes at Walpole, "the populace went to their Liberty pole . . . and cryed aloud Liberty is gone." They cut the pole "down and at the fall Huzza'd aloud for King George and His Laws."[58]

If Vermont's foreign policy reflected a consensus that statehood required recognition and protection, the implementation of that policy undermined those premises. The loss of legitimacy in higher authorities subverted their ability to legitimize—or destroy—the new state. Early in the war, for instance, the people of Vermont seemed "disposed to acquiesce in the decision of Congress," whatever that might be.[59] As late as 1780, "there are very few but what will readily acquiesce."[60] Thereafter, however, calls for congressional decision were joined by calls for armed intervention; the people of Vermont were no longer expected to submit to the will of Congress, unless it was supported by force. The amount of force thought necessary was a good measure of declining congressional prestige. "One year ago," Jacob Bayley wrote in 1781, "ten men would have subdued all that would oppose" Congress, but now "two thousand will not [do] and I am afraid they will still increase."[61] Now, Vermonters would "join the enemy on a mere suspicion that Congress would judge against them." If Congress were to find for New York, "the continent must be involved in a war to enforce" its determination.[62]

Hostility to Congress encouraged a revival of pro-British sentiment, yet this was a highly interested and calculated species of "loyalism," as the Haldimand negotiators were quick to recognize. After all, Vermonters had participated actively in the American war effort. They grew disenchanted with Congress as it became apparent that it would not guarantee the new state's existence or secure Vermonter land claims; they now turned to Britain in order to achieve these goals, not because they suddenly recognized the legitimacy of British authority. At war's end, the British lost what little interest they had had in enlisting Vermont's support. Meanwhile, as congressional prestige plummeted to new lows throughout the United States, Vermonters were assured that "no coercive measures will be pursued."[63] Vermont appeared more likely to survive than Congress itself.

The end of the American Revolution left a power vacuum in the Vermont region which the new state was prepared to fill. The ineffectiveness of both Congress and the Crown, and the very fact that the state's allegiance to one or the other came to be seen as negotiable and contingent, helped minimize the political liabilities of nonrecognition.

Through membership in Congress, the American states sought to secure their interests and gain recognition of their jurisdictional claims. Boundary agreements were crucial to the survival of the American state system; without secure, recognized boundaries, it would be impossible to establish durable institutions and enduring loyalties. Though the states in Congress were not immune to boundary disputes, such controversies were treated as legal issues that could be resolved by establishing the relative validity or priority of conflicting claims. Force or the threat of force was never invoked by one state in prosecuting its claims against another. Nor were the states willing to consult affected populations, through plebiscites, about which state they would consent to join.

But Vermont was not recognized by the United States and therefore was not bound by the same formal and informal conventions that normalized interstate relations. Because its neighbors would not even recognize its right to exist, there was no reason for Vermont to respect their territorial rights. As a result, the jurisdiction and claims of the new state were in a constant state of flux, causing considerable instability in Vermont as well as in New York and New Hampshire. As George Washington warned President Mesech Weare of New Hampshire, "so long as this Dispute of Territory subsists, the parties, Divisions and Troubles, both external and internal, will . . . encrease."[64] With uncertain boundaries, domestic factionalism in Vermont shaded imperceptibly into schemes to annex frontier areas of adjacent states—or to establish the claims of those states in Vermont. Governor Chittenden told Washington that Vermont expansionism was designed "to qui[e]t some of their own internal Divisions, occasioned by the Machinations" of New Hampshire and New York, and to let "them experience the Evils of intestine Broils."[65] If anything, the Eastern and Western unions exacerbated Vermont's "internal divisions," but the attempt to export Vermont's tumultuous politics was a tremendous success.

Volatile loyalties and constantly changing boundaries subverted the authority of all states in the Vermont region. Furthermore, the process of drafting the first state constitutions led to disputes over the basic organization of power in the revolutionary states and appeared to make their territorial limits negotiable as well. In the subsequent confusion, Vermont often enjoyed a relative advantage over its competitors, offering favorable terms of union—or backing its claims with superior force. But the popular perception of the "tyranny" of New Hampshire and New York did not mean that Vermont's authority would be seen as legitimate. Rather, the skill with which Vermonters combined appeals to interest and threats of reprisal served to emphasize the expediency of submitting to Vermont, not its right to govern. In fact, the loss of legitimacy in state governments throughout greater Vermont was mutually exacerbating. The Connecticut Valley towns grew accustomed to "anarchy" as they were "deserted by the states."[66] "What can we expect but to see our states crumble to pieces?" asked Jacob Bayley of Newbury.[67]

Individual towns and groups of towns meeting in convention undertook negotiations with the contending states; sometimes they appealed directly to Congress or to General Washington for resolution of the claims controversy and protection from the enemy. Towns strung along the east bank of the Connecticut River refused to join New Hampshire without adequate representation in its legislature.[68] Virtually every town in Cheshire and Grafton counties rejected the proposed constitution of 1779 and declined to sit in subsequent conventions and assemblies. Some towns collected New Hampshire taxes but impounded them in town treasuries "to be disposed of hereafter as the town shall judge proper."[69] These towns were also interested, with their counterparts on the west bank, in securing "union of the [New Hampshire] Grants on both sides of Connecticut River."[70] This led a large number of towns into union with Vermont in 1778 and again in 1781.[71] Moretown, on the west side, proclaimed it "our desire to be a New State but [we] are willing to submit the matter to Congress" and, if refused, to "be annex'd to the State of New Hampshire."[72] Thetford also voted to consider "itself belonging to the State of Vermont," but Newbury, another west bank town, voted to be under New Hampshire.[73]

To the south, adjacent towns in Cumberland/Windham County (New York/Vermont) pledged allegiance to different states. Even Yorker partisans asserted their "full liberty" to look elsewhere for protection if New York could not establish effective jurisdiction. The county convention told New York in 1776 that it would also consider an alliance with Massachusetts.[74] Such stipulations in a request for protection were an "insult" to the dignity of New York; but even when dropping the offensive reservation in favor of another state, the Yorkers would not "preclude ourselves from the privilege of presenting our petition to . . . Congress" for separation.[75] Nor did they hesitate to register serious misgivings about the New York constitution. In 1778, another Yorker convention acknowledged "ourselves bound by the most sacred of human ties" to New York; nonetheless, their opposition to Vermont was premised on the "inexpedience" of a separate government "in the present time," the "poverty" of the people, and the lack of local legal talent to draft a "new and equitable system of laws."[76] In 1779, the Cumberland Yorkers warned that they would submit to Vermont if New York did not govern effectively. The threat was made good two years later, when many Yorkers participated in negotiations with the new state leaders resulting in the second Vermont union with towns on the east bank of the Connecticut.[77] Given the failure of New York to protect its citizens, petitioners from Guilford argued that it was "justifiable" for the oppressed Yorkers "to procure their own redress and relief by terms of composition with their oppressors."[78] Of course, this submission to Vermont was also contingent. The "unconstitutional" dissolution of the Eastern Union (February 1782) set "the subjects of New York State . . . free from Vermont." Ironically, the Yorkers were now assuming the doctrinal stance of the Vermonters themselves; they were under no authority at all, though "at least three quarters of the people east of the Green Mountains *want* to return to New York." But they would do so only if civil government were established and military protection were extended.

Popular hostility to New Hampshire on its western frontier and to New York on its northeastern frontier paved the way for Vermont's expansion east and west. "The idea of the Tyranny of New Hampshire is immovably fixed" in the river towns; "the General Assembly, the Compilers of the Constitution, and the Executive authority have combined together to enslave the People."[79] Vermont recruited an "outrageous mob" to its cause in Albany County, New York, but it was also true that many leading men favored the annexation.[80] New York had been "remiss" in not offering protection against the British. The staunchest supporters of New York were exasperated by its failure to do anything. A Cumberland County petition stated, "We esteem [New York's help] not one farthing's better than what Congress" has done—that is, nothing.[81]

Yet Vermont's grasp on popular loyalty was also shaky. Before the annexations of 1781, support for the new state had declined precipitously.[82] The eastern counties enthusiastically supported the Eastern Union with New Hampshire towns, but the western counties, fearing a radical shift in power within the state, were considerably less enthusiastic.[83] Expansion in the west reestablished the balance, but these new Vermonters—known as "Cattermounters"—were extremely unpopular in the east. "Grate division" was reported in Vermont in the wake of the unions.[84] The Cattermounters "are supported only by the Governor, Council and a few hot-headed people"; many Vermonters were "daily falling off from their new state."[85] Disenchantment reached new depths when the Haldimand negotiations were widely publicized in early 1782. Yorkers reported that their Vermont tormentors were now "heartsick of Vermont."[86] According to Charles Phelps, "nothing has so sunk the spirit of Vermonters as the proof of their treasonable confederacy with the enemy."[87]

In the long run, however, Vermont stood to gain most by the delegitimation of state authority and the related collapse of congressional prestige. What was being destroyed, after all, was the notion that political community was a given and that states had legitimate claims to obedience under all circumstances. Lacking recognition and a given status as a state, Vermont was forced to rely entirely on popular consent. And nowhere in America did local communities become so thoroughly accustomed to such a high degree of political self-determination. At the same time, political imperatives were clarified to an unusual degree. Americans in the greater Vermont region needed to secure a modicum of law and order; they needed to be protected from foreign invaders and, most of all, from each other.

The solution to ineffective state government was to adapt revolutionary infrastructure—county militia, committees of safety, and county conventions—to fill the jurisdictional vacuum. The new state of Vermont itself came into being after a series of such conventions which were superseded by general assemblies beginning in 1778.[88] But in the Connecticut Valley, particularly in Cheshire and Grafton counties (New Hampshire) and Windham/Cumberland (Vermont/New York), conventions continued to sit throughout the war. Conventions derived their sanction from the interruption of legitimate authority and, at least inferentially, from the sovereignty of the people. As intermediaries between towns and the contending states or Congress, the conventions were supposed to facilitate the transition to legitimate authority. Yet one of the hallmarks of American constitutional development, reflecting the crisis of legitimacy in the new state governments, was to identify legitimate, constituent authority with the conventions themselves, to grant constitutional as well as temporal priority to these extralegal—supralegal—and temporary organizations.[89]

In greater Vermont, the convention movement had a continuing vitality throughout the war precisely because of the low repute of state governments, including Vermont's. But the claims of the new state were inextricably linked with the convention movement (through sheer lack of any other justification for its existence), and as conventions acquired prestige and legitimacy, other kinds of claims to state jurisdiction identified with the pretensions of the "claiming states" suffered corresponding losses. According to the emerging standards of American constitutionalism, Vermont's claims to self-government became increasingly credible. The "right" was not derived from history or from higher authority; it came from its own constitution.

Vermont became a state because the people "consented" to its creation, even when that consent was coerced by force. Indeed, statehood implied coercion; effective authority depended on a monopoly of power. Vermont propagandists recognized this in their enthusiasm for the classic natural law doctrine that "allegiance must be founded on a reciprocal protection."[90] During the course of the war, all parties in the Vermont controversy came to identify jurisdiction with the exercise of force. The Vermont leadership had to proceed cautiously at the outset because of widespread doubts about the legitimacy and durability of the state and the dubious loyalty if not outright hostility of the eastern counties. But it was apparent to Yorkers as early as 1779 that "they will establish their State by the sword."[91] With typical bravado, Ethan Allen made the same point. If the United States withheld recognition from Vermont, it would be compelled to support its claims "by right of Conquest!"[92] Still, no definitive move was made against the Yorker towns until 1782 and 1783, when punitive expeditions under Allen's leadership crossed the Green Mountains "with weapons of terror."[93] The display of force was followed by vigorous prosecution of Yorker dissidents in the Vermont courts, leading to the imprisonment or exile of several key leaders and the political conversion of many others. Allen was supposed to have agreed that "it was a savage way to support government as he did, but they could not carry the point without it."[94] Jailed Yorkers suffered loss of property and threats to their lives; they also had to submit to the taunts and boasts of their captors. Allen would "march into Albany with the Green Mountain Boys, and set up and be absolute monarch of all America," according to one reported harangue

—obviously intended for the edification of New York Governor George Clinton.[95]

The expeditions against Windham County Yorkers represented a definitive contribution to the sustained debate over the nature of legitimate authority: what was a state supposed to be? The attack on the Yorkers was also of course an attack on New York State. The vindication of New York's claims had long ceased to be one of legal right to Yorkers—though, for their part, the state's politicians continued to devote an inordinate amount of energy to proving the validity of its pretensions to Congress. Yorker partisans in Vermont knew that only a show of force would be effective against the separatists. This realistic appraisal combined with their own predisposition, apparent since 1776, to treat statehood as a negotiable issue—in which rights necessarily gave way to more expedient calculations—meant that Yorkers and Vermonters saw their respective problems in similar terms, equally remote from, if not hostile to, New York's assertions of territorial right or the similarly theoretical claims of New York City speculators to Vermont lands. The Vermonters' violent language—and the language of their violence—struck even the most sympathetic congressmen (attuned to the pretense that the controversy was among title claims which Congress would adjudicate) as a brazen admission of the moral bankruptcy of the Vermonters, tantamount to treason to the common cause.[96] Certainly, Vermonters had learned not to take Congress very seriously, but Yorkers had learned the same lesson. They had warned that without adequate support they would come to terms with Vermont, that their loyalty to New York was contingent. The Allen expeditions were shaped by these expectations; their violence was not gratuitous or unexpected. If they convinced many congressmen that Vermont should not be a state, they convinced the Yorkers that it was one.

Vermont's survival as a state was made possible by the inability of the claiming states to enforce their jurisdictional claims. As a result, the kinds of claims made by those states—based on "legal" precedent—were radically devalued. Similarly, the impotence of Congress helped delegitimize congressional authority. The Vermont leadership could not easily overcome the pervasive conviction that the security and legitimacy of the new regime rested on the recognition and protection of higher authority. But playing one side against the other taught the leaders of the new state as well as the people in general to look on loyalty as a contingent matter.[97] And in the aftermath of war, only Vermont could govern Vermonters.

Only Vermont could provide institutions responsive to local self-determination and coercive force sufficient to establish and maintain law, order, and land titles.

Outside the union, Vermont could not make the kinds of claims to statehood so essential to the pretensions of the United States. Only in Vermont was the concept of a state as a self-constituted political community fully and radically tested against, rather than in tandem with, orthodox notions of legitimate state authority, premised on succession to the claims of colonial communities, and recognized and guaranteed by other states in Congress. In this sense, Vermont was the only true American republic, for it alone had truly created itself.

PART · THREE

ORIGINS · OF THE · FEDERAL REPUBLIC

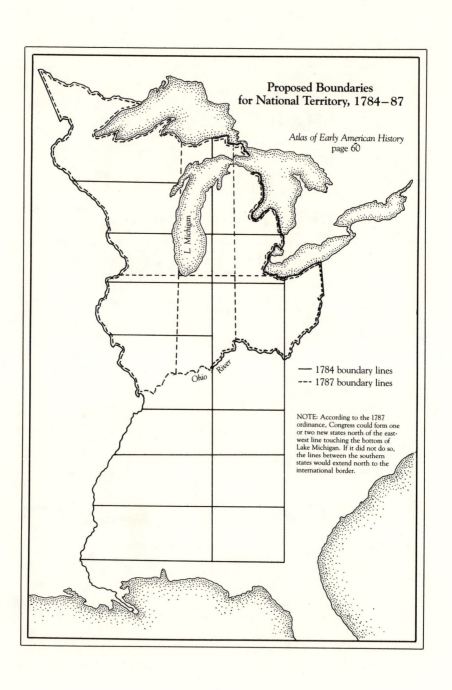

**Proposed Boundaries
for National Territory, 1784–87**

Atlas of Early American History
page 60

L. Michigan

Ohio River

—— 1784 boundary lines
--- 1787 boundary lines

NOTE: According to the 1787
ordinance, Congress could form one
or two new states north of the east-
west line touching the bottom of
Lake Michigan. If it did not do so,
the lines between the southern
states would extend north to the
international border.

· 7 ·

New States and the New Nation: American Territorial Policy in the "Critical Period"

The revolutionary war effort gave the American states a "common cause" and helped contain claims controversies and conflicts of interest. With the end of the war, however, the weaknesses of the American state system became all too apparent. States openly looked to their own advantage, in and out of Congress. Increasing demands on Congress to protect or promote state interests, combined with growing pessimism about its ability to act disinterestedly—or to act at all—undermined the prestige and threatened the survival of central government. But at the same time, many Americans came to believe that only a vigorous national government could prevent the disintegration of the states themselves. In 1787 one writer epitomized the dilemma of American politics. "The breath of jealousy has blown the cobweb of our confederacy asunder," he wrote. Still, "we pretend to dread the growing power of Congress." [1]

The fundamental problem was not that the American people had turned against their own governments—though they often did. The crisis of legitimate authority was ultimately rooted in the new governments themselves, in their unenlightened pursuit of self-interest at each other's expense and at the expense of the union. As Richard Dobbs Spaight of North Carolina complained, the northern states would "sacrifice our national strength and dignity in hopes of rendering themselves more conspicuous," though, he conceded, "I do not think they wish for a dissolu-

149

tion of the Confederacy."[2] (The compliment was amply returned by small, landless states, which saw the selfishness of large, landed states like North Carolina as the chief impediment to a stronger union.[3]) Interstate conflict jeopardized state authority, particularly when jurisdiction itself was at issue. Pervasive mistrust crippled Congress, which therefore was unable to support and legitimize particular state claims or uphold the interests of the states collectively. As nationalist propagandists had long argued, the pursuit of particular interests unleashed centrifugal forces that could destroy the union.

The anticipated "horrors of a civil war" or of warfare among the states—categories not easily distinguished—were repeatedly cited by reformers.[4] Spaight predicted, for instance, that "the seeds of dissension" sown in Vermont and the Wyoming Valley "will not end without a Civil War."[5] If such "distinctions . . . prevail among us," Richard Peters warned, "we shall fall a prey either to Domestic Ambition or foreign invasion."[6] As a Boston writer put it, "The welfare, and even existence of the American states depend on the federal government: for the states to trifle any longer, is to sport with their existence, and to offer themselves a prey to any invader, or to a tyrant, or to anarchy."[7]

Prophesies of imminent bloodshed proved unfounded, but they did contribute to the pervasive sense of political crisis after the Revolution. As much as possible, Americans had postponed controversial issues during the war years; thus they avoided debate about the nature of American federalism.[8] This was fortunate because inherited concepts did not describe contemporary political practice. When nationalists did bring conventional logic to bear on the American state system, they could prove that federalism was a contradiction in terms. They argued that the fragmentation of authority, "*imperium in imperio*," was the underlying cause of instability in American politics. Americans had to choose between one national sovereignty and thirteen distinct and necessarily hostile sovereignties. The United States and the states separately "cannot both be perfectly sovereign and independent at the same time," said Stephen Higginson.[9] For the nationalists there really was no choice. It was of course "absurd, that there should be thirteen states . . . each a sovereign power."[10] Yet many Americans would reach another conclusion, if they had to choose. Arthur Lee of Virginia argued that the states were "sovereign free and independent" before Congress even existed, and remained so except in "what they voluntarily gave to Congress by the Confederation."[11] If Congress overstepped its mandate, Virginia might be forced to withdraw from the union.

The shared conviction that present political arrangements were ephemeral—however divergent the predicted outcomes—undermined the credibility and legitimacy of existing authorities. Ideological polarization taught Americans to see anarchy and impermanence in American politics; it also justified the identification (or confusion) of narrow self-interest and broad constitutional issues. Americans liked to argue that their state's particular claims were compatible with the true interests of the union, properly understood. At the same time, they were quick to see through such pretenses in others; it was natural for states, like other interest groups, to pursue their own interests, patriotic professions notwithstanding. But if all Americans joined in such condemnations, no practical compromises (which were logically inconceivable in any case) were soon forthcoming. Americans persisted in exempting themselves from their pessimistic judgments on each other.

Americans interpreted each other's behavior according to a set of assumptions that constituted a nearly self-fulfilling prophecy of doom. The comforting illusion that disputes among Americans were the unnatural results of the imperial connection was soon dissipated.[12] Patriots came to agree with their opponents that the states were bound to compete for relative advantage, though they were able to put aside many of their differences during the war. Americans were prepared to be demoralized after the war, not only by their exaggerated claims for the regenerative powers of republican governments but also by an underlying pessimism about the "real" motives of men and states.[13] Fears about interstate conflict were compounded by the assumption that the states competed for fixed stakes, that one's gain was another's loss. Relations between Congress and the states were also seen in such terms. Therefore, even though most Americans agreed in principle that a stronger central government was the last and best hope for the states' survival in a deteriorating state system, the belief that the states would have to give up more extensive powers, thus "conceding a part of our separate independency," suggested an immanent contradiction.[14] Would a powerful central government whittle away at state powers until they no longer existed?

Struggles over western land claims established the idea that disparities in the size of the American states constituted the leading source of danger to the union. This issue was at the heart of the protracted impasse over the Articles of Confederation and was kept alive by acrimonious debate over the terms of, or need for, western land cessions. There was still "an ample theatre for hostile pretensions" "in the wide field of Western territory," Hamilton warned in the seventh *Federalist*.[15] Large states with large populations would overawe their smaller neighbors (according to the small states), or small states would combine their forces in Congress to seize the western lands (according to the large states).

The expectation that long-standing jurisdictional controversies would degenerate into border wars was a crucial component in the perception of the postwar years as a critical period. Persisting inequalities among the states, declining congressional prestige, and the disappearance of a unifying common cause made Americans fear for the worst. But dire prophecies were not fulfilled; even the assumptions on which they were based had begun to erode. Extensive but ungovernable territorial claims could not be seen as an unmitigated blessing to large states, or as a grave threat to the survival of small states. The traditional equation of state size and power was no longer compelling. For this reason, boundary controversies could be dissociated from the zero-sum model—the gain or loss of territory by one state or another was inconsequential to the balance of power in the union.

A growing awareness of divergent sectional interests gradually supplanted the old concern with correcting disparities in state size and power.[16] From this perspective, the division of large states did not necessarily weaken them; rather, it could advance their interests by increasing sectional voting power in Congress. In the short run, sectionalism exacerbated doubts about congressional independence and about the very existence of a national political community. But sectionalism also shifted attention away from states' rights. It was assumed that states could continue to cooperate, at least on a regional scale. Meanwhile, state land cessions to Congress began to correct the grossest inequalities among the states. Congress finally gained control of a national domain and began planning for the formation of new western states. A static conception of the union was no longer appropriate. A new political geography rendered the old calculations obsolete.

Not surprisingly, changing conditions and perceptions were only belatedly reflected in formal political discourse. This delay was itself a factor in making the postwar era seem critical. A new concept of union, as much as any substantive reallocation of powers, was the "reform" that would preserve the American republics from destruction and legitimate the great changes wrought by the Revolution. Eventually, the static, competitive model of the American state system was superseded by a dynamic and expansive conception that muted interstate rivalries and enhanced the authority and prestige of the central government as creator of new states and guarantor of collective interests. Federalist proponents of the new Federal Constitution fully articulated and exploited this new view. But their ideas had been anticipated by westerners who advocated the creation of new states. A redefinition of the union was also implicit in the development of congressional policy for the government of its new territories.

Though Americans disagreed about their boundaries, they did agree in principle that stable boundaries were essential to the survival of the union. Now was "the time," Congress resolved in April 1784, "when our Confederacy, with all the territory included within its limits should assume its ultimate and permanent form." [17] But the states' willingness to guarantee each other's claims was qualified by the belief that the states should be more or less equal in size. Boundaries would not be secure, in any case, without a balance of power between the states they distinguished. Alexander Hamilton predicted in 1781, "Some of the larger states, a small number of years hence, will be in themselves populous, rich and powerful, in all those circumstances calculated to inspire ambition and nourish ideas of separation and independence." [18] Therefore, according to a Kentucky writer at the time of the Philadelphia Convention, "the having some states too large, [and] others more ridiculously small" was one of the chief "defects" of the Confederation; the failure to fix state boundaries "by precise limits" was a function of this inequality. [19] The small states could at least refuse to recognize large-state pretensions. [20]

Just as nationalists argued for congressional sovereignty, opponents of large-state claims called for a general negotiation of state boundaries. One of the leading attractions of a stronger central government for the small states was the promise that it would neutralize or redress disparities among the states. James Madison, representing Virginia—the largest state— argued that the "gradual partition of the large, & junctions of the small States will be facilitated" by a "Gen[era]l Gov[ernmen]t" with "sufficient energy & permanency," eventually leading to "that equalization, which is wished for by the small States, now, but can never be accomplished at once." [21] New state promoters in frontier areas also favored redrafting boundaries, "so that the component parts of the [American] Empire might be nearer on a footing of equality." [22] But defenders of state territorial rights feared the augmentation of national power that the determination and enforcement of new boundaries implied. The campaign to equalize the states was also rendered suspect by the machinations of land company speculators and separatists, overlapping interests groups whose success depended on circumventing state jurisdiction. "It is much to be lamented," William Grayson of Virginia wrote in 1787, "that the desire of dismembering States prevails in so great a degree among the citizens of the Union; if a doctrine of this sort is allowed, it will go directly to the destruction of all government." Such threats to state territorial integrity prompted Grayson and other large state leaders to insist on "the propriety of defining in the most accurate manner the limits of the States" prior to, or as part of, any redefinition of powers in a new federal compact.[23]

Most Americans agreed that the solution to "competitions and encroachments" among the states, "whether in commerce or territory," was to strengthen the central government. Nationalists like "Harrington" thought the states should "come forward, and first throw their sovereignty at the feet of the [constitutional] convention."[24] But state leaders—from large and small states alike—were determined to establish the terms of relations among the states before chartering expansive national powers. Americans had to resolve the underlying theoretical and practical problem of how to combine states of disparate size and power into an effective federal union.

The western land cessions represented a first step toward resolving the problem of state inequalities without attacking the states themselves, while simultaneously underwriting the expansion of congressional power through the creation of a national domain. The reconception of congressional politics in sectional terms led to a new receptivity to the formation of new states; the proliferation of new states would diminish the significance of differences among the original states. James Monroe of Virginia was at first reluctant to promote new western states which, he supposed, would have no interest in remaining in the union.[25] But by late 1786 he "earnestly wish[ed] the admission of a few additional States into the Confederacy in the Southern Scale."[26] Maine separatists hoped to capitalize on a similar impulse to build northern voting power in Congress; the New England states—and even some New Yorkers—encouraged the Vermont separatists for the same reason.[27]

The willingness to countenance new states was symptomatic of a growing sectional polarization that threatened to immobilize the union. New state proponents discovered that sectionalism could frustrate their aspirations even while promoting them. "Jealousy of the growing importance of the western country, and an unwillingness to add a vote to the Southern Interest" would keep Kentucky out of the union, John Brown reported, unless a new northern state "is brought forward at the same time."[28] Still, it was clear that the American states did not oppose new states on principle, but did so only when their own claims or sectional interests were in jeopardy. Coalitions of states of unequal size and power were possible; indeed, disunionist scenarios increasingly postulated the emergence of regional confederacies.[29] A new concept of union was implicit in these predictions, a concept that gradually replaced the older idea that interstate conflict would necessarily and inevitably stretch and snap the federal bonds.

Westerners were quick to grasp the connections among the creation of new states, equalization of the states, and the growth of national power. A petition to the Virginia Assembly received in late 1784 or early 1785 (probably drafted by Arthur Campbell) included an incisive analysis of the basic problem of the American state system and a solution to it that anticipates Madison's famous argument in the tenth *Federalist*:

> It is as possible that one state shall aim at an undue influence over others, as that any individual should aspire after the aggrandisement of himself. The danger of the evil in both cases will be lessened by the increase of obstacles: and therefore our security as citizens of America will be promoted not only by the increase of number as individuals, but also by the increase of states which form the general union. . . . Your memorialists conceive that an increase of states in the federal union will conduce to the strength and dignity of that union, just as our increase of individual citizens will increase the strength and dignity of a state.[30]

Thomas Jefferson repeated the same argument in a letter from Paris in early 1786. "Our present federal limits are not too large for good government," he told Archibald Stuart, "nor will the increase of votes in Congress produce any ill effect. On the contrary it will drown the little divisions at present existing there."[31] "Publius" (Madison) subsequently expanded the argument to appeal to minority interests threatened by majority rule. The "extent of the Union" was their best security. "Extend the sphere and you take in a greater variety of parties and interests"; "the greater number of citizens and extent of territory . . . renders factious combinations less to be dreaded." Madison drew on David Hume's authority, but he echoed Arthur Campbell's logic, with which he was certainly familiar. Americans did not need to rely on the genius of Hume, or Madison, to discover "a republican remedy for the diseases most incident to republican government."[32]

New state proponents were able to use republican arguments—including Montesquieu's famous dictum that republics had to be small—against the territorial monopoly of the original states.[33] Ironically, separatists said they sought to protect the common people against the tyranny of eastern aristocrats in precisely the same way Madison later promised to defend endangered minorities against the people.[34] New state propagandists delighted in portraying the old states as hotbeds of aristocratic reaction; if these overlarge states were not divided, they would extend their "aristocratical domination" throughout their extended claims and liberty would be lost.[35] (Federalists were equally disenchanted with the old state governments, though for the opposite reason; they were supposed to be too democratic.[36]) According to the separatists, the formation of new western states would prevent aristocracy from rearing its ugly head; it would also undermine the preponderant power of the large states in the federal councils. The resulting equality of the states, like the equality of citizens, would "perpetuate good will and reciprocal benefits."[37]

From the traditional, static perspective, inequalities among the states could be redressed only by direct assaults on particular states that would deprive them of territory or sovereignty. But by the mid 1780s, Congress already had jurisdiction, or was expected to gain it soon, throughout western America. The multiplication of states would correct the old imbalances in state power without challenging states' rights. Therefore, westerners like Arthur Campbell could reject the alternatives that had emerged in the postwar debate over the location of sovereignty:

> I cannot agree with the politicians, who urge, that we must ere long have a consolidated Empire under one head, and abolish the different legislatures. Equally extravagant it appears, for one, or a few States, to erect a separate government, and dissolve the present Confederacy. Is not there much less difficulty, and far less danger, to limit the large States to a convenient, and suitable bounds; and then parcel out the Western territory, into proper divisions for free Communities. . . . Then may not twice thirteen States, if so many there be, unite in the closes[t] bands of amity, and reciprocal good offices, as to all national purposes, leaving to each of the Members of the Union, sovereignty and independence, as to internal legislation, and judiciary decisions.[38]

Americans need not sacrifice their states to the union, or their union to the states.

The separatists' concept of statehood was not only compatible with, but depended on, a strong national government. They simultaneously called for "the protecting arm of the federal government and the priviledges of

. . . independent state[s]."[39] Congress, "guardian for the whole" union, would sponsor the establishment of new states.[40] The central government's role in a confederation of thirteen states struggling for relative advantage was increasingly problematic. But this dynamic conception of an expanding union suggested a much broader, positive role for Congress.

"Solon," a Maine separatist, argued that a break with Massachusetts would encourage "Growth, popularity [population], and wealth . . . beneficial to our brethren in the other parts of the Commonwealth as well as ourselves, and also to the Union at large."[41] In dismissing the obligations of state citizenship, separatists liked to argue that they were "American" citizens, a conceit that depended on the existence of a national political community. Gordon Wood has shown that belief in such a community was central to the "federalist persuasion." James Wilson, who developed the argument "more boldly and fully than anyone else," asserted that "the supreme power . . . did not rest with the state governments. It *resides* in the PEOPLE, as the fountain of government."[42] But this fusion of populist, democratic rhetoric and political centralization was already full-blown in separatist propaganda. Separatists, like the Federalists, saw American federalism in vertical, or hierarchical, terms. State governments were limited from below, by the sovereign rights of American citizens, and from above, by the superior claims of the whole union. "Solon" thus suggested that "a town is public compared with an individual; a county, compared with a town; a state, compared with a county; and the Union at large, compared with a State."[43] Each jurisdiction had its distinct sphere and character; these complementary authorities had no reason to compete with one another. Madison invoked this argument at Philadelphia. While states should retain jurisdiction over their internal affairs, they would be, in their mutual relations, "mere counties of one entire republic, subject to one common law."[44] As Virginian separatists had previously argued, "every particular state is therefore as much indebted to the continental establishment as any individual of that state is indebted to his own government."[45] A "sacred regard for the principles of the continental union" was "the only security of the independency of each of the United States."[46] Thus, western patriots were "ready to resign all partial consideration of private interest or the interests of particular states when they should undermine the interests of the Confederacy."

The separatist formulation, though designed to promote the interests of embryonic new states, inevitably diminished statehood claims in general as well as the territorial claims of specific states. The rights of citizens were absolute, and their loyalty to particular states was contingent. At the same time, the United States as a whole could make legitimate claims on American citizens, again at the expense of the states. But this new conception of the union was not widely accepted as long as it was identified with opposition to state claims. Congress refused to entertain separatist petitions, and even small-state leaders were reluctant openly to encourage assaults on their larger neighbors. The separatists' ideas gained currency only when they were distinguished from separatist political ambitions and when the old states were guaranteed against further encroachments. It is not clear how these ideas were transmitted. Madison and his fellow Virginians were doubtless all too well acquainted with Arthur Campbell's arguments. But the genealogy of the new conception of the union is not important; it expressed an underlying consensus about the nature of American politics.[47] Separatists did not use these arguments because they were brilliant theorists but because the arguments came so easily to hand. In the same way, the authors of congressional territorial policy eventually embraced the notion of a dynamic, expanding union not from any profound philosophical inclination but simply because the creation of new states was incompatible with the traditional, static conception of the American state system. By bringing this same logic to bear on the actual organization of power in the United States, Federalists were able to overcome the contradictions immanent in American political theory and practice under the Articles of Confederation.

The reconception of the American union and the corollary devaluation of statehood claims suggested a solution to the problem of disparities among the states—a problem of diminishing significance in any case. But it failed to deal with deeper, less tractable sectional divisions. "Little divisions" in Congress could be effectively neutralized in an expanding union, but sectional rivalries would only be given a broader compass. Paradoxically, the new paradigm of American politics that sectionalism made possible permitted Americans to solve what were supposed to be the classic dilemmas—according to the paradigm it supplanted. Thus, as long as Americans continued to believe or pretend that inequalities among the states were critical, they could see the federal Constitution, and the new federal system, as the answer to their problems.

There were several sources of resistance to the new ideas of union promoted by frontier separatists or congressional policymakers. Large landed states naturally sought to block efforts to circumscribe their claims; antiseparatist writers played on endemic fears that the American states were on the verge of disintegration. Easterners doubted the loyalties of westerners, arguing that a natural diversity of interests could be counteracted only by upholding the extensive claims of the original states. If anything, the United States was thought to be too large to sustain republican governments, or to hold together at all. Separatist agitation and rumors of a counterrevolutionary conspiracy involving frontiersmen and foreign powers seemed to justify these pessimistic assessments and so to validate traditional assumptions about the American state system. A new, dynamic, and expansive conception of the union—and perhaps even the survival of the union itself—depended on the implementation of an effective western policy. It had to be shown that the expansion of the union through the formation of new states was not necessarily synonymous with disunion and anarchy.

The association of new states with attacks on the jurisdiction of the old states by separatists was one of the biggest obstacles to wide acceptance of this new conception of the union. According to the antiexpansionist, antiseparatist view, the division of old states and the creation of new states would pull the union apart. Should Maine separatists "now be countenanced in their movements," one hostile commentator suggested, "such attempts would become so frequent, as totally to annihilate all the force and vigour of the United States."[48] Governor Alexander Martin of North Carolina believed that the Franklin separation would be "a precedent . . . for every district, and every County of the State to claim the right of separation and independency."[49] As the states disintegrated, they would become impotent. "The more *we diminish the state*" of Virginia, James Monroe warned in 1785, "*the less consequence she will have in the union.*"[50] "Nothing but madness could induce" the people of Kentucky to separate from the "powerful state" of Virginia, according to a writer in the *Kentucky Gazette*; both areas would be weakened by the split.[51] Similarly, one writer from Maine thought that separation of the district would "lessen the weight of Massachusetts in Congress, and thereby give the southern States the advantage."[52] Maine would "become an insignificant, contemptible state, of no weight in the union." The sum of the new parts would be less than the former whole.

States with extended claims resisted the formation of new states at their expense. But some easterners believed that opening the West constituted a threat to the union, regardless of who exercised jurisdiction. Rufus King considered "every emigrant to that country from the Atlantic States, as forever lost to the Confederacy."[53] Westerners demanded free navigation of the Mississippi, but if they got it they would have little interest in remaining in the union. Archibald Stuart suggested, "The Interests of that

Country and the Atlantick States Will certainly interfere."[54] Ironically, the size of the United States was thus supposed to be its chief liability. According to "Nestor" (Benjamin Rush), "there is but one path that can lead the United States to destruction; and that is their extent of territory. It was probably to effect this, that Great Britain ceded to us so much waste land [at the Paris peace treaty]."[55]

There were two related premises in the antiexpansionist argument: first, that power diminished as it was divided (anarchy was the ultimate expression of this tendency); and second, that a weakened United States would fall prey to one of the great imperial powers. A Jamaican writer predicted, "If the original union of the Americans should continue to be thus divided and subdivided . . . surely they will be shortly ripe for that punishment they so justly merit."[56] Small, weak new states on the frontier would inevitably fall under the influence of Britain or Spain. Separatists from Vermont to Franklin exploited this threat. If the Mississippi were not opened, for instance, the westerners' "allegiance will be thrown off, and some other power applied to. Great Britain stands ready, with open arms, to receive and support us."[57] Even "Inhabitant," the Kentucky antiseparatist, accepted this logic. "If there were any other country that we could be united to, from which we could receive more compleat aid in time of distress," he would be prepared to separate from the "powerful state" of Virginia.[58]

New states would not be able to stand on their own. But if new states were bound to be mere satellites, they might just as easily be drawn into the American orbit. The federal role depended on who took the initiative in state-making. This was the crucial question for the expansion of the American state system and thus for the emergence of a new, dynamic conception of the union. If separatists, speculators, small states, or Congress itself sought to force the large states to divide, the large states would attempt to uphold their claims at all costs. Until the Virginia cession of 1784, the western lands controversy conformed to this pattern, reinforcing the traditional "zero-sum" conception of interstate relations. But if the new states were created by Congress out of national territory, ceded to Congress by Virginia and other landed states for that very purpose, the United States could expand without jeopardizing state sovereignty.

Congress's acceptance of the Virginia cession represented the belated convergence of congressional and Virginian western policy goals. It broke the protracted deadlock over western land claims; Congress could at last begin to implement a national territorial policy that would commit the

United States to create and admit new members. At least in theory, Congress embraced an optimistic and expansive idea of the union. But from 1784 to 1787, while its territorial policy was still being defined—and thus remained merely prospective—it was unclear who could qualify for statehood and how they would go about doing it. The limits of the national domain, in which Congress was supposed to create the new states, were not yet fixed. Indeed, Congress had pledged itself to form new states in 1780, when it called for state land cessions, before there even was a national domain.[59] Because the Virginia cession was seen as a precedent for additional offers—by Virginia as well as by the other landed states—the first territorial government ordinance, adopted on April 23, 1784, articulated a general policy, not only for "the territory ceded but *to be ceded.*" According to Jefferson, the ordinance showed "how and when" new states "shall be taken into the union."[60] Inasmuch as it specified new state boundaries throughout the West, regardless of state claims, the ordinance inspired, or justified, a new wave of separatist activity. Westerners interpreted the ordinance as a quasi-constitutional compact for the nationalization of the frontier and the creation of new states.[61] Its wording sanctioned this interpretation: "the preceding articles shall be formed into a charter of compact . . . and shall stand as fundamental constitutions between the thirteen original states, and each of the several states now newly described."[62]

Jefferson apparently believed that the government ordinance would apply to existing settlements, as well as to future settlements in the West. As he explained to Madison, the cessions constituted the ceding states' agreement to circumscribed boundaries, and the ordinance committed Congress to establish the new states prescribed in the cessions; "there is no body then to consult but the people to be severed."[63] But Madison did not accept this interpretation, and his disagreement with Jefferson reveals the source of much confusion about new state formation. Madison insisted that settled areas could not be ceded, because "a cession of the *jurisdiction* to Cong[res]s can be proper only where the Country is vacant of settlers." The erection of a new state in the Kentucky District, for instance, "and an incorporation of it into the union," was "a work to which all three [Virginia, Kentucky, and Congress] must be parties."[64] Franklinite separatists objected to North Carolina's cession offer of 1784 on these very grounds. The eastern part of the state had unilaterally cut off the west; this unconstitutional abrogation of the social compact justified the westerners' claims to independent statehood.[65]

According to Madison, states as political communities could not be divided without the consent of the original parties to the social compact, even though states could limit their claims to unsettled territories as they pleased. "Senex," an opponent of Maine separatism, stated succinctly, "When a social compact is once formed, it is binding, or it is not." The constitution of Massachusetts, including the Maine District, should be as "binding in conscience, as a private contract between two individuals."[66] "The fact is," an antiseparatist writer told readers of the *Kentucky Gazette*, "we are a part of the *same whole* [as Virginia], governed by the *same laws*, in the making of which . . . we have an equal voice."[67] Madison did not invoke this doctrine to preclude authorized separations. But, as he wrote Richard Henry Lee, the creation of a new state in Kentucky would represent the "first instance of a voluntary dismemberment of a State" and "should . . . form a salutary precedent." "No interval whatever should be suffered between the release of our hold on that Country, and its taking on itself the obligations of a member of the federal Body."[68]

Madison considered cessions inappropriate for regions like Virginia's Kentucky District, with relatively large and growing populations. Jefferson's vision of ten new states presupposed cessions that were in fact long delayed or simply not forthcoming; he overlooked the differences between hypothetical new states in unsettled areas and new states in areas that were already settled and politically active. Virginians at home were beginning to negotiate terms of separation with the Kentucky people and had little patience with Jefferson's approach, which was consistent with the state's western policy down to the time of the cession—before there was significant support for Kentucky statehood. In fact, Jefferson was not interested in actually making new states in the immediate future; his preeminent concern was to secure state boundaries and establish a single, legitimate mode for forming new states at some future date. But Madison saw that actual settlements could not be ceded and that the settlers would not be denied; their status was a political problem, involving rights and obligations of states and citizens, not simply a question of jurisdictional claims. In any case, the United States had no incentive to accept cessions that were already covered by private grants.[69]

The 1780s were a "critical period" for the American West, and for the emergence of a dynamic, expansive conception of the union, because Jefferson's new state policy—as incorporated in the 1784 ordinance—prevailed, while the aspirations of new state proponents in unceded areas were thwarted, even when they were encouraged by their old states. As an attempt to resolve jurisdictional controversies, the territorial government ordinance backfired; Congress's apparent commitment to form new states and the landed states' apparent willingness to circumscribe their claims led to an outburst of anticipatory attacks by separatists on state jurisdictions. But these attacks only hardened the resolve of the states to maintain their claims. The antiseparatist reaction, combined with dilatoriness on further cessions and a growing sense of sectional alienation on the question of Mississippi navigation, threatened to throw the western settlements into turmoil.

The major thrust of congressional territorial policy after 1784 was to undo the damage done by the ambitious sweep of the first government ordinance. Not only were provisions for congressional control over the territories elaborated, but the scope of successive revisions culminating in the Northwest Ordinance of 1787 was finally limited to areas already under congressional jurisdiction. Congressmen disavowed any solicitude for spontaneous, unauthorized state divisions that separatists might have read into the 1784 ordinance. In 1785, the Massachusetts delegates, seconded by Virginia, proposed a resolution condemning separations as "unconstitutional attempts to destroy the fundamental principles of the Union." [70] The Virginia delegates reported that everyone at Congress was compelled "to acknowledge . . . the propriety of the measure whenever it should be brought forward . . . as the desire of any one or more of the legislatures of the larger States." [71] At the same time, Congress defeated a proposal by the Rhode Island delegates to revise the Articles in order to permit the formation and admission of new states through the voluntary division of the old states and agreement of Congress. This formula anticipated provisions in the Federal Constitution and would have made possible the establishment of new states in Kentucky and Vermont. But the large states were determined that Congress would offer no plausible pretext for separatist agitation; it would only create new states in national territory at some distant date, and it was unwilling to consider the formation of new states elsewhere, even where a state consented to its own division. As a result, the political aspirations of western Americans that had been aroused in 1784 were frustrated in subsequent years; the promise of new states in an expanding union was, thus far, an empty one.

The separatists' confusion about Congress's intentions, as articulated in the 1784 ordinance, was understandable. But Jefferson and his fellow committeemen did not mean to encourage the political aspirations of settlers in the West. The careful delineation of new state boundaries suggested that states would be made for the westerners, that westerners would not make their own states. As Robert Berkhofer has shown, Jefferson had a vision of "ideological geography," of a union of small republics balanced against each other and bound to the original states by common commitments and institutions. "The Ordinance of 1784 was merely a framework of general rules for the establishment of government in the West," according to Berkhofer. Jefferson recognized that "a specific system had yet to be worked out." His plan for territorial government was thus prospective and hypothetical; it was not supposed to take effect immediately.[72]

The 1784 ordinance promised to transform the American state system, but the promise was effectively withdrawn by a reluctance to accord powers to the central government that new state formation would require, and by a determination to uphold state claims against separatists. As a result, while Congress endorsed new states in principle, it delayed putting the principle into practice. Districts seeking recognition as new states were rebuffed, and statehood for settlers in national territory became an increasingly distant prospect as Congress drafted specific government regulations. The 1784 ordinance did not transform the union; instead it suggested what the union should be like, at some distant future date. (The distinction was too subtle for most westerners.) Americans stood at the brink of a new kind of union, but they held back.

Jefferson's committee proposed constitutional provisions for new state formation, but it was beyond Congress's power to enact them. The Articles of Confederation were radically defective on the question of new states, according to Jefferson; the 1784 ordinance "has pointed out what *ought* to be agreed on."[73] A state would be admitted "whensoever any of the said states shall have, of free inhabitants, as many as shall then be in any one of the least numerous of the thirteen Original states," *provided* that the "consent of so many states in Congress is first obtained as may at the time be competent to such admission."[74] The proviso effectively negated the preceding offer; in fact, the Articles would have to be amended, by the unanimous action of all the state legislatures, in order to admit a single new state. The ordinance was a prescription for constitutional revision without any constitutional standing; it was not a carte blanche for the separatists.

The territorial interests of the old states were guaranteed by the requirement that state claims be ceded before any new state could be organized. This was such a crucial aspect of Jefferson's scheme for new state creation that he convinced himself that Virginia would make or even "has by this time [January 1786] made a second cession of lands to Congress" in order to permit the erection of a new state in Kentucky.[75] All that would be then necessary would be the presumably unanimous "consent of the several assemblies." Significantly, Congress itself, beyond pointing out "what ought to be agreed on," would play no role in this transaction. Jefferson was wary of the expansion of congressional power; the initiative in formulating western policy was to be with the landed states, depending on their willingness to cede their western claims. Jefferson thus hoped that "Virginia will concur in that plan [the 1784 ordinance] as to her territory South of the Ohio"—by making another cession—"and not leave to the Western country to withdraw themselves by force and become our worst enemies instead of our best friends."[76] Even when he learned that Virginia planned to sponsor the formation of a new state in Kentucky, without a cession, Jefferson insisted that all new states should "come into the union in the manner" set down in the ordinance, and therefore "without any disputes as to their boundaries."[77] The determination of boundaries, and not liberal provisions for frontier self-government, was the crucial feature of Jefferson's western policy. Together with cessions, through which the old states unilaterally set their own western boundaries, the ordinance—which depended on the cessions—was supposed to prevent future jurisdictional controversies. Congress did not exceed its powers when it set "state" boundaries in the national domain, provided it did not presume to admit those states into the union without constitutional authorization.

Jefferson's ultimate vision of American political geography was undoubtedly in accord with "liberal" republican principles. Yet his strict-constructionist approach to the process of new-state formation shared important features with antiseparatist arguments against new states. Constitutional scruples were prominent in both cases. The "13 States formed ye body politic," Nathan Dane argued in opposing the Maine separatists; with the exception of Canada or any other British colony, "no other States can be admitted." Otherwise, "it would be in the power of nine States to ballance the union at pleasure by dividing old states and making new ones."[78] This was the same worst-possible case that landed states like Virginia had invoked in defense of their claims and of their right to set the terms for ceding them. Separatism was yet another challenge to the integrity of state claims, similar to earlier attacks by land speculators and landless states in Congress. It was not surprising then that Jefferson should make boundaries the highest priority and thus advocate a second cession by Virginia finally to "bound our country to the Westward."[79] After all,

were also prospective. Committeeman David Howell reported that future "settlers will always readily know in which of the states they are, for the states are to be named as well as numbered"; their boundaries were drawn in advance.[84] If there already were settlements in the eastern tier of proposed new states, the new states' boundaries were not drawn with them in mind, as separatists subsequently complained.[85]

Given the generally low estimation of the political character of the "rude people" expected to settle the West and the well-understood danger to public lands in unbridled emigration, it is doubtful that even Jefferson thought that the first settlers in the new states should be left to their own devices.[86] The settlers themselves agreed. The Franklinites, for instance, complained that the aborted North Carolina cession of 1784 left them on "the verge of anarchy." "The influence of the Law . . . became almost a nullity," and they were left unprotected "against the common Enemy—that always infest this part of the World."[87] Though the Franklinites seized on the territorial government ordinance to justify their independence, they also counted on congressional protection. They agreed that there was a dangerous constitutional hiatus between the cession, its acceptance by Congress, and the institution of government under congressional authority. Jefferson's protégé Monroe believed that subsequent territorial government committees would have to fill this lacuna. The issue, as he defined it for Jefferson, was the extent of "authority Congress will exercise over the people who may settle within the bounds of either of the new States previous to the establishment of a temporary gov[ernmen]t."[88] The 1784 ordinance had not answered this question.

The best that could be said for the 1784 ordinance was that it articulated "liberal" general principles for the expansion of the United States.[89] But Jefferson and the other authors of the ordinance assumed that the problem of the union could be reduced to a question of boundaries defining state jurisdictions and to the establishment of an equilibrium among the states according to their relative size. The implicit conception of the union was an abstraction from interstate relations up to that time, with the source of conflict—disputed claims—carefully removed. Jefferson's thinking was clearly shaped by the western lands controversy; his idea of the union was rooted in the past. This is why Jefferson was an "old-fashioned" proponent of new states whose ideas were so much closer to those of antiseparatists and antiexpansionists than to those of the separatists who claimed him for an ally. It also explains the sense that the drafters of the Northwest Ordinance had that they were not simply amending the

1784 ordinance, or the modifications proposed by later territorial government committees. A new conception of the union, of how the new territories and states were connected to the original states, was central to the 1787 ordinance. The new ordinance represented a radical departure from its predecessor, equivalent to the supersession of the Articles of Confederation by the Federal Constitution.

The boundary proposals of the 1784 ordinance soon came under fire. Jefferson's ten new states met the size requirements of the Virginia cession, which in turn embodied Congress's own stipulation of October 1780 that new states should be between 100 and 150 miles square. Congress considered itself bound by this cession compact, and thus to a vision of the expanding union that paid little heed to actual conditions in the West.[90] Monroe became convinced that the West would never support a large enough population for any of these small, new states to qualify for admission to the union.[91] The 1784 boundaries combined with pressure to increase minimum population requirements for statehood led Monroe to believe in a conspiracy to keep westerners "out of the confederacy," just when southerners were beginning to see advantages in new state creation. The controversy over the navigation of the Mississippi brought these fears to a head; the "occlusion" of that river would retard emigration to the West, Monroe told Patrick Henry, and "effectually . . . exclude any new State."[92] The self-interested policy of the eastern (northern) states would throw westerners "into the hands of Britain."[93]

Monroe and other southerners were increasingly anxious to strengthen their sectional voting power in Congress through the creation of new states. Meanwhile, in Europe, Jefferson continued to belabor the question of the size of new states, expressing "serious apprehensions of the severance of the Eastern and Western parts of our confederacy" if the new states were too large—that is, his correspondents replied, large enough to hope for admission into the union.[94] Jefferson remained trapped by an outmoded and highly abstract theory of union; he was isolated from the rising tide of sectional feeling that shaped attitudes in the North as well as the South toward new state-making.

Virginian delegates at Congress pressed for a revision of their state's cession act in order to permit the creation of larger new states. "A Division of the Country into many Small States would effectually disappoint the design of Virginia"—which by now was to gain allies in Congress—because none of these new states was ever likely to achieve a large enough population to be admitted into the union.[95] The westerners themselves were not deeply moved by Jefferson's concern, on their behalf, for establishing small, self-governing republics. As Edward Carrington explained to Jefferson, it would have been "disgusting" to the westerners to be kept out of the union, whatever the reason.[96] Indeed, many observers were convinced that frontier settlers would willingly forfeit their status as "republicans," if one of the imperial powers offered satisfactory terms.[97]

A workable new state policy would have been impossible if only one section stood to gain by the admission of new states. In the midst of the Mississippi crisis, many southerners had good reason to believe that northerners opposed the expansion of the union; but by 1787, northerners had discovered their own political and private, speculative reasons for favoring new states. Pressure from land companies, dominated by ex-military men from the North, as well as from surplus population, counteracted a traditional hostility to expansion in that region. At least the first of the three to five states projected for the Northwest Territory in the 1787 ordinance "will no doubt be settled chiefly by Eastern people," said Nathan Dane of Massachusetts. "There is, I think, full an equal chance of its adopting Eastern politics."[98] At the same time, southerners remained convinced that the creation of new states in the West would ultimately strengthen their bloc. These differing though not necessarily incompatible assessments made it possible for statesmen from both sections to plan for new states without a sense of betraying their interests. Staughton Lynd has written, "in place of a West vaguely attractive or dangerous, the Ordinance made available a West just sufficiently specific that each section could read in it the fulfillment of its political dreams."[99] Implicit in this cooperative effort—symbolized by the nearly unanimous adoption of the Northwest Ordinance (opposed only by Abraham Yates of New York who appeared, according to Dane, "not to understand the subject at all")—was the understanding that the sectional equilibrium would be maintained. It was this extraconstitutional principle that permitted the admission of Vermont and Kentucky to the union, as well as the subsequent coupling of "northern" and "southern" new states.

Sectional politics, and not Jefferson's "ideological geography," precipitated a new attitude toward new states, and therefore to the union itself. American statesmen were not primarily concerned with spreading the beneficent reign of republican institutions, or with meeting the self-evidently legitimate demands of the westerners for political rights. Indeed, the emergence of a new, workable western policy was accompanied by increasingly pessimistic views of the "uninformed, and perhaps licentious people" likely to move West.[100] This contempt for westerners justified the adoption of "strong-toned," even "colonial," governments for the territories, but it did not lead to rejection of the new-state principle. Emigration to the West would not be contained in any case, and as hostile commentaries implicitly suggested, westerners could and would take initiatives that might prove "inconvenient for the [American] Empire."[101] Most important, the new sectionalist paradigm made it possible to see new states not just as potential problems or as a source of weakness but rather as auxiliaries in the struggle for national political power. This focus on congressional politics—at a time when Congress itself barely functioned—revealed a fundamental reconception of the union. Sectional politics had shifted attention away from the old struggles between particular states, as well as from such ephemeral groups as those combining large and landed states, or small and landless states.

The committee that drafted the Northwest Ordinance "found [itself] rather pressed," according to Dane's account.[102] Land companies had laid proposals before Congress for the purchase of millions of acres of Ohio lands. Richard Henry Lee, another committeeman, saw an effective government ordinance as a necessary "measure preparatory to the sale of the Lands." Quick sales to the companies, rather than the painfully slow survey and sale of federal lands under the terms of the Land Ordinance, could alone help "demolish . . . the Ocean of public Securities."[103] At first, Dane told Rufus King, "we tried . . . to patch up M[onroe]'s . . . system." But it soon became apparent that it would be necessary to "abolish the old system" and implement entirely "new ideas" for the organization of new western states. Accordingly, the 1787 ordinance "declared null and void" the 1784 ordinance.[104] "The former act is repealed *absolutely*," William Grayson told Monroe, adding that the new ordinance was "something different," a "departure" from the proposals of Monroe's committee as well.[105] But, Grayson counseled, Monroe should support the new ordinance, because it was consistent with the essential interests of Virginia and the other southern states.

What were the most important innovations in the new system? The articulation of a neo-colonial scheme of government in the pre-statehood period may have been most striking to contemporaries. "The form of this government," Lee was satisfied to say, "is much more tonic than our democratic forms on the Atlantic are."[106] The self-designated "compact" provisions, securing settlers' legal rights and outlawing slavery, also raised eyebrows. These provisions doubtless were designed to appeal to potential emigrants, particularly to the many New Englanders waiting impatiently in the wings. Southerners accepted the ban on slavery in order to curb competition in labor-intensive staple production; perhaps they expected even nonslaveholding new states to be drawn into their orbit.[107] The most important result, whether the southerners who supported the ordinance intended it or not, was to encourage expansionist sentiment in the North and to commit the United States as a whole to the creation of new states. Unlike the 1784 ordinance, the Northwest Ordinance took effect immediately, providing at last for the West's "easy passage into permanent State Governments."[108] The Northwest Ordinance also broke out of the constitutional straitjacket in which the earlier ordinance had confined itself. In a crucial change of wording during the drafting process, the proviso that "the consent of so many states in Congress is first obtained, as may at that time be competent to such admission," was dropped.[109] Statehood automatically followed, once a population of 60,000 was attained, and the enlarged new states were likely to reach that figure at an early date.

Congress defined a central role for itself in the government of national territory. State legislatures would no longer be able to thwart the admission of new states—unless, of course, they chose to challenge the constitutionality of the ordinance, as they well might. But whether or not Congress arrogated new powers to itself, not authorized by the Articles, widespread support for the new ordinance suggested that Americans had reached agreement on what to do about the West. This agreement presupposed the same dynamic and expansive conception of the union that underlay the new Federal Constitution.

During the debates at the Philadelphia Convention, the emerging sectionalist paradigm contended with the traditional, static conception of American politics. Most delegates still supposed that the dangerous preeminence of large states, and vulnerability of small states, constituted the major liability of the American state system. The debate over representation, pitting large-state proponents of proportional representation against small-state proponents of representation by states, raised these older assumptions to the fore—arguably, the assumptions survived as artifacts of the debate itself. But as Madison suggested on June 28, the delegates were ignoring the real problem:

If there was a real danger [from large states], I would give the smaller states the defensive weapons—But there is none from that quarter. The great danger to our general government *is the great southern and northern interests of the continent, being opposed to each other. Look to the votes in Congress, and most of them stand divided by the geography of the country, not according to the size of states.*[110]

Still, Madison's analysis—echoed by other delegates in subsequent weeks—did not lead to a decisive turn in the debate; indeed, it had been invoked in order to advance the case for proportional representation. Madison and other "nationalists," all those who remained convinced that there still was a national interest, probably inflated the sectional threat and the danger of regional confederacies in order to make national constitutional reform seem a moderate alternative. (It is interesting that Madison ignored sectionalism in his supposedly prescient tenth *Federalist*.)

Sectionalism was undoubtedly an important factor at Philadelphia, as it had been in the recent history of Congress. As Staughton Lynd has suggested, sectional differences, particularly on the sensitive slavery question, were worked out at Congress and in the convention in a largely concealed "Compromise of 1787."[111] But sectionalism had indirect consequences that were equally important. Identification with broader regional interests permitted delegates to reconceive relations among the states, and between the states and the central government—once those interests were adequately secured. Thus, a true compromise on the representation question was possible, a compromise that was equally distasteful to traditional nationalists (like Madison) and defenders of states' rights.[112] The important point, as Madison had noted, was that the question of state size was *not* a fundamental one, and therefore concessions could be made on either side without real risk.[113] Yet it was important for the founding fathers, and for later historians, to believe that a "miracle" had taken place in Philadelphia. Given traditional assumptions about the intractability of interstate conflict and the centrality of disparities in the size of states, a constitutional compromise securing large and small states alike was by definition a miracle. Intentionally or not, the founding fathers' persistence in conceiving of the dilemma of American politics in terms of state size, or in terms of equally artificial and exaggerated fears of democracy or aristocracy run rampant, validated and legitimized—and made seem heroic—what was otherwise truly an unremarkable achievement. The Constitution simply articulated and embodied a conception of the union, and of the states, that had become common currency among American statesmen during the "critical period," a conception that had deep roots in popular notions of citizenship and in loyalty to the American revolutionary cause.

· 8 ·

Constitutional Crisis

The Federal Constitution embodied conceptions of statehood and the union that had emerged in the decade after independence and were implicit in provisions for territorial government. The struggle between friends and opponents of the new union did not betray fundamental differences in the definitions of these key terms. Federalists and Antifederalists drew on the same stock of political ideas, tirelessly and often indiscriminately invoking the authority of Montesquieu and other "celebrated writers."[1] Few Americans advocated full jurisdictional autonomy for the states. According to Rufus King's memorable characterization, "the States were not 'Sovereigns'" in any accepted sense of the word. "As political Beings, they were dumb . . . they were deaf . . . and they had not even the organs or faculties of defence or offence. . . ."[2] On the other hand, most Americans were too attached to their states to make any consolidationist scheme possible. "The affairs of so extensive a Country are not to be thrown into one mass," Edward Carrington wrote James Madison. Any "attempt to confederate upon terms materially opposed to the particular Interests would in all probability occasion a dismemberment."[3] The limits of what was politically acceptable as well as theoretically conceivable thus pointed to the creation of a "complicated" government for the United States that was, as Madison put it, neither an "absolute consolidation" nor a "mere confederacy."[4] It would be a mistake, however, to minimize the extent of

173

disagreement between proponents and opponents of the Constitution. Different rhetorical emphases suggested radically different ways of applying the conventional wisdom to the realities of American politics.

The Federalists' biggest challenge was to overcome the pervasive fear that constitutional innovation masked a conspiracy against American liberties; reform could be justified only if it could be shown that the states were otherwise headed for certain disaster. Constitutional reformers thus promoted the notion that the United States were in the throes of a "critical period." The "crisis" resulted from their juxtaposition of various domestic and international disorders; Shays's Rebellion provided an organizing motif. Though they could not deny the existence of these disturbances, Antifederalists did question the Federalist contention that they constituted related symptoms of a general political pathology.

Divergent interpretations of recent American history were matched by different schemes for calculating the relative advantages and disadvantages that ratifying or rejecting the Constitution would entail. Federalists argued that a more powerful central government would secure the rights and interests of the states as well as of the people at large. The Constitution would expand the stock of available political values; everyone would gain a larger slice from a growing pie. The logic of the debate led Antifederalists to emphasize potential sacrifices to particular interests. Though such predictions were often inconsistent with each other, they shared a common premise: the stock of values was finite and inevitably would be depleted under the proposed government. At best, the states could hold on to their present shares; at worst, they would struggle over diminishing shares of a contracting pie. Antifederalists thus combined an idealization of the recent past with a concern for preserving existing rights and interests. Federalists argued that future conditions would render such calculations obsolete. Americans needed a central government that could accommodate the growth of population, expansion of settlement, and creation of new states.

Shays's Rebellion was the focus of the anxieties about the future of American republicanism that Federalists encouraged and exploited. Insurgent farmers, oppressed by mounting debts and by the state government's hard money policies, shut down courts in Northampton (August 1786), Springfield (September), and Worcester (November).[5] Similar disturbances were reported throughout New England, spreading consternation across the continent. "The Danger indeed extends immediately to all the

Eastern States," delegate Charles Pettit wrote President Benjamin Franklin of Pennsylvania. "The Consequences cannot be unimportant to the other States in the Union."[6] Another frightened observer feared that this "wild fire" would "cause a conflagration" that would consume the United States.[7]

Actual events did not justify such overblown fears. Americans abroad, determined to uphold the good name of their countrymen, asserted that "the most trifling events have been Magnified into Monstrous outrages." Jefferson's friend Uriah Forrest, writing from London, wondered whether "the next generation" would "Credit Us that, in the first twelve Years of the Independence of thirteen free powerful and separate States, only one Rebellion happend . . . ?"[8] Besides, thought Jefferson—safely ensconced in Paris—"a little rebellion now and then is a good thing."[9] Even John Adams, who was less prone to such outbursts, seemed unperturbed. "All will be well," he wrote, adding prophetically that "this Commotion will terminate in additional Strength to Government."[10]

A commentator's vantage point was crucial. From a distance, the American "Commotions" did not add up to much, particularly in light of routine popular disturbances elsewhere. But in the context of American politics, agrarian troubles had ominous implications. The states' earlier success in maintaining order made agitation in the mid-1780s all the more conspicuous. The survival of the American republics was supposed to depend on the "virtue" of the people; the states could not resort to force to keep the peace when the instruments of force were so broadly distributed. In theory, the people need never employ extraconstitutional means to express their grievances under republican governments.[11] But republican ideals were like a house of cards, vulnerable to the slightest breeze. Faith in popular virtue did not run deep. Shays's Rebellion soon became paradigmatic for many Americans, not because it was typical but because it validated their basic assumptions about human nature and political behavior. The rebellion offered a concrete image of what they already knew was wrong with American politics.

The troubles in Massachusetts demonstrated that Americans were not a new species of men, immune to the corruptions postulated by contemporary theorists. The "critical period" was characterized by the emergence of a pessimistic "realism" that had never been far below the surface of republican optimism. Yet neither of these related modes could render a satisfactory account of American conditions. A sense of "crisis," grounded in traditional assumptions, encouraged Americans to reexamine and reconstitute American politics. But the attempt to define and balance conflicting interests and to determine the nature and limits of political community within and among the United States led to a transformation in political thought. Once Americans began to think about distinctively American problems, they broke out of their conceptual ruts.

Nationalist reformers had always believed that a constitutionally "imbecilic" Congress, unable to muster a quorum for weeks on end, would be unable to prevent the eventual outbreak of interstate warfare. The want of *"energy & stability"* in the state governments, which could barely maintain the rudiments of public order, was supposed to lead to chaos and anarchy.[12] These predictions were apparently incompatible: how could the states make war on each other if they could not govern their own people? Antifederalists exploited the contradiction. "Surely it could not be supposed" that the New England states "would make war" upon New York, Melancton Smith argued; they would be too busy keeping their own insurgents at bay.[13] But, the Federalists replied, the states would not survive in their present form. "The languishing condition of all the States, large as well as small, w[oul]d soon be transformed into vigorous & high toned Gov[ern-men]ts," said Madison.[14] The inevitability of change was a central theme in reform rhetoric. The apparent peacefulness within and among the states was no security for the future, when the underlying problems of American politics would become manifest.

Congress's loss of power and prestige was particularly ominous. The survival of the union was essential to the peaceful coexistence of the states. "The Union has great weight in the Minds of the People," John Adams thought.[15] States were restrained because popular loyalties were divided between the states and the union. Belief in the union facilitated the resolution of conflicts among the states. But how long could anyone sustain belief in a union that barely existed and was unlikely to survive the current crisis? The "natural instability of the common people" was already apparent in many states.[16] Edmund Randolph was "satisfied . . . that a rooted distrust of Congress pretty generally prevailed."[17] As Madison suggested, the question before the American people was "whether the Union shall or shall not be continued."[18] This question implied another: What would happen to the American states in the event of disunion? To Federalists it was obvious that without a union the states would begin to resemble their European counterparts. A chronic "state of war" would ultimately prevail.

Proponents of constitutional reform predicted that the real "critical period" was yet to come. With the collapse of their union, Americans would lose their immunity to the general laws of political science. A chain of necessary consequences would lead straight from "anarchy" to "despotism." Finding the absence of order intolerable, the people would "enroll themselves under the banners of some enterprising ruffian."[19] Such predictions were the stuff of classical political theory.[20] The challenge to reformers was to translate them into American terms. Shays's Rebellion made this possible.

Americans equated tyranny and monarchy. Pessimists believed that, at some more or less distant date, monarchy would be reestablished in America. But how could a king possibly exercise authority over the present generation of republican revolutionaries, no matter how lost to virtue?[21] Perhaps some "Caesar or Cromwell" would rise up on the backs of the people.[22] But Daniel Shays, whatever his actual intentions, offered a much more plausible model of a genuinely American, democratic despot. If not for the Grace of God—and his own incompetence—Shays would have become "the monarch and tyrant of America."[23] Before the insurgency was suppressed, many people in Massachusetts "should have been glad to snatch at any thing that looked like a government."[24] Whether Shays himself became "monarch," or another strong man should arise who "was able to protect us" from him, Americans would lose their liberties.

Shays's Rebellion, as seen through the eyes of frightened contemporaries, provided a powerful image of America after its fall from political grace. Shays himself became the exemplary antihero, the type for dissident leaders elsewhere. John Franklin, chief troublemaker in the Wyoming Valley, was supposed to be a "western Shays."[25] And, according to Oliver Ellsworth, it was "some future Shays" who would be—in the event of disunion—"the tyrant of your children."[26] The conditions that had made Shays's ascendancy possible were present everywhere and would become progressively more acute. It was not generally known "on what a perilous tenure we held our freedom and independence" at the time of the rebellion, James Wilson asserted. "The flames of internal insurrection were ready to burst out in every quarter."[27] Significantly, commentators in other states, where dissidence was equally pervasive and often more protracted and politically advanced, devoted little attention to their own troubles. Pennsylvania's Wilson did not allude to the Wyoming controversy at the Pennsylvania ratifying convention. In North Carolina, William R. Davie held forth on "the rebellion in Massachusetts," rather than "dwelling on the unhappy commotions in our own back counties"—which had functioned as the independent state of Franklin since 1784.[28]

Shays's Rebellion assumed the stature of a national event because it offered a model for domestic dissidence in every state. New state movements in frontier areas were irritating and even potentially dangerous, particularly when Americans began to consider their precarious international situation. Separatist movements usually grew out of interstate claims controversies. New state proponents could thus count on sympathy, if not open support, from other states. Frontier settlers were supposed to be unruly and, as good republicans, could legitimately demand the division of the large states. But Shays's Rebellion struck at the authority of the leading northern state within its universally recognized boundaries. The insurgents' goals could not be reconciled with republican theory. They "certainly mean the abolition of debts" and a "division of property," a program that would gain support everywhere state fiscal policies pressed hard on debt-ridden farmers.[29]

The language used to describe Shays's Rebellion encouraged generalizations about the critical condition of all the American states. The rebellion was most frequently likened to a "fire" or "conflagration." "Combustible materials, both physical and moral, are heaped up" throughout America, Henry Muhlenberg wrote in his journal.[30] "The flame has caught in Vermont," Samuel Parsons reported in November 1786.[31] General Benjamin Lincoln warned Governor George Clinton that New Yorkers were also "ripe to commit any outrage."[32] Disease was another favorite metaphor for popular dissidence. Henry Lee was persuaded that "the contagion will spread and may reach Virginia."[33] The underlying premise was the same, whatever the image. The troubles could not be contained by state boundaries. State governments might respond differently with differing success, but their problems were identical.

Reactions to Shays's Rebellion betrayed a growing fear that popular discontent was national in scope. The idea that the "people" constituted an homogeneous group was at least partially justified by their mobility; common folk tended to move more often than their social superiors. The diaspora of the Shaysites was a particularly salient case in point. The rebels infested border areas of neighboring states, most notably Vermont, and posed a continuing threat to Massachusetts as well as to their more or less unwilling hosts.[34] Insurgents in Pennsylvania's Wyoming Valley expected to be reinforced by Shaysite refugees. Ethan Allen promised that his Green Mountain Boys from Vermont would also join the Wyoming uprising.[35]

Dissidents in different states were supposed to constitute a kind of national "anticommunity." Defenders of law and order found themselves ill-equipped to deal with them, particularly when they crossed state lines. The Articles of Confederation were premised on the existence of thirteen distinct political communities and effectively barred a coordinated response to national political problems. Many Americans therefore became convinced that the United States had to be formed into a single state in order to maintain peace at home as well as respect abroad.

The concept of American citizenship, and of a national political community, emerged in tandem with the perception of popular disorder on a national scale. Significantly, the separatist opponents of state authority, who were responsible for much of this disorder, were among the first to consider themselves "American citizens."[36] The vastly exaggerated vision of domestic dissidence spreading throughout America, regardless of state boundaries, thus prefigured—and continued to inform—the Federalist notion that the "union" ought to embrace the American people, not the states.

Domestic dissidence was not the only threat to the success of the Revolution. Foreign powers were thought to be eagerly awaiting the opportunity to exploit divisions among Americans. Incipient "anarchy" would lead to tyranny; it would also lead to foreign adventurism. The fear of counterrevolution, orchestrated by Great Britain, was especially prominent in "critical period" rhetoric. Many people even thought the troubles in Massachusetts could be traced to British influence.

Contemporary political thought encouraged Americans to connect—and confuse—domestic and international politics. The "state of nature" was a particularly protean concept that was invoked in countless, inconsistent contexts. States and nations could be in a "state of nature"; this was the normal condition in international society. In theory, individuals could also find themselves in such a state, in the absence of organized political societies. The distinction was easily lost. Thus the statement that the American states were "on the eve of war"[37]—in a state of nature—was virtually interchangeable with the statement that the American people were "fast verging on anarchy and confusion."[38] When Noah Webster wrote that "the present situation of our American states is very little better than a state of nature," he could have been referring to the situation of the states themselves, or of the people, but probably did not intend to make a distinction at all.[39]

The use of the word "war" was also ambiguous. Sometimes writers meant wars between or among the states; perhaps the "thirteen contemptible single governments . . . will fall upon each other."[40] The same causes that drove European nations to war would operate in America. Alexander Hamilton warned in the sixth *Federalist*, "Vicinity, or nearness of situation, constitutes nations natural enemies."[41] Usually, however, the precise nature of future violence was left undefined. A "civil war" might involve individual states or groups of states, but it could also suggest "anarchy," the collapse of order within the states. In Edmund Randolph's colorful terminology, if "we reject the Constitution, the Union will be dissolved, the dogs of war will break loose, and anarchy and discord will complete the ruin of this country."[42]

The states would have ample motive to make war on each other if the union dissolved. They would not long lack the means. According to John Jay, "every State would be a little nation, jealous of its neighbors, and anxious to strengthen itself by foreign alliances."[43] Thus, just as interstate warfare could not be distinguished from the collapse of civil order, it also implied a broadening of conflict that would involve foreign powers. Foreigners would "play the states off one against another," Oliver Ellsworth predicted, and "when friends become enemies, their enmity is the most virulent."[44] Promoters of the new constitution emphasized the vulnerability of particular states. New Hampshire "will be the first to fall" under Britain's sway;[45] New York was a "weak state" and would "probably be the theatre of . . . operations" in the next war;[46] without the combined strength of the states, South Carolina must "soon fall."[47] Archibald Maclaine of North Carolina thought it "impossible for any man in his senses to think that we can exist by ourselves, separated from our sister states."[48] "Each state is fully sensible, that she cannot protect herself."[49] "The teeth of the [British] lion will be again made bare," New Hampshire readers were warned.[50] The British "stand ready to attack and devour these states, one by one."[51]

The premise shared by all these predictions was that all America would share in the coming cataclysm. The sources of future conflict were systemic, not idiosyncratic; disorder of any kind would be quickly communicated throughout the states. The synthetic view of domestic dissidence as a national phenomenon was matched by the belief that great power politics would draw every state into its vortex. Thus Americans had a common destiny, or "union," whether they liked it or not. The question was what sort of union would be established. "This Country must be united," according to Gouverneur Morris. "If persuasion does not unite it, the sword will."[52] Future Antifederalist Elbridge Gerry agreed; if the Philadelphia Convention could not secure the union, "some foreign sword will probably do the work for us."[53] According to Ellsworth, the "daring genius" who would "step forth" and restore order would create union with his "iron hand."[54] Anything short of a complete union—including existing arrangements—was inherently unstable. The Federalist ideal of a constitutional union was thus counterpointed to the union that would otherwise be established by force. In any case, the present Confederation could not survive, for, as Henry Knox wrote in January 1787, "the poor poor Federal government is sick almost unto death."[55]

When Americans talked about "war," they could mean any and every kind of violent conflict, domestic or foreign, actual or potential. It provided powerful images for the instability and changeability of American politics. As long as "war" was possible, change was inevitable. And change, according to the conventional wisdom, was bound to be for the worse.

Awareness of the threat of foreign intervention grew in the months before the Philadelphia Convention. One Canadian wrote in October 1786, "A storm is gathering over your republics."[56] Many Americans were ready to run for cover. But there was nothing new about counterrevolutionary activity, particularly along the northern and western frontiers. What was new was the dawning realization that the core areas of the states were vulnerable *through* their frontiers. During the protracted struggle for control of the western lands, American statesmen had not worried much about foreign influence. Instead, their anxieties centered on the ambitions of other states, land speculators, or Congress itself. Frontier disaffection was recognized as a problem only when settlement spread rapidly after the war and settlers began to take political matters into their own hands. Even then, frontier disorders were usually considered little more than embarrassments to the affected states. With the Mississippi crisis, however, the "West" emerged as a distinct section in contemporary discourse; scattered settlements and hitherto unrelated problems began to coalesce into a new synthesis. The continuing union of East and West, and even of North and South, was supposed to depend on whether Congress would uphold American claims to the river's navigation or barter them away for trade concessions. As westerners exhibited symptoms of disloyalty, they were naturally identified with the renegade state of Vermont. The Vermonters, in turn, were said to be in league with the Shaysites, thus completing a vicious circle around the states. British influence was believed to be the common denominator.

A new round of negotiations between Vermont and Great Britain was widely reported in late 1786.[57] At the same time, the British were "already . . . tampering" with the Kentucky settlements.[58] Madison feared that the westerners "will slide like Vermont insensibly into a communication and latent connection with their British neighbours."[59] Conditions were ripe for exploitation: the vulnerability of frontier settlers to Indian attacks and to the vagaries of changing imperial policies was matched by their inflated estimation of their "rights." This peculiar mixture of weakness and bravado was apparent in widely publicized threats to quit the union. If the Mississippi were abandoned, westerners "will look upon themselves relieved from all Federal Obligations and fully at Liberty to exact alliances & Connections wherever they find them."[60] New western states could not hope to go it alone. Instead, many westerners "talk very strongly of becoming Spanish subjects,"[61] or attended closely to "favorable proposals . . . by Great Britain."[62] John Brown, a leading proponent of Kentucky statehood, warned that if the United States would not guarantee "equal Protection—Rights & Benefits" to his countrymen, they would seek these "wherever they are to be found."[63] Similarly, if the Wyoming insurgents "found themselves unable to stand against the States," they would not hesitate to "call for the assistance of the British."[64]

The political behavior of the adventurers, speculators, and office-seekers who crowded the new western settlements could be seen as a preview of American politics in general, in the event of disunion. The British, "infernal foes" of American independence, were already hard at work sowing "the seeds of discord and dissension."[65] The unrestrained pursuit of self-interest, barely concealed by the overblown language of natural rights, made it easy for foreign powers to gain influence in the chaotic political conditions that prevailed in the West. And there, but for the attenuating authority of the state governments, went the rest of America. Again, Shays's Rebellion made it easier to connect frontier disorder with the future of the states. In effect, the insurgency turned the American frontier outside in; it gave the enemy access to the heart of the country. No one could doubt "*that great Britain will be in readiness to improve any advantage which our derangements may present for regaining her lost dominions*," Edward Carrington of Virginia wrote.[66] Rumored negotiations between Sir Guy Carleton (Lord Dorchester), the new British governor of

Canada, Shaysite rebels, and the Vermonters facilitated the identification of domestic dissidence and foreign "intrigue."[67] Henry Lee was convinced, without benefit of hard evidence, that the Shaysites "contemplate a reunion with G[reat] Britain"—provided they would not have to repay their private debts![68] Even after the rebellion was crushed, Shays was supposed to be preparing to descend from Canada with a large force.[69]

The fears that united Americans during the "critical period" may have been exaggerated or misplaced. Predictions that America would "roll in blood" at some not far distant date had little empirical basis.[70] It was absurd to blame the British for Shays's Rebellion; in fact, the British were not prepared to invest heavily in counterrevolution. They knew from experience that frontier malcontents made dubious allies. Nonetheless, the idea that dissidents throughout America were forming an unholy alliance with the British to destroy the United States did accurately reflect a crisis of legitimate authority—and long-standing jurisdictional muddle—within and among the states. Americans were groping for language adequate to express their justifiable anxieties for the future. Shays's Rebellion provided concrete images that permitted this synthetic revaluation of American politics.

Constitutional reformers recognized the propaganda value of the troubles in Massachusetts; some even regretted that they had not continued a little longer, fearing that the American people would relapse into complacency.[71] But Shays's Rebellion had helped change the way Americans thought about politics, and there was no changing back. It was clear to most observers, including Antifederalist William Grayson, that "the temper of America is changed beyond conception. . . . I believe they were ready to swallow almost any thing."[72] "I never saw so great a change in the public mind," Stephen Higginson reported in November 1786. The people would soon be ready for "anything . . . wise and fitting."[73] A year later, the "fear of anarchy" still prevailed, prompting many Americans to support the new Constitution.[74]

The crucial change in American political thought was a general acceptance that a "crisis" existed and that immediate steps would have to be taken to prevent disaster. "*The inefficiency of Government has been felt by its friends as well as enemies,*" said Edward Carrington.[75] Henry Knox reported that "the mass of the people feel the inconveniences of the present government, and ardently wish for . . . alterations."[76] Even Antifederalists were compelled to concede that "our situation is critical."[77] Political opportunists were also convinced that the United States were about to collapse; "internal and external enemies to American Independence" were ready to act.[78]

Shays's Rebellion was an inspiration to dissidents elsewhere who hoped to make the most out of "anarchy." If the rebellion were not suppressed, "we shall be flung into a State of Anarchy, from which a new form of Government must Grow." Even if monarchy were reestablished, the Wyoming people would probably be able to escape the tyranny of the "Land Jobing Jockying State of Pennsylvania."[79] A Maine separatist thought that "now is the golden opportunity" to drive Massachusetts "into a compliance, by threatening to join in the insurrection."[80]

The rout of the Shaysites may have restored a superficial calm, but many commentators were convinced that worse was yet to come. The rebels "submit to events," Major William North told Knox, "but appear to look forward to a time when they shall again take arms."[81] Later in 1787, one writer asserted that "licentiousness" still "advances nigh to a contempt of all order and subordination."[82] Such gloomy assessments had become conventional by then; it was no longer necessary to produce evidence for them. If disturbances subsided in one place, they were bound to break out elsewhere. The proposition was virtually axiomatic; the people were "licentious" and revolt-prone, while American governments were too weak to keep them under control. "It is for the want of energy" in government "that we see *banditties* rising up against law and good order in all quarters of our country."[83] "The peculiar circumstances of the United States have encouraged bad men in several of them to throw off their allegiance" and attempt to erect new states.[84]

Terms like "civil war" and "anarchy" performed an important synthetic function in "critical period" rhetoric. They did not necessarily falsify "reality"—though it is doubtful that there was any measurable increase in the incidence of disorder. The new rhetoric created a new reality by juxtaposing and synthesizing different and previously unconnected kinds of violence and disorder and by treating them all as symptoms of an underlying constitutional problem. American "anarchy" thus included everything from common lawlessness (with a hitherto unsuspected political content) to rebellion against state authority and treason against the United States. These disorders could not be fully distinguished because the relative situation of citizens, states, and the union had not yet been adequately defined. Americans had been able to live with this lack of defi-

nition as long as they did not see it. Shays's Rebellion dramatically illuminated this formerly obscure terrain: a coherent account of America's
troubles revealed the incoherence of American politics. The political situation was "anarchic," whether or not insurgents were actually up in arms,
because nothing was fixed and anything could happen. Thus, when Madison asserted that the United States was "rapidly approaching to anarchy"
that word suggested a realm of meaning that transcended the conventional
image of bloodshed and strife.[85]

A "state of war" could, like "anarchy," exist in the absence of actual
hostilities. Commentaries on the present crisis in American politics and
predictions of future turmoil merged imperceptibly. The states were already making something like war on each other. "Like thirteen conten-
tious neighbors, we devour and take every advantage of each other,"
Oliver Ellsworth claimed.[86] The comparison of states and "neighbors" suggested the confusion of private and public spheres that destroyed republics.
In a similar vein, another writer suggested that "individuals *and* states
have all been privateering upon each other."[87] "Privateering" expressed
the ambiguous character of political behavior in a world verging on
"anarchy."

The union was an increasingly frail barrier between the peaceful coexistence of the states and the outbreak of war. "If such a barrier was removed," Rufus King argued, and the United States could not interpose to
uphold state authority in one instance, "every other government would
eventually be swept away."[88] Governor James Bowdoin of Massachusetts
warned that a "Civil War" in his state "may extend not only to the neighboring States, but even to the whole Confederacy, and finally destroy the
fair temple of American liberty."[89] The whole nation was involved when
insurrection broke out in any state. Thus, the primary problem was the
organization of the union, and only derivatively the constitution of the
state governments.

Federalists argued that the proposed Federal Constitution would resolve
the crisis of American politics, as it had been defined and imagined in the
"critical period." Properly constituted, the American union would spread
across the continent, a model and inspiration to the whole world. The
United States would be exempted from the inevitable cycle of decay and
corruption that marked the career of every other state in history.

· 9 ·

Making a "Miracle":
The Reconstitution of American Politics

The "duty" of the union was "to protect and secure the states."[1] Proponents and opponents of the new Constitution began with this identical premise. But what did it imply? What state claims or rights should the other states be obliged to defend? What powers had to be vested in the central government so that it could perform its "duty"?

Though the Antifederalists cast themselves as guardians of states' rights, state "sovereignty" was not well enough defined to be defended in doctrinaire fashion. The clearest difference between Antifederalists and Federalists was over the nature of threats to the political stability and survival of the states. Federalists believed that these dangers were pervasive under the near anarchic conditions that had already begun to prevail; Americans had to guard against foreign intervention and domestic dissidence, as well as interstate conflict. Antifederalists promoted a narrower interpretation. The most immediate dangers to the states could be traced to the other states, or to groups of states. Particular states or sections would seek to extend their advantage through a stronger central government, established on unequal terms. Given such suspicions, attempts to concentrate power in the central government could be seen as the chief challenge to state authority.

Antifederalists minimized dangers to the states at home and abroad. Taken to its logical extreme—which it usually was not—their conception of the union finally led to its own negation. Luther Martin of Maryland, the most vigorous exponent of states' rights at Philadelphia, conceded that the union had to "defend the whole ag[ain]st foreign nations," but he was most concerned that it "defend the lesser States ag[ain]st the ambition of the larger."[2] Martin thought the proposed Constitution would sacrifice the small states to large-state consolidationists. Antifederalists in the large states followed the same reasoning to opposite conclusions: state equality in the Senate gave the small states an unequal advantage. Notwithstanding the inconsistency of such complaints, Antifederalists everywhere shared an overriding concern with the relative situation of states that were supposed to be competing for fixed stakes.[3] Any reconstitution of the union would produce a new set of winners—and losers.

The Antifederalist conception of American politics as a competition for limited advantage was neatly expressed by William Grayson of Virginia. "The little states gain in proportion as we [in the large states] lose," he told the state ratifying convention.[4] While the terms were reversed, the same objection was turned against the Virginia Plan at the Constitutional Convention. According to Gunning Bedford of Delaware, the "large States [were] evidently seeking to aggrandize themselves at the expense of the small."[5] Similar logic justified fears of growing national power. If Congress gained the taxing power, the states would lose it.[6] "Will not the diminution" of the states' "power and influence be an augmentation of those of the general government?"[7] Congress and the states could not both be sovereign. Thomas Tredwell of New York charged that the Federalist notion of "coordinate sovereignties" was as "supreme an absurdity, as that two distinct separate circles can be bounded exactly by the same circumference."[8] It was "a solecism in politics."[9]

Fears that particular states or sections would gain preponderant power, or that a "consolidated empire" would be erected on the "ruins of the present compact between the states," reflected recent American experience as well as the persistence of traditional patterns of thought.[10] Competition among the states to avoid tax burdens or to gain control of scarce resources in fact constituted the normal course of affairs under the Confederation; it was taken for granted that one state's gain was another's loss. According to conventional political logic, power itself was a scarce and finite resource. Sovereignty was unitary and indivisible because power was not expansible; to attempt to divide sovereign authority was to destroy it.

Antifederalists were bound to argue that their opponents had blown the current "crisis" all out of proportion. "Europe is engaged and we are tranquil," said James Winthrop. Suppression of the recent agrarian disturbances provided "decisive evidences of the vigour" of American republican governments.[11] Another Massachusetts writer put it, "We are in a much better situation [now] . . . than we were at this period the last year."[12] "We are at peace with all the world," Melancton Smith wrote. "The state governments answer the purposes of preserving the peace" and "our condition as a nation is in no respect worse than it has been for several years past."[13] If the political situation in 1788 was really no different from what it had been in previous years, the old rules of the game still applied. The Federalists' attempt to refute or transcend the old assumptions of American politics was therefore nothing but a smoke screen for a power grab. "The weakest will be in the end obliged to yield to the efforts of the strongest." The states would be "annihilated," and the American people would lose their liberties to a "despotic aristocracy."[14]

Antifederalist logic led to a crucial paradox. According to Martin, the "Union was meant to support . . . the sovereignties of the particular states."[15] Yet the union also represented a potential source of danger to them. Federalists reasoned that if the central government was to protect the states from one another, it was an "absurdity" to "deny them the means."[16] No government could exist without "the power of the *purse* and the *sword*," Rufus King asserted.[17] But this power could be turned against the states. The more this possibility worried the Antifederalists, the less they were willing to trust the central government to fulfill its original mandate. Instead, they argued that the American states needed a weaker, or at least more effectively limited, central government, not the more powerful government advocated by the Federalists.

The dangers of union on unequal terms made disunion less unthinkable. If the union collapsed, the small states would have "nothing to fear" from their overlarge and impotent neighbors.[18] At the same time, no one would dare "disturb" the mighty dominion of Virginia. Grayson was reported to have told a courthouse crowd that the states that had already ratified the Constitution "when compared to Virginia . . . are no more than this Snuff Box . . . to the Size of a Man."[19] These wildly contradictory assessments of the relative situation of the states lent an air of unreality and incoherence to the Antifederalist position. Antifederalists expressed and exploited a growing hostility among states and sections, but by doing so they inadvertently helped justify the Federalists' call for a more effective union. Antifederalism could be equated with disunionism—particularly when Patrick Henry and his friends broached the possibility of separate confederacies along sectional lines—and was therefore symptomatic of the very problem Federalist reformers set out to redress.[20]

Antifederalists discounted the many threats to the safety of the states so vividly portrayed in reform rhetoric. Even interstate conflict paled in comparison with the dangers of consolidation and the new aristocratic class that would rise to power. Federalists promoted the Constitution as the best possible compromise, given the "jarring interests of the States."[21] But Antifederalists claimed that the compromise was more apparent than real. According to Martin, the real "source" of the ratification campaign was "the pride, the ambition and the interests of individuals." The states and the people as well stood to lose their most precious rights to these would-be aristocrats.

Antifederalist writers invariably recurred to the supposed dangers of incipient aristocracy. This concern may have reflected an authentic rift between well-born and common folk, but the social origins of Antifederalist leaders argue against this interpretation.[22] Ironically, Antifederalist logic also subverted the putative class distinction. According to their argument, American "aristocrats" were at the present time still powerless to realize their selfish ambitions. The proposed Constitution would in effect create an aristocracy—the much maligned Articles of Confederation had kept would-be aristocrats at bay. But if aristocrats were such an ineffectual and powerless group, anti-aristocratic feeling could not have run very deep. Antifederalists emphasized the dangers of aristocracy because this was the conventional way to discredit political opponents. At the same time, such name-calling was so far abstracted from contemporary political reality that it could disguise conflicts of interests and ideas within the Antifederalist camp. Hypothetical future dangers enabled Antifederalists to divert attention from their adversaries' "critical period" and so uncover the "real" constituency for constitutional reform. In fact, opponents of the Constitution could do little more than revive the old political and social anxieties—the fear of power and of a corrupt officeholding aristocracy—that had inspired the revolutionary generation.

Federalists argued that the American political crisis called for an entirely new agenda for American politics. The states were supposed to be under siege from every possible direction and could not hope to survive unless the union was completely reconstituted. It was imperative, as Thomas McKean put it, that "some power should exist capable of collecting and directing the national strength against foreign force, Indian depredations," and "domestic insurrection."[23] "Harmony between the States

[was] no less necessary than harmony between foreign states and the United States," Edmund Randolph added.[24]

While Antifederalists conceded that some unspecified "authority . . . to decide disputes between States" was required, they insisted that the powers of the central government had to be carefully limited.[25] But Federalists were convinced that such limitations were the cause of the present union's "imbecility." The central government had to be able to command adequate military force and collect sufficient revenue ("Money is universally acknowledged to be the Sinews of war"),[26] as well as to exercise a well-defined and enforceable judicial supremacy. "Tranquillity among the states," William R. Davie explained, depended on "impartiality in decisions" by a fully competent federal judiciary.[27] "Even a *wrongful decision*" would be preferable to none, said Pelatiah Webster.[28] America could resign itself to perpetual conflict, approaching anarchy, or it could "institute a supreme power with full and effectual authority to controul the animosities, and decide the disputes" among states, and between the states and the federal government. It was particularly important for the central government to be able to establish and enforce a national commercial policy.[29]

Federalists came to the conclusion that the central government would have to exercise power over the states. The "general judiciary ought to be competent to the decision of all questions which involve the general welfare or peace of the Union," Davie argued.[30] Proponents of the Constitution interpreted this mandate broadly, including not only enforcement of treaties and resolution of interstate conflict, but commercial regulation and the defense of the states against domestic dissidence as well. Antifederalists indeed might wonder what was left for the states. Melancton Smith predicted that "the state governments, without object or authority, will soon dwindle into insignificance." "I am . . . at a loss to know how the *state legislatures* will spend their time."[31]

Power over the states implied power over individual citizens. In Hamilton's opinion, "the radical vice in the old Confederation is, that the laws of the Union apply only to states in their corporate capacity."[32] But according to Madison, "the practicability of making laws, with coercive sanctions, for the States as Political bodies, had been exploded on all hands."[33] Under the Articles the only sanction against a state that refused to meet its obligations was violence. Would Congress attempt to coerce the noncomplying states and "hazard a civil war?" Hamilton asked.[34] A "coercive principle" was essential to the survival of the union. Oliver Ellsworth put it,

> The only question is shall it be a coercion of law or a coercion of arms? There is no other possible alternative. Where will those who oppose a coercion of law come out? Where will they end? A necessary consequence of their principles is a war of the states, one against another. I am for coercion by law, that coercion which acts only upon delinquent individuals. This Constitution does not attempt to coerce sovereign bodies, states in their political capacity. . . . If we should attempt to execute the laws of the Union by sending an armed force against a delinquent state, it would involve the good and bad, the innocent and guilty, in the same calamity.[35]

The Federalists' basic premise was that the United States constituted a single political community. Neither states nor individuals could be allowed to evade its jurisdiction. "There can be no free, good, and secure government but where every man is under the coercive power of law."[36]

The inevitable conclusion was that the framers of the Constitution intended to form "one new nation out of the individual states."[37] One hostile critic noted, "It is not merely (as it ought to be) a CONFEDERATION of STATES, but [it is also] a GOVERNMENT of INDIVIDUALS. . . . The powers of Congress extend to the *lives,* the *liberties,* and the *property* of every citizen."[38] Patrick Henry wondered "who authorized" the framers "to speak the language of, *We, the people,* instead of, *We, the states?*" The result would be not a confederation but rather "one great, consolidated, national government, of the people of all the States."[39]

If Antifederalists verged on disunionism, Federalists betrayed consolidationist tendencies. Opponents of the Constitution welcomed this polarization, because it justified their view of politics as a competition for fixed stakes, in which one side or another would emerge victorious. But Federalists, whatever their secret inclinations, moved to occupy a middle ground, arguing that everyone—states included—would benefit from a proper constitutional settlement. The Federalists' main task was to transcend the conventional logic, which the Antifederalists now commanded, and to articulate a new conception of the American union.

Conventional political wisdom did more to muddle than to clarify recent American experience. Indeed, it suggested that the United States itself was something of a logical impossibility. Hamilton found himself at an uncharacteristic loss for words when considering "the amazing extent of

Country."[40] Independent Americans would have to maintain a large military force in order to guarantee their extensive claims; they might even have to sacrifice some of their precious rights in exchange for security—the same argument that gained Thomas Hutchinson such notoriety.[41] Perhaps, Hamilton thought, "the British Gov[ernmen]t is the only proper one for such an extensive Country." James Wilson agreed that the "extent" of the country "seems to require the vigour of Monarchy," though, he added, Americans manners were "purely republican."[42] (Unlike Hamilton, Wilson believed that there was a solution to this conundrum.) James Monroe also asserted that the United States was "too extensive to be governed but by a despotic monarchy."[43]

The "ablest writers" were agreed that "no extensive empire can be governed upon republican principles" but must inevitably "degenerate to a despotism."[44] American experience in the British Empire was sufficient to demonstrate the truth of this proposition. But if this was an iron law of political development, how could the United States survive? Many well-read Americans doubted that it would; Americans could maintain their liberties, or their extensive territories, but not both. Some sort of future division of the states was therefore widely anticipated. Nathaniel Gorham, for instance, wondered whether it could be seriously supposed "that this vast Country including the Western territory will 150 years hence remain one nation."[45]

Antifederalists argued that the United States was already too large for a "consolidated" government. James Winthrop, writing as "Agrippa," asserted that it was "impossible for one code of laws to suit Georgia and Massachusetts."[46] No "single legislature" could "fully . . . comprehend the circumstances of the different parts of a very extensive dominion."[47] The problem of size was implicit in the Antifederalists' appeals to aggrieved or endangered state or sectional interests; it was their most powerful argument against the national political community contemplated by the framers of the Constitution. In a large polity, according to the conventional wisdom, power was supposed to concentrate at the center, in the commercial and bureaucratic metropolis. Great Britain presented a typical case. "The extremes of the empire will, like Ireland and Scotland, be drained to fatten an overgrown capital."[48] Robert Yates and John Lansing, Jr., the delegates from New York who withdrew from the Constitutional Convention in protest, argued that it would be impossible to keep "the extremities of the United States . . . in due submission" without resorting to force.[49] "The middle states . . . would enjoy great advantages" under the proposed constitution, the "Federal Farmer" warned. "The benefits of government would collect in the centre." Discriminatory taxation and commercial legislation would direct the flow of wealth from the peripheries of the American "empire," causing Boston to languish and Philadelphia to wax prosperous and powerful. Economic loss would be matched by political debasement; soon the distant parts of the continent would be held in union by force alone.[50]

The virtue of this line of argument, like the argument against aristocracy, was that it conjured up dangerous consequences that were supposed to flow from the Constitution against which all good republicans should unite. But there was a fundamental contradiction in Antifederalist opposition to a stronger, expanding union that played into the hands of constitutional reformers. The threat of domination by the central states was overshadowed by the great division between "*southern and northern interests*," the "real distinction" in American politics.[51] The clash between North and South provided Antifederalists with a limitless supply of arguments against the Constitution that were much more compelling than the theoretical danger of a central metropolis draining wealth from the provinces. Northern Antifederalists suggested that the South had gained the upper hand in the slavery compromises, while southerners came to the opposite conclusion about the commerce clause.[52] But these charges were not only inconsistent with each other, they were also incompatible with the classic argument against large polities. The "extremes" would not be sacrificed to the center; instead, one extreme was in danger of being sacrificed to the other. The real problem, therefore, was not the size of the union but rather the balance—or imbalance—of sectional interests.

Antifederalists failed to reconcile arguments drawn from theory with arguments drawn from experience. They worried about how particular states or sections might take advantage of a stronger central government, while inveighing against the dangers of such a government to *all* the states. But to dwell on relative advantages and disadvantages was to accept the Federalists' formulation of the problem: how could conflicting interests best be secured, where possible, and compromised, where necessary. The new Constitution was promoted as the mechanism through which balance, and therefore union, was achieved. With interests properly balanced, the general government could be strengthened in the general interest.

According to Antifederalist logic, the creation of a "consolidated" republic would lead to the concentration of power at the center and a corresponding loss of political energy at the periphery. The scope of the union's effective authority would necessarily contract. But the Federalists' union—and the union implicit in Antifederalist denunciations of sectional imbalance—was infinitely expansible. The union depended on multiple and overlapping balances; there was no single point at which all power would be centered.

The western lands controversy encouraged Americans to equate a state's power with the extent of its claims and to consider balance among the states as essential to the survival of the union. The Federalist conception of union exploited this continuing concern with the relative size of the states. The focus on the limits of jurisdiction, rather than on powers incidental to jurisdiction, enabled promoters of the new Constitution to escape the logical impasse presented by traditional definitions of "sovereignty." If sovereignty were unitary and indivisible, separate sovereign states would inevitably drift apart and into war; if a sovereign national government were established, the states would be destroyed. But if the states were defined by boundaries that were guaranteed by a powerful central government, they would never have to exercise sovereign powers—preeminently those of war and peace—to uphold their "sovereignty." This diminutive notion of state sovereignty was the natural product of the adjustment of state claims under the Confederation. Americans had grown accustomed to seeing the ambitious designs of other states as the leading threat to their own; the possibility of encroachments by an "imbecilic" Congress was hypothetical at worst.

Small-state delegates at Philadelphia were vigorous proponents of the idea that equality with other states was the essence of state sovereignty. William Paterson of New Jersey argued, "Sovereignty and Equality are convertible Terms."[53] "A confederacy supposes sovereignty in the members composing it & sovereignty supposes equality."[54] "Equality" in this context meant primarily the equal representation of the states regardless of size that had been the rule in the Confederation Congress. But it also referred to the relative size of the states. Paterson's colleague, David Brearly, thus suggested that "a map of the U[nited] S[tates] be spread out, [and] that all the existing boundaries be erased," so that thirteen equal states could be established.[55] Such proposals were designed to make equal representation more attractive—the large states would presumably prefer to concede the point and remain large. But the "desirability" of equalization was not disputed by large-state delegates. "If there was a probability of equalizing the states," Wilson of Pennsylvania "would be for it."[56] Gorham of Massachusetts "hoped to see all the States made small by proper divisions," and Virginia's Madison promised that such an "equalization" would take place once the new union was established.[57]

The "balance and security of interests among the States" was the most critical problem in reconstituting the union, according to Pierce Butler of South Carolina.[58] In Paterson's opinion, either "state distinctions must cease, or the states must be equalized."[59] Otherwise, large states would devour small states. A balance of power was crucial for the maintenance of peace among nations, and the same principle applied to the American states. Vattel suggested in his *Law of Nations*, "The surest means of preserving a balance of power would be to bring it about that no State should be much superior to the others, that all the States, or at least the larger part, should be about equal in strength. . . . Confederations would be a sure means of preserving the balance of power and thus maintaining the liberty of Nations."[60] But the American Confederation could not maintain the rights of its member states because of disparities in state size and power. "Even as Corporations," Hamilton contended, "the extent of some" states—notably Virginia and Massachusetts—was "formidable," and therefore dangerous to the smaller states.[61]

The argument for the equalization of the states presupposed that the larger states were proportionately more powerful than the smaller ones. Large-state delegates pointed to the recent western land cessions and to the imminent division of old states and formation of new states as guarantees against large-state aggression. Gorham thus assured the convention that "Pennsylvania can never become a dangerous state" because it would eventually be divided. When the western territory was "separated from her . . . her power will be diminished."[62] New states would also be established in Maine and Kentucky, so reducing the power of Massachusetts and Virginia respectively.[63] Small-state delegates were less sanguine about the likelihood of future state divisions; in Luther Martin's view, the Constitution was a transparent scheme to preserve otherwise untenable jurisdictional claims.[64] Small-state defenders of state sovereignty were determined to secure their equality, through representation or by the redistribution of territory, as a central feature and sine qua non of any constitutional settlement; large-state nationalists hoped to dissociate the equalization issue from provisions for representation in the federal legislature. But the principle of state equality itself was unexceptionable, and it was finally incorporated in the new Constitution through equal representation in the Senate.

The concern for state equality was related to a preference for small states that was grounded in American experience as well as republican theory. Small-state delegates insisted that "the largest States are the worst Governed" and that "the people are more happy in small than large States."[65] "The States that please to call themselves large" were, in Martin's opinion, "the weekest in the Union."[66] Indeed, "the large States were weak at present in proportion to their extent"—a complete reversal of the equalization argument.[67] According to Jefferson, "a tractable people may be governed in large bodies";[68] Americans, however, were anything but "tractable." Martin suggested that "wherever new settlements have been formed in large states, they immediately want" to set up their own governments "nearer home."[69] Given the character of the American people, Roger Sherman concluded, small states simply "have more vigor in their Gov[ernmen]ts than the large ones."[70]

The arguments for state equality and small states were apparently contradictory. If small states were so vigorous and well governed, why should they be concerned about the extensive, ungovernable claims of their large neighbors? Antifederalists seized on the issue of state size in defense of the constitutional status quo. "Our small and separate governments are not only admirably suited in theory," James Winthrop claimed, "but have been remarkably successful in practice."[71] And if some of the *states* were "almost too great for . . . a republican form of government," "Cato" wondered how a consolidated union could avoid plunging into despotism?[72] It is significant, however, that Winthrop (of Massachusetts), "Cato" (of New York), and most other leading Antifederalists—with the vociferous exception of Luther Martin—came from large states, suggesting that their partiality for smallness was a rhetorical affectation. Most small-state politicians became ardent nationalists, once the principle of state equality was built into the Constitution. They reconciled their preference for small states with their call for a stronger union by drawing a distinction—which Antifederalists refused to recognize—between the kind of political community to be established on the national level and the state polities that the union was designed to protect.

Republics were supposed to be small. As republics, the small states could better command the loyalties and resources of their citizens than their large neighbors. But the small states had no guarantee that the large states would remain republics; their present weakness, manifest in separatist movements and other domestic disorders, suggested that a transformation was imminent. Federalists predicted that, without the union, republican governments would collapse throughout the states. The large states would be all too well situated to exploit the subsequent confusion. According to Ellsworth of Connecticut, there would be nothing "to hinder" them from "oppressing" their small neighbors.[73]

Federalists resolved the problem of size by embracing an apparent paradox. States should be small, but the union should be large and powerful. Republican government would thrive within the states while the states collectively would guarantee harmony among themselves and respect abroad. But the formula made sense only if this superintending authority were not seen as a "state," according to the conventional definition, subject to the same laws of political development that governed the fate of nations.

The tendency to conceive of state sovereignty in increasingly diminutive terms facilitated the distinction between state and union. It is significant that small state delegates were the leading defenders of state sovereignty at the Constitutional Convention, even though their vulnerability to large-state domination also made them proponents of a stronger union. But "state "sovereignty," as they defined and defended it, virtually withered away. "Give N[ew] Jersey an equal vote," Charles Pinckney quipped, "and she will dismiss her scruples, and concur in the Nati[ona]l system."[74] Consistency was not a strong suit on either side. If small-state defenders of state sovereignty were really "nationalists," large state "nationalists" betrayed a solicitude for states' rights when small-state delegates set out to circumscribe their claims or to demolish the states altogether. Representatives of the large states heaped abuse on the "phantom of *State* sovereignty," while dismissing small-state claims to equal representation.[75] But attacks on large-state claims inspired different sentiments. Elbridge Gerry "did not think . . . that the large States ought to be cut up," lest through continuing division they "be reduced to the size"—and presumably the status—"of Counties."[76] Wilson of Pennsylvania reacted angrily to partition threats: "Nothing . . . would give greater or juster alarm than the doctrine, that a political society is to be torne asunder without its own consent."[77] Thus almost every American politician of the founders' generation could find himself cast in the role of a defender of states' rights. What is remarkable is that their conception of these rights should be so modest and that, once they were supposed to be properly secured—through equal representation or through the constitutional guarantee of state claims—the same politicians should become such ardent nationalists.

The debasement of state sovereignty was a crucial component in rethinking and reconstituting the American union. But it was also necessary to articulate new images of the union that would resolve the apparent paradox of sovereign states in a sovereign union. This was the Federalists' greatest achievement.

Federalists had to show that a stronger union would secure individual rights, strengthen the union, provide for the creation of new states, and guarantee America against foreign intervention. In order to prove that this new government would not itself become a danger to the survival of the states, promoters of the Constitution could adopt one of two strategies: they could distinguish the objects of the new central government from those of the states, or they could try to show that the character of the governments themselves was fundamentally different.

Edmund Pendleton argued that "the two governments are established for different purposes, and act on different objects. . . . They can no more clash than two parallel lines can meet." [78] This argument for distinct spheres was unexceptionable, with a venerable pedigree in American efforts to define a safe place for the colonies in the British Empire. The role of the central government had also been carefully circumscribed under the Articles of Confederation. But because there was relatively little disagreement about what the national government should do, the distinct-sphere argument begged the question. The real controversy was over what the new government *could* or *would* do, according to the way it was constituted. The Federalists' determination to establish the supremacy of the central government and to remodel the union itself into something like a "state" was the weakest point in their rhetorical position. If the powers of the state and national governments were identical—as the complicated structure of the proposed government suggested—the argument for distinct spheres was subverted. Antifederalists insisted that the projected distribution of authority would lead to a death struggle for supremacy between the states and the union. [79] To assert that state and national governments possessed "coordinate sovereignties" served only to illuminate the apparent contradiction. Proponents of the new Constitution therefore had to abandon the language and logic of "sovereignty" altogether, or risk rhetorical suicide.

Nationalists traditionally had argued that the perpetuation of state distinctions jeopardized the survival of the union and thus of independence itself. Hamilton expressed this view at the Constitutional Convention. "The general power . . . must swallow up the State powers. Otherwise it will be swallowed up by them. . . . Two Sovereignties can not co-exist within the same limits."[80] Gunning Bedford of Delaware also believed that there was "no middle way between a perfect consolidation and a mere confederacy of the States."[81] Old-line nationalists were convinced that "the powers of the union must be increased, and those of the States individually must be abridged; they cannot both be perfectly Sovereign and independent at the same time."[82] Benjamin Rush of Pennsylvania eagerly anticipated the day when the new federal government "like a new continental wagon will overset our state dung cart."[83]

Federalists who pursued this logic justified Antifederalist anxieties about consolidation. The use of social-contract doctrine also exacerbated Antifederalist fears. Federalists frequently compared the formation of the new union to the creation of civil society from a state of nature. Wilson argued, "More liberty is gained by associating, than is lost by the natural rights which it absorbs."[84] But if Americans were in a true state of nature, then the American states did not truly exist; contract theory thus suggested the kind of radical change that Federalists disclaimed. Furthermore, it was unclear who the contracting parties were supposed to be. Contracts implied distinct parties, with distinct interests, negotiating from equal strength. The appeal to contract theory therefore reinforced the conventional competitive conception of politics that justified Antifederalist arguments against the Constitution. Individuals—or states—would have to "give up such share of our rights as to enable government to support, defend, and preserve the rest."[85] But such exchanges might favor some interests more than others. Contract theory thus conjured up fears of absolute loss—in the exchange of freedom for protection—and relative disadvantage. These fears were central to the Antifederalist appeal.

Federalists like Wilson were well aware of the limitations of contract theory. He emphatically denied that the Constitution set up a government "founded upon compact." The new government "is founded upon the power of the people," Wilson asserted.[86] Therefore, the elaborate contrivances of the complicated new government proposed by the Constitution did *not* provide for the distribution of sovereign authority, which "remains and flourishes with the people."[87] Sovereignty might, by its conventional definition, remain fixed, finite, and indivisible. But the proliferation of institutions through which sovereign authority could be exercised, and therefore the scope of that authority, was infinitely expansible. Federalists thus were able to escape the constraints of traditional theory in which politics was seen as a closed system and effective, legitimate power was supposed to contract and deflate. Instead, they promoted an inflationary view of politics: everyone would benefit under the new dispensation.

Proponents of the Constitution argued that the new federal government was directly grounded on the sovereignty of the people and therefore was legitimate in a way that the Confederation Congress never had been. In this respect at least, it was advantageous to portray the new union as a state, in which power was effectively checked and balanced. The imputation of ultimate authority to the people also laid to rest the old question of whether the states or the union were sovereign, and so superseded the traditional competitive model of politics.[88] The people, as a collective sovereign, could not compete with itself. Because the distribution of authority itself was not involved, the problems presented by constitution-making were supposed to be merely mechanical.

But if the Federalists' invocation of popular sovereignty enabled them to evade the force of conventional political logic, it was also necessary to develop a new logic to sanction the new constitutional order. It was not sufficient to argue that neither state nor national governments were sovereign; the role of each had to be described in positive terms. Federalists had to show that the Federal Constitution was "well framed to secure the rights and liberties of the people and for preserving the governments of the individual states."[89]

Characterizations of the existing union provided a rhetorical contrast to the new union envisaged by constitutional reformers. The present union was compared to a "cobweb" or "chain" in which each state was a link.[90] Both these images expressed the weakness of the federal bands under the Articles. A chain was only as strong as its weakest link, and the American chain abounded in weak links. Oliver Ellsworth complained, "A single state can rise up and put a *veto* upon the most important public measures."[91] A "cobweb" was particularly vulnerable to dangerous winds from abroad, just as, in Hugh Williamson's elaborate figure, the United States, "like a dark cloud, without cohesion or firmness" was "ready to be torn asunder . . . by every breeze of external violence, or internal commotion."[92] The union, according to these images, was nothing more—and perhaps was less—than the sum of its parts. Wilson described it as a loaf of bread; each state "endeavoured to cut" its own "slice" at the expense of the others.[93] Edmund Randolph suggested that the union "has been unable to defend itself against the encroachments made upon it by the states. Every one of them has conspired against it; Virginia as much as any."[94]

Constitutional reformers believed that the very structure of the present union encouraged a mutually destructive competition for fixed, if not diminishing, stakes. And, like a chain, cobweb, or rain cloud, the union was structurally undifferentiated; no inherent principle of superordination or subordination held its component parts together. George Washington complained that there was no "power" under the Articles that could "pervade the whole Union."[95] This fundamental defect made the states vulnerable to each other as well as to foreign powers. Furthermore, because the terms of the existing union were fixed, while its advantages were supposed to be finite, the United States could not expand.[96] If the union had been defined according to the way distinct spheres of authority were coordinated, rather than as a specific combination of states, the addition of new states would have posed no problems. But the United States, as constituted by the Articles of Confederation, would not simply have been enlarged by new states—it would have been fundamentally transformed.[97]

Antifederalists claimed that conflict among the states, and between the states and the national government, was inevitable. The terms of this conflict would be unequal under the proposed Constitution; some states or sections would gain at the expense of others, and the union itself would overpower all the states. For all its defects, the present union did enable the member states to defend their rights and interests. Patrick Henry said, "The southern parts of America have been protected by that weakness so much execrated."[98] Antifederalists thus embraced a minimalist conception of the union: the states would be held together by bonds of friendship and reciprocal advantage, not by power. This benign vision of interstate harmony was totally at odds with the supposed conflicts of interest that Antifederalists invoked against the Constitution. But their point was that if the relationship among the states were not voluntary and uncoerced, "union" itself was a contradiction in terms.[99]

Federalists sought to convince Americans that everyone would benefit from a more powerful union. According to "One of the People," the Constitution did not undermine the authority of the states; instead, "it supports and adds a dignity to every government in the United States."[100] Pelatiah Webster explained, "The new Constitution leaves all the Thirteen States, complete republics, as it found them."[101] Without the union, these republics would not survive.[102] James Wilson best expressed the Federalist contention that the fate of the states and the fate of the union were indissolubly linked in a positive rather than adversarial relation. If Americans rejected the Constitution, everyone would lose; if they ratified it, the states' "respectability and power will increase with that of the general government." [103]

Federalists maintained that "the General & State Gov[ernmen]ts were not enemies to each other," as John Langdon put it at the Philadelphia Convention. [104] But the history of interstate conflict and resulting suspicions about the misuse of federal power appeared to disprove this crucial proposition. It was therefore necessary to redefine statehood and union in ways that would make harmony and cooperation among the states seem possible. The wide variety of images invoked by proponents of the Constitution suggested the broad outlines and implications of this redefinition. Comparisons of the American union to a human body, or even to a hand (each finger was a state), expressed the closeness of ties that made Americans in some respects members of one inclusive political community. [105] Better yet, the states could be seen as members of a single family; "why should members of one and the same family clash, while the interests of the family are the same?" [106]

Organic or familial imagery left the role of the states unspecified. Antifederalists seized on the implication that the proposed Constitution would bypass the states altogether and establish one "grand body politic" on the supposed sovereignty of the people. [107] Friends of the Constitution were compelled to argue that the new union would uphold state distinctions. Hamilton thus distinguished "the rights of a state," which the Constitution secured, from its selfish "interests." "We are attempting, by this Constitution, to abolish factions," he explained, playing on the contemporary prejudice against partisanship. [108] The integrity of the states, whose legitimate claims were guaranteed by the union, was suggested by the comparison of states to planets in the solar system. Unlike comets with their "conflicting orbits," the states would, like planets, move "harmoniously" within their "proper sphere," James Wilson argued. [109] The image also emphasized the crucial role of the central government. Madison said that the states "will continually fly out of their proper orbits" if not held in check by a higher authority. [110]

Celestial imagery was flattering to Americans, [111] but it failed to capture the dynamic and expansive character of the American union, as many Federalists understood it. Furthermore, the comparison failed to suggest any distinctive role for the sovereign people. Structural imagery was better suited to articulating the Federalists' conception of the union. James Wilson likened the union to a "pyramid," resting on as "broad a basis" of popular authority "as possible."[112] As he developed the comparison at the Pennsylvania ratifying convention, the federal pyramid "is laid on the broad basis of the people; its powers gradually rise, while they are confined, in proportion as they ascend, until they end in that most permanent of all forms."[113]

The pyramid image successfully established "a chain of connection" between the people and a powerful federal government, but it also betrayed Wilson's lack of concern about states' rights. In order to allay popular misgivings about "consolidation," it was necessary to show that "the general government . . . depends for support upon the individual states" as well as upon the sovereign people.[114] The idea that the states were like "great massy pillars on which this political fabric was to be extended and supported" was admirably suited to this purpose.[115] According to Oliver Wolcott, the Constitution "effectually secures the states in their several rights. It must secure them for its own sake, for they are the pillars which uphold the general system."[116] Richard Law, speaking after Wolcott at the same session of the Connecticut convention, developed the image. The general government would be "like a vast and magnificent bridge built upon thirteen strong and stately pillars. Now the rulers, those who occupy the bridge, cannot be so beside themselves as to knock away the pillars which support the whole fabric."[117]

All Federalists did not use the same language in describing the proposed union, but the multiplicity of images suggested, if nothing else, that it would not be the simple despotism projected by opponents of the constitution. Nor could the new national government be compared to the state governments. As John Page explained to Jefferson, the Constitution would set up a

> complicated Government, of 13, perhaps 30 States which were to be *united*, so as to be *one* in Inter[est] Strength and Glory [while] . . . severally sovereign and independent, as to their municipal Laws, and local Circumstances. . . . I found that the Objections which might be made to a single State thus governed, would not apply to this great delicate and complicated Machinery of Government.[118]

The new union was unprecedented in world history. "Where," asked John Dickinson, "was there ever a confederacy of republics, in such territory, united, *as these states are to be* by the proposed constitution?" Dickinson agreed with Montesquieu "that extensive territory has in general been arbitrarily governed." But it was just "as true," he added, "that a number of republics, in such territory, loosely connected, must inevitably rot into despotism."[119] The new union alone could avoid the pitfalls of consolidation or disunion.

Warnings about the impossibility of establishing effective government over an extensive territory helped Federalists make their case for a new union. If Antifederalists were really convinced by their own logic, Pelatiah Webster wrote, then the only "conclusion . . . must be *against any union at all*."[120] Federalists believed that the American crisis resulted from the failure to institute a successor to the imperial government that could keep the peace among the states and guarantee them all against foreign aggression. The existing union was woefully inadequate to these tasks, but the Constitution would finally establish "a government whose powers will be coequal with its extent."[121]

The key premise in the Federalist argument was that interstate conflict could be contained without destroying the states. Antifederalists were reduced to denying either the existence of such conflict or the desirability of union itself. Federalists rejected the notion that Americans faced a choice between freedom and power, or between state and federal sovereignty. Their union was a government both for the states and for the people of the states. As Robert Livingston put it, the state and general governments were "different deposits" of the people's power; "their liberty acquires an additional security from the division." The states also gained "additional security" from a strong central government.[122] Thus, in the Federalists' inflationary scheme, power was not inversely related to liberty—as was conventionally supposed. The strength of the central government, properly checked by the authority of the people, was the best guarantee of everyone's rights.

The states had always been an embarrassment to nationalists. But the structure of the debate over the Constitution suggested a new role for them. Ellsworth argued at Philadelphia, "It would be impossible to support a Republican Gov[ernmen]t over so great an extent of Country" without the "co-operation" of the state governments.[123] Montesquieu's point was taken, and turned to advantage. A "single Gov[ernmen]t" could not maintain order "throughout the U[nited] States," just as large states were unable to govern their own extensive claims. But the states and union would be perfectly complementary. Francis Corbin argued in the Virginia convention,

The extent of the United States cannot render this government oppressive. The powers of the general government are only of a general nature, and their object is to protect, defend, and strengthen the United States; but the internal administration of government is left to the state legislatures, who exclusively retain such powers as will give the states the advantages of small republics, without the danger commonly attendant on the weakness of such governments.[124]

Indeed, Nathaniel Gorham suggested, "the strenghth of the General Gov[ernmen]t will lie not in the largeness, but in the smallness of the States."[125] Small states would be ideally suited to republican self-government; a large and powerful union was the best guarantee for their survival.

According to Federalist logic, the larger the union the better. "*Its true size,*" Alexander Hanson asserted, "*is neither greater nor less than that, which may comprehend all the states, which, by their contiguity, may become enemies, unless united under one common head, capable of reconciling all their differences.*"[126] General William Heath told the Massachusetts convention that the Constitution was "not for the present people of the United States only—but, in addition to these, for all those states which may hereafter rise into existence within the jurisdiction of the United States, and for millions of people yet unborn. . . . Every thing depends on our union."[127] Antifederalist calculations of relative advantage presupposed continuing competition among the same states or sections for the same, limited stakes. But the Federalists understood that the expansion of settlement and the proliferation of new states was one of the central facts of American politics. These new states need not be connected to the old, as the case of Vermont demonstrated. But, John Dickinson wrote, the "consequences" of the failure to extend the union "are evident." Americans had to create a system "that will communicate equal liberty and assure just protection" to new states as well as old.[128] It was not enough to compromise existing interests—which itself was more than the more pessimistic Antifederalists thought possible. It was also necessary to establish principles of government that would be appropriate to an incomparably different future.

If the Federalists' system was unprecedented, it was not unanticipated. Montesquieu, Vattel, and before them, a whole series of early world federalists had imagined a world of confederated states, freed from war.[129] The Constitution would set up the kind of federal republic advocated by Montesquieu, James Wilson claimed. The new union "consists in assembling distinct societies, which are consolidated into a new body capable of being increased by the addition of other members; an expanding quality peculiarly fitted to the circumstances of America."[130] A "true federal republic," Hanson added, "is always capable of accession by the peaceable and friendly admission of new single states."[131]

Federalists thus embraced a dynamic vision of expansion and growth. It was significant that this expansion was understood in terms of the creation of new states. States were essential components of the new system. Not only would the union support the states, but the states would support the union. The growing size of the union would also help guarantee the interests of the existing states. George Nicholas of Virginia asserted that "every new state will bring an accession of security" against any treaty that might jeopardize the South and West.[132] Dickinson believed that "THE EXTENT of our territory, and the NUMBER of states within it, vastly increase the difficulty of any political disorder diffusing its contagion."[133]

Antifederalists feared that expansion would weaken the union. They could not conceive of the United States extended across time and space. Melancton Smith thought that "in three or four hundred years" there might be a hundred million Americans, constituting "two or three great empires . . . totally different from our own."[134] Thus, he reasoned, there was no point in looking too far ahead. But Federalists believed that the Constitution—with its provisions for regular censuses, reapportionment, and the admission of new states—was ideally suited for future generations. Daniel Clymer of Pennsylvania confidently predicted that "the extended embrace of fraternal love shall enclose three millions, and ere fifty years are elapsed thirty millions, as a band of brothers!"[135] According to James Wilson, the delegates at the Pennsylvania ratifying convention were "representatives . . . not merely of the present age, but of future times; not merely of the territory along the seacoast, but of regions immensely extended westward. We should fill, as fast as possible, this extensive country, with men who shall live happy, free, and secure."[136] Southern Federalists appealed to less exalted emotions when they predicted that "we shall soon outnumber" northerners, and therefore would gain an edge in representation.[137] But even then, Federalists believed that political calculations should take into account the growth of population and the passage of time.

It was this willingness to embrace the future, not their disinterestedness, that most distinctly differentiated friends of the Constitution from their opponents. The Antifederalists' concern with securing existing interests encouraged them to think of politics in static terms: every gain was matched by a loss. Given such logic, the only safe course was to do nothing at all. Federalists, for no less interested reasons, were convinced that something had to be done. But their Constitution was more than a simple answer to the impending horrors of "anarchy"; it was also supposed to be the key to unlocking America's future greatness. American power would expand with American population. "It ought to be a maxim with us," James Wilson said, "that the increase of numbers increases the dignity, the security, and the respectability of all governments."[138] Federalists thus thought of politics in dynamic terms. The doctrine of popular sovereignty was crucial to this new mode of thought; not only did it permit Federalists to multiply the authorities to whom power was delegated, it also made it possible to think of sovereignty itself, like population, as expansible. Every gain was a gain for everyone. As Wilson said, "The interest of the whole must, on the great scale, be the interest of every part."[139]

Federalists addressed themselves to the problem of political legitimacy, while Antifederalists focused on the defense of rights against the encroachments of power. Legitimacy, or the public acceptance of the lawfulness of government, can expand or contract. Federalists portrayed the "critical period" as a time when there was a loss of legitimate authority at every level of American politics. The Constitution was supposed to reverse this disastrous trend so that local, state, and national governments would all be strengthened. But Antifederalists doubted that governmental power could be "legitimate"; at best, it could be checked and balanced so that it would not endanger liberty. Rights in civil society were by definition limited; history demonstrated that they were easily lost, but rarely recovered. Politics thus presented a tragic paradox: man found himself poised between anarchy (too much freedom) and despotism (too much power).

The doctrine of popular sovereignty provided Federalists with a neat solution to the problem of freedom and power: the "people" never relinquished their authority at all. Strong government did not therefore require a corresponding diminution of rights, nor did one government necessarily extend its jurisdiction at the expense of others. Antifederalists commanded the conventional wisdom, but the Federalists successfully appealed to American experience with overlapping authority in the British Empire and after independence. Furthermore, if Americans could withdraw their support from their governments so that there was no effective authority anywhere, they could just as well extend their support to those same governments. Federalists assumed that legitimacy was expansible. Antifederalists believed that their rights were in constant danger of being throttled to death by governmental power.

But legitimacy presented its own problems. Why should Americans pledge their allegiance to the new regime, when they had withheld it from the old one, and when so many saw so much in the Constitution to arouse anxiety? Federalists needed a "miracle," or a philosopher's stone, to transform the base substance of American politics into gold. The Constitution assumed this function in Federalist rhetoric.

Federalists attempted to show not only that America in general was in the midst of a political crisis, but also that the framers of the Constitution had had to overcome enormous obstacles. Their "miraculous" success, measured against the intractability of conflicting interests, was the secret of the Constitution's authority; it gave Americans something to believe in.[140] William Pierce cited the "variety of local circumstances, the inequality of states, and the dissonant interests of the different parts of the Union" that the convention had to reconcile;[141] Madison alluded to "the jarring interests of States,"[142] William Davie to "a multiplicity of discordant and clashing interests,"[143] and Charles Pinckney to "jarring interests and prejudices."[144] The great debate between large and small states over representation, as well as the delicate negotiations between carrying and non-carrying states and slave and (relatively) free states were repeatedly invoked. The convention was seen as a microcosm of the whole country: if the framers could unite behind a plan, why could not the American people as a whole do so?

The Antifederalist fixation on the conflict of interest among states and sections helped the Federalists make their case. The deeper the disagreement within the convention and in the country at large, the more miraculous the Constitution seemed. The constitutional myth was thus grounded in a consensus about the supposed pervasiveness and depth of conflict in the United States. The Antifederalists helped legitimize the Constitution by predicting dire consequences upon its adoption. It was easy to exaggerate the differences between Federalists and Antifederalists over the powers that had to be vested in the union, or over the authority that should remain in the states. Their most important disagreement centered on whether or not they believed in the possibility of an expanding union. The Antifederalists had little faith in the union: their pessimism provided a striking background for the "miracle" at Philadelphia. Without the pessimism there was no miracle.

The Constitution was the product of many compromises. Federalists were thus able to promote it by appealing to interest groups that were supposed to be beneficiaries. Slavery was protected; small states gained equality in the Senate; merchants would benefit from a coherent commercial policy. But it was the process of compromise itself that provoked the most fulsome rhetoric. Madison thought "the degree of concord" was nothing less than a "miracle";[145] Washington thought the constitutional settlement "little short of a miracle,"[146] and Wilson was filled with "astonishment, in beholding so perfect a system formed from such heterogenous materials."[147] If the founders themselves soon achieved godlike status, Federalists argued that God himself had had an "influence" in the proceedings of the convention.[148] The compromises embodied in the Constitution were so "equitable" and "politic" that an "angel" could not have been a truer "umpire."[149] Pinckney was "struck with amazement. Nothing less than that superintending hand of providence, that so miraculously carried us through the war" could have produced such a happy result.[150]

Ultimately, the Constitution was self-legitimizing. It was not so much that the Federalists cleverly appropriated the doctrine of popular sovereignty to make a strong central government acceptable to suspicious republicans. Instead, acceptance of the Constitution reflected the people's eagerness to believe in the Herculean achievements of the founding fathers who had been able to overcome a conflict of interests that supposedly had immobilized American politics in the "critical period." Americans of all political persuasions soon embraced the founding myth. They were willing to believe the worst about themselves in the dark days before the Philadelphia Convention in order to hope for the best under the new constitutional dispensation. Revisionist historians have demonstrated that the "critical period" was largely a creation of contemporary rhetoric. But Federalists did correctly diagnose and exploit a crisis of confidence in American government; they were also able to tap a reservoir of fellow-feeling and a faith in the future that had inspired the American revolutionaries.

The Constitution could be all things to all people because all things were possible to those who would believe them so. The success of the Constitution was grounded on faith, or on what contemporaries would call "virtue."[151] Americans experienced a rapid inflation of power under the Constitution because they accepted the legitimacy of power. In the realm of public opinion, the Constitution did indeed accomplish miracles. But its greatest accomplishment was to articulate an underlying consensus about what the American union should be like. The Constitution would not have been possible without prior development of concepts of statehood and union. It could not have been a "miracle" without the "critical period." America's founding myth explained the transformation of "anarchy" into order; it established the legitimacy of republican government.

Notes

INTRODUCTION

1. The literature is reviewed in James H. Hutson, "Country, Court, and Constitution: Antifederalism and the Historians," *William and Mary Quarterly*, 3d ser., 38 (1981): 337–68. See also the essays collected in parts 5 and 6 of Jack P. Greene, ed., *The Reinterpretation of the American Revolution* (New York, 1968).

2. Andrew McLaughlin, "The Background of American Federalism," *American Political Science Review* 12 (1918): 215–40. See also Westel Willoughby, *The American Constitutional System* (New York, 1919), 29 and passim; and Robert G. McCloskey, *The American Supreme Court* (Chicago, 1960), 11–13.

3. Bernard Bailyn, *The Ideological Origins of the American Revolution* (Cambridge, Mass., 1967). On Bailyn's impact, see Robert E. Shalhope, "Toward a Republican Synthesis: The Emergence of an Understanding of Republicanism in American Historiography," *William and Mary Quarterly*, 3d ser., 29 (1972): 49–80; and idem, "Republicanism and Early American Historiography," ibid., 39 (1982): 334–56.

CHAPTER 1: CONGRESS AND THE STATES

1. Carter Braxton to Landon Carter, April 14, 1776, in Paul H. Smith, ed., *Letters of the Delegates to Congress*, 9 vols. to date (Washington, D.C., 1976–   ), 3:520–23. Josiah Tucker predicted that "the moment a separation [from Britain] takes effect, intestine quarrels will begin: For it is well known, that the Seeds of Discord and Dissention between Province and Province are now ready to shoot forth." *The True Interest of Great Britain, Set Forth in Regard to the Colonies* (Norfolk, Va., 1774), 61–62.

2. John Randolph, *Considerations on the Present State of Virginia* (Williamsburg, 1774), 11.

3. For an early statement of this view, see Alexander Hamilton to James Duane, September 3, 1780, in Harold C. Syrett, ed., *The Papers of Alexander*

Hamilton, 26 vols. (New York, 1961–79), 2:404: "The disputes about boundaries &c, testify how flattering a prospect we have of future tranquillity, if we do not frame in time a confederacy capable of deciding the differences and compelling the obedience of the respective members." See also Hamilton's "Continentalist" III, August 9, 1781, in ibid., 2:660–61: "Competitions of boundary and rivalships of commerce will easily afford pretexts for war." According to Richard Peters, "we shall be despised abroad and convulsed at home if something is not speedily done to support our tottering union"; Peters to Oliver Wolcott, July 13, 1783, Oliver Wolcott Papers (Connecticut Historical Society, Hartford), 3:152. "Dissension" in Vermont and the Wyoming Valley "will not end without a civil war," predicted Richard Dobbs Spaight in a letter to Gov. Alexander Martin, October 16, 1784, in William L. Saunders, Walter Clark, and Stephen B. Weeks, eds., *Colonial and State Records of North Carolina*, 26 vols. (Raleigh, Winston, Goldsboro, and Charlotte, 1886–1914), 17:172–75. According to Hamilton's "Federalist" no. 6, in *Hamilton Papers*, 4:317, "vicinity, or nearness of situation, constitutes nations natural enemies." See "Federalist" no. 7, in ibid., 319–22, for a review of the western lands controversy ("an ample theatre for hostile pretensions") and of disputes in Wyoming and Vermont. The dangers of domestic "insurrection" are treated in no. 28, in ibid., 439–43. On the conviction of Hamilton and John Jay "that among separate sovereign states there is a constant possibility of war," see the discussion in Kenneth Waltz, *Man, the State, and War* (New York, 1959), 208, 237. In an interesting variation on this theme, Oliver Ellsworth argued at the Connecticut ratifying convention that only a powerful central government "which acts only upon delinquent individuals" could avoid making war against states in order to preserve the union; in Jonathan Elliott, ed., *The Debates of the Several State Conventions on the Adoption of the Federal Constitution*, 5 vols. (Philadelphia, 1876), 2:197. For a good introduction to early American thought on international relations, with which interstate relations were easily confused, see Felix Gilbert, *To the Farewell Address* (Princeton, 1961), and Gerald Stourzh, *Alexander Hamilton and the Idea of Republican Government* (Stanford, 1970).

4. Sir William Holdsworth, *A History of English Law*, 16 vols. (London, 1922–66), vol. 11; Joseph L. Smith, *Appeals to the Privy Council from the American Plantations* (New York, 1950).

5. Charles James Fox's prediction, quoted in "Sketches of the Present Times in North America," *The Times* (London), February 2, 1786.

6. According to a writer in ibid., January 29, 1785. "America seems to be this moment on the point of falling into that anarchy which generally attends a country torn from an ancient state, before it has time to form a wise system of government."

7. The sentiment was inspired by reports of impending conflict in the Wyoming Valley, *State Gazette of South Carolina*, April 13, 1786.

8. A "Dialogue" ("Whig" speaking), *Falmouth Gazette* (Falmouth/Portland, Massachusetts/Maine), March 23, 1786.

9. Jefferson to James Madison, January 30, 1787, in William T. Hutchinson et al., eds., *The Papers of James Madison*, 13 vols. to date (Chicago and Charlottesville, 1962–), 9:247–52.

10. See, e.g., resolutions adopted on June 30, 1777, and May 23, 1780, in Worthington C. Ford, ed., *Journals of the Continental Congress* (hereafter JCC), 34 vols. (Washington, D.C., 1904–37), 8:508–13; 17:452. According to the latter resolution, "the lands contained within the limits of the United States are . . . under the jurisdiction of some one or other of the thirteen states."

11. This was true of the controversies between Virginia and Pennsylvania and between Connecticut and Pennsylvania. On the former, see Boyd Crumrine, "The Boundary Controversy Between Pennsylvania and Virginia, 1748–1785," in Carnegie Institution, *Annals of the Carnegie Museum*, vol. 1 (Pittsburgh, 1901), 505–24; and Thomas Perkins Abernethy, *Western Lands and the American Revolution* (New York, 1937), 227, 254, 269–70. On Wyoming, see the documents collected in Julian P. Boyd and Robert J. Taylor, eds., *The Susquehannah Company Papers*, 11 vols. (Wilkes-Barre and Ithaca, 1930–71); and James E. Brady, "Wyoming: A Study of John Franklin and the Connecticut Movement into Pennsylvania" (Ph.D. diss., Syracuse University, 1973). These disputes are discussed in Chapter 3.

12. Knox to George Washington, October 23, 1786, Knox Papers (microfilm ed., Massachusetts Historical Society, Boston), XIX.

13. James Warren was "mortified by the Imbecility and Inattention with which our public Affairs have been Conducted," according to his letter of October 22, 1786, to John Adams, inspired by Shays's Rebellion, in Worthington C. Ford, ed., *Warren-Adams Letters*, 2 vols. (Boston 1917–25), 2:279. For an excellent analysis of the political significance of the rebellion, see J. R. Pole, *Political Representation in England and the Origins of the American Republic* (1966; paperback ed., Berkeley, Calif., 1971), 226–44. The "Vices of the [American] System" are discussed in Gordon Wood, *The Creation of the American Republic, 1776–1787* (Chapel Hill, 1969), 393–429.

14. John Adams's notes on debates, August 2, 1776, in L. H. Butterfield, ed., *Diary and Autobiography of John Adams*, 4 vols. (Cambridge, Mass., 1961), 2:249. See James Brown Scott, *The United States of America: A Study in International Organization* (New York, 1920); and James Brown Scott, ed., *Judicial Settlement of Controversies Between States of the American Union*, 2 vols. (Washington, D.C., 1918), a collection of cases. Both works devote considerable attention to the colonial period.

15. Pauline Maier, *From Resistance to Revolution: Colonial Radicals and the Development of American Opposition to Britain, 1765–1776* (1972; paperback ed., New York, 1974), 198ff.; Pauline Maier, "The Beginnings of American Republicanism, 1765–1776," in *The Development of a Revolutionary Mentality* (Washington, D.C., 1972), 99–117.

16. See esp. Jack N. Rakove, *The Beginnings of National Politics: An Interpretive History of the Continental Congress* (New York, 1979).

17. "Nestor" (Benjamin Rush), *American Herald* (Boston), June 19, 1786, reprinted from *Independent Gazeteer* (Philadelphia), June 3. See also "Tullius," in *Three Letters Addressed to the Public* (Philadelphia, 1783), 8: "Each of the States, if indeed it can properly be denominated a *Sovereignty*, has only a limited, territorial one . . . because in Congress alone resides the power of making war and peace, and treating in a sovereign capacity with other nations." Congress should have "complete sovereignty," according to Hamilton's letter to Duane, cited in note 3, above.

18. Braxton to Carter, cited in note 1, above.

19. Carter Braxton, *Address to the Convention of Virginia* (Philadelphia, 1776), 23–24; *Virginia Gazette* (Dixon and Hunter), June 8, 1776.

20. George Ross to Lancaster Committee of Correspondence, May 30, 1775, in *Letters of the Delegates*, 1:421–22.

21. On the Virginia separatists, see William S. Lester, *The Transylvania Colony*

(Spencer, Ind., 1935), and the discussion in Chapter 4, below. For the background and early history of agitation against New York in its northeastern counties, see Matt Bushnell Jones, *Vermont in the Making, 1750–1777* (Cambridge, Mass., 1939) and Chapter 6, below.

22. Report submitted November 4, 1775, *JCC* 3:321.

23. According to Roger Sherman, in a letter to Zebulon Butler, calling for peace in the Wyoming Valley, January 19, 1776, in *Letters of the Delegates*, 3:116.

24. Virginia and Pennsylvania Delegates to the Inhabitants West of the Laurel Hill, July 25, 1775, in ibid., 1:665–66; order of Congress, June 1, 1775, *JCC* 2:76.

25. Connecticut Delegates to Butler et al., August 2, 1775, in *Letters of the Delegates*, 1:693.

26. Deane to Thomas Mumford, October (16?), 1775, in ibid., 2:188–91.

27. Smith to Arthur St. Clair, September 5, 1775, in William Henry Smith, ed., *The St. Clair Papers*, 2 vols. (Cincinnati, 1882), 1:360.

28. According to Ethan Allen's *Animadversary Address to the Inhabitants of Vermont* (Hartford, 1778), 5, the "Tories . . . to a man, through the whole State, are . . . in favour of the government of *New-York.*" Jacob Bayley suggested in a letter to the president of the New York convention on February 19, 1777 (in E. B. O'Callaghan, ed., *The Documentary History of the State of New York*, 4 vols. [Albany, 1849–51], 4:930–31) that "these Counties are in danger of Ministeriall protection." Subsequently, New York partisans circulated rumors about negotiations between Vermont and the British. See, e.g., the published resolutions of the town of Guilford, March 13, 1782, James Phelps Scrapbook (Vermont Historical Society, Montpelier).

29. Eliphalet Dyer to William Judd, July 23, 1775, in *Letters of the Delegates*, 1:654–55.

30. Deane to Mumford, October (16?), 1775, in ibid., 2:188–91. See also the Connecticut Delegates' Memorial to Congress, [December 12?, 1775], in ibid., 476–77; and the Subscription List for the Defense of Pennsylvania Claims, October 9, 1775, in *Susquehannah Company Papers*, 6:366.

31. Smith diary, September 30, 1775, in *Letters of the Delegates*, 2:82–83.

32. St. Clair to John Penn, September 15, 1775, in *St. Clair Papers*, 1:361. See also James Wilson to John Montgomery, September 14, 1775, in *Letters of the Delegates*, 2:58n.

33. Recorded by John Adams in his notes on debates, October 7, 1775, in *Adams Diary*, 2:200.

34. Connecticut Delegates' motion for a "Committee [to] be appointed out of the other colonies" to resolve the Wyoming dispute, October 14, 1775, *JCC* 3:295.

35. Richard Smith diary, December 18, 20, 21, 23, 1775, in *Letters of the Delegates*, 2:494, 500–501, 503–4, 517–18; December 23, *JCC* 3:452–53.

36. Connecticut Delegates' proposed resolution [October 17(?), 1775], in *Letters of the Delegates*, 2:196.

37. Richard Smith diary, September 25, 1775, in ibid., 2:57–58.

38. Resolution of November 27, 1775, *JCC* 3:377.

39. For a typical complaint to this effect, see George Clinton to John Jay, June 23, 1779, in Hugh Hastings, ed., *The Public Papers of George Clinton, First Governor of New York*, 10 vols. (New York, 1899–1914), 5:93–95.

40. The "anarchy" in this region is described by Silvanus Ripley in a letter to

John Phillips, December 6, 1780, Wheelock Papers (New Hampshire Historical Society, Concord). See the discussion in Chapter 6, below.

41. Resolution of April 15, 1776, JCC 4:283.

42. Adams to John Penn [before March 27, 1776], in Robert J. Taylor, ed., *The Papers of John Adams*, 4 vols. to date (Cambridge, Mass., 1977–   ), 4:78–86, at 83. See also Wood, *Creation of the American Republic*, 125–389, and for a good discussion of the lack of interest in the organization of power on the national level, see Rakove, *Beginnings of National Politics*, 183–91.

43. According to Adams's notes on debates, July 25, 1776, in *Adams Diary*, 2:241.

44. Noah Webster, *An Examination into the . . . Constitution* (Philadelphia, 1787), 51.

45. According to Adams's notes, July 30, 1776, in *Adams Diary*, 2:247–48.

46. John Adams, *Thoughts on Government* (Boston, 1776), reprinted in *Adams Papers*, 4:86–93, at 92. See the discussion in Rakove, *Beginnings of National Politics*, 139–51.

47. JCC 5:546–56, at 549–51.

48. Statements in this and the following paragraph are taken from Adams's notes on debates, July 25 (Wilson and Jefferson) and August 2, 1776 (Chase, Stone, and Huntington), in *Adams Diary*, 2:241–42, 249.

49. *Ordinances Passed at a General Convention of Delegates and Representatives . . .* (Williamsburg, 1776), 5–13. See Chapter 4, below.

50. Jefferson quoted in Adams's notes, July 25, 1776, in *Adams Diary*, 2:241.

51. The Sherman, Harrison, and Huntington quotations in this and the following paragraph are taken from Adams's notes, August 2, 1776, in ibid., 2:249.

52. Wood, *Creation of the American Republic*, 197–225; Jackson Turner Main, *The Sovereign States, 1775–1783* (New York, 1973), 143–85.

53. See, e.g., the proposal by the Rhode Island Delegates, June 23, 1778, JCC 11:639, that Congress assume jurisdiction over Crown lands. Also "Lucius Quintus Cincinnatus," *The Mote Point of Finance, or the Crown Lands, Equally Divided* (broadside, Philadelphia, September 21, 1779); Alexander Hamilton, "Continentalist" VI, July 4, 1782, in *Hamilton Papers*, 3:105.

54. John Adams to James Warren, October 1775, in *Adams Papers*, 3:266–67. Louise B. Dunbar, *A Study of "Monarchical" Tendencies in the United States from 1776 to 1801* (Urbana, Ill., 1922).

55. John Adams, "Novanglus," March 6, 1775, reprinted in Bernard Mason, ed., *The American Colonial Crisis: The Daniel Leonard–John Adams Letters to the Press, 1774–1775* (New York, 1972), 208 and passim; Edmund Pendleton to Joseph Jones, July 26, 1779, in David John Mays, ed., *The Letters and Papers of Edmund Pendleton, 1734–1803*, 2 vols. (Charlottesville, 1967), 2:334; Edmund Randolph's "Brief on American Claims," August 20, 1782, JCC 23:516. For a discussion of American concepts of sovereignty, see Peter S. Onuf, ed., *Maryland and the Empire, 1773* (Baltimore, 1974), introduction.

56. James D. Richardson, *A Compilation of the Messages and Papers of the Presidents, 1789–1902*, 12 vols. (Washington, D.C., 1903–9), 1:9–18.

57. Rhode Island Delegates to Gov. William Greene, April 16, 1782, in Edmund Cody Burnett, ed., *Letters of the Members of the Continental Congress*, 8 vols. (Washington, D.C., 1921–36), 6:329. See Chapter 6, below.

58. *Freeman's Journal* (Philadelphia), January 21, 1783. See also Robert R.

Livingston to Lafayette, January 10, 1783, in *Susquehannah Company Papers*, 7:252; and for a comprehensive account of the trial, see Robert J. Taylor, "Trial at Trenton," *William and Mary Quarterly*, 3d ser., 26 (1969): 521–47.

59. July 12, 1776; October 27, 1777; November 15, 1777. JCC 5:550; 9:841–43, 915–16.

60. Both disputes were resolved by bilateral negotiations; JCC 33:617–29, 466–74. On the expediency of avoiding an Article IX proceeding, see Gov. James Bowdoin's speech to the General Court, June 2, 1786, in James Phinney Baxter, ed., *The Documentary History of the State of Maine* (Portland, 1916), 21:188–98.

CHAPTER 2: FROM COLONY TO TERRITORY

1. Andrew McLaughlin, "The Background of American Federalism," *American Political Science Review* 12 (1918): 215–40; Richard Koebner, *Empire* (Cambridge, Eng., 1961), 105–237.

2. Gordon S. Wood, *The Creation of the American Republic, 1776–1787* (Chapel Hill, 1969), 344–89; Peter S. Onuf, ed., *Maryland and the Empire, 1773* (Baltimore, 1974), 4–12.

3. Jackson Turner Main, *The Sovereign States, 1775–1783* (New York, 1973), 144–85; Wood, *Creation of the American Republic*, 125–389.

4. Jackson Turner Main, *Political Parties Before the Constitution* (Chapel Hill, 1973); Stephen E. Patterson, *Political Parties in Revolutionary Massachusetts* (Madison, 1973), esp. 3–32, on traditional "antipartisan theory."

5. James H. Kettner, *The Development of American Citizenship, 1608–1870* (Chapel Hill, 1978), esp. 173–209.

6. Bertrand de Jouvenel, *Sovereignty* (Chicago, 1959); F. H. Hinsley, *Sovereignty* (London, 1966).

7. John Jay to George Washington, June 27, 1786, in Jared Sparks, ed., *Correspondence of the Revolution: Being Letters of Eminent Men to George Washington*, 4 vols. (Boston, 1853), 4:136.

8. "Crazy Jonathan," *Cumberland Gazette* (successor to *Falmouth Gazette*, Falmouth/Portland, Massachusetts/Maine), September 27, 1787.

9. Thomas Perkins Abernethy, *Western Lands and the American Revolution* (New York, 1937); Frederick Jackson Turner, "Western State-Making in the Revolutionary Era," *American Historical Review* 1 (1895–96): 70–87, 251–69.

10. "Massachusettensis" (Daniel Leonard), "To the Inhabitants of Massachusetts Bay," February 20, 1775, reprinted in Bernard Mason, ed., *The American Colonial Crisis* (New York, 1972), 67. For an excellent general treatment, see Pauline Maier, *From Resistance to Revolution: Colonial Radicals and the Development of American Opposition to Britain, 1765–1776* (1972; paperback ed., New York, 1974). On British anticipations of the colonies' independence, see J. M. Bumsted, "'Things in the Womb of Time': Ideas of American Independence, 1633 to 1763," *William and Mary Quarterly*, 3d ser., 31 (1974): 533–64.

11. Thomas Fitch, *Reasons Why the British Colonies in America, Should Not Be Charged with Internal Taxes* (New Haven, 1764), 18.

12. British writers emphasized the distinctness of the colonies more than Americans did. See, e.g., Sir William Blackstone's assertion that the colonies "were no part of the mother country, but distinct, though dependent dominions," in *Commentaries on the Laws of England*, 4 vols. (Oxford, 1765–69), 2:112. For a

fuller discussion of this point, see Peter Onuf, "Toward Federalism: Virginia, Congress, and the Western Lands," *William and Mary Quarterly*, 3d ser., 34 (1977): 353–74, at 359–60.

13. The quotation is from Adams, "Novanglus," March 6, 1775, in *American Colonial Crisis*, 207. Wilson, *Considerations on the Nature and Extent of the Legislative Authority of the British Parliament* (Philadelphia, 1774), 34n, located Britain's superintending authority in the royal prerogative to conduct foreign policy.

14. Malachy Postlethwayt, *The Universal Dictionary of Trade and Commerce, Translated from the French of the Celebrated Monsieur Savary*, 2 vols. (London, 1766), 1:lviii, proposed a "commercial union" between Britain and the colonies. It may not "improperly be considered as a NEW TREATY OF COMMERCE BETWEEN GREAT BRITAIN AND HER AMERICAN COLONIES AND PLANTATIONS." Thomas Pownall, *The Administration of the Colonies* (1764; London, 1766), 91, suggested putting the colonies "on a true and constitutional basis." The point is also discussed at 15, 201–2, and appendix, 17.

15. H. Trevor Colbourn, *The Lamp of Experience: Whig History and the Intellectual Origins of the American Revolution* (Chapel Hill, 1965). See also J. G. A. Pocock, *The Ancient Constitution and the Feudal Law* (Cambridge, Eng., 1957); and for a good introduction to the significance of such thought in early modern revolutions, see J. H. Elliott, "Revolution and Continuity in Early Modern Europe," *Past and Present* 42 (1969): 35.

16. Adams, in *American Colonial Crisis*, 207.

17. Thomas Jefferson, *A Summary View of the Rights of British America* (Williamsburg, 1774), 8.

18. Bernard Bailyn, *Ideological Origins of the American Revolution* (Cambridge, Mass., 1967), 55–93 and passim.

19. Jefferson to Edmund Randolph, August 18, 1799, in Andrew A. Lipscomb and Albert E. Bergh, eds., *The Writings of Thomas Jefferson*, 20 vols. (Washington, D.C., 1903), 10:127–28.

20. D. P. O'Connell, *The Law of State Succession* (Cambridge, Eng., 1956); Ian Brownlie, *Principles of Public International Law* (Oxford, 1966). For the Supreme Court's subscription to the doctrine, see *U.S. v. Perchmen*, 7 Peters 61 (1834). State succession doctrine has been moving away from the American model in recent decades; O'Connell, *Law of State Succession*, 78–101.

21. Pendleton to Joseph Jones, February 10, 1781, in David John Mays, ed., *The Letters and Papers of Edmund Pendleton, 1734–1803*, 2 vols. (Charlottesville, 1967), 2:328–38, at 334.

22. Petition of Laurel Hill Inhabitants to Congress, read January 27, 1783, Papers of the Continental Congress (hereafter PCC) (National Archives, Washington, D.C.), 48:251. See also Observations of Barbé-Marbois on the Western Boundary of the United States, October 6–16, 1780, in William T. Hutchinson et al., eds., *The Papers of James Madison*, 13 vols. to date (Chicago and Charlottesville, 1962–), 2:115: "The charters of the Colonies [interfere with each other,] most of them having disputes not only with neigh[bours, but with those] at a distance." Madison suggested that Daniel of St. Thomas Jenifer of Maryland may have contributed to the drafting of the Observations. For another attack on charter claims, see Roger Sherman, *Remarks on a Pamphlet Entitled A Dissertation on the Political Union . . .* (New Haven, 1784), 16–17 and passim. Sherman believed that Congress succeeded to "the prerogatives of the Crown of Great Britain" over territorial questions (p. 18).

23. As reported in Joseph Chew to Jared Ingersoll, August 10, 1763, in Julian P. Boyd and Robert Taylor, eds., *The Susquehannah Company Papers*, 11 vols., Wilkes-Barre and Ithaca, 1930–71), 2:265. Franklinite separatists mocked North Carolina's charter claims: "Why do you not insist *positively*, on the full extent of your original charter . . . for you know the state of North Carolina was not represented at the Treaty of Versailles." Justificative Memorial of the State of Frankland, answering Governor Martin's Manifesto, June 13, 1785, *American Herald* (Boston), January 2 and 9, 1786.

24. "The contested territory" between New York and Massachusetts "would add greatly to the weight and importance of this state," Elbridge Gerry told the Massachusetts House and Senate; the "lands retained would be a valuable fund for sinking . . . a very considerable part, of our public debt"; speech of October 25, 1784, in James T. Austin, *The Life of Elbridge Gerry*, 2 vols. (Boston, 1828), 1:461. Conversely, "if Massachusetts should unfortunately prove successful," according to a New York writer, "little more would belong to this State than a barren name"; article dated New York, November 17, 1784, *Virginia Gazette* (Hayes), December 4, 1784.

25. Laurel Hill petition, cited in note 22, above. According to a letter from the Association of Southwestern Virginia separatists, accompanying a petition to Congress (June 1785), PCC 48:287, "individuals are not created for the pleasure of government, but government [is] instituted for the happiness of men." If Americans had the right to emigrate, they also had the right to "introduce alterations . . . as they think will increase their happiness . . . where they live."

26. The insufficient number of "gentlemen of learning, especially in republican knowledge," was cited by "A Friend to the Massachusetts," *Falmouth Gazette*, September 17, 1785. On the prohibitively high expenses of a new government for Maine, see the proceedings of North Yarmouth town meeting, January 2, 1786, in ibid., March 9, 1786. Gov. Richard Caswell of North Carolina argued that the Franklinites "are not yet of strength and opulence sufficient to support an independent state"; Caswell to Gov. John Sevier of Franklin, February 23, 1787, in William L. Saunders, Walter Clark, and Stephen B. Weeks, eds., *Colonial and State Records of North Carolina*, 26 vols. (Raleigh, Winston, Goldsboro, and Charlotte, 1886–1914), 20:617–19. "Inhabitant," an opponent of Kentucky separation, thought that "nothing but madness could induce us to separate from a powerful state" (*Kentucky Gazette*, September 8, 1787).

27. The people of York were "parties to the Constitution of Massachusetts, and could not, consistently therewith, appoint a delegate, for the express purpose of its destruction"; report of town meeting, *Falmouth Gazette*, December 10, 1785. According to "Cornplanter," an opponent of Kentucky separation from Virginia, "we are a part of the same whole governed by the same laws, in the making of which . . . we have an equal voice" (*Kentucky Gazette*, September 13, 1788).

28. Copy of a letter from a gentleman to his friend in the county of York, *Falmouth Gazette*, February 2, 1786.

29. See Jefferson's discussion of the use of the "Vermont doctrine" in the Virginia Assembly in Jefferson to Edmund Randolph, February 15, 1783, in Julian P. Boyd, ed., *The Papers of Thomas Jefferson*, 20 vols. to date (Princeton, 1950–   ), 6:247–48.

30. Because the western part of Massachusetts was "but a step from anarchy," the eastern counties should not "add to the confusion" by pressing for Maine separation; Falmouth town meeting, *Cumberland Gazette*, August 31, 1786.

31. Richard Buel, Jr., "Democracy and the American Revolution: A Frame of Reference," *William and Mary Quarterly*, 3d ser., 21 (1964): 165–90; J. R. Pole, *Political Representation in England and the Origins of the American Republic* (New York, 1966; paperback ed., Berkeley, Calif., 1971).

32. "A Lad," *Falmouth Gazette*, March 30, 1786. "D.A.," writing in *Cumberland Gazette*, May 25, charged that "Lad's" logic denied "the sovereignty of the people." The leading men of Boston invoked "the *sacred* compact which holds us in one society" in their plea for order during the turmoil of Shays's Rebellion; Address to the Towns, September 11, 1786, ibid., September 28, 1786. For further discussion of this point, see Ronald M. Peters, *The Massachusetts Constitution of 1780: A Social Compact* (Amherst, 1978), 65–114.

33. Dane to Samuel Phillips, January 20, 1786, Nathan Dane Miscellaneous Manuscripts (Library of Congress, Washington, D.C.).

34. "Senex," *Cumberland Gazette*, November 24, 1786. The assertion was vigorously contested by "Scribble-Scrabble" (George Thatcher), ibid., December 8, 1786.

35. See, e.g., the "Abstract of Yeas and Nays for [a New] State," submitted by Maine separatists, March 15, 1788, in James Phinney Baxter, ed., *The Documentary History of the State of Maine* (Portland, 1916), 21:459–60; 22:14–15.

36. Neither Congress nor the states could claim constitutional priority; their claims were interdependent. Jack N. Rakove, *The Beginnings of National Politics: An Interpretive History of the Continental Congress* (New York, 1979), 49, 77–79, 81–82.

37. September 24, 1779, Worthington C. Ford, ed., *The Journals of the Continental Congress* (hereafter JCC), 34 vols. (Washington, D.C., 1904–37), 15:1096.

38. "Tullius," *Three Letters Addressed to the Public* (Philadelphia, 1783), 7. See also Noah Webster, *Examination into the Constitution* (Philadelphia, 1787), reprinted in Paul Leicester Ford, ed., *Pamphlets on the Constitution of the United States* (Brooklyn, 1888), 46; and Pelatiah Webster, *The Weakness of Brutus Exposed* (Philadelphia, 1787), in ibid., 127.

39. *American Herald* (Boston), June 19, 1786, reprinted from *Independent Gazeteer* (Philadelphia), June 3, 1786.

40. Item dated Boston, July 19, 1786, *State Gazette of South Carolina*, August 24, 1786.

41. Gov. John Sevier of Franklin did not expect Gov. Patrick Henry of Virginia "to correspond with us until our Government is Recognized by Congress"; letter of July 19, 1785, in William R. Palmer, ed., *Calendar of Virginia State Papers*, 11 vols. (Richmond, 1875–93), 4:42–43. See the various petitions to Congress collected in PCC 48.

42. See, e.g., James Duane to Robert R. Livingston, August 11, 1780, in Edmund Cody Burnett, ed., *Letters of the Members of the Continental Congress* (hereafter LMCC), 8 vols. (Washington, D.C., 1921–36), 5:321: "The Doctrine that our jurisdiction over Vermont is to be sacrifised for the publick Tranquillity is pretty fully established."

43. Thomas Donaldson, *The Public Domain: Its History with Statistics . . .* (Washington, D.C., 1884), 82, 86–88; Merrill Jensen, "The Cession of the Old Northwest," *Mississippi Valley Historical Review* 23 (1936): 27–48; and Jensen, "The Creation of the National Domain, 1781–84," ibid., 26 (1939): 323–42.

44. Franklin Assembly to Gov. Alexander Martin of North Carolina, March

22, 1785, reprinted in Samuel Cole Williams, *History of the Lost State of Franklin* (New York, 1933), 63–65. The "right of conquest" was the source of a collective United States title in the West, according to the Rhode Island delegates, in a letter to Gov. William Greene, October 13, 1782, *LMCC* 6:503. On the Crown lands see, e.g., "Lucius Quintus Cincinnatus," *The Mote Point of Finance, or the Crown Lands, Equally Divided* (broadside, Philadelphia, September 21, 1779), and a petition from residents of Kentucky (1780), PCC 48:245.

45. Campbell to Gov. Richard Caswell, November 30, 1786, reprinted in Williams, *Lost State of Franklin*, 115.

46. Copy of a letter, May 21, 1785. A correspondent from New Hampshire (*Cumberland Gazette*, May 25, 1786) suggested that boundaries should be established according to "nature"; that is, Maine should be annexed to New Hampshire and New Hampshire should cede "a line or two of townships on the southern border" to Massachusetts.

47. Lafayette to Washington, February 5, 1783, in *Correspondence of the Revolution*, 3:548.

48. Extracts from an Address to the Western Inhabitants, enclosed in Charles Cummings to President of Congress, April 7, 1785, PCC 48:289.

49. "Scribble-Scrabble," *Cumberland Gazette*, April 27, 1786. "Scribble-Scrabble" (Thatcher) elaborated on this theme in ibid., June 8, 1786: large land grants in Europe "have produced lords and barons, with their opposites, slaves and dependents." "A Sketch" (ibid., August 10, 1786) anticipated that a new state would make small land grants and pass an "agrarian law," "according to the genuine spirit of republicanism."

50. Ethan Allen, *An Animadversary Address to the Inhabitants of the State of Vermont* (Hartford, 1778), 16.

51. Town of Chesterfield instructions to Michael Creasy, December 12, 1776, in *State Papers of New Hampshire*, vol. 10 (Concord, 1877), 239–40.

52. Caleb Wallace to James Madison, July 12, 1785, in *Madison Papers*, 8:320–23.

53. Justificative Memorial of the State of Frankland, *American Herald* (Boston), January 2 and 9, 1786; extract of a letter from Virginia, dated Washington, June 1, 1785, *Pennsylvania Packet*, October 3, 1785.

54. Herbert J. Storing, *What the Anti-Federalists Were For*, vol. 1 of *The Complete Anti-Federalist*, 7 vols. (Chicago, 1981), 15–23; Cecelia Kenyon, "Men of Little Faith: The Anti-Federalists on the Nature of Representative Government," reprinted in Jack P. Greene, ed., *The Reinterpretation of the American Revolution, 1763–1789* (New York, 1968), 527–66, esp. 529–30.

55. *Freeman's Journal* (Philadelphia), June 15, 1785. A "Farmer" writing in *Falmouth Gazette*, March 5, 1785, suggested that the government of Massachusetts was "too extensive to be look'd well to in every part by one body." This was an "unanswerable reason" for a separation, according to "Impartialis Secundus," ibid., June 11, 1785.

56. *Pennsylvania Herald*, June 11, 1785.

57. Extracts of the Journals of the Convention, August 8, 1785, in Temple Bodley, ed., *Littel's Political Transactions in and Concerning Kentucky*, Filson Club Publications, no. 31 (Louisville, 1926), 66–70.

58. Franklin Assembly to Governor Martin, March 22, 1785, reprinted in Williams, *Lost State of Franklin*, 65.

59. Copy of a letter from a gentleman to his friend in the county of York,

Falmouth Gazette, February 2, 1786; Judge David Campbell to Gov. Richard Caswell, November 30, 1786, reprinted in Williams, *Lost State of Franklin*, 116.

60. Instructions to Maryland delegates, December 15, 1778, laid before Congress May 21, 1779, JCC 14:619–22, quote at 621. "They affect to fear our power, and they are certainly envious of the wealth they suppose may flow from this source," Richard Henry Lee wrote Patrick Henry, November 15, 1778 (in James Curtis Ballagh, ed., *The Letters of Richard Henry Lee*, 2 vols. [New York, 1911], 1:452–53).

61. "Outline and Preamble of Argument on Virginia's Claim" (1782), possibly by Jefferson, *Jefferson Papers*, 6:665. See also Joseph Jones to Jefferson, June 30, 1780, ibid., 3:473: "Virginia . . . certainly is already full large for vigorous Government."

62. Jay to Gov. George Clinton, October 7, 1779, in Hugh Hastings, ed., *The Public Papers of George Clinton, First Governor of New York*, 10 vols. (New York, 1899–1914), 5:311–15.

63. The thought was inspired by Maryland's arguments, in a letter to Horatio Gates, June 1, 1779, LMCC 4:243–44. But Lovell's response to the New York–Vermont impasse was significantly different: "I hope our State will never let Congress be a Tribunal to decide Bounds and Right of Soil"; Lovell to Samuel Adams, September 29, 1779, LMCC 4:458.

64. *Freeman's Journal* (Philadelphia), June 15, 1785.

65. Hugh Williamson to Governor Martin, November 18, 1782, LMCC 6:545.

66. Dane to Phillips, January 20, 1786, Dane Manuscripts.

67. Report of the committee, convention of towns in Cheshire County, November 15, 1780, in *New Hampshire State Papers*, 10:381–83. "Jonathan of the Valley" argued against Maine separatism for the same reason; *Falmouth Gazette*, November 12, 1785: "Should they now be countenanced in their movements, such attempts would become so frequent, as totally to annihilate all the force and vigour of the United States."

68. Extract of a letter from a gentleman in York to his friend in Biddeford, December 5, 1785, *Falmouth Gazette*, December 31, 1785. Such divisions would be attended with "fatal consequences"; report from Machias, November 21, 1786, *American Herald* (Boston), January 1, 1787. Governor Martin of North Carolina warned against the dangerous "precedent" set by the Franklin separation "for every district, and even every county of the state, to claim the right of separation" (Martin's Manifesto, April 25, 1785, reprinted in Williams, *Lost State of Franklin*, 70).

69. Jefferson to Richard Henry Lee, July 12, 1785, in *Jefferson Papers*, 8:287. According to a Jamaican correspondent, "if the original union of the Americans should continue to be thus divided and subdivided into petty dominations . . . they will be shortly ripe for that punishment they so justly merit" (dated July 25, 1785, *Falmouth Gazette*, September 10, 1785).

70. Jones to James Madison, October 2, 1780, in *Madison Papers*, 2:105–6.

71. See Rufus King to Elbridge Gerry, June 4, 1786, LMCC 8:380–82; James Monroe to Patrick Henry, August 12, 1786, in William Wirt Henry, *Patrick Henry: Life, Correspondence, and Speeches*, 3 vols. (New York, 1891), 2:296–97.

72. See the discussion and citations in Robert F. Berkhofer, Jr., "The Northwest Ordinance and the Principle of Territorial Evolution," in John Porter Bloom, ed., *The American Territorial System* (Athens, Ohio, 1973), 45–55, at 50–51.

73. Letter from Suffolk, Virginia, dated June 1, 1785, *London Chronicle*, August 6, 1785, reprinted in Williams, *Lost State of Franklin*, 87–88. However, "it is policy on the side of England to recede from any overture," according to a writer in *The Times* (London), January 31, 1785.

74. Carrington to Gov. Edmund Randolph, December 8, 1786, in *Virginia State Papers*, 4:195–99. Henry Lee thought the Shaysites meant to set up "a new government" and perhaps seek a "re-connexion with G[reat] B[ritain]" (Lee to James Madison, October 19, 1786, in *Madison Papers*, 9:143–45). See also Henry Knox to Samuel Parsons, November 19, 1786, Knox Papers (microfilm ed., Massachusetts Historical Society, Boston), XIX; and William Grayson to Madison, November 22, 1786, in *Madison Papers*, 9:173–75.

75. Documents relating to the Haldimand negotiations can be found in *Collections of the Vermont Historical Society*, 2 vols. (Montpelier, 1870–71), vol. 2. In general, see Charles R. Ritcheson, *Aftermath of Revolution: British Policy Toward the United States, 1783–1795* (Dallas, 1969; paperback ed., New York, 1971), 147–63.

76. "Loyolus," dated December 19, 1785, *Falmouth Gazette*, December 24, 1785.

77. *A Declaration of Rights, Also, the Constitution . . . Agreed to . . . by the . . . Freemen of the State of Frankland . . . 14th of November, 1785* (Philadelphia, 1786), 7–9.

78. Memorial to Congress, read January 13, 1785, reprinted in Williams, *Lost State of Franklin*, 47.

79. Letter from Association of Southwestern Virginians, accompanying a petition to Congress (June 1785), PCC 48:287.

80. For Ira Allen's complaint to this effect, see his "Information," May 11, 1781, *Vermont Collections*, 2:122. "A majority of the Inhabitants" of Franklin "disapproved the scheme of assuming power without first applying to Congress," according to Arthur Campbell, in a letter to Henry, June 15, 1785, in *Virginia State Papers*, 4:37–38.

81. Laurel Hill petition, read January 27, 1783, PCC 48:251.

82. Thomas Young, *To the People of the Grants*, Philadelphia, April 11, 1777.

83. Committee report of second Franklin convention, Jonesborough, December 14, 1784, reprinted in Williams, *Lost State of Franklin*, 40. See also report of August 1785 session of Franklin Assembly, *Freeman's Journal* (Philadelphia), January 4, 1786, calling for a constitutional convention; and Franklin Memorial to Congress, presented May 16, 1785, reprinted in Williams, *Lost State of Franklin*, 82–83, which alludes to the "friendly disposition of Congress" to "new states."

84. Extract of a letter from a gentleman in Frankland to his friend in Virginia, August 17, 1785, *The Times* (London), December 31, 1785. Jefferson's inspiration was also cited by Arthur Campbell in a letter to Patrick Henry, July 26, 1785, in *Life of Henry*, 3:308–10.

85. Address to the Western Inhabitants, enclosed in Charles Cummings to the President of Congress, April 7, 1785, PCC 48:289. Maine separatists like "Impartialis Secundus" (*Falmouth Gazette*, July 9, 1785) believed that Congress would "think our number sufficient to intitle us to a seperation, with power of sending Delegates to act in Congress," because of their "declared Sentiments concerning the ten new states."

86. Jefferson to Madison, April 25, 1784, in *Madison Papers*, 8:23.

87. Jefferson to Washington, March 15, 1784, in *Jefferson Papers*, 7:25–26, suggesting a further cession by Virginia. Madison to Jefferson, March 16, 1784 (in

Madison Papers, 8:9), argued that a settled area could only be "separated" from the state and incorporated into the union by the agreement of all parties. Jefferson to Madison, April 25, 1784 (in ibid., 23–24), clarified his position.

88. Governor Sevier to Governor Caswell, May 14, 1785, reprinted in Williams, *Lost State of Franklin*, 73–76; Sevier to Caswell, October 28, 1786, reprinted in J. G. M. Ramsey, *The Annals of Tennessee to the End of the Eighteenth Century* (Kingsport, Tenn., 1926), 348–49.

89. Extract of a letter from Virginia, dated Washington, June 1, 1785, *Pennsylvania Packet*, October 3, 1785. See also William Cocke to Benjamin Franklin, June 15, 1786, reprinted in Williams, *Lost State of Franklin*, 104. According to "Impartialis Secundus," a Maine separatist writing in *Falmouth Gazette*, June 11, 1785, "we must remember it is to Congress, the Supreme Council of the nation, that we are to apply to constitute us a distinct State."

90. For complaints about the failure of state governments to maintain law and order, see Franklin Assembly to Governor Martin, March 22, 1785, reprinted in Williams, *Lost State of Franklin*, 63–65. Sentiment for separatism in Kentucky was directly related to Virginia's ability to administer justice and offer defense against the Indians; Walker Daniel to Gov. Benjamin Harrison, May 21, 1784, in *Virginia State Papers*, 3:584–88.

91. Frankland Justificative Memorial, *American Herald* (Boston), January 2 and 9, 1786.

92. Charles Cummings to President of Congress, on behalf of residents of Washington County, Va., April 7, 1785, PCC 48:297.

93. Petition to Virginia Assembly, n.d., *Freeman's Journal* (Philadelphia), January 12, 1785.

94. Vermonters claimed that a charter had been issued to Philip Skene to establish a new colony; Hiland Hall, *The History of Vermont, from Its Discovery to Its Admission into the Union in 1791* (Albany, 1868), 195–96. A similar plan was supposed to have been in contemplation for Maine, according to a "Farmer," *Falmouth Gazette*, July 23, 1785. Maine separatists also made much of the Gorges patent to part of their district; the charter was reprinted in full in the *Falmouth Gazette*, July 30 and August 6 and 13, 1785.

95. Frankland Justificative Memorial (cited in n. 91, above) argued for the "authority of the English Government" to alter "old, inconsistent charters." The U.S. Congress succeeded to that jurisdiction.

96. The motion of October 7, 1785, was referred to the states; Virginia delegates to Governor Henry, November 7, LMCC 8:250; JCC 29:810–12. At the same time, a motion to draft an article to allow for the admission of new states was defeated. Even the small states were reported to "acknowledge . . . the propriety" of the antiseparatist resolution. The text of the resolution is in PCC 36: iv, 53–55.

97. Vermont was the "only innovation on the system of Apr. 23, 1784, which ought ever possibly to be admitted," according to a letter to Richard Henry Lee, July 12, 1785, in *Jefferson Papers*, 8:287. Following this logic, a writer from Franklin thought the Kentucky separation convention was "a dangerous expedient" because it "contravene[d] the act of Congress of April 23, 1784; especially in aiming at unreasonable territory"; letter dated September 2, 1785, *Freeman's Journal* (Philadelphia), January 4, 1786.

98. Kentucky's admission was delayed for many years despite Virginia's sponsorship. "An opinion begins to prevail that a State has no right to dismember itself with[ou]t the previous consent of the U[nited] S[tates]," William Grayson reported

to Madison, August 21, 1785; *Madison Papers*, 8:348–49. Attempts to gain the admission of Vermont or Kentucky aroused constitutional scruples as well as sectional suspicions. See Samuel A. Otis to Theodore Sedgwick, June 6 and 22, 1788, Sedgwick Manuscripts (Massachusetts Historical Society, Boston), A148 and A154; and John Brown to George Muter, July 10, 1788, in *Littel's Political Transactions*, xxxiii: "The jealousy of the growing importance of the western country, and an unwillingness to add a vote to the southern interest, are the real causes of opposition."

99. For a recent general treatment, see Joseph L. Davis, *Sectionalism in American Politics 1774–1787* (Madison, 1977). "Impartialis," writing in *Falmouth Gazette*, May 14, 1785, believed that Massachusetts would consent to Maine's separation but that "Congress . . . will not readily consent to double the influence of Massachusetts." The same point was made by Dane in a letter to Phillips, January 20, 1786, Dane Manuscripts.

100. JCC 26:274–79. See editorial notes and resolution drafts, March 1 and 22, and April 23, 1784, in *Jefferson Papers*, 6:581–617. I am indebted to Robert F. Berkhofer, Jr., "Jefferson, the Ordinance of 1784, and the Origins of the American Territorial System," *William and Mary Quarterly*, 3d ser. 29 (1972): 231–62.

101. Francis Philbrick, *The Laws of the Illinois Territory, 1809–1818* (Illinois State Historical Society *Collections* 25, Springfield, 1950), introduction; Arthur Bestor, "Constitutionalism and the Settlement of the West: The Attainment of Consensus, 1754–1784," in Bloom, *The American Territorial System*, 13–44.

102. See various petitions, PCC 30:453, 459, 463–64; 48:215.

103. Timothy Pickering to Elbridge Gerry, March 1, 1785, in Charles H. King, ed., *The Life and Correspondence of Rufus King*, 6 vols. (New York, 1894–1900), 1:72–73.

104. October 15, 1783, JCC 25:693–94.

105. Jefferson thought that the small size of the new states was crucial for the "happiness" of the westerners; in large states "we treat them as subjects, we govern them, and not they themselves" (Jefferson to James Monroe, July 9, 1786, in *Jefferson Papers*, 10:112–13).

106. Monroe thought the number of new states would have to be reduced and their boundaries enlarged if there were to be new states at all; Monroe to Jefferson, January 19, 1786, in *Jefferson Papers*, 9:189–90. "It would accord with my judgement if natural boundaries had been more attended to," Arthur Campbell wrote Arthur Lee, October 18, 1784 (in Paul Hoffman, ed., *The Lee Family Papers* [microfilm ed., Charlottesville, 1966], reel 7, 411).

107. Richard Henry Lee to George Washington, July 15, 1787, *LMCC* 8:620; see also Dane to Rufus King, July 16, *LMCC* 8:621–22.

108. Monroe to Jefferson, May 11, 1786, in *Jefferson Papers*, 9:511.

109. For the text of the ordinance, see Clarence E. Carter and John Porter Bloom, eds., *The Territorial Papers of the United States*, vol. 2 (Washington, D.C., 1934), 39–50, or JCC 32:334–43. See also Jack Ericson Eblen, *The First and Second United States Empires: Governors and Territorial Government, 1784–1912* (Pittsburgh, 1968), 17–51. James Monroe was beginning to think of western territories as "colonies" as early as April 20, 1786, in a letter to John Jay, *LMCC* 8:342.

110. William Grayson to Lt. Gov. Beverley Randolph, June 12, 1787, *LMCC* 8:609–10.

111. E.g., copy of a letter from a gentleman at the Falls of the Ohio, *Cumber-*

land Gazette, July 19, 1787: "Some states [are] too large, others more ridiculously small."

112. James D. Richardson, *A Compilation of the Messages and Papers of the Presidents, 1789–1902,* 12 vols. (Washington, D.C., 1903–9), 1:30–31.

113. It is revealing that Virginian William Grayson treated charter claims with such contempt after Virginia's cession had been accepted. See his attack on Connecticut's cession offer, recorded in Thomas Rodney Diary, May 4, 1786, *LMCC* 8:353–54: "The Crown did no more with respect to the Quebeck bill than they did in grant of N[ew] Y[ork] and Pensylvania, by Taking away, what had been granted before. Therefore the Canada Bill having fixt the right in the Crown belongs to the United States by Conquest etc."

114. This point is developed in Peter S. Onuf, "Territories and Statehood," in Jack P. Greene, ed., *Encyclopedia of American Political History* (forthcoming).

CHAPTER 3: STATE AND CITIZEN

1. See William Blathwayt's Draft of the Charter of Pennsylvania [February 24, 1681] and the editorial material in Richard S. Dunn and Mary Maples Dunn et al., *The Papers of William Penn,* 2 vols. to date (Philadelphia, 1981–   ), 2:61–77. The charter passed the great seal on March 4, 1681. See also the discussion in Charles M. Andrews, *The Settlements,* vol. 3 of *The Colonial Period of American History,* 4 vols. (New Haven, 1934–38), 278–82, 292–96.

2. *Penn v. Lord Baltimore* (1745–50), in James Brown Scott, ed., *Judicial Settlement of Controversies Between States in the American Union,* 2 vols. (New York, 1918), 1:585–600.

3. In a letter to the president of Congress, March 24, 1780, Minutes of the Supreme Executive Council, *Pennsylvania Colonial Records,* 16 vols. (Philadelphia and Harrisburg, 1852–53), 12:290–92.

4. On the controversy with Virginia, see Boyd Crumrine, "The Boundary Controversy Between Pennsylvania and Virginia, 1748–1785," in Carnegie Institution, *Annals of the Carnegie Museum,* vol. 1 (Pittsburgh, 1901); Robert Foster, "The Pennsylvania and Virginia Controversy," in *Pennsylvania Archives,* 3d ser., 3 (Harrisburg, 1894): 485–504; and Thomas Perkins Abernethy, *Western Lands and the American Revolution* (New York, 1937), 227, 254, 269–70. The Wyoming controversy can be followed through the documents collected in Julian P. Boyd and Robert J. Taylor, eds., *The Susquehannah Company Papers,* 11 vols. (Wilkes-Barre and Ithaca, 1930–71). See also Oscar Jewell Harvey and Ernest Gray Smith, *A History of Wilkes-Barre,* 6 vols. (Wilkes-Barre, 1909–30); James E. Brady, "Wyoming: A Study of John Franklin and the Connecticut Movement into Pennsylvania" (Ph.D. diss., Syracuse University, 1973); and Oscar Zeichner, *Connecticut's Years of Controversy, 1750–1776* (Chapel Hill, 1949), passim.

5. Proponents of the Connecticut claims frequently discussed ways of consolidating the colony's pretensions. See, e.g., Pelatiah Webster to Silas Deane, April 2, 1774, in *Susquehannah Papers,* 6:160, arguing against "sending a party on discovery to [the] Mississippi"—it was first necessary to make "a fast lodgement on the Delaware and Susquehannah."

6. So characterized in Gov. John Penn's proclamation of October 12, 1774, in Neville B. Craig, *The Olden Time* (Cincinnati, 1876), 1:507–8.

7. Zeichner, *Connecticut's Years*, 30–35, 103–10, 143–58; Resolution to Support Western Claim, October 16 and 21, 1773, and Act Erecting the Town of Westmoreland, January 1774, in *Susquehannah Papers*, 5:175–77, 177–79, 268–69. For a defense of Connecticut's claims, see Gov. Jonathan Trumbull to Governor Penn, March 24, 1774, Shippen Papers, Force Transcripts (microfilm ed., Library of Congress, Washington, D.C.), reel 72; Benjamin Trumbull, "To the Public," *Connecticut Courant*, April 1, 5, 12, 19, 26, 1774, in *Susquehannah Papers*, 6:68–114; and Answers of the Colony of Connecticut Regarding Her Boundaries, October 1774, ibid., 6:290–91.

8. Governor Dunmore's Proclamation, September 17, 1774, in Craig, *Olden Time*, 1:506. For a defense of Pennsylvania's claims, see Governor Penn to Dunmore, March 31, 1774, *Pa. Archives*, 4th ser., 12 vols. (Harrisburg, 1900–1902), 3:464–71.

9. See the discussion in Lawrence Henry Gipson, *American Loyalist: Jared Ingersoll* (New Haven, 1920; paperback ed., New York, 1971), 317n. The lands were purchased from the Six Nations, though occupied by Delawares.

10. Webster to Silas Deane, April 2, 1774, in *Susquehannah Papers*, 6:161. As William Smith suggested in *An Examination of the Connecticut Claim* (Philadelphia, 1774), *Susquehannah Papers*, 6:1–59, at 25, the Massachusetts claims "were once as exorbitant" as Connecticut's.

11. Penn to [Henry Wilmot], April 2, 1774, in *Susquehannah Papers* 6:158.

12. Report from Philadelphia, dated January 23, 1782, *Connecticut Courant*, February 5, 1782, in *Susquehannah Papers*, 7:98–99.

13. Governor Penn to Governor Trumbull, February 24, 1774, in *Pa. Archives*, 4th ser., 3:459–60; Trumbull to Penn, March 24, 1774, Shippen Papers; Penn to Trumbull, April 11, 1774, in *Susquehannah Papers*, 6:193–94.

14. Penn to [Wilmot], April 2, 1774, in *Susquehannah Papers* 6:158; Penn's petition to the King, April 9, 1774, in ibid., 6:188–93. The Pennsylvania Assembly continued to rely on a decision by Privy Council as late as September 30, 1775, even while simultaneously appealing to Congress "to quiet the minds of the good people of this Province" (ibid., 6:360). Worthington C. Ford, ed., *Journals of the Continental Congress* (hereafter JCC), 34 vols. (Washington, D.C., 1904–37), 3:283.

15. Webster to Deane, April 2, 1774, in *Susquehannah Papers*, 6:161; "B. Schemer," *Connecticut Courant*, March 25, 1774, in *Susquehannah Papers*, 6:64–68.

16. James Tilghman and Andrew Allen to Dunmore, May 23, 1774, and Dunmore to Tilghman and Allen, May 24, 1774, in Craig, *Olden Time*, 1:485–88.

17. In Council, March 24, 1780, in *Pa. Colonial Records*, 12:289–90.

18. Smith to Johnson, April 9, 1774, in *Susquehannah Papers*, 6:187. Anti-Susquehannah interests in Connecticut also predicted that "bloody Tragedies may Ensue," if the colony did not withdraw its claim (Petition and Remonstrance of the Middletown Convention, March 30, 1774, ibid., 6:149). The Pennsylvania Assembly intimated in resolves of October 27, 1775, that it might resort to coercive measures if congressional intervention failed (ibid., 6:382–83).

19. Governor Penn to Lady Juliana Penn, April 5, 1774, in ibid., 6:171–72; and see Memorial of William Smith et al. to Assembly, October 25, 1775, in ibid., 6:376–81.

20. "The Pennsylvania Examiner," April 23, 1774, *Pennsylvania Gazette*, April 27, 1774, in *Susquehannah Papers*, 6:119.

21. Penn to William Crawford et al., April 22, 1774, in *Pa. Archives*, 4th ser., 3:473–74.

22. Subscription of Pennsylvania Claimants to Lands on the West Branch, October 9, 1775, in *Susquehannah Papers*, 6:366; Deane to Thomas Mumford, October 16, in Paul H. Smith, ed., *Letters of the Delegates to Congress*, 9 vols. to date (Washington, D.C., 1976–   ), 2:188–91; Connecticut Delegates' Memorial to Congress, [December 12(?), 1775], in ibid., 2:476–77. See also Brady, "Wyoming," 78–85.

23. William Smith, "Examination of the Connecticut Claim," in *Susquehannah Papers*, 6:57.

24. William Smith to Governor Trumbull, October 10, 1774, in *Letters of the Delegates*, 1:170.

25. When compensation for proprietary lands was being discussed, the Radicals contended that "the proprietor and his successors were . . . the people's trustees," but the argument was rejected. Robert L. Brunhouse, *The Counter-Revolution in Pennsylvania, 1776–1790* (Harrisburg, 1942), 79. For a statement of the trusteeship argument, with respect to Crown lands, see Thomas Jefferson, *A Summary View of the Rights of British America* (Williamsburg, 1774), 21.

26. As Oliver Wolcott wrote John Laurens, December 27, 1780 (in *Susquehannah Papers*, 6:76–77), "the same Act of the Crown which constituted the once Colony of Connecticut with the Powers of Government vested the Colony with the Fee of the Land which the State now Claims." The anti-Susquehannah forces in Connecticut argued that the colony's western claims jeopardized the colony's self-government under the charter (Zeichner, *Connecticut's Years*, 152–54).

27. James H. Hutson, *Pennsylvania Politics, 1746–1770: The Movement for Royal Government and Its Consequences* (Princeton, 1972); Richard Alan Ryerson, *The Revolution Is Now Begun: The Radical Committees of Philadelphia, 1765–1776* (Philadelphia, 1978).

28. It was a favorite conceit of Connecticut propagandists that Pennsylvania's claims were supported only by Tory land speculators. "The Governor of Pennsylvania is a Tory . . . and would do all that lies in his power to break the union of the Provinces," [?] to Zebulon Butler, December 10, 1775, in *Susquehannah Papers*, 6:406. On the political persuasions of the Pennsylvania claimants, who appear to have been equally divided between Patriots and Loyalists, see the sources cited in note 22, above.

29. See the discussion of Dunmore's motives in Thomas Smith to Arthur St. Clair, September 5, 1775, in William Henry Smith, ed., *The St. Clair Papers*, 2 vols. (Cincinnati, 1882), 1:360. Also see the discussion in Chapter 1, above.

30. September 10 and 23, November 24, 1779, in *Minutes of the Third General Assembly of the Commonwealth of Pennsylvania* (Philadelphia, 1778), 124, 133–34, 167–70. The bill, which passed by a vote of 40 to 7, may be found in *The Acts of the General Assembly of the Commonwealth of Pennsylvania* (Philadelphia, 1782), chap. 129, November 27, 1779, 258–63. See also the petition of the Pennsylvania Council to Congress, July 20, 1781, in *Susquehannah Papers*, 7:88: "By an act of Assembly passed the twenty-seventh day of November, 1779, the right and title to all and singular the premises, is now become duly vested in the Commonwealth"; and the Pennsylvania Agents' brief at the Trenton Trial, December 9, 1782, ibid., 7:181. Proponents of the Connecticut claim exploited the weakness of Pennsylvania's position; according to "The Claims of Connecticut to Lands West of the Delaware" (*Connecticut Courant*, January 4–February 15, 1785, in *Susquehannah*

Papers, 8:165–90, at 176), "the fact is, the Assembly has usurped the rights of the proprietaries, and their *strength* and *violence* constitute the *sole legality* of their title."

31. Smith, "Examination of the Connecticut Claim," in *Susquehannah Papers* 7:57; Penn to Trumbull, February 24, 1774, in *Pa. Archives*, 4th ser., 3:459–60.

32. *Connecticut Journal*, April 8, 1774, in *Susquehannah Papers*, 6:179–83, at 182. On the Connecticut people's attachment to fee-simple landownership, see William Samuel Johnson to Richard Jackson, May 30, 1772, cited in Zeichner, *Connecticut's Years*, 144: "None but the most worthless of Mankind will stay below and labour upon the Lands of others."

33. Dyer to William Judd, July 23, 1775, in *Letters of the Delegates*, 1:655.

34. Memorial of October 25, signed by William Smith et al., in *Susquehannah Papers*, 6:376–81, at 378.

35. Edward Countryman, "'Out of the Bounds of the Law': Northern Land Rioters in the Eighteenth Century," in Alfred Young, ed., *The American Revolution* (DeKalb, Ill., 1976), 37–69. For a suggestive discussion of popular fears of landlordism see Richard Bushman, "Massachusetts Farmers and the Revolution," in Richard Jellison, ed., *Society, Freedom, and Conscience: The Coming of the Revolution in Virginia, Massachusetts, and New York* (New York, 1976), 77–124. See also Rowland Berthoff and John M. Murrin, "Feudalism, Communalism, and the Yeoman Freeholder: The American Revolution as a Social Accident," in Stephen G. Kurtz and James H. Hutson, eds., *Essays on the American Revolution* (Chapel Hill, 1973), 256–88, particularly 266–68, on proprietary claims in Pennsylvania.

36. Deane to Henry, January 2, 1775, in *Susquehannah Papers*, 6:303.

37. Dyer to Judd, July 23, 1775, in *Letters of the Delegates*, 1:654. See also Jared Ingersoll to Jonathan Ingersoll, March 12, 1774, in *Jared Ingersoll Papers, New Haven Colony Historical Society Papers*, vol. 9 (New Haven, 1918), 446; New Englanders were seen as a "Set of Goths & Vandals who may one day overrun these Southern Colonies."

38. "B. Schemer," *Connecticut Journal*, March 25, 1774, in *Susquehannah Papers*, 6:66.

39. William Maclay to Joseph Shippen, Jr., September 22, 1775, in *Susquehannah Papers*, 6:352–53.

40. John Ormsby to Joseph Shippen, March 11, 1774, Shippen Papers, reel 72.

41. Governor Dunmore to Governor Penn, March 3, 1774, in Craig, *Olden Time*, 1:452–53; Penn to Dunmore, March 31, 1774, in *Pa. Archives*, 4th ser., 3:464–71.

42. Aeneas Mackay to Governor Penn, April 4, 1774, in Craig, *Olden Time*, 1:476–78.

43. Address to Residents of Pittsburgh area, enclosed in Arthur St. Clair to Governor Penn, February 2, 1774, in ibid., 1:473–75.

44. For the proprietors' concern with boundaries, see Governor Penn to [Wilmot], May 1, 1774, in *Susquehannah Papers*, 6:233–35; and William Baker and Lady Juliana Penn to Tilghman, April 5, 1775, in ibid., 6:309–10.

45. Colden to Penn, August 22, 1774, in ibid., 6:278–79. See also Colden to Penn, September 24, 1774, in ibid., 6:283–84.

46. Tilghman and Allen to Governor Dunmore, May 23, 1774; Dunmore to Tilghman and Allen, May 24, 1774, in Craig, *Olden Time*, 1:485–88; Deane to Mumford, October [16?], 1775, in *Letters of the Delegates*, 2:188–91; Connecticut Delegates' Proposed Resolution, [October 17(?), 1775], in ibid., 2:196; Reso-

lution of the Pennsylvania Assembly, October 27, 1775, in *Susquehannah Papers*, 6:382–84.

47. Trumbull to the Connecticut Delegates, October 9, 1775, in *Susquehannah Papers* 6: 368–69.

48. Virginia delegates at Congress to the Speaker of the Pennsylvania Convention, July 15, 1776, in Julian P. Boyd, ed., *The Papers of Thomas Jefferson*, 20 vols. to date (Princeton, 1950–   ), 1:466.

49. Trumbull to John Hancock, November 11, 1775, in *Susquehannah Papers*, 6:387–88.

50. Deane to Zebulon Butler, July 24, 1775, in *Letters of the Delegates*, 1:660–61; July 31 and August 1, JCC 2:235, 238. See also Connecticut Delegates to Zebulon Butler et al., August 2, in *Letters of the Delegates*, 1:693. The Wyoming people adopted Articles of Association on September 21, 1775 (in *Susquehannah Papers*, 6:350–52), pledging to support "our Country" (that is, America) and not to disturb Pennsylvania settlers.

51. Butler to Ellis Hughes, Northumberland County magistrate, August 21, 1775, in *Susquehannah Papers*, 6:345–46.

52. Proceedings of Commissioners to Settle the Pennsylvania–Virginia Boundary, August 27–31, 1779, in *Jefferson Papers*, 3:77; George Bryan to Pres. Joseph Reed, August 31, 1779, in William B. Reed, *The Life and Correspondence of Joseph Reed*, 2 vols. (Philadelphia, 1847), 2:133–35. Pennsylvanians had hoped to extend their jurisdiction behind Maryland to 39°, interpreting the charter to include the entire 40th degree. The Mason-Dixon line, drawn at 39°30′, compromised a similar claim against Maryland. Bryan felt that a "compromise" with Virginia on this basis would preclude "further discussion with Maryland."

53. June 23, 1780, *Journal of the House of Delegates*, 1780 session (Williamsburg, 1780), 60–61; September 23, 1780, in *Pa. Archives*, 1st ser., 12 vols. (Philadelphia, 1852–56), 8:570–71.

54. Petition of Pennsylvania Council to Congress, July 20, 1781, in *Susquehannah Papers*, 7:87–88; November 3, 1781, JCC 21:1092.

55. *Connecticut Courant*, February 5, 1782, in *Susquehannah Papers*, 7:98–99.

56. See the excellent discussion in Robert J. Taylor, "Trial at Trenton," *William and Mary Quarterly*, 3d ser., 26 (1969): 521–47. Documents of the proceedings are collected in *Susquehannah Papers*, 7:144–246.

57. Council Minutes, January 24, 1783, in *Susquehannah Papers*, 7:257–58; John Dickinson to Assembly, January 23, 1783, in *Pa. Archives*, 4th ser., 3:876–77. For other comments on the decision, see Robert R. Livingston to Lafayette, January 10, in *Susquehannah Papers*, 7:252; *Freeman's Journal*, January 22, 1783, cited in Taylor, "Trial at Trenton," 546; and *Virginia Gazette*, January 25, 1783.

58. Baker and Lady Juliana Penn to Tilghman, April 5, 1775, in *Susquehannah Papers*, 6:309–10.

59. Captain William Strawder to President Dickinson, March 29, 1783, *Pa. Archives*, 1st ser., 10:23.

60. Timothy Pickering to John Pickering, November 11, 1787, in Harvey, *History of Wilkes-Barre*, 3:1618.

61. Reed to Assembly, February 5, 1779, in *Pa. Archives*, 4th ser., 3:714.

62. Gen. Edward Hand to Jasper Yeates, August 25, 1777, in Reuben Thwaites and Louise Kellogg, eds., *Frontier Defense on the Upper Ohio, 1777–1778* (Madison, 1912), 48–49; Lachlan McIntosh to the Magistrates of Westmoreland

County, October 21, 1778, in Louise Kellogg, ed., *Frontier Advance on the Upper Ohio, 1778–1779* (Madison, 1916), 147–48; McIntosh to Bryan, December 29, 1778, ibid., 188–90.

63. Reed to Thomas Scott, December 29, 1779, in *Pa. Archives*, 1st ser., 8:63–64.

64. Reed to William Amberson, August 5, 1780, in ibid., 1st ser., 8:487–88.

65. Irvine to Washington, December 2, 1781, in Jared Sparks, ed., *Correspondence of the Revolution: Being Letters of Eminent Men to George Washington*, 4 vols. (Boston, 1853), 3:452–60, at 459.

66. Jefferson to Brodhead, October 12, 1780, in *Pa. Archives*, 1st ser., 8:641–42.

67. Excerpt of a letter from Pittsburgh, July 18, 1783, in *Pa. Archives*, 1st ser., 10:72; B. Johnston to Gov. Benjamin Harrison, August 4, 1783, in William R. Palmer, ed., *Calendar of Virginia State Papers*, 11 vols. (Richmond, 1875–93), 3:520–21; Memorial of John Campbell to Virginia Executive, December 1784, in ibid., 3:631.

68. September 6 and October 10, 1780, JCC 17:806–8; 18:915–16; Scott to President Reed, January 24, 1781, in *Pa. Archives*, 1st ser., 8:713–16.

69. An Act to Prevent the Erecting Any New and Independent State Within the Limits of This Commonwealth, *Laws Enacted in the Third Sitting of the Sixth General Assembly* (Philadelphia, 1782), 121–23; James Madison to Edmund Randolph, December 3, 1782, in William T. Hutchinson et al., eds., *The Papers of James Madison*, 13 vols. to date (Chicago and Charlottesville, 1962–   ), 5:358. See the discussion in Abernethy, *Western Lands*, 269–70.

70. June 23, 1780, *Journal of the House of Delegates*, 1780 sess., 60–61.

71. Eliphalet Dyer to Governor Trumbull, November 8, 1782, *Collections of the Massachusetts Historical Society*, 7th ser., 3 (1902):398.

72. See, e.g., petition of Zebulon Butler et al. to Congress, May 1, 1784, in *Pa. Archives*, 1st ser., 10:613–17; and memorial of John Franklin et al. to Connecticut General Assembly, October 20, 1784, in *ibid.*, 1st ser., 10:681–83. On successful efforts to neutralize Connecticut's patronage of the Susquehannah claimants, see documents and notes in *Jefferson Papers*, 6:501–7, and Pennsylvania Delegates to Pres. Benjamin Franklin, May 7, 1786, in Edmund Cody Burnett, ed., *Letters of the Members of the Continental Congress*, 8 vols. (Washington, D.C., 1921–36), 8:357.

73. Petition of the Inhabitants on the West Side of the Laurel Hill, read January 27, 1783, in Papers of the Continental Congress (hereafter PCC) (National Archives, Washington, D.C.) 48:251; Madison's notes on debates, January 27, 1783, in *Madison Papers*, 6:133–34; Madison to Randolph, January 28, 1783, in ibid., 6:156.

74. Samuel Wharton to William Trent, November 15, 1782, cited in Abernethy, *Western Lands*, 269; Wharton to George Read, November 17, 1782, in William Thompson Read, *Life and Correspondence of George Read* (Philadelphia, 1870), 373–74: many legislators "are of opinion that this State would be large enough if it was confined to the Allegheny Mountain. . . ."

75. Scholars have differed widely on the seriousness of new state proposals. Robert J. Taylor, in his introduction to vol. 8 of *Susquehannah Papers*, discounts new state agitation; but, for another view, see Julian P. Boyd, "Attempts to Form New States in New York and Pennsylvania, 1786–89," *New York State Historical*

Association Quarterly Journal 12 (1931):257–70; and Brady, "Wyoming," 212–13.

76. Brady, "Wyoming," 223–33; Harvey, *History of Wilkes-Barre*, 3:1579–97, 1650–59. The Confirming Act was suspended in 1788 and repealed in 1790, and rights recognized under the act were overturned by the U.S. Supreme Court (*Van Horne's Lessee v. Dorrance*, 2 Dallas 304 [1795]). Nonetheless, the Connecticut settlers were never driven from their lands; subsequent legislation offered compensation to Pennsylvania titleholders.

77. Instructions to Finley, February 6, 1783, in *Pa. Archives*, 1st ser., 10:163–65; Finley to (?), March 18, 1783, in ibid., 1st ser., 10:41–44.

78. Finley to President Dickinson, April 28, 1783, in ibid., 1st ser., 10:40–41.

79. Petition of the Inhabitants West of Laurel Hill, PCC 48:251.

80. Griswold to Dickinson, December 20, 1784, in *Susquehannah Papers*, 8:162.

81. Petition of John Jenkins et al. to Pennsylvania Assembly, February 20, 1785, in ibid., 8:210–15, at 212.

82. Brunhouse, *Counter-Revolution*, 16–17 and passim.

83. Queries enclosed in Randolph to Harrison, April 22, 1782, in *Virginia State Papers*, 3:133–36, at 135.

84. Brunhouse, *Counter-Revolution*, 112–14. A "temporary line" was ratified by the Assembly on March 24, 1783, and proclaimed by President Dickinson on March 26, 1783, in *Pa. Archives*, 4th ser., 3:884–85, resolving any ambiguity about the extent of the state's jurisdiction. The line was formally completed in 1785.

85. Pa. Assembly Committee to Zebulon Butler et al., May 6, 1783, in Harvey, *History of Wilkes-Barre*, 3:1469.

86. David Jackson to Bryan, July 18, 1785, in *Susquehannah Papers*, 8:431.

87. Protest of various assemblymen against a Northumberland election, November 1783, in ibid., 7:316–17. The protest applauded the "precedent" of recognizing the citizenship of former Virginians in the West. On residence and citizenship in general, see James H. Kettner, *The Development of American Citizenship, 1607–1870* (Chapel Hill, N.C., 1978), 182–84 and passim.

88. Washington to Brodhead, March 22, 1779, in John C. Fitzpatrick, ed., *The Writings of George Washington*, 39 vols. (Washington, D.C., 1931–44), 14:281.

89. Hand to Col. David Shepherd, June 3, 1777, in Thwaites and Kellogg, eds., *Frontier Defense*, 1–3.

90. McIntosh to the Westmoreland magistrates, October 21, 1778, in Kellogg, ed., *Frontier Advance*, 147–48.

91. Petition of Nathan Denison et al. to Pennsylvania Assembly, January 18, 1783, in *Susquehannah Papers*, 7:256.

92. Smith to Zebulon Butler, July 28, 1786, in ibid., 8:376–77.

93. Petition of Pittsburgh inhabitants, [April 1781?], in Louise Kellogg, ed., *Frontier Retreat on the Upper Ohio, 1779–1781* (Madison, 1917), 360–63.

94. Minutes of the meeting held at Kingston, July 20, 1786, in *Susquehannah Papers*, 8:372.

95. *An Address from the Inhabitants of Wyoming* (broadside, September 12, 1786), in *Susquehannah Papers*, 8:401.

96. In Council, March 24, 1780, *Colonial Records*, 12:289–90. For a contemporaneous expression of this sentiment by the Wyoming settlers, reminding the Connecticut government of its duty to them, see the petition of Jenkins et al. to

the Connecticut Assembly, April 25, 1780, in *Susquehannah Papers*, 7:59–62: "your Petitioners in fact conceive they have a Right to Protection from this State, or that they cannot be bound to pay any obedience."

97. Petition of Jenkins et al. to Pennsylvania Assembly, February 20, 1785, in *Susquehannah Papers*, 8:213–14.

98. David Mead to Pennsylvania Council, February 6, 1785; deposition of Constable Thomas Parks, February 5, 1785, enclosed in above, in Harvey, *History of Wilkes-Barre*, 3:1464.

99. Excerpt of a letter from Pittsburgh, July 18, 1783, in *Pa. Archives*, 1st ser., 10:72.

100. Judd to Butler, June 1, 1786, in *Susquehannah Papers*, 8:356–57.

101. Petition and Remonstrance of Connecticut Settlers to Pennsylvania Assembly, November 18, 1783, in ibid., 7:328.

102. Report of meeting held November 15, reported in *Pennsylvania Packet*, March 21, 1786. Brady, "Wyoming," 216, calls this meeting a "definite move toward independence."

103. Petition to Pennsylvania Assembly, February 21, 1786, in Harvey, *History of Wilkes-Barre*, 3:1492–93. The petition asked that "*this settlement . . . be set off as a distinct county.*"

104. Judd to Butler, January 11, 1787, in *Susquehannah Papers*, 9:5–6. But see the counterargument by Timothy Pickering, in a letter to Simon Spaulding et al., January 10, in ibid., 9:3: "If their residence and their oaths do not, in their apprehension, bind them to submit unconditionally to the laws, surely the bare giving in of their votes . . . will not do it." For a list of oath-takers, see *Susquehannah Papers*, 9:13–17, including 140 signatures, January 13–February 1, 1787.

105. Jefferson to Samuel Huntington, president of Congress, February 9, 1780, in *Jefferson Papers*, 3:289. For another view of what Virginia meant to accomplish, see Scott to President Reed, November 29, 1779, in ibid., 3:207–8, and Reed to the Pennsylvania Delegates, *Pa. Archives*, 1st ser., 8:46–47. "We have seen the State of Virginia in progressive Encroachments advancing upon the old allowed Territory of this State"; it was now "seduc[ing] our Inhabitants" by the "low Price of Lands in their Office." In response to this letter, Congress resolved, December 27, 1779, (JCC 15:1411) to ask both states "not to grant any part of the disputed lands." See also President Reed's Proclamation, December 28, 1779, *Pa. Archives*, 4th ser., 3:747–50, publishing this resolution.

106. Mason to Joseph Jones, July 27, 1780, in Robert A. Rutland, ed., *The Papers of George Mason*, 3 vols. (Chapel Hill, 1970), 2:656–59.

107. Jenkins to Pennsylvania Commissioners, April 23, 1783, in *Pa. Archives*, 1st ser., 10:33–34.

108. Minutes of meeting held in Wyoming, July 20, 1786, in *Susquehannah Papers*, 8:372.

109. Petition to Assembly (drafted by Timothy Pickering), February 5, 1787, in Harvey, *History of Wilkes-Barre*, 3:1557.

110. The Susquehannah Company, at its meeting of July 13, 1785, offered half-shares in the company to settlers who would emigrate to Wyoming; these settlers could not hope to have their claims recognized by Pennsylvania. According to William Montgomery (in a letter to the Pennsylvania Council, May 20, 1786, in *Susquehannah Papers*, 8:336), "their encroachments, like the feudal system of old, will furnish the reward of their adherents and followers." See the discussion in Brady, "Wyoming," 212–13.

111. Smith to Timothy Pickering, February 21, 1787, in *Susquehannah Papers*, 9:67.

112. Franklin to Sheriff Lord Butler, April 11, 1787, in Harvey, *History of Wilkes-Barre*, 3:1562; Franklin to [Samuel Huntington], April 14, 1787, in *Susquehannah Papers*, 9:101.

113. Petition of Inhabitants West of Laurel Hill, PCC 48:251.

114. Christopher Hays to President Dickinson, May 12, 1784, in *Pa. Archives*, 1st ser., 10:264–65.

115. Resolutions, Remonstrance, and Circular Letter from the Town of Easton, May 21, 1787, in *Susquehannah Papers*, 9:136. The Resolutions were condemned as "seditious" by the Pennsylvania Council, which directed that the attorney general commence prosecutions against the perpetrators (Council Minutes, June 13, 1787, ibid., 9:144–45).

116. Scott to President Reed, January 24, 1781, in *Pa. Archives*, 1st ser., 8:713–15.

117. "It was suggested that a Second Vermont might Save the Dear Country," Judd wrote Zebulon Butler, February 1, 1782 (in *Susquehannah Papers*, 7:97–98). According to a deposition by Preserved Cooley, received at Congress, January 14, 1785 (in ibid., 8:197), "they meant to hold it as New Vermont."

118. Allen to Butler et al., October 27, 1785, in ibid., 8:270–71.

119. Anonymous to Allen, August 4, 1785, in ibid., 8:254–55.

120. An Appeal to the Susquehannah Company, February 1, 1786, *Connecticut Courant*, March 6, 1786, in *Susquehannah Papers*, 8:286–89; meeting at Kingston, November 15, 1786, in Harvey, *History of Wilkes-Barre*, 3:1489–90. If Wyoming were to become a new state, it would be only because of outside initiatives. Brady suggests ("Wyoming," 314), "These people were uncomfortable without the sanction of some superior authority."

121. Pickering to John Swift, October 4, 1787, in Harvey, *History of Wilkes-Barre*, 3:1588–89.

122. Smith to Jonathan Corey and James Lasley, May 4, 1787, in *Pa. Archives*, 1st ser., 11:104; Smith, "A Serious Address to the Inhabitants of Wyoming," May 4, 1787, in Harvey, *History of Wilkes-Barre*, 3:1500.

123. William Hooker Smith, Samuel Hover, and Abraham Westbrook to William Montgomery, May 14, 1786, in *Susquehannah Papers*, 8:326–27.

124. Report from Philadelphia, August 29, 1787, *Connecticut Courant*, September 10, 1787, in *Susquehannah Papers*, 9:188.

125. Judd to Butler, January 11, 1787, in ibid., 9:5–6.

126. Samuel Richards, Jr., to Eliphalet Richards, September 25, 1787, in ibid., 9:206–7: "Vermont rose in such a storm too strong to fear an attack."

127. Hosmer to John Paul Schott, February 2, 1787, in ibid., 9:21–22.

128. Timothy Pickering to George Clymer, November 1, 1787, in ibid., 9:256.

129. Rush to Timothy Pickering, August 30, 1787, in L. H. Butterfield, ed., *Letters of Benjamin Rush*, 2 vols. (Princeton, 1951), 1:439–40.

130. May 24 and 25, 1786, JCC 30:299–304, 307–11. The deed may be found in Clarence E. Carter and John Porter Bloom, eds., *The Territorial Papers of the United States*, vol. 2 (Washington, D.C., 1934), 22–24. The cession did not include the Western Reserve, an area extending 120 miles west of Pennsylvania. See also James Monroe to Richard Henry Lee, May 24, 1786, in *Letters of the Members*, 8:365–66; William Grayson to Washington, and to Madison,

May 27 and 28, 1786, in ibid., 8:371–72, 372–73; and Charles Pettit to Jeremiah Wadsworth, May 27, 1786, in *Susquehannah Papers*, 8:349–51. Pettit stated, "It is understood that the State of Connecticut will on her part give no farther Countenance to the Claims of the State or of her Companies within Penns[ylvani]a." It was erroneously reported that Congress had made a cession to the Susquehannah Company (*Pennsylvania Packet*, June 21, 1786; *New York Daily Advertiser*, June 23).

131. Petition of John Franklin to Connecticut Assembly, May 10, 1787, seeking intervention on behalf of the Wyoming settlers, in *Susquehannah Papers*, 9:131.

132. For the use of the word "empire" to describe the United States, see Matthew Griswold to John Dickinson, December 20, 1784, in ibid., 8:162.

133. Letter from an Officer of Distinction, October 12, 1785, *Carlisle Gazette* (Carlisle, Pa.), December 7, 1785. For similar sentiments, see Governor Harrison to President Dickinson, June 12, 1783, in *Pa. Archives*, 1st ser., 10:56–57; settlement of the boundary was "not among the most inconsiderable of the Blessings of Peace."

CHAPTER 4: VIRGINIA AND THE WEST

1. The best general account is Thomas Perkins Abernethy, *Western Lands and the American Revolution* (New York, 1937). On the Indian boundaries, see Louis De Vorsey, Jr., *The Indian Boundary in the Southern Colonies, 1763–1775* (Chapel Hill, 1961); and John Richard Alden, *John Stuart and the Southern Colonial Frontier: A Study of Indian Relations, War, Trade, and Land Problems in the Southern Wilderness, 1754–1775* (Ann Arbor, 1944). Literature on the land companies includes Shaw Livermore, *Early American Land Companies: Their Influence on Corporate Development* (New York, 1939); George E. Lewis, *The Indiana Company, 1763–1798: A Study in Eighteenth-Century Frontier Land Speculation and Business Venture* (Glendale, Calif., 1941); Max Savelle, *George Morgan: Colony Builder* (New York, 1932), 18–110; K. L. Bailey, *The Ohio Company of Virginia and the Westward Movement, 1748–1792* (Glendale, Calif., 1939); and Lois Mulkearn, ed., *George Mercer Papers Relating to the Ohio Company of Virginia* (Pittsburgh, 1954).

2. The various state claims are outlined in the cession proposals reprinted in Thomas Donaldson, *The Public Domain: Its History with Statistics . . .* (Washington, D.C., 1884), 82, 86–88.

3. Remonstrance of the Virginia General Assembly, December 14, 1779, in William Waller Hening, ed., *The Statutes at Large: Being a Collection of All the Laws of Virginia, from the First Session of the Legislature, in the Year 1619* (Richmond, 1809–23), 10:557–59.

4. *Ordinances Passed at a General Convention of Delegates and Representatives . . .* (Williamsburg, 1776), 5–13. In an earlier draft of the constitution, Thomas Jefferson used even stronger language, calling for "new colonies" which "shall be free and independant of this colony and of all the world" (Julian P. Boyd, ed., *The Papers of Thomas Jefferson*, 20 vols. to date [Princeton, 1950–   ], 1:362–63).

5. Lee to Patrick Henry, November 15, 1778, in James Curtis Ballagh, ed., *The Letters of Richard Henry Lee*, 2 vols. (New York, 1911), 1:452–53.

6. Abernethy, *Western Lands*, passim; Merrill Jensen, "The Cession of the Old Northwest," *Mississippi Valley Historical Review* 23 (1936):27–48; and Jensen, "The Creation of the National Domain, 1781–1784," ibid., 26 (1939): 323–42.

7. Land-company membership lists may be found in the Thomas Jefferson Papers, (Library of Congress, Washington, D.C.), 7:1164 (Vandalia), 1166 (Indiana and Illinois-Wabash). Maryland's key role in opposing the Virginia claims is discussed by Herbert B. Adams, *Maryland's Influence upon Land Cessions to the United States*, Johns Hopkins University Studies in Historical and Political Science, 3d. ser., vol. 1 (Baltimore, 1885), 1–54. The arguments against Virginia are developed in the Maryland assembly's Declaration and delegate Instructions of December 15, 1778, which were laid before Congress on May 21, 1779; in Worthington C. Ford, ed., *Journals of the Continental Congress* (hereafter JCC), 34 vols. (Washington, D.C., 1904–37), 14:619–22. The Declaration is reprinted in *Va. Statutes at Large*, 10:549–52.

8. For background on this competition, see Savelle, *George Morgan*, and the other sources cited in note 1, above. The controversy was still seen in such terms by a Virginia delegate writing to an unnamed correspondent on December 10, 1781, published in *Freeman's Journal* (Philadelphia), January 4, 1786: "The Pennsylvanians will have the chief of the back country, if they succeed in their schemes."

9. For Virginia's increasingly extensive claims in the West, see the governors' reports to the Board of Trade for 1742, Colonial Office 5/1325, 113–19, Public Record Office of Great Britain, (hereafter PRO, CO) for 1743, 1744, and 1747, CO 5/1326, 12–19, 103–10, 234–44; for 1749 and 1750, CO 5/1327, 778–83, 105–12; for 1755, R. A. Brock, ed., *The Official Records of Robert Dinwiddie, Lieutenant Governor of Virginia, 1751–1758*, 2 vols. (Richmond, 1883–84), 1:381; and for 1763, King's Manuscript 205, 255–76, British Library. The Burgesses passed acts in 1752, 1753, and 1754, "encouraging persons to settle on the waters of the Mississippi" (*Va. Statutes at Large*, 6:258, 355–56, 417–20).

10. De Vorsey, *Indian Boundary in Southern Colonies*, 48–92.

11. William Nelson to Hillsborough, October 18, 1770, CO 5/1348, 321–30. The plight of actual settlers had been periodically invoked in Virginian objections to the Proclamation of 1763: Governor Fauquier to Lords of Trade, February 13, 1764, CO 5/1345, 319; Fauquier to Shelburne, November 18, 1766, ibid., 313–14, and May 20, 1767, King's Manuscript 206, 141–57.

12. Thomas Jefferson, *A Summary View of the Rights of British America* (Williamsburg, 1774), 21.

13. Resolution on Land Grants, March 27, 1775, in *Jefferson Papers*, 1:162.

14. "Extracts from the Virginia Charters" (ca. July 1773), in Robert A. Rutland, ed., *The Papers of George Mason*, 3 vols. (Chapel Hill, 1970), 1:163–85.

15. The "Vindication of Virginia's Claim Against the Proposed Colony of Vandalia" is printed in *Jefferson Papers*, 6:656–63. The text is often identical with Mason's "Remarks."

16. *Mason Papers*, 1:163–85. If Indian treaties were invoked in support of Virginia's title, a basis would be established for promoting land-company claims. The Fort Stanwix Treaty of 1768, for instance, apparently supported the colony's claims south of the Ohio, yet the Indiana grant had been transacted at the same treaty. Thus reliance on the treaty would confirm the Indiana Company's claims. See Carter Braxton, "Address to the Convention of Virginia," *Virginia Gazette* (Dixon and Hunter), October 8, 15, 1776. Arthur Lee premised his defense of state claims in part on Indian cessions at Lancaster and Loggs-town in 1744 and 1752. See Lee, "Concise View of the Title of Virginia to the Western Lands in Refutation of the Pamphlet Called Public Good" (ca. 1782), in Paul P. Hoffman, ed., *The Lee Family Papers, 1742–1795* (microfilm ed., Charlottesville, 1966), reel 7, 280. But such a

defense served only to make company pretensions, also based on Indian transactions, all the more plausible. Edmund Randolph thought it "rank suicide *to oppose* the *title of* the *natives* to *the claims* of the *companies*," and such dangerous
doctrines were generally suppressed. Randolph to James Madison, May 10, 1782,
in William T. Hutchinson et al., eds., *The Papers of James Madison*, 11 vols. to date
(Chicago and Charlottesville, 1962–   ), 4:226.

17. Jefferson, *Summary View*, 8. For similar arguments against the Quebec Act,
see Edmund Randolph's brief on territorial claims, August 20, 1782: "Even if it
[that act] had been designed to abridge the boundaries of the colonies, the right of
the British parliament to do so must be denied" (*JCC* 23:510–11).

18. "Vindication," *Jefferson Papers*, 6:656–63, at 660.

19. Pendleton to Joseph Jones, February 10, 1781, in David John Mays, ed.,
The Letters and Papers of Edmund Pendleton, 1734–1803, 2 vols. (Charlottesville,
1967), 1:334.

20. *Ordinances Passed at a Convention*, 5–13.

21. Pendleton to Virginia delegation, July 14, 1776, in *Jefferson Papers*, 1:464.

22. Pendleton to Jefferson, August 3, 1776, in ibid., 484.

23. *Proceedings of the Convention of Delegates . . .* (Richmond, 1816), 63. On
the Transylvania Company, see William S. Lester, *The Transylvania Colony* (Spencer, Ind., 1935), and Julian Boyd's note in *Jefferson Papers*, 1:564–69. George
Morgan protested on behalf of the Indiana Company that the resolutions "laid a
foundation for calling in question . . . the validity of the title" of the company
(petition of March 12, 1777, Draper Manuscripts [Wisconsin Historical Society,
Madison], 1CC [Kentucky Papers], 140–46).

24. Pendleton to Jefferson, August 3, 1776, in *Jefferson Papers*, 1:484.

25. *Jefferson Papers* 2:139–42.

26. The bill was passed by the lower house on June 17, 1779, and by the Senate
on June 22; *Journal of the House of Delegates* (hereafter *JHD*) (May 1779 sess.; rept.
Richmond, 1827), 53, 61, and is printed in *Va. Statutes at Large*, 10:50–65. See
the discussions in Abernethy, *Western Lands*, 228, and Merrill D. Peterson,
Thomas Jefferson and the New Nation (1970; paperback ed., New York, 1975),
120–22.

27. Jefferson to Pendleton, August 13, 1776, in *Jefferson Papers*, 1:492. John
Todd wrote William Preston on June 22, 1776, Draper Manuscript 4QQ (Preston
Papers), 52, that "weak Kentucky . . . is distracted with the clashing interests of
cabinning and surveying." "Reason tells us that the Occupant must prevail."

28. Jefferson to Samuel Huntington, president of Congress, February 9, 1780,
in *Jefferson Papers*, 3:286–89.

29. Edmund Randolph, *History of Virginia*, ed. Arthur H. Shaffer (Charlottesville, 1970), 272–73.

30. On the development of Jefferson's thought on this subject, see Robert F.
Berkhofer, Jr., "Jefferson, the Ordinance of 1784, and the Origins of the American
Territorial System," *William and Mary Quarterly*, 3d. ser., 29 (1972): 231–62.

31. Reply of the Committee of the Transylvania House of Representatives to
the Proprietors, May 25, 1775, reprinted in George W. Ranck, *Boonesborough: Its
Founding, Pioneer Struggles, Indian Experiences, Transylvania Days, and Revolutionary
Annals*, Filson Club Publication, no. 16 (Louisville, 1901), 202–3.

32. James Hogg to Richard Henderson, January 1776, in ibid., 224–29. See
also L. H. Butterfield, ed., *Diary and Autobiography of John Adams*, 4 vols. (Cambridge, Mass., 1961), entry for October 25, 1775, 2:218.

33. Pendleton to Virginia's congressional delegation, July 15, 1776, in *Jefferson Papers*, 1:462–64.

34. *JHD* (October 1776 sess.; rept. Richmond, 1828), 31; *Va. Statutes at Large*, 9:257–58. For petitions from loyal inhabitants of the Kentucky District, dated June 15 and 20, 1776, seeking Virginia's protection, see James Alton James, ed., *George Rogers Clark Papers, 1771–1781*, vol. 3 of Illinois State Historical Society *Collections* (Springfield, 1912), 11–15; October 8, *JHD* 4.

35. According to Jefferson's "Notes on my title to 485 acres of land surveyed for me Mar. 27, 1788," *Jefferson Papers*, 2:138.

36. The original draft is in ibid., 2:155–67. The bill was finally passed by the lower house on June 16, 1779, and agreed to by the senate on June 17, *JHD* (May 1779 sess.; rept. Richmond, 1827), 50–51, 53, and may be found in *Va. Statutes at Large*, 10:35–50.

37. Petition of June 15, 1776, reprinted in Lester, *Transylvania Colony*, 139. Documents on the house's hearings on the Henderson claim are collected in *Jefferson Papers*, 2:64–111. See also Henderson's petition to the house, October 29, 1778, *JHD* (October 1778 sess.; rept. Richmond, 1827), 36. The house resolved to compensate Henderson on November 4, 1778; a special committee recommended 800,000 acres compensation on November 23, 1778. For these and subsequent deliberations, reducing the size of the grant, see *JHD* 42, 79, 91, 100, 105, and *Va. Statutes at Large*, 9:57–72.

38. On the Loyal claim see *JHD* (October 1778 sess.; rept. Richmond, 1827), November 9 and 26, 1778, 53–54, 88. In 1783 the Virginia Court of Appeals upheld confirmation of lands actually granted by the company; Daniel Call, ed., *Reports of Cases Argued and Decided in the Court of Appeals*, 6 vols. (Richmond, 1803–33), 4:21–37.

39. Hearings on the Indiana claim were held at Pittsburgh in February and March 1777; William R. Palmer, ed., *Calendar of Virginia State Papers*, 11 vols. (Richmond, 1875–93), 1:276–82. The company's position was outlined in petitions read before the house in October 1776 and June 1777; Draper Manuscripts 1CC 140–46; *JHD* (May 1777 sess.; Williamsburg, 1777), 74–75. Prominent Virginians who supported the Indiana claim at one time or another included Patrick Henry, Edmund Randolph, James Mercer, and Edmund Pendleton. Samuel Wharton, *Plain Facts: Being an Examination into the Rights of the Indian Nations of America . . .* (Philadelphia, 1781), 102–4; Pendleton's "Opinion Relating to George Croghan's Title," July 19, 1777, *Pendleton Papers*, 1:216–17; Edmund Randolph's speech at the Virginia ratifying Convention in 1788, in Jonathan Elliot, ed., *The Debates in the Several State Conventions on the Adoption of the Federal Constitution*, 5 vols. (Philadelphia, 1876), 3:574.

40. Wharton, *Plain Facts*, 145, gave the final vote against the Indiana claim as 50 to 28. George Morgan claimed in a letter to the Virginia delegates, November 16, 1780, in *Madison Papers*, 2:176–77, that on a vote on whether to offer compensation to the company, "the House of delegates were equally divided, untill the Speaker gave the Casting Vote against them." The Indiana claim was considered in a joint session of the house and senate, June 7, 8, 9, and 18; *JHD* (May 1779 sess.; rept. Richmond, 1827), 38, 39, 40, 56, 57. The house rejected two different compensation resolutions, the first recognizing a "just claim" by the company, the second making no reference to the company's title. It is likely that Wharton's tally refers to the first and Morgan's to the second resolution. For a succinct review of these events see Abernethy, *Western Lands*, 217–19.

41. Petition of March 12, 1777, Draper Manuscripts 1CC 140–46.

42. Wharton, *Plain Facts*, 145.

43. *Va. Statutes at Large*, 10:549–52. Maryland's Instructions were laid before Congress on May 21, 1779; JCC 14:619–22. They were an "indecent performance," according to William Fleming, in a letter to Jefferson, May 22, in *Jefferson Papers*, 2:269.

44. Ratification act dated February 3, 1781, laid before Congress on February 12, 1781, JCC 19:138–40.

45. Lee to Patrick Henry, May 26, 1777, in *Richard Henry Lee Letters*, 1:301.

46. Cornell to Gov. William Greene, June 18, 1780, in William R. Staples, *Rhode Island in the Continental Congress* (Providence, 1870), 294–96. John Armstrong of Pennsylvania wrote George Washington on January 12, 1780, "I cou'd sincerely wish the policy of Virginia respecting their Land-Office and extent of territory were otherwise timed and more disinterested" (Edmund Cody Burnett, ed., *Letters of the Members of the Continental Congress* [hereafter LMCC], 8 vols. [Washington, D.C., 1921–36], 5:9).

47. Timothy Pickering to John Pickering, June 13, 1780, Timothy Pickering Papers (Massachusetts Historical Society, Boston), 5:175–76.

48. Madison minimized land company influence in letters to Joseph Jones, October 17 and November 21, 1780, in *Madison Papers*, 2:136–39, 190–93. Ezekiel Cornell of Rhode Island wrote that "both parties have their advocates" but that Congress "have little to do in the affair"; Cornell to Governor Greene, October 24, 1780, LMCC 5:425–26.

49. In the letter cited in note 47, above.

50. Lee to Henry, November 15, 1778, in *Richard Henry Lee Letters*, 1:452–53.

51. Jones to Washington, October [2?] 1780, LMCC 5:396.

52. "Outline and Preamble of Argument on Virginia's Claim" [1782], in *Jefferson Papers*, 6:665.

53. Mason to Jefferson, September 27, 1781, in ibid., 6:120–21.

54. Patricia Watlington, *The Partisan Spirit: Kentucky Politics, 1779–1792* (New York, 1972), 23–34 and passim.

55. Henry to the Speaker of the Maryland house, March 17, 1778, LMCC 3:133.

56. September 14 and October 29 and 30, 1779, JCC 15:1063–64, 1223–24, 1226–30. Congress ignored Virginia's protest and resolved to ask the state to "reconsider their late act of assembly for opening their land office."

57. *Va. Statutes at Large*, 10:557–59.

58. Morgan to the delegates, November 16, 1780, and Delegates to Morgan, November 20, 1780, in *Madison Papers*, 2:176–77, 188.

59. Mason to Jefferson, September 27, 1781, in *Jefferson Papers*, 6:120–21.

60. According to a letter by a Virginia delegate writing to an unnamed correspondent, December 10, 1781, published in *Freeman's Journal* (Philadelphia), January 4, 1786.

61. Remonstrance dated June 16, 1778, laid before Congress, June 25; JCC 11:650. Similar arguments were developed by other opponents of Virginia's claims, including the Indiana Company in its memorial of September 14, 1779 (ibid., 15:1063–64), and petitioners from the Kentucky District, asking permission to set up a new government across the Ohio, in a memorial laid before Congress August 23, 1780. Papers of the Continental Congress (hereafter PCC)

(National Archives, Washington, D.C.), 48:245; JCC 17:760. See also "Lucius Quintus Cincinnatus," *The Mote Point of Finance, Or the Crown Lands, Equally Divided* (broadside, Philadelphia, September 21, 1779).

62. Thomas Paine, *Public Good: Being an Examination into the Claims of Virginia to Vacant Western Territory . . .* (Philadelphia, December 30, 1780), 10, 18, 24, 27, 28.

63. At least two full-length replies were drafted, though not published, by Virginians. See Arthur Lee's "Concise View," in *Lee Family Microfilms,* reel 7, 280; and Edmund Pendleton to Joseph Jones, February 10, 1781, in *Pendleton Papers,* 1:328–38.

64. September 19, 1778, JCC 12:931–33.

65. Lee to Henry, November 15, 1778, in *Richard Henry Lee Letters,* 1:452–53.

66. According to the Remonstrance of December 14, 1779, *Va. Statutes at Large,* 10:557–59.

67. Mason to Joseph Jones, July 27, 1780, in *Mason Papers,* 2:656.

68. Walker to Jefferson, July 11, 1780, in *Jefferson Papers,* 3:484.

69. *Laws of the State of New York, Commencing with the First Session . . .* (Poughkeepsie, 1782), 3d sess., 2d meeting (February–March 1780), chap. 38, 103–4. See Chapter 5, below, for a fuller discussion.

70. September 6, 1780, JCC 17:806–7.

71. Lee to Samuel Adams, September 10, 1780, in *Richard Henry Lee Letters,* 2:201.

72. Jones to Jefferson, June 30, 1780, in *Jefferson Papers,* 3:473.

73. Jones to Washington, October [2?], 1780, LMCC 5:396.

74. Walker to Jefferson, July 11, 1780, in *Jefferson Papers,* 3:484.

75. Mason to Jones, July 27, 1780, in *Mason Papers,* 2:656.

76. See Jones's letters to Washington, September 6, 1780, LMCC 5:364; to Madison, December 2, 1780, in *Madison Papers,* 2:220; and to Theodorick Bland, January 2, 1781, in Charles Campbell, ed., *The Bland Papers: Being a Selection from the Manuscripts of Colonel Theodorick Bland, Jr.,* 2 vols. (Petersburg, Va., 1840), 2:43–44.

77. September 6, 1780, JCC 17:808.

78. Jones to Madison, October 9, 1780, in *Madison Papers,* 2:119–20.

79. Lee to Samuel Adams, September 10, 1780, in *Richard Henry Lee Letters,* 2:201.

80. Madison to Jones, September 19, 1780, in *Madison Papers,* 2:89–90.

81. JCC 18:915–16.

82. Madison to Jones, November 21, 1780, in *Madison Papers,* 2:191. See also Madison to Jones, October 17, 1780, in ibid., 2:136–39.

83. Mason to Jones, July 27, 1780, in *Mason Papers,* 2:656–62.

84. The 1781 cession act may be found in JCC 25:559–63. See also *JHD* (May 1780 sess.; rept. Richmond, 1828), 80–81.

85. The connection between the Virginia cession and Maryland's ratification was generally assumed. See, e.g., Madison to Jones, December 19, in *Madison Papers,* 2:249. But a more likely cause of Maryland's capitulation was pressure from the French minister, La Luzerne. St. George L. Siousatt, "The Chevalier de la Luzerne and the Ratification of the Articles of Confederation by Maryland, 1780–1781," *Pennsylvania Magazine of History and Biography* 60 (1936):391–418.

86. Virginia delegates to Governor Jefferson, January 30, 1781, in *Madison Pa-*

pers, 2:300. See also Theodorick Bland to Richard Henry Lee, March 5, 1781, LMCC 6:7.

87. According to Madison's notes on congressional debates, April 18, 1783, in *Madison Papers*, 6:471.

88. See Chapter 3, above.

89. According to Madison, in a letter to Edmund Randolph, November 5, 1782, in *Madison Papers*, 5:243.

90. The Connecticut act was received on January 31, 1781 (JCC 19:99), and the Illinois-Wabash memorial was referred to the committee on March 12, 1781 (JCC 19:253). The Indiana memorial was read and committed July 24 (JCC 21:784). The committee's report was delivered to Congress on June 27, 1781, and may be found in PCC 30:561. The suggestion to set western boundaries was adopted from a report by the Ways and Means Committee of May 14, 1781 (JCC 20:502, 704).

91. August 22, 1781, JCC 21:895.

92. The committee consisted of Elias Boudinot of New Jersey, James M. Varnum of Rhode Island, Daniel of St. Thomas Jenifer of Maryland, Thomas Smith of Pennsylvania, and Samuel Livermore of New Hampshire (JCC 21:1032).

93. The protest, submitted to Congress on October 10, 1781, may be found in *Madison Papers*, 3:284–86. For Virginia's futile attempt to block congressional consideration of land-company petitions on October 16, see JCC 21:1057–58.

94. The report may be found in PCC 30:1–13, and in JCC (for May 1, 1782) 22:225–32. For a typical Virginian response to the report, see Arthur Lee's comments, n.d., *Lee Family Microfilms*, reel 7, 601–2: "What can prevail upon Congress to offer such an insult to the Sovereignty and Jurisdiction of one of the States in the Union?"

95. Arthur Lee's motions of April 18 and May 1, 1782, that "each member do declare upon his honour, whether he is, or is not personally interested . . . in the claims of any company," were ruled out of order on May 2 (JCC 22:191–94, 223, 234). Theodorick Bland moved on September 5 that Congress accept all three cessions (by New York, Connecticut, and Virginia) "with the conditions therein named," but was also ruled out of order (JCC 23:550).

96. Randolph to Governor Nelson, November 7, 1781, LMCC 6:259–60. See also delegates to Nelson, October 23, 1781, in *Madison Papers*, 3:293.

97. Madison to Jefferson, November 18, 1781, in *Madison Papers* 3:308.

98. On September 6, 1782, Congress approved John Witherspoon's motion "that in case of a compliance" with the congressional call for unconditional cessions, "no determinations of the particular states relating to private property of lands within those cessions, shall be reversed or altered without their consent," except by an Article IX proceeding between two states (JCC 23:552–53). Madison was optimistic that a compromise could be reached on this basis, according to his letter to Edmund Randolph, September 10, 1782 (in *Madison Papers*, 5:115–16). But Congress resolved to strike the proviso on September 25, 1782 (JCC 23:604–6).

99. Carroll to Daniel of St. Thomas Jenifer, LMCC 6:498.

100. JCC 23:694.

101. Madison to Jefferson, April 16, 1782, in *Madison Papers*, 4:154.

102. Madison to Edmund Randolph, November 5, 1782, in ibid., 5:242.

103. Ezra L'Hommedieu to Gov. George Clinton, November 5, 1782, LMCC 6:531.

104. North Carolina delegates to Gov. Alexander Martin, September 26, 1783, LMCC 7:313.

105. According to Edmund Randolph to Madison, May 9, 1783, in *Madison Papers*, 7:33. See also Mason to Randolph, October 19, 1782, in *Mason Papers*, 2:746–56.

106. *Virginia Gazette* (Hayes), May 30, 1783.

107. Speech by Abraham Clark of New Jersey, August 27, 1782, Charles Thomson's notes on congressional debates, LMCC 6:458.

108. Jefferson to Madison, June 17, 1783, in *Jefferson Papers*, 6:277.

109. Harrison to the delegates, July 4, 1783, in *Madison Papers*, 7:208.

110. The problem was discussed in a letter from the Western Commissioners to Harrison, March 9, 1783 (in *George Rogers Clark Papers*, 2 [1926]: 216).

111. Harrison to the Delegates, September 26, 1783, in *Madison Papers*, 7:358; Delegates to Harrison, November 1, in ibid., 7:392.

112. The memorial was laid before the assembly on May 21, 1783 (*JHD* [May 1783 sess.; Richmond, 1783], 23). It was referred to the Committee on Propositions and Grievances, which reported it "reasonable" on June 13 (ibid., 91), but was then committed to the Committee of the Whole House, which agreed on June 27 to delay consideration until the cession question was resolved (ibid., 171).

113. Jones to Madison, June 8, 1783, in *Madison Papers*, 7:119–20.

114. For a fuller discussion, see Peter S. Onuf, "Sovereignty and Territory: Claims Conflict in the Old Northwest and the Origins of the American Federal Republic" (Ph.D. diss., Johns Hopkins University, 1973), 355–68, and Chapter 7, below.

115. Madison's notes on debates, April 18, 1783, in *Madison Papers*, 6:471; April 23, 1783, JCC 24:271–72; delegates to Governor Harrison, April 29, 1783, in *Madison Papers*, 6:502.

116. James Wilson of Pennsylvania and Daniel Carroll of Maryland were dropped; Gunning Bedford of Delaware and John Rutledge of South Carolina remained from the original committee; Nathaniel Gorham of Massachusetts, Oliver Ellsworth of Connecticut, and Madison were added (JCC 24:381).

117. Daniel Carroll moved that a "committee be appointed to report the territory lying without the boundaries of the several states" and on the establishment of new states, but was supported by only Maryland and New Jersey (JCC 25:554–59). The June 1783 report and vote and the September 13, 1783, vote are in JCC 25:559–64. The adopted report omitted an explicit invalidation of Indian purchases, but upheld Virginia's policy by a broader interpretation of the "common benefit" condition in the cession. This was clearly understood to be a capitulation to Virginia's demands.

118. Jones to Madison, October 30, 1783, in *Madison Papers*, 7:388.

119. Madison to Jefferson, December 10, 1783, in ibid., 7:401.

120. George Nicholas for the Committee of the Whole House reported favorably on the new terms on December 8, 1783 (*JHD* [October 1783 sess.; Williamsburg, 1783], 97). A week later, Jones presented the cession act for a first reading. Amendments were read and agreed to on December 18, 1783; the lower house passed the act the next day and the Senate concurred on December 20, 1783 (ibid., 115, 119, 123, 129, 130, 131, 148). Jones told Jefferson in a letter of December 29, 1783 (in *Jefferson Papers*, 6:428) that the success of the cession in the Senate was "contrary to my expectation." The form of the cession—which, following New York's precedent, was a deed of conveyance—aroused some misgivings

in the house, "as the Congress not being a corporate Body could not take a title by conveyance." Jones dismissed these objections, "conceiving as I do the cession to be a conventional act between sovereign and independent States and not to be scanned by the rules of municipal law."

121. Howell to Jonathan Arnold, February 21, 1784, *LMCC* 7:451.

122. JCC 26:110–11.

123. JCC 26:116–17.

124. Jefferson to Harrison, March 3, 1784, in *Jefferson Papers*, 7:4.

125. JCC 26:117.

126. Higginson to Theophilus Parsons, Jr., April [7?], 1783, *LMCC* 7:123.

127. Madison's notes on debates, April 9, 1783, in *Madison Papers*, 6:442–43.

128. New York delegates to Governor Clinton, September 19, 1783, *LMCC* 7:300–301.

CHAPTER 5: AN UNBOUNDED STATE

1. Virginia's western land cession of January 2, 1781, was adopted on the same day the British began their invasion of the state (*Journal of the House of Delegates* [October 1780 sess., 1828 ed.], 80; Thomas Perkins Abernethy, *Western Lands and the American Revolution* [New York, 1939], 244–45). See also the discussion in Chapter 4, above. The willingness of the southern states to recognize Vermont was attributed to the British invasion (Ezra L'Hommedieu to Gov. George Clinton, September 8, 1781, in Edmund Cody Burnett, ed., *Letters of the Members of the Continental Congress* [hereafter LMCC], 8 vols., [Washington, D.C., 1921–36], 6:212).

2. For the background of this dispute, see Matt Bushnell Jones, *Vermont in the Making, 1750–1777* (Cambridge, Mass., 1939); and Irving Mark, *Agrarian Conflicts in Colonial New York, 1711–1775* (New York, 1940).

3. E. Wilder Spaulding, *His Excellency George Clinton, Critic of the Constitution* (New York, 1938), 142–50; Edward Countryman, *A People in Revolution: The American Revolution and Political Society in New York, 1760–1790* (Baltimore, 1981), 154–59, 175–77, 211 (on Clinton's role); Edward P. Alexander, *A Revolutionary Conservative: James Duane of New York* (New York, 1938), 68–92 and passim.

4. Scott to James Duane, February 2, 1780, James Duane Papers (New-York Historical Society, New York).

5. Scott to Clinton, September 26, 1780, in Hugh Hastings, ed., *The Public Papers of George Clinton, First Governor of New York*, 10 vols. (New York, 1899–1914), 6:254–56.

6. New York Delegates to Governor Clinton, September 21, 1782, *LMCC* 6:489–90.

7. Philip Schuyler warned that Congress intended to negotiate a land cession from the Iroquois (Schuyler to the Lieutenant Governor and Speaker of the House, January 29, 1780, *LMCC* 5:21; Abernethy, *Western Lands*, 243). Robert R. Livingston claimed credit for suggesting the cession. Livingston to Gouverneur Morris, January 18, 1781, Letters to Livingston [Bancroft Collection, New York Public Library]). See Livingston to Clinton, November 30, 1779, *LMCC*, 4:530, suggesting a cession. Livingston's role is discussed in George Dangerfield, *Chancellor Robert R. Livingston of New York, 1746–1813* (New York, 1960), 118–19.

8. Jay to Clinton, October 7, 1779, in *Clinton Papers*, 5:311–15. Jay later added that it would "be proper for New York to establish Posts in that Country, and in every respect treat it as . . . [our] own" (Jay to Clinton, October 25, 1779, in Richard B. Morris, ed., *John Jay: The Making of a Revolutionary, Unpublished Papers 1745–1780* [New York, 1975], 659–60).

9. *Laws of the State of New York, Commencing with the First Session . . .* (Poughkeepsie, 1782), 3d sess., 2d meeting (February–March 1780), chap. 38, 103–4. February 8, 12, 14, 1780, *Votes and Proceedings of the House* (hereafter *House Journal*) (1779–80), 98, 106, 107; February 6, 7, 8, 9, 14, *Votes and Proceedings of the Senate* (hereafter *Senate Journal*) (1779–80), 64, 66, 67, 76–77.

10. The cession deed was laid before Congress on March 7, but was not executed until March 1, 1781 (Worthington C. Ford, ed., *Journals of the Continental Congress* [hereafter JCC], 34 vols. [Washington, D.C., 1904–37], 19:208–13). The deed may also be found in Papers of the Continental Congress (hereafter PCC) (National Archives, Washington, D.C.), 67:250. The Declaration is reprinted in Thomas C. Donaldson, *The Public Domain: Its History with Statistics . . .* (Washington, D.C., 1884), 66.

11. Burke to the Committee of Correspondence of the New York Assembly, August 2, 1774, *The Letters and Papers of Cadwallader Colden*, 9 vols. (New York, 1917–37), 7:232–39.

12. Board of Trade to Duke of Bedford, January 10, 1751, Colonial Office 5/1344, 96–99, Public Record Office of Great Britain; John Huske, *The Present State of North-America* (London, 1755), 17. For a discussion of this point and further citations, see Peter S. Onuf, "Sovereignty and Territory: Claims Conflict in the Old Northwest and the Origins of the American Federal Republic" (Ph.D. diss., Johns Hopkins University, 1973), 150–61. Elsewhere in America the English generally relied on charter claims (Max Savelle, *The Origins of American Diplomacy: The International History of Anglo-America, 1492–1763* [New York, 1967], 208–9). For a brief review of early Iroquois diplomacy, see Barbara Graymont, *The Iroquois in the American Revolution* (Syracuse, 1972), 26–47.

13. Philip J. Schwarz, *The Jarring Interests: New York's Boundary Makers, 1664–1776* (Albany, 1979), 168–74 and passim.

14. Morris to R. R. Livingston, received January 1781, Letters to Livingston.

15. See, e.g., R. R. Livingston's "Considerations on the Land Claims of Massachusetts" (1781), Livingston Papers (New-York Historical Society, New York); and Duane's "State of the Evidence and Argument in Support of the Territorial Rights and Jurisdiction of New York . . ." (1781), in *Collections of the New-York Historical Society*, 2d ser., 3 (1870): 1–75, and "Collection of Evidence in Vindication of the Territorial Rights and Jurisdiction of the State of New York Against the Claims of . . . Massachusetts and New Hampshire . . . ," ibid., 2 (1869), 277–528.

16. On the Virginia charter, see Arthur Lee, "Concise View of the Title of Virginia to the Western Lands . . ." (ca. 1782), in Paul P. Hoffman, ed., *The Lee Family Papers, 1742–1795* (microfilm ed., Charlottesville, 1966), reel 7, 280; and "Extracts from the Virginia Charters" (ca. July 1773), in Robert A. Rutland, ed., *The Papers of George Mason*, 3 vols. (Chapel Hill, 1970), 1:163–85.

17. For typical Vermont attacks on the 1764 boundary, see Ethan Allen and Jonas Fay, *A Concise Refutation of the Claim of New Hampshire and Massachusetts-Bay to the Territory of Vermont* (Hartford, 1780), 10–14; Ira Allen to the Pennsylvania Council, January 20, 1780, in E. P. Walton, ed., *Records of the Governor and*

Council of the State of Vermont (hereafter *Governor and Council*), 8 vols. (Montpelier, 1873–74), 2:236–37; and Representation of Peter Olcott and Bezaleel Woodward to Congress, read February 7, 1780, in *Clinton Papers*, 5:486–89.

18. The Indiana Memorial was read in Congress on September 14, 1779 (*JCC* 15:1063–64). Virginia's Remonstrance of December 14, 1779, against congressional reception of the memorial may be found in William Waller Hening, *The Statutes At Large: Being a Collection of All the Laws of Virginia*, 13 vols. (Richmond, 1809–23), 10:557–59. A petition from Kentucky, dated May 19, 1780 (PCC 48:237–44), was read in Congress on August 24, prompting the Virginia delegation to move that it be referred to that state (William T. Hutchinson et al., eds., *The Papers of James Madison*, 13 vols. to date [Chicago and Charlottesville, 1962–ۜ], 2:65).

19. Morris to R. R. Livingston, March 14, 1781, *LMCC* 6:26n.

20. See Duane to Clinton, October 7 and 18, 1780, *LMCC* 5:410–11, 424–25. On Roger Sherman's support for the separatists, see Christopher Collier, *Roger Sherman's Connecticut, Yankee Politics and the American Revolution* (Middletown, Conn., 1971), 148–56. Sherman apparently did not have any interest in Vermont lands, though his associates did. Elias Boudinot of New Jersey asserted that he was not influenced by his small holdings. George Adams Boyd, *Elias Boudinot: Patriot and Statesman, 1740–1821* (Princeton, 1952), 98–99.

21. Jay to Clinton, September 25, 1779, in *Clinton Papers*, 5:283–85n.

22. Ten Broeck to the President of Congress, January 20, 1777, in E. B. O'Callaghan, ed., *The Documentary History of the State of New York* (hereafter *DHSNY*) 4 vols. (Albany, 1849–51), 4:928–30.

23. See the comprehensive account of Duane's interests in Alexander, *Revolutionary Conservative*. Duane discussed his involvement in New York grants in Vermont in a speech to the General Assembly, June 1781, Duane Papers, insisting that he was not influenced by them.

24. Duane, "State of the Evidence," 30. Also see New York delegates to Governor Clinton, May 21, 1780, *LMCC* 5:160: Congress was "the only body who can preserve the peace of the confederacy."

25. James Madison to Edmund Pendleton, October 30, 1781, in *Madison Papers*, 3:296–98; Virginia delegates to Gov. Thomas Nelson, October 23, 1781, in ibid., 293.

26. Jay to Governor Clinton, September 25, 1779, in *Clinton Papers*, 5:283–85n.

27. Extract of a letter to the New York Committee of Safety, July 2, 1777, Records of the States of the United States (microfilm ed., Library of Congress, Washington, D.C.), Vermont E, reel 1; Egbert Benson to Jay, July 6, 1779, in *Clinton Papers*, 5:113–16.

28. Clinton to Jay, June 7, 1779, in *Clinton Papers* 5:54–57, objecting to the projected visit of a congressional committee to Vermont, pursuant to resolves of June 1, 1779, *JCC* 14:673–74.

29. Egbert Benson to Jay, June 23, 1779, in *Jay Papers*, 605; according to Jay and Duane, writing to Clinton, June 16, 1779 (in *Clinton Papers*, 5:89–90), "Any Decisions of Congress made ex-parte would have less weight than if made after hearing these people."

30. Jay to Clinton, September 25, 1779, in *Clinton Papers* 5:283–85n.

31. Clinton to Jay, June 6, 1778, in ibid., 3:417.

32. See the letter cited in note 30, above.

33. Daniel of St. Thomas Jenifer to Thomas Johnson, Jr., June 8, 1779, *LMCC* 4:253. See the discussion in H. James Henderson, *Party Politics in the Continental Congress* (New York, 1974), 307–9.

34. American military leaders were too prone to deal with the Vermonters and thus "inflame [their] . . . ambition," according to Duane in a letter to Clinton, February 20, 1779, *LMCC* 4:78. See also Duane to Jay, August 22–24, 1778, in *Jay Papers*, 494, and Clinton to Jay, June 7, 1779, in *Clinton Papers*, 5:54–57.

35. Clinton to Jay, June 23, 1779, in *Clinton Papers*, 5:93–95.

36. Jay to Clinton, December 19, 1779, in ibid., 4:406.

37. This point is developed in Chapter 6.

38. Bezaleel Woodward to the president of Congress, August 31, 1781, in *State Papers of New Hampshire*, vol. 10 (Concord, N.H., 1877), 374–75. See also note 27, above.

39. Duane to Clinton, June 14, 1779, in *Clinton Papers*, 5:84–85; emphasis mine.

40. Morris to Clinton, March 4, 1778, in *Governor and Council*, 3:291–92. These "splendid acts" should include the abolition of quit rents and the guarantee of New Hampshire titles: "We want *subjects* not *land.*"

41. Robert R. Livingston to Clinton, July 27, 1778, Livingston Papers.

42. Jay to Clinton, August 27, 1779, in *Clinton Papers*, 5:117–19.

43. February 6 and 21, *House Journal* (1777–78), 46, 58, 59, 60, 61; February 21, *Senate Journal* (1777–78), 64–66; October 24, 1778, *House Journal* (1778–79), 22; October 26 and 28, 1778, *Senate Journal* (1778–79), 139–41, 143. For Governor Clinton's proclamation of February 23, 1778, see *DHSNY* 4:951–55. The legislative history is discussed in Edward P. Countryman, "Legislative Government in Revolutionary New York, 1777–1788" (Ph.D. diss., Cornell University, 1971), 187–96.

44. Governor Clinton's Message, June 22, 1778, in *House Journal* (1777–78), 111–13.

45. *To the People of the Grants*, Philadelphia, April 11, 1777, reprinted in *DHSNY* 4:934–36.

46. June 23, 25, 28, 30, 1777; *JCC* 8:491, 497, 507, 508–13, quote at 512. See also the delegates' letter to the Committee of Safety, cited in note 27, above.

47. Clinton to Henry Laurens, President of Congress, April 7, 1778, in *Clinton Papers*, 3:145.

48. Congressional resolutions of June 16 demanded that the Vermonters release imprisoned New York officers (*JCC* 14:741–42). For a note on Jay's role, see *Jay Papers*, 510–11.

49. September 17, 20, 22, 23, 24, 1779; *JCC* 15:1078–80, 1090, 1094, 1095–99. See also Jay to Clinton, September 25 and 29, in *Clinton Papers*, 5:283–85n, 290.

50. Vermont's agents had indicated a willingness to have the controversy "fully laid before the Grand Council of America" (in a letter to Congress, July 1, 1779, in John A. Williams, ed., *The Public Papers of Governor Thomas Chittenden* [vol. 17 of *Vermont State Papers*] [Montpelier, 1969], 468–69). It was falsely assumed that the Vermonters had no choice but to submit and would be grateful for a hearing on any terms. But the Vermont Assembly resolved (October 21, 1779, *Journals and Proceedings of the General Assembly of the State of Vermont* [4 vols., Bellows Falls, 1924–29], 1:82–83) to "support their right to independence, at Congress, and to the World, in the character of a free and independent State."

51. Jay to Clinton, September 29, 1779, in *Clinton Papers*, 5:290.

52. Peabody to President Mesech Weare, October 26, 1779, *LMCC* 4: 498–99.

53. William Whipple to Josiah Bartlett, August 3, 1779, *LMCC* 4:351.

54. According to Woodbury Langdon, in a letter to Weare, October 12, 1779, *LMCC* 4:486.

55. For L'Hommedieu's suspicions about Massachusetts, see his letters to Governor Clinton, February 22 and March 15, 1780 (quote), *LMCC* 5:45, 75. See also Jay to Clinton, October 5, 1779, in *Jay Papers*, 652 (enclosing draft act for granting jurisdiction to Congress), and Benson to R. R. Livingston, January 3, 1780, Letters to Livingston.

56. Benson to R. R. Livingston, March 20, 1780, Letters to Livingston.

57. Jay to Clinton, May 6, 1780, in *Clinton Papers*, 5:685.

58. Address of September 4, 1779, *House Journal* (1779–80), 18.

59. Instructions to New York delegates, August 27, 1779, *DHSNY* 4:987–92, at 988; *House Journal* (1779–80), 10.

60. Clinton to Jay, June 7, 1779, in *Clinton Papers*, 5:54–57; Jay to Clinton, September 2, 1779, *LMCC* 4:400.

61. Clinton to James Duane, October 29, 1780, Duane Papers.

62. Clinton to the delegates, May 9, 1780, Duane Papers.

63. March 2 and 21, 1780, *JCC* 16:222, 222n, 273. On the "disagreeable Situation" of the New York delegates who found themselves unprepared to proceed, and on the absence of Samuel Livermore, New Hampshire's agent, who had been inoculated with smallpox, see delegates to Governor Clinton, February 9, 1780, and L'Hommedieu to Clinton, February 22, 1780, *LMCC* 5:31–32, 45. For a review of subsequent delays, largely owing to "the want of a competent representation," see R. R. Livingston to Schuyler, May 26, 1780, and delegates to Clinton, June 2, 1780, *LMCC* 5:170, 182. For a discussion of New Hampshire's attitude toward the hearings, see Charles P. Whittemore, *A General of the Revolution: John Sullivan of New Hampshire* (New York, 1961), 153–59.

64. June 2, 1780, *JCC* 17:482–84; Duane and John Morin Scott to Clinton, June 5, 1780, in *Clinton Papers*, 5:797–99.

65. John Sullivan to President Weare, September 16, 1780, in Otis G. Hammond, ed., *The Letters and Papers of Major General John Sullivan*, 3 vols. (Concord, 1930–39), 3:188.

66. See, e.g., Thomas Chittenden to Samuel Huntington, President of Congress, July 25, 1780, in *Chittenden Papers*, 326–30; and Ira Allen and Stephen R. Bradley, Remonstrance to Congress, September 22, 1780, in Records of the States, Vermont A, reel 2: "Needless would it be for us to inform Congress that by the mode of trial now adopted the State of Vermont can have no hearing without denying itself."

67. According to Sullivan in the letter cited in note 65, above.

68. Samuel Adams to James Lovell, March 25, 1780, in Harry Alonzo Cushing, ed., *The Writings of Samuel Adams*, 4 vols. (New York, 1904–8), 4:184–85.

69. Lovell to Samuel Adams, February 1, 1780, *LMCC* 5:24.

70. Samuel Holten to Jeremiah Powell, President of Massachusetts Council, May 30, 1780, *LMCC* 5:176–77; Ezekiel Cornell to Gov. William Greene, September 19, 1780, *LMCC* 5:379.

71. Jenifer to Gov. Thomas Sim Lee, June 5, 1780, *LMCC* 5:192–93.

72. Duane to Clinton, November 14, 1780, *LMCC* 5:444; Nathaniel Folsom to Weare, June 13, 1780, *LMCC* 5:213.

73. See the realistic assessment of Benson in a letter to R. R. Livingston, March 20, 1780, Letters to Livingston. For a comprehensive account of Yorker opposition to the new state, see Benjamin H. Hall, *History of Eastern Vermont from Its Earliest Settlement to the Close of the Eighteenth Century*, 2 vols. (Albany, 1865).

74. John Sullivan to Weare, October 2, 1780, *LMCC* 5:397; James Warren to John Adams, November 22, 1780, in Worthington C. Ford, ed., *Warren-Adams Letters*, 2 vols. (Boston, 1917–25), 2:150–51. The threat of such an alliance was implicit in Governor Chittenden's letter to the President of Congress, cited in note 66, above.

75. Sullivan to Weare, December 11, 1780, *LMCC* 5:481.

76. By Samuel Huntington, according to Duane's notes on debates, October 6, 1780, *LMCC* 5:408–9.

77. Ibid. For analyses of these debates, see Duane to Clinton, October 7, 1780, *LMCC* 5:410–11; and Scott to Clinton, September 26, 1780, in *Clinton Papers*, 6:254–56.

78. See, e.g, Sullivan to Weare, September 16, 1780, in *Sullivan Papers*, 3:187–90. Governor Clinton had long been "jealous of a premeditated intention to make a sacrifice of this State to answer the political views of others and of interested individuals" (Clinton to Duane, October 29, 1780, Duane Papers).

79. Madison, in a speech of October 6, 1780, in *Madison Papers*, 2:113.

80. Morris to Clinton, March 4, 1778, in *Governor and Council*, 3:291–92. For a brief account of Morris's attitude toward Vermont, and his resulting political difficulties, see Max M. Mintz, *Gouverneur Morris and the American Revolution* (Norman, Okla., 1970), 135–36.

81. Morris to Clinton, June 6, 1778, in *Clinton Papers*, 3:420.

82. Morris to Livingston, received in January 1781, Letters to Livingston.

83. See the hostile account of this treaty in the Report of the Cheshire Convention, November 15–16, 1780, in *New Hampshire State Papers*, 10:381–83. The Eastern Union is discussed in chapter 6.

84. In the letter cited in note 82, above.

85. Philip Schuyler to George Washington, January 21, 1781, in Jared Sparks, ed., *Correspondence of the Revolution: Being Letters of Eminent Men to George Washington*, 4 vols. (Boston, 1853), 3:212–14; Alexander Hamilton to John Laurens, February 4, 1781, in Harold C. Syrett, ed., *The Papers of Alexander Hamilton*, 26 vols. (New York, 1961–79), 2:549–51. See also the discussion in Merrill Jensen, *The New Nation: A History of the United States During the Confederation, 1781–1789* (1950; paperback ed., New York, n.d.), 48–51.

86. Message to the House, February 5, 1781, *House Journal* (1781, 1820 ed.), 9. Chittenden to Clinton, November 22, 1780, may be found in *Clinton Papers*, 6:430–31. Schuyler told Hamilton in a letter of November 12, 1780 (*Hamilton Papers*, 2:500) that he intended to press for "a final Settlement" of the Vermont controversy at the next meeting of the Assembly.

87. *Senate Journal* (1780–81), 52–53; *House Journal* (1781, 1820 ed.), 34–35.

88. Message of February 27, 1781, *House Journal* (1781, 1820 ed.), 43.

89. Clinton was citing the House's address to him, October 15, 1778, in *House Journal* (1778–79), 8. For Clinton's account of these events, see his letter to Alexander McDougall, April 6, 1781, *Clinton Papers*, 6:741–45.

90. L'Hommedieu to William Floyd, August (28?), 1781, LMCC 6:202; Samuel Livermore to Weare, August 14, 1781, LMCC 6:184; Roger Sherman to Bartlett, July 31, 1781, in *Governor and Council*, 3:293–94n; L'Hommedieu to Clinton, July 31, 1781, in *Clinton Papers*, 7:149–51.

91. Clinton to McDougall, cited in note 89, above.

92. July 1, 1781, *House Journal* (1780–81, unpaginated); June 30, 1781, *Senate Journal* (1780–81), 111–12.

93. Benson to Jay, November 27, 1781, in Henry P. Johnston, ed., *The Correspondence and Public Papers of John Jay, 1763–1826*, 4 vols. (New York, 1890), 2:149–53.

94. Schuyler to Washington, July 7, 1781 (George Washington Papers [Library of Congress, Washington, D.C., microfilm ed.]), repeating sentiments developed at greater length in an earlier letter to Washington, May 4, 1781 (in John C. Fitzpatrick, ed., *The Writings of George Washington*, 39 vols. [Washington, D.C., 1931–44], 22:82n). But compare Schuyler to Clinton, May 4, 1781, in *Clinton Papers*, 6:841, in which he confesses that his "faith in the political virtue" of the Vermonters is "staggered" and makes no mention of his continuing support for the recognition of Vermont.

95. Duane and L'Hommedieu to Clinton, August 7, 1781, in *Clinton Papers*, 7:174–76.

96. Congressional motives are comprehensively surveyed in Madison to Pendleton, August 14, 1781, in *Madison Papers*, 3:224. Also see Elias Boudinot to Gov. William Livingston, August 25, 1781, LMCC 6:197–98, and Pendleton to Madison, August 27, 1781, in *Madison Papers*, 3:234–35. As Jenifer had written on July 24, 1781, to John Hall, LMCC 6:155, "If we do not soon make" the Vermonters "independant the British will endeavor to do it." The Massachusetts General Court's resolution of March 8, 1781, may be found in *Chittenden Papers*, 538.

97. L'Hommedieu to Clinton, July 31, 1781, and Duane and L'Hommedieu to Clinton, August 7, 1781, in *Clinton Papers*, 7:149–51, 174–76. Clinton anticipated that the Vermonters "are to be a State" (Clinton to McDougall, April 6, 1781, ibid., 6:745). He suggested that it would be in New York's interest to have the new state extend across the Connecticut River.

98. Delegates to Clinton, August 9, 1781, LMCC 6:173.

99. Duane to R. R. Livingston, August 11, 1781, LMCC 6:176; the letter also appears in LMCC 5:321, where it is misdated August 11, 1780. See also Duane to Clinton, August 20, 1781 (in *Clinton Papers*, 7:232), which betrays some anxiety about the western boundary.

100. August 20 and 21, 1781, JCC 21:886–88, 892–93. A congressional committee reported on July 20 (JCC 20:770–72) in favor of asking New York and New Hampshire to follow Massachusetts's example and relinquish their claims. But, as the New York delegates wrote Clinton on September 9, 1781 (LMCC 6:213), "any Decision was preferable to Delay: and that as internal Dissentions would arise from a Reference to our own Legislature, it would not be expedient to shift the ultimate Admission or Rejection of the Claim from the United States to those which were immediately interested."

101. Delegates to Clinton, August 21, 1781, LMCC 6:192.

102. Delegates to Clinton, September 26, 1781, in *Clinton Papers*, 7:359–60; delegates to Clinton, September 9, 1781, LMCC 6:213.

103. On the growth of anti-Vermont feeling in the New York Assembly, see Clinton to John Tayler, November 18, 1781, in *Clinton Papers*, 7:507–8. The concurrent resolves may be found in ibid., 7:516–19. See also November 15, 1781, *Senate Journal* (1781–82), 23–24, and November 19, 1781, *House Journal* (1781–82), 38–41.

104. L'Hommedieu to Clinton, September 8, 1781, LMCC 6:212.

105. Congressional committee's queries for Vermont agents, August 18, 1781, LMCC 6:188–89; Agents to Committee, August 18, 1781, in *Governor and Council*, 2:317–18.

106. WS (?) to Gov. William Tryon, April 12, 1781, PRO, CO 5/158, 220.

107. February 19 and 22, 1782, *Vermont Assembly Journal*, 2:60–65.

108. Floyd to Clinton, January 31, 1782, LMCC 6:297–98.

109. Floyd to Clinton, February 26, 1782, LMCC 6:306; R. R. Livingston to Schuyler, February 13, 1782, LMCC 6:306n.

110. JCC 22:105–14.

111. Delegates to Clinton, March 5, 1782, LMCC 6:309–11.

112. Delegates to Clinton, March 12, 1782, LMCC 6:313–14.

113. Madison to Pendleton, January 22, 1782, in *Madison Papers*, 4:38–39. Joseph Jones argued in a letter to Pendleton (March 19, 1782, LMCC 6:319) that the "fair construction" of the Articles of Confederation required the "assent of the whole" (all thirteen states) to the admission of a new state.

114. Arthur Lee to James Warren, April 8, 1782, LMCC 6:326–27. See also Madison to Pendleton, cited in note 113, above.

115. In a letter to James Bowdoin, March 8, 1782, Bowdoin-Temple Papers (Massachusetts Historical Society, Boston, microfilm ed.), reel 48.

116. Madison to Edmund Randolph, May 1, 1782, in *Madison Papers*, 4:197. According to Lee, in a letter to Samuel Adams, April 21, 1782 (LMCC 6:331–32), "Every Motion relative to Vermont and the Cessions of the other States is directed by the interests of these Companies." See also New York delegates to Clinton, March 29, 1782 (Vermont Council of Safety Papers [Force Transcripts, Library of Congress, Washington, D.C.]), citing the influence of "landjobbers" and the desire of the New England states to "increase their weight in the Seat of the Union."

117. Rhode Island delegates to Governor Greene, April 16, 1782, LMCC 6:329.

118. Butler to James Iredell, April 5, 1782, LMCC 6:327n.

119. Lee to Samuel Adams, cited in note 116, above. Lee suggested that Vermont be made a state without "a voice in Congress" in the letter to Warren cited in note 114, above.

120. Madison's "Observations," May 1, 1782, in *Madison Papers*, 4:200–202. On sectional alignments, see also Livermore to Weare, March 12, 1782, LMCC 6:312.

121. Floyd to Clinton, February 26, 1782, LMCC 6:306.

122. Osgood to Lovell, March 2, 1782, LMCC 6:308–9.

123. Livermore to Weare, March 2, 1782, LMCC 6:308.

124. April 17, 1782, JCC 22:185–90; Madison to Randolph, April 23, 1782, in *Madison Papers*, 4:181.

125. Madison to Randolph, November 5, 1782, in *Madison Papers*, 5:243. See also Duane to Clinton, October 30, 1782, in *Clinton Papers*, 8:49.

126. Duane to Clinton, November 15, 1782, *LMCC* 6:541–42.

127. *JCC* 23:765–67; *Hamilton Papers*, 3:204–6.

128. Madison, December 3, 1782, in *Madison Papers*, 5:351–52.

129. Ibid. New Jersey adopted instructions on November 1, 1782, against us-ing force in Vermont, in response to a letter from Boudinot to Gov. William Livingston, October 23, 1782 (*LMCC* 6:522–24). The Rhode Island Assembly adopted similar instructions in February 1783; William R. Staples, *Rhode Island in the Continental Congress* (Providence, 1870), 431.

130. According to Clinton to Hamilton, December 29, 1782, in *Hamilton Papers*, 3:230–31. See also Clinton to Floyd, February 6, 1783, in *Clinton Papers*, 8:64.

131. Hamilton and Floyd to Clinton, December 9, 1782, in *Hamilton Papers*, 3:208–9.

132. Floyd to Clinton, May 22, 1782, *LMCC* 6:354; Scott to Clinton, May 21, 1782, *LMCC* 6:353–54; Livermore to Weare, March 12, 1782, *LMCC* 6:312.

133. Clinton to Scott, June 6, 1782, in *Clinton Papers*, 8:7–8. New York acts "For pardoning certain offences . . ." and "For quieting the minds of the in-habitants . . ." may be found in *New York Laws*, chaps. 43 and 44, 5th sess. (1781–82).

134. R. R. Livingston to Livermore, September 10, 1782, Livingston Papers.

135. According to the delegates, in the letter to Clinton cited in note 116, above.

136. Hamilton to Clinton, January 1 and 12, 1783, in *Hamilton Papers*, 3:236, 241.

137. Extract from a letter dated February 18, 1783, in *Governor and Council*, 3:289.

138. In a letter to Duane, August 5, 1782, Duane Papers, Clinton suggested that it would be necessary to "collect the sentiments of our friends in that quarter" before dealing with New Hampshire. For New Hampshire papers on the partition proposal, see *New Hampshire State Papers* (Concord, 1874), 8:943–44; 10:490. A New York House committee on a letter from President Weare of New Hampshire appointed July 15, 1782, apparently never reported (*House Journal* [1781–82], 110–11).

139. Clinton to Hamilton, February 24, 1783, in *Hamilton Papers*, 3:266–67.

140. Clinton to Floyd, February 23, 1783, in *Clinton Papers*, 8:79–81.

141. Hamilton to Clinton, July (23?), 1783, in *Governor and Council*, 3:291.

142. Hamilton to Clinton, July 27, 1783, in *Hamilton Papers*, 3:418–19; the date is given as July 14 in *Governor and Council*, 3:290.

143. See Clinton to the delegates, August 23, 1783, in *Governor and Council* 3:279, and editorial note.

144. The present author seconds the view of Linda Grant DePauw, *The Elev-enth Pillar: New York State and the Federal Constitution* (Ithaca, 1966), 11–13, that New York did not contemplate any measures against the new state after 1783. On Vermont's admission to the union, see Chilton Williamson, *Vermont in Quandary, 1763–1825* (Montpelier, 1949), 165–84.

145. Julius Goebel, Jr., ed., *The Law Practice Of Alexander Hamilton*, 4 vols. (New York, 1964–80), 1:553–84.

CHAPTER 6: THE NEW STATE OF VERMONT

1. In general, see Chilton Williamson, *Vermont in Quandary, 1763–1825* (Montpelier, 1949), and for the colonial background, Matt Bushnell Jones, *Vermont in the Making, 1750–1777* (Cambridge, Mass., 1939).

2. Page Smith, *A New Age Now Begins*, 2 vols. (New York, 1976), 2:891–947; Charles Jellison, *Ethan Allen: Frontier Rebel* (Syracuse, 1969), 102–20.

3. June 11 and October 21, 1778, *Journals and Proceedings of the General Assembly of the State of Vermont*, 4 vols. (Bellows Falls, 1924–29) (the 4 vols. constitute vol. 3 of *The State Papers of Vermont*), 1:24, 41–45 (hereafter *Vt. Assembly Journal*). See also Ira Allen's broadside *Address to the Inhabitants of Vermont*, Dresden, November 27, 1778 (copy in Brattleboro Public Library), and Josiah Bartlett to Pres. Mesech Weare, September 26, 1778, miscellaneous manuscripts (Vermont Historical Society [hereafter, VHS], Montpelier), reporting on congressional reaction to the union.

4. April 5 and June 16, 1781, *Vt. Assembly Journal*, 1:213–14, 242–44.

5. For a good general treatment, see Williamson, *Vermont in Quandary*, 90–126. Documents relating to the talks may be found in *Collections of the Vermont Historical Society* (hereafter *Collections*), 2 vols. (Montpelier, 1870–71), vol. 2.

6. August 20 and 21, 1781, in Worthington C. Ford, ed., *Journals of the Continental Congress* (hereafter JCC), 34 vols. (Washington, D.C., 1904–37), 21:886–88, 892–93.

7. The dissolution of the unions caught many Vermont leaders by surprise; February 19 and 22, 1782, *Vt. Assembly Journal*, 2:60–65. A letter from George Washington to Gov. Thomas Chittenden, January 1, 1782 (in John A. Williams, ed., *The Public Papers of Governor Thomas Chittenden* [vol. 17 of *Vermont State Papers*] [Montpelier, 1969], 573–75), advising dissolution, apparently had a great impact on the Assembly. For congressional inaction on Vermont's renewed application, see April 17, 1782, JCC 22:185–90.

8. Vermonters' scruples about the legality of their constitution are discussed in Gordon S. Wood, *The Creation of the American Republic, 1776–1787* (Chapel Hill, 1969), 307–8.

9. September 24, 1779, JCC 15:1096.

10. For a recent discussion of this point, see Garry Wills, *Inventing America* (Garden City, 1978), 44–48. See also Jack Rakove, *The Beginnings of National Politics* (New York, 1979), 164–76 and passim.

11. The resolution was in direct reponse to the Vermont separation: June 23, 25, 28, and 30, 1777, JCC 8:491, 497, 507, 508–13, quotation at 509.

12. May 23, 1780, JCC 17:452.

13. According to Article XI, Canada would be admitted into the union by "acceding to this confederation." Any other colony would be admitted by the vote of nine states; no mention was made of "states." (James D. Richardson, ed., *A Compilation of the Messages and Papers of the Presidents*, 12 vols. [Washington, D.C., 1903–6], 1:9–18.) For examples of contemporary constitutional scruples, see James Madison to Edmund Pendleton, January 22, 1782, in William T. Hutchinson et al., eds., *The Papers of James Madison*, 13 vols. to date (Chicago and Charlottesville, 1962–   ), 4:38–39, citing the opinion of several states that there was a "want of power" in Congress to admit new states; also, Ezra L'Hommedieu to Gov. George Clinton, September 8, 1781, in Edmund Cody Burnett,

ed., *Letters of the Members of the Continental Congress* (hereafter *LMCC*), 8 vols. (Washington, D.C., 1921–36), 6:212: "Many gentlemen from the Southward are fully of opinion that Congress has no authority to admit those people [of Vermont] into the Federal Union as a separate State on the present principles."

14. For an extensive discussion of this point, see C. C. Langdell, "The Status of Our New Territories," *Harvard Law Review* 12 (1899): 365–92.

15. Hugh Williamson to Alexander Martin, November 18, 1782, *LMCC* 6:545.

16. Phelps to New York Assembly, September 21, 1779, in E. B. O'Callaghan, ed., *The Documentary History of the State of New York* (hereafter *DHSNY*), 4 vols. (Albany, 1849–51), 4:999.

17. Governor Chittenden's Proclamation, June 3, 1779, in *Chittenden Papers*, 458–59.

18. Thomas Jefferson to Edmund Randolph, February 15, 1783, in Julian P. Boyd, ed., *The Papers of Thomas Jefferson*, 20 vols. to date (Princeton, 1950–   ), 6:247–48.

19. Chittenden to the President of Congress, January 9, 1783, in *Chittenden Papers*, 601.

20. Chittenden to John Jay, President of Congress, August 5, 1779, in ibid., 470–72.

21. Ethan Allen, *A Vindication of the Opposition of the Inhabitants of Vermont to the Government of New York* (Dresden, 1779), 47–48, 12–13.

22. Gouverneur Morris's notes on congressional debates, May 29, 1779, Gouverneur Morris Collection (Columbia University Library, New York).

23. Ethan Allen, *An Animadversary Address to the Inhabitants of the State of Vermont* (Hartford, 1778), 4. For a colorful account of the struggle between Yankees and Yorkers, see Jellison, *Ethan Allen*, 18–101; and on the origins of this enmity, see esp. Edward Countryman, "'Out of the Bounds of the Law': Northern Land Rioters in the Eighteenth Century," in Alfred F. Young, ed., *The American Revolution* (DeKalb, Ill., 1976), 37–69.

24. Allen, *Animadversary Address*, 16; Aaron Hutchinson, *A Well-Tempered Self-Love a Rule of Conduct Toward Others* (Dresden, 1777), sermon preached at Windsor convention, reprinted in *Collections*, 1:67–101, at 85; Ira Allen, *Miscellaneous Remarks on the Proceedings of the State of New York Against the State of Vermont* (Hartford, 1777), reprinted in *Collections*, 1:135–44, at 141–42.

25. Ethan Allen, *Vindication*, 52.

26. Allen to Samuel Huntington, President of Congress, March 9, 1781, in *Chittenden Papers*, 345–47.

27. Ethan Allen and Jonas Fay, *A Concise Refutation of the Claim of New Hampshire and Massachusetts-Bay to the Territory of Vermont* (Hartford, 1780), 10–14.

28. Jones, *Vermont in the Making*, passim.

29. Ethan Allen and Fay, *Concise Refutation*, 14.

30. For a brief discussion of the supposed charter, see Hiland Hall, *The History of Vermont, from Its Discovery to Its Admission into the Union in 1791* (Albany, 1868), 195–96.

31. Ira Allen to Frederick Haldimand, July 11, 1782, in *Collections*, 2:283–86.

32. Ethan Allen and Fay, *Concise Refutation*, 27.

33. According to Ira Allen at negotiations with British agents at Isle au Noix, May 2–25, 1781, in *Collections*, 2:110 (emphasis mine).

34. Ethan Allen(?) to Haldimand, June 16, 1782, in ibid., 2:275–76.

35. Report of Dr. George Smith, enclosed in Philip Schuyler to Washington, May 24, 1781, in ibid., 2:132.

36. Jenifer to John Hall, July 24, 1781, LMCC 6:155.

37. *To the People of the Grants*, Philadelphia, April 11, 1777, reprinted in DHSNY 4:934–36.

38. Compare with the original wording of the congressional resolves, May 10, 1776, JCC 4:342: "That it be recommended to the respective assemblies and conventions of the United Colonies, where no government sufficient to the exigencies of their affairs have been hitherto established, to adopt such government as shall, in the opinion of the representatives of the people, best conduce to the happiness and safety of their constituents in particular, and America in general."

39. In a letter to Jay, President of Congress, August 5, 1779, in *Chittenden Papers*, 470–72.

40. Ethan Allen, *Vindication*, 55.

41. October 13, 1780, *Vt. Assembly Journal*, 1:127.

42. Chittenden to Samuel Huntington, President of Congress, July 25, 1780, in *Chittenden Papers*, 326–30.

43. Chittenden to Clinton, November 22, 1780, in Hugh Hastings, ed., *The Public Papers of George Clinton, First Governor of New York*, 10 vols. (New York, 1899–1914), 6:430–31; to Gov. Jonathan Trumbull of Connecticut and Gov. John Hancock of Massachusetts, both December 12, 1780, Vermont Council of Safety Papers (Force Transcripts, Library of Congress, Washington, D.C.) (hereafter Council Papers); to President Weare of New Hampshire, December 12, 1780, in *Chittenden Papers*, 335–37.

44. Schuyler to Washington, November 12, 1780, George Washington Papers (Library of Congress, Washington, D.C., microfilm ed.).

45. The transcription of Ira Allen's information, May 11, 1781, in *Collections*, 2:122, differs slightly from the original Stevens transcript in Haldimand Manuscripts (Secretary of State's Office, Montpelier).

46. Report of negotiations at Isle au Noix, May 8–25, in *Collections*, 2:112.

47. Micah Townshend's abstract of intelligence from Col. Samuel Wells, in a letter to Henry Clinton, April 10, 1781, Colonial Office 5/158, Public Record Office of Great Britain.

48. Vermont historians have gone to extraordinary lengths to exonerate the Allens of charges of disloyalty. See, e.g., John Williams's notes to *Chittenden Papers*, esp. 332, where it is asserted that "documentary evidence abundantly proves the loyalty of Ira Allen, Governor Chittenden and their associates." But there is no question that the reinforcing interests of the state's civil and military establishments and of Vermont land grantees made reunion with Britain desirable; sources cited throughout this chapter provide abundant documentation.

49. One of the British agents to Ira Allen(?), February 28, 1782, in *Collections*, 2:250–51.

50. See proposed proclamation, ca. October 1, 1781, in ibid., 2:181–82.

51. Affidavits of Dirck Swart and Maj. Daniel Dickenson, December 20, 1781, in *Clinton Papers*, 7:613–14. On Tichenor's earlier attitude, see John Lansing, Jr., to Philip Schuyler, July 26, 1780, Philip Schuyler Papers (Bancroft Collection, New York Public Library): "he admires the State of New York, and I believe, cordially wishes that the Grants may remain under New York."

52. Answers of Vermont Loyalists to Queries Concerning the Haldimand Ne-

gotiations, August 18, 1781, Allen Papers (University of Vermont, Burlington; photocopy of original at British Library).

53. Haldimand to Sir Guy Carleton, June 22, 1781, in *Collections*, 2:280–81.

54. See note 6 above; see also congressional committee queries to Vermont agents, August 18, 1781, *LMCC* 6:188–89; and Vermont agents to Committee, August 18, 1781, citing their inability to "perform any public act" exclusive of the Eastern and Western unions, in E. P. Walton, ed., *Records of the Governor and Council of the State of Vermont* (hereafter *Governor and Council*), 8 vols. (Montpelier, 1873–74), 2:317–18.

55. Benjamin Baker's declaration, January 10, 1782, reporting statement of Josiah Arms of Brattleborough, December 3 or 4, 1781, Council Papers.

56. Thomas Baker and David Lamb affidavit, sworn before Samuel Bixby at Halifax, September 9, 1782, in *Governor and Council*, 3:240.

57. For a collection of such sentiments, see Benjamin H. Hall, *History of Eastern Vermont from Its Earliest Settlement to the Close of the Eighteenth Century*, 2 vols. (Albany, 1865), 2:478–79.

58. Luke Knowlton to General Haldimand, January 10, 1783 (VHS; transcript of original at British Library).

59. Egbert Benson to Jay, July 6, 1779, *Clinton Papers*, 5:114.

60. Bezaleel Woodward to President of Congress, August 31, 1781, *State Papers of New Hampshire*, vol. 10 (Concord, 1877), 374–75.

61. Bayley to Washington, February 26, 1781, Washington Papers.

62. Jacob Bayley so suspected the loyalty of Vermonters, but John Sullivan thought his "reasoning is Truly ridiculous," in a letter to President Weare, December 11, 1780, *LMCC* 5:481; but it was Sullivan who thought a "war" would be necessary (in another letter to Weare, September 16, 1780, in Otis G. Hammond, ed., *The Letters and Papers of Major General John Sullivan*, 3 vols. [Concord, 1930–39], 3:187–90).

63. For Alexander Hamilton's anxieties about the union, see his letter to Governor Clinton, February 14, 1783, in Harold C. Syrett, ed., *The Papers of Alexander Hamilton*, 26 vols. (New York, 1961–79), 3:256: "It is the first wish of my heart that the Union may last; but feeble as the links are, what prudent man would rely upon it?" Madison had predicted that "the present union will little survive the present war," in a letter to Pendleton, October 31, 1781, *LMCC* 6:252. On the "collapse" of Congress at this time, see Merrill Jensen, *The New Nation: A History of the United States During the Confederation, 1781–1789* (1950; paperback ed., New York, n.d.), 67–84. For the failure to use force against Vermont, see Governor Clinton to William Floyd, February 6, 1783, in *Clinton Papers*, 8:64. Washington was particularly reluctant to send his forces against Vermont; see Washington to Joseph Jones, February 11, 1783, in *Chittenden Papers*, 608–10.

64. Washington to Weare, July 31, 1782, in John C. Fitzpatrick, ed., *The Writings of George Washington*, 39 vols. (Washington, D.C., 1931–44), 24:449–50.

65. Chittenden to Washington, November 14, 1781, in *Chittenden Papers*, 381.

66. Silvanus Ripley to John Phillips, dated Dresden, December 6, 1780, Wheelock Papers (New Hampshire Historical Society, Concord).

67. Bayley to Washington, February 26, 1781, Washington Papers.

68. In general, see Jackson Turner Main, *The Sovereign States, 1775–1783* (New York, 1973), 214–17, 354–56; and Jere R. Daniell, *Experiment in Republicanism: New Hampshire Politics and the American Revolution* (Cambridge, Mass.,

1970), 164–79. For details, see microfilm copies of town records, New Hampshire State Library, Concord (hereafter NHSL). And for an early statement of the idea that "every body politic" (i.e., town) "whether large or small are, legally the same," see *An Address of the Inhabitants of Plainfield . . .* (Norwich, Conn., 1776), dated July 31, 1776, reprinted in *New Hampshire State Papers*, 10:229–35, at 231.

69. Cornish town meeting, June 28, 1781, NHSL.

70. Charlestown town meeting, April 2, 1781, NHSL.

71. *Governor and Council*, 1, Appendix G; April 5, 1781, *Vt. Assembly Journal*, 1:213–14.

72. Moretown town meeting, May 25, 1779, *New Hampshire State Papers*, 10:340.

73. Thetford town meeting, June 11, 1782, in *Governor and Council*, 3:283; Memorial of New Hampshire General Court by Convention of town committees from Newbury, Bradford, Norwich, and Hartford, May 31, 1782, ibid., 3:281–82; Newbury town meeting, May 31, 1782, Council Papers.

74. Instructions to delegates to New York Provincial Congress, June 11–21, 1776, and Cumberland Committees to Provincial Congress, June 21, 1776, in Hall, *History of Eastern Vermont*, 1:258–61.

75. In a letter to the New York Convention, November 6, 1776, in ibid., 1:278.

76. Protest of the Inhabitants of Guilford, Brattleboro, Putney, New Fane, Hinsdale, Rockingham, Westminster, and Weathersfield to the Vermont General Assembly, June 4, 1778, Allen Papers (photocopy of original at New-York Historical Society).

77. Petition of Cumberland Committees, May 4, 1779, *DHSNY* 4:957–60; Cumberland Convention, October 31, 1780, meeting with New Hampshire towns at Charlestown, November 8, 1780, and at Walpole, November 15, 1780, in Hall, *History of Eastern Vermont*, 2:401 and passim. On the wavering loyalties of Yorkers, see Micah Townshend to Clinton, April 12, 1780, in *Clinton Papers*, 5:616–17.

78. Guilford Address to Congress, Clinton, and New York General Assembly, January 8, 1782, in Hall, *History of Eastern Vermont*, 2:415; manuscript address, n.d. (early 1782?), James H. Phelps Collection (VHS). Rumors of the impending dissolution preceded the event, February 11 and 21, 1782, in *Vt. Assembly Journal*, 2:44, 45, 59, 60, 61, 62.

79. Thomas Sparhawk and Benjamin Bellows to Committee of Safety, dated Walpole, July 30, 1782, in *New Hampshire State Papers*, 10:491–93.

80. Solomon Pendleton to Clinton, dated Albany, December 7, 1781, in *Clinton Papers*, 7:556–59. See also Brinton Paine to Clinton, dated Stillwater, April 16, 1781, in ibid., 6:775–77.

81. Petition to Governor Clinton, June 3, 1783, James Phelps Scrapbook (VHS).

82. See extracts of letters from agents for negotiating with the people of Vermont, August 2–18, 1781, in *Collections*, 2:148–50: the majority of the population was "under very little, if any, subjection to their nominal leaders."

83. Beverley Robinson to Haldimand, dated New York, May 8, 1781, in ibid., 2:119–20; New York delegates to Governor Clinton, September 9, 1781, *LMCC* 6:213.

84. John Younglove to Clinton, dated Cambridge, N.Y., June 20, 1781, in *Clinton Papers*, 7:34–36.

85. Petition to Governor Clinton, cited in note 81, above.

86. Petition and Remonstrance, March 23, 1782, Phelps Scrapbook; see also petition of May 17, 1782, in ibid.

87. Phelps to Clinton, April 27, 1782, ibid. See also Hall, *History of Eastern Vermont*, 2:421. Resolutions of Brattleboro (March 12, 1782) and Guilford (March 13, 1782) publicizing the negotiations were printed and distributed by the Yorkers; Phelps Scrapbook.

88. Records of the early conventions, July 24, 1776 (Dorset), September 25, 1776 (adjourned session, Dorset), October 30, 1776 (adjourned session, Westminster), January 15, 1777 (adjourned session, Westminster), June 4, 1777 (adjourned session, Windsor), July 2, 1777 (Windsor), are collected in *Chittenden Papers*, 5–54.

89. R. R. Palmer, "The American Revolution: The People as Constituent Power," reprinted in Jack P. Greene, ed., *The Reinterpretation of the American Revolution, 1763–1789* (New York, 1968), 338–61.

90. Governor Chittenden's Annexation Proclamation, July 18, 1781, in *Chittenden Papers*, 541–43.

91. Samuel Minott to Clinton, dated Brattleboro, May 25, 1779, *DHSNY* 4:965–66.

92. James Duane to Jay, August 22–24, 1778, in Richard B. Morris, ed., *John Jay: The Making of a Revolutionary, Unpublished Papers, 1745–1780* (New York, 1975), 494, reporting conversation between Ethan Allen and Robert R. Livingston. See also Governor Clinton's sarcastic comments on the "conquest" right in a letter to Duane, September 18, 1778, in *Clinton Papers*, 4:46.

93. Charles Phelps to Clinton, July 10, 1782 (abstract), in *Collections*, 2:286.

94. Samuel Bixby et al. to Clinton, dated Halifax, September 22, 1782, Council Papers. "I yield to brute force," Timothy Phelps announced to the Vermont Court at Marlborough, February 4–11, 1783 (in Hall, *History of Eastern Vermont*, 2:492–94).

95. Timothy Phelps to Clinton, dated Bennington Jail (May–June?) 1783, in ibid., 2:496–98.

96. See, e.g., Connecticut delegates to Governor Trumbull, January 21, 1782, *LMCC* 6:294–95.

97. James H. Kettner, *The Development of American Citizenship, 1608–1870* (Chapel Hill, 1978), 173–209.

CHAPTER 7: NEW STATES AND THE NEW NATION

1. Letter from New York, April 23, 1787, *Carlisle Gazette* (Carlisle, Pa.), May 9, 1787, reprinted from *Massachusetts Centinel*. For a similar analysis, see Jonathan Gould Journal and Diary (Maine Historical Society, Portland).

2. Spaight to Gov. Alexander Martin, October 16, 1784, in William L. Saunders, Walter Clark, and Stephen B. Weeks, eds., *The Colonial and State Records of North Carolina*, 26 vols. (Raleigh, Winston, Goldsboro, and Charlotte, 1886–1914), 17:172–75.

3. North Carolina delegates to Martin, September 26, 1783, in Edmund Cody Burnett, ed., *Letters of the Members of the Continental Congress* (hereafter LMCC), 8 vols. (Washington, D.C., 1921–36), 7:313; Spaight to Martin, April 30, 1784, *North Carolina Records*, 17:65–66.

4. Stephen Higginson to Henry Knox, February 8, 1787, Knox Papers (Mas-

sachusetts Historical Society, Boston), XIX. See also Higginson to Knox, February 13, 1787, ibid., and Hugh Williamson to William Samuel Johnson, February 14, 1787, in Julian P. Boyd and Robert J. Taylor, eds., *The Susquehannah Company Papers*, 11 vols. (Wilkes-Barre and Ithaca, 1930–71), 9:60–62.

5. Spaight to Martin, October 16, 1784, *North Carolina Records*, 17:172–75.

6. Peters to Oliver Wolcott, July 13, 1783, Oliver Wolcott Papers (Connecticut Historical Society, Hartford), 3:152.

7. Boston, July 19, 1786, *State Gazette of South Carolina*, August 24, 1786.

8. See the excellent discussion in Jack Rakove, *The Beginnings of National Politics: An Interpretive History of the Continental Congress* (New York, 1979), 158–76. See also Andrew McLaughlin, "The Background of American Federalism," *American Political Science Review* 12, (1918): 215–40.

9. Higginson to Knox, February 8, 1787, Knox Papers, XIX.

10. Tullius, *Three Letters Addressed to the Public* (Philadelphia, 1783), 8.

11. As reported in Charles Thomson's notes of congressional debate on a petition from Kentucky, August 27, 1782, LMCC 6:457.

12. See discussion in Chapter 1.

13. Gordon Wood, *The Creation of the American Republic, 1776–1787* (Chapel Hill, 1969), 91–124; J. G. A. Pocock, *The Machiavellian Moment: Florentine Political Thought and the Atlantic Republican Tradition* (Princeton, 1975), 506–52; Gerald Stourzh, *Alexander Hamilton and the Idea of Republican Government* (Stanford, 1970).

14. Higginson to Knox, February 8, 1787, Knox Papers, XIX; Extract of a Letter from Dr. (Richard) Price to a Correspondent in Philadelphia, January 26, 1787, *Carlisle Gazette*, June 6, 1787.

15. Jacob E. Cooke, ed., *The Federalist Papers* (Middletown, Conn., 1961), 38; see also the sixth and eighth numbers.

16. Staughton Lynd, "The Compromise of 1787," reprinted in *Class Conflict, Slavery, and the United States Constitution* (Indianapolis, 1967), 185–213; Joseph L. Davis, *Sectionalism in American Politics, 1774–1787* (Madison, 1977).

17. Report recommending cessions, adopted April 29, 1784, Worthington C. Ford, ed., *Journals of the Continental Congress* (hereafter JCC), 34 vols. (Washington, 1904–37), 26:316.

18. Hamilton, in the "Continentalist" III, August 9, 1781, in Harold C. Syrett, ed., *The Papers of Alexander Hamilton*, 26 vols. (New York, 1961–79), 2:660–61.

19. Copy of a letter from a gentleman at the Falls of the Ohio, dated Baltimore, July 3, 1787, *Cumberland Gazette* (Portland, Massachusetts/Maine), July 19, 1787.

20. For an early statement of this position, see John Witherspoon's comments in debate, August 27, 1782, LMCC 6:458–59.

21. Speech of June 28, 1787, in Max Farrand, ed., *The Records of the Federal Convention of 1787*, 4 vols. (New Haven, 1911–37), 1:449.

22. "Authentic copy" of a letter from Arthur Campbell to John Edmiston, August 26, 1785, in William R. Palmer, ed., *Calendar of Virginia State Papers*, 11 vols. (Richmond, 1875–93), 4:100–101; copy of a letter, *Falmouth Gazette* (predecessor of *Cumberland Gazette*, Portland, Massachusetts/Maine), May 21, 1785.

23. Grayson to Lt. Gov. Beverley Randolph, June 12, 1787, LMCC 8:609–10.

24. "Harrington" to the Freemen of the United States, *Carlisle Gazette*, July 4, 1787.

25. See Monroe to Thomas Jefferson, January 19, 1786, in Julian P. Boyd, ed., *The Papers of Thomas Jefferson*, 20 vols. to date (Princeton, 1950–   ), 9:189–90.

26. Monroe to James Madison, September 3, 1786, in William T. Hutchinson et al., eds., *The Papers of James Madison*, 13 vols. to date (Chicago and Charlottesville, 1962–   ), 9:104. See also James Monroe to Patrick Henry, August 12, 1786, in William Wirt Henry, *Patrick Henry: Life, Correspondence, and Speeches*, 3 vols. (New York, 1891), 2:296–97, and Monroe to Madison, August 14, 1786, in *Madison Papers*, 9:104. Southerners like William Grayson had been long aware that northerners feared the augmentation of southern power through the admission of new states; see his letter to George Washington, May (8?), 1785, LMCC 8:118.

27. "Impartialis," *Falmouth Gazette*, May 14, 1785, suggested that Maine's separation would "undoubtedly be the interest of Massachusetts," because it would "double the influence" of the state in Congress, but expected that the other states would oppose it for that very reason. See also Nathan Dane to Samuel Phillips, January 20, 1786, Nathan Dane Miscellaneous Manuscripts (Library of Congress, Washington, D.C.). Philip Schuyler of New York argued for recognition of Vermont as part of a strategy to form an eastern alliance. See the discussion in Chapter 5, above.

28. Brown to George Muter, July 10, 1788, in Temple Bodley, ed., *Littel's Political Transactions in and Concerning Kentucky*, Filson Club Publications, no. 31 (Louisville, 1926), xxxi–xxxiii; Brown to John Smith, July 9, 1788, John Mason Brown Papers (Yale University Library, New Haven), citing the "opposition of the Eastern States."

29. Monroe to Madison, August 14, 1786, in *Madison Papers*, 9:104; Extract of a letter from Dr. Price, January 26, 1787, *Carlisle Gazette*, June 6, 1787; *New York Daily Advertiser*, February 23, 1787; Madison to Edmund Pendleton, February 24, 1787, in *Madison Papers*, 9:294–96.

30. Report in *Freeman's Journal* (Philadelphia), January 12, 1785. See also Madison to Jefferson, January 9, 1785, in *Madison Papers*, 8:232.

31. Jefferson to Stuart, January 25, 1786, in *Jefferson Papers*, 9:218.

32. Cooke, ed., *Federalist Papers*, no. 10, 63–64; Douglass G. Adair, "'That Politics May Be Reduced to a Science': David Hume, James Madison, and the Tenth Federalist," reprinted in Trevor Colbourn, ed., *Fame and the Founding Fathers: Essays by Douglass Adair* (New York, 1974), 93–106.

33. See the discussion in Cecelia Kenyon, "Men of Little Faith: The Anti-Federalists on the Nature of Representative Government," reprinted in Jack P. Greene, ed., *The Reinterpretation of the American Revolution* (New York, 1968), 526–66, at 529–33.

34. The ease with which one threat could be substituted for, and even identified with, another is apparent in contemporary rhetoric. See, e.g., "Harrington's" promise in *Carlisle Gazette*, July 4, 1787, that a strong central government would offer security and relief to those "who have suffered under aristocratic or democratic juntos."

35. Extracts of an address of the Western Inhabitants to Congress (1785), Papers of the Continental Congress (hereafter PCC) (National Archives, Washington, D.C.), 48:289; speech in Frankland Assembly (August 1785), *New York Gazetteer*, January 24, 1786.

36. Wood, *Creation of the Republic*, 409–13, passim.

37. Arthur Campbell to Edmiston, August 26, 1785, in *Virginia State Papers*, 4:100–101.

38. Campbell to Madison, October 28, 1785, in *Madison Papers*, 8:383.

39. Charles Cummings to President of Congress, April 7, 1785, PCC 48:297.

40. Arthur Campbell to Edmiston, August 26, 1785, in *Virginia State Papers*, 4:100–101; Westerners' Association (June 1785), PCC 48:287; "Impartialis Secundus," *Falmouth Gazette*, June 11, 1785.

41. *Falmouth Gazette*, April 7, 1786; Report of Second Separation Convention, January 4–5, 1786, ibid., January 7, 1786. New states would relieve the old states of some of the burden of the national debt (Campbell to Arthur Lee, October 18, 1784, in Paul Hoffman, ed., *The Lee Family Papers, 1742–1795* [microfilm ed., Charlottesville, 1966], reel 7, 411).

42. *Creation of the Republic*, 519–64, quote at 530.

43. *Cumberland Gazette*, April 7, 1786.

44. Speech of June 28, 1787, in Farrand, ed., *Records of the Convention*, 1:449. See also Noah Webster, *Sketches of American Policy* (Philadelphia, 1785), 35: "As towns and cities are, as to their general concerns, mere subjects to the State; so let the several States, as to their own police, be sovereign and independent, but as to the common concerns of all, let them be mere subjects of the federal head."

45. Petition to Virginia Assembly, late 1784 or early 1785, *Freeman's Journal*, January 12, 1785.

46. Westerners' Association (June 1785), PCC 48:287.

47. As Westel Willoughby pointed out in *The American Constitutional System* (New York, 1919), 29, Americans saw "no difficulty whatever . . . in the existence of a sovereign national state composed of constituent sovereign states."

48. "Jonathan of the Valley," from a late Boston paper, *Falmouth Gazette*, November 12, 1785.

49. Martin's Manifesto, April 25, 1785, in *North Carolina Records*, 17:440–45.

50. In a letter to Jefferson, August 25, 1785, in *Jefferson Papers*, 8:442.

51. "Inhabitant," *Kentucky Gazette*, September 8, 1787.

52. "A Friend to Massachusetts," *Falmouth Gazette*, September 17, 1785.

53. King to Elbridge Gerry, June 4, 1786, LMCC 8:380.

54. Stuart to Jefferson, October 17, 1785, in *Jefferson Papers*, 8:646.

55. "To the People of the United States," *Carlisle Gazette*, July 5, 1786.

56. Letter dated Kingston, Jamaica, July 25, 1785, *Falmouth Gazette*, September 10, 1785. For a similar analysis, see another letter, also dated Kingston, December 3, 1785, ibid., February 16, 1786.

57. Extract of a Letter from Louisville, December 4, 1786, *Cumberland Gazette*, July 19, 1787; John Campbell to Madison, dated Pittsburgh, February 21, 1787, in *Madison Papers*, 9:287–88; Capt. John Sullivan to Gardoquoi, March 1, 1787, *Kentucky Gazette*, November 10, 1787.

58. *Kentucky Gazette*, September 8, 1787.

59. September 6, October 10, 1780, JCC 17:806–8; 18:915–16.

60. Jefferson to Madison, April 25, 1784, in *Jefferson Papers*, 7:118. For the development of the ordinance, see Julian Boyd's editorial notes and the documents in ibid., 6:599–605, 607–9, 613–15; also March 15, April 19, 20, 21, 23, 1784, JCC 26:142–43, 246–52, 255–60, 274–79.

61. See, e.g., Resolutions of Franklin Assembly, August 1785, reprinted in *Boston Gazette*, February 20, 1786; and "Freelander," Justificative Memorial of the State of Frankland, June 13, 1785, *American Herald* (Boston), January 2 and 9, 1786.

62. JCC 26:278.

63. Jefferson to Madison, April 25, 1784, in *Jefferson Papers*, 7:118.

64. Madison to Jefferson, March 16, 1784, in *Madison Papers*, 8:9.

65. Franklin Assembly to Governor Martin, February 22, 1785, and Gov. John Sevier to Martin, March 22, 1785, in *North Carolina Records*, 17:601–4, 623–25.

66. *Cumberland Gazette*, November 24 and 31, 1786. Madison invoked "social Compact" theory to support Virginia's jurisdiction in Kentucky (Comments in Congress, August 27, 1782, in *Madison Papers*, 5:83).

67. "Cornplanter," *Kentucky Gazette*, September 13, 1788.

68. Madison to Lee, July 7, 1785, in *Madison Papers*, 8:314. See also Lee's reply, August 11, in ibid., 8:339.

69. Hugh Williamson believed that western Carolinians would "lose the prospect of becoming a Separate State" if North Carolina proceeded to sell its western lands. Congress would then have no reason to accept a cession; without a cession there could be no new state. Williamson to Governor Martin, September 30, 1784, LMCC 7:596–97.

70. October 7, 1785, JCC 29:810–12; PCC 36, 4:53–55.

71. In a letter to Governor Henry, November 7, 1785, LMCC 8:250.

72. "Jefferson, the Ordinance of 1784, and the Origins of the American Territorial System," *William and Mary Quarterly*, 3d ser., 29 (1972):231–62, quote at 260.

73. Answers to Démeunier's First Queries, January 24, 1786, in *Jefferson Papers*, 10:14 (emphasis mine). See also Answers to Additional Queries, January–February, 1786, in ibid., 10:27–28.

74. JCC 26:277–78. This clause was substituted for one that required nine states to "agree to such admission, according to the reservation of the eleventh of the Articles of Confederation." Jefferson in his Answers to Démeunier, cited in note 73 above, suggested that the eleventh article, providing for the admission of Canada or any other former British colony, did not apply. Instead, new state admission came under the thirteenth article, stipulating that all state legislatures agree to any alteration of the Confederation.

75. Answers to Démeunier, in *Jefferson Papers*, 10:14.

76. Jefferson to Lee, July 12, 1785, in ibid., 8:287.

77. In a letter to David Hartley, September 5, 1785, ibid., 8:483.

78. Dane to Samuel Phillips, January 20, 1786, Dane Manuscripts.

79. Jefferson to Madison, April 25, 1784, in *Jefferson Papers*, 7:118.

80. Peter Onuf, "Toward Federalism: Virginia, Congress, and the Western Lands," *William and Mary Quarterly*, 3d ser. 39 (1977):353–74; Peter S. Onuf, "Sovereignty and Territory: Claims Conflict in the Old Northwest and the Origins of the American Federal Republic" (Ph.D. diss., Johns Hopkins University, 1973).

81. Jefferson was thus characterized in an Extract of a Letter from a Gentleman in Frankland to his Friend in Virginia, August 17, 1785, reprinted in *The Times* (London), December 31, 1785.

82. May 20, 1785, JCC 28:375–81. For a brief discussion, see Francis S. Philbrick, *The Rise of the West, 1754–1830* (New York, 1965), 120–33.

83. Pickering to Gerry, March 1, 1785, in Charles H. King, ed., *The Life and Correspondence of Rufus King*, 9 vols. (New York, 1894–1900), 1:72–73.

84. Howell to Jonathan Arnold, February 21, 1784, in William R. Staples, ed., *Rhode Island in the Continental Congress* (Providence, 1870), 480; Berkhofer, "Origins of the Territorial System," 255. John Fitch published a map of the western country, "generally distinguished by the *Ten New States*," *New York Daily Advertiser*, September 28, 1785.

85. See, e.g., Arthur Campbell to Arthur Lee, *Lee Family Microfilms*, reel 7, 411.

86. The characterization is by Richard Henry Lee in a letter to William Lee, July 30, 1787, *LMCC* 8:629–30. See Robert F. Berkhofer, Jr., "The Northwest Ordinance and the Principle of Territorial Evolution," in John Porter Bloom, ed., *The American Territorial System* (Athens, Ohio, 1973), 45–55.

87. Franklin Assembly to Governor Martin, February 22, 1785; Governor Sevier to Governor Richard Caswell, May 14, 1785, in *North Carolina Records*, 17:601–4, 446–49.

88. Monroe to Jefferson, June 16, 1785, *LMCC* 8:144.

89. For discussions of constitutional and political aspects of the ordinance, see Francis Philbrick, *The Laws of the Illinois Territory, 1809–1818* (Illinois State Historical Society *Collections*, 25, Springfield, 1950), introduction; Arthur Bestor, "Constitutionalism and the Settlement of the West: The Attainment of Consensus, 1754–1784," in Bloom, *American Territorial System*, 13–44; and Jack Ericson Eblen, *The First and Second United States Empires: Governors and Territorial Government, 1784–1912* (Pittsburgh, 1968), 17–51.

90. July 7, 1786, *JCC* 30:390–94; Secretary of Congress to Governor Henry, July 11, *LMCC* 8:403. The Northwest Ordinance, adopted July 13, 1787, would not become operative until "Virginia shall alter her act of cession" (*JCC* 32:319).

91. Monroe to Jefferson, January 19 and May 11, 1786, *LMCC* 8:285–86, 359–60; Committee Reports, March 24 and May 10, 1786, *JCC* 30:13–35, 251–55. A deleted paragraph in the motion of July 7, calling for revision of the Virginia cession, cited in note 90 above, summarizes this argument (*PCC* 30:569).

92. Monroe to Henry, August 12, 1786, in *Life of Henry*, 2:296–97.

93. Monroe to Jefferson, July 16, 1786, *LMCC* 8:404.

94. Jefferson to Madison, December 16, 1786, in *Jefferson Papers*, 10:603. See also Jefferson to Monroe, July 9, 1786, in ibid., 10:112–13.

95. Delegates to Gov. Edmund Randolph, November 3, 1787, in *Madison Papers*, 10:238.

96. Carrington to Jefferson, October 23, 1787, in *Jefferson Papers*, 12:256.

97. John Campbell to Madison, February 21, 1787, in *Madison Papers*, 9:287–88; Samuel Otis to Theodore Sedgwick, June 6, 1788, Sedgwick Papers (Massachusetts Historical Society, Boston), A148. Westerners frequently alluded to the possibility. See, e.g., Brown to Madison, June 7, 1788, in *Madison Papers*, 11:88–90.

98. Dane to Rufus King, July 16, 1787, *LMCC* 8:621–22. See also William Wetmore to a Massachusetts delegate(?), May 9, 1787, Wetmore Family Papers (Yale University Library, New Haven): "are you likely to lose ye whole western territory, by not proceeding with proper vigour . . .?"

99. Lynd, "Compromise of 1787," *Class Conflict and the Constitution*, 210.

100. Richard Henry Lee to Washington, July 15, 1787, *LMCC* 8:620.

101. Carrington to Jefferson, October 23, 1787, in *Jefferson Papers*, 12:256. For the use of the word "colonial" in reference to the territories, see Monroe to John Jay, April 20, 1786, *LMCC* 8:342, and Monroe to Jefferson, May 11, 1786, in *Jefferson Papers*, 9:510–11.

102. Dane to King, July 16, 1787, *LMCC* 8:621–22.

103. Richard Henry Lee to Washington, July 15, 1787, *LMCC* 8:620.

104. For the text of the ordinance, see *JCC* 32:334–43.

105. Grayson to Monroe, August 8, 1787, *LMCC* 8:631–32. Compare the

Monroe committee report of July 13, 1786, with the report of the new committee, September 19, 1786, and the adopted ordinance, *JCC* 30:402–6; 31:669–72.

106. Richard Henry Lee to William Lee, July 30, 1787, *LMCC* 8:629–30.

107. See the discussion in Lynd, "Compromise of 1787."

108. Carrington to Jefferson, October 23, 1787, in *Jefferson Papers*, 12:256.

109. May 10, 1787, *JCC* 32:283.

110. Madison's speech, in *Records of the Convention*, 1:446–49. Madison saw that sectional conflict was the true obstacle "to *an augmentation of the federal authority*" (Madison to Jefferson, August 12, 1786, in *Madison Papers*, 9:97). As he wrote George Nicholas, May 17, 1788 (ibid., 9:45), the strengthening of the central government was essential to overcoming the centrifugal force of sectionalism, and to binding "together the Western and Atlantic States."

111. Lynd, "Compromise of 1787."

112. Wood, *Creation of the Republic*, 524ff.

113. Historians have been puzzled by the discontinuity between the debates at Philadelphia and the subsequent ratification debates in the states. Cecelia Kenyon wrote in "Men of Little Faith," 523n: "Curiously enough, the Big-Little State fight, which almost broke up the Convention, played very little part in the ratification debates."

CHAPTER 8: CONSTITUTIONAL CRISIS

1. For a recent review of the literature, see James H. Hutson, "Country, Court, and Constitution: Antifederalism and the Historians," *William and Mary Quarterly*, 3d ser., 38 (1981): 337–68. For a recent, comprehensive treatment of Antifederalist thought, see Herbert J. Storing, *What the Anti-Federalists Were* For, vol. 1 of *The Complete Anti-Federalist*, 7 vols. (Chicago, 1981). On Antifederalist agreement about the need for some kind of "Complex Government," see Storing's discussion in ibid., 53–63. The authoritative editions of Antifederalist writings collected in vols. 2–6 were not available when the present volume was being written. See also the seminal essay by Cecelia Kenyon, "Men of Little Faith: The Anti-Federalists on the Nature of Representative Government," *William and Mary Quarterly*, 3d ser., 12 (1955): 3–43. On the "Federalist Persuasion," see Gordon S. Wood, *The Creation of the American Republic, 1776–1787* (Chapel Hill, 1969), 519–64. The quote is from The Dissent of the Minority of the Pennsylvania Convention, *Pennsylvania Packet*, December 18, 1787, in Merrill Jensen et al., eds., *The Documentary History of the Ratification of the Constitution*, 4 vols. to date (Madison, 1976–   ), 2:617–40, at 625.

2. King, speech of June 19, 1787, in *Notes of Debates in the Federal Convention of 1787 Reported by James Madison*, intro. by Adrienne Koch (Athens, Ohio, 1966; reprint of C. C. Tansill ed., Washington, D.C., 1927), 152.

3. Carrington to Madison, June 13, 1787, in William T. Hutchinson et al., eds., *The Papers of James Madison*, 13 vols. to date (Chicago and Charlottesville, 1962–   ), 10:52–53.

4. Speech of June 6, 1788, in Virginia Convention, ibid., 12:85. The limits of political possibility are emphasized in John P. Roche, "The Founding Fathers: A Reform Caucus in Action," *American Political Science Review* 55 (1961):799–816.

5. For a recent account, see David P. Szatmary, *Shays' Rebellion: The Making of an Agrarian Insurrection* (Amherst, 1980). Also Robert J. Taylor, *Western Massa-*

chusetts in the Revolution (Providence, 1954), 103–67. Robert Feer, "Shays's Rebellion and the Constitution: A Study in Causation," *New England Quarterly* 42 (1969): 388–410, minimizes the impact of the insurrection on contemporary thought. But see also William Wiecek, *The Guarantee Clause of the United States Constitution* (Ithaca, 1972), and Frederick W. Marks III, *Independence on Trial: Foreign Affairs and the Making of the Constitution* (Baton Rouge, 1973).

6. Pettit to Franklin, October 18, 1786, in Edmund Cody Burnett, ed., *Letters of the Members of the Continental Congress* (hereafter *LMCC*), 8 vols. (Washington, D.C., 1921–36), 8:487–88.

7. Henry Muhlenberg Journals, February 3 and March 2, 1787, cited in Szatmary, *Shays' Rebellion*, 126.

8. Forrest to Jefferson, December 11, 1787, in Julian P. Boyd, ed., *The Papers of Thomas Jefferson*, 20 vols. to date (Princeton, 1950–   ), 12:416–17.

9. Jefferson to Madison, January 30, 1787, in ibid., 11:93.

10. Adams to Jefferson, dated London, November 30, 1786, in Lester J. Cappon, ed., *The Adams-Jefferson Letters . . .* , 2 vols. (Chapel Hill, 1959), 1:156.

11. Wood, *Creation of the Republic*, 319–28; J. R. Pole, *Political Representation in England and the Origins of the American Republic* (New York, 1966; paperback ed., Berkeley, Calif., 1971), 238–39.

12. Madison to Philip Mazzei, October 8, 1788, in *Madison Papers*, 11:278–79.

13. Speech of June 20, 1788, in Jonathan Elliot, ed., *The Debates in the Several State Conventions on the Adoption of the Federal Constitution*, 5 vols. (Philadelphia, 1876), 2:223–24.

14. Speech of June 29, 1787, in *Madison's Notes*, 214.

15. Adams to John Jay, May 8, 1787, in *Documentary History of the Constitution of the United States*, 5 vols. (Washington, D.C., 1901–5), 5:137.

16. Timothy Pickering to George Clymer, November 1, 1787, in Julian P. Boyd and Robert J. Taylor, eds., *The Susquehannah Company Papers*, 11 vols. (Wilkes-Barre and Ithaca, 1930–71), 9:255–60.

17. Randolph, speech of June 16, 1787, in *Madison's Notes*, 129.

18. Madison to Edmund Pendleton, February 21, 1788, in ibid., 10:532.

19. "A Plain Citizen," *Independent Gazetteer* (Philadelphia), November 22, 1787, in Jensen, ed., *History of Ratification*, 2:289–92.

20. See the discussion in J. G. A. Pocock, *The Machiavellian Moment: Florentine Political Thought and the Atlantic Republican Tradition* (Princeton, 1975), 75–80.

21. "Philadelphiensis" XI, *Independent Gazetteer*, March 8, 1788, in Cecelia Kenyon, ed., *The Antifederalists* (Indianapolis, 1966), 79–85. See also Louise B. Dunbar, *A Study of "Monarchical" Tendencies in the United States, from 1776 to 1801* (Urbana, Ill., 1922).

22. [Noah Webster], *An Examination into the Leading Principles of the Federal Constitution* (Philadelphia, October 10, 1787), 52.

23. "Landholder" (Oliver Ellsworth) V, *Connecticut Courant*, December 3, 1787, in Jensen, ed., *History of Ratification*, 3:482. See also William R. Davie's speech in the North Carolina Convention, July 24, 1788, in Elliot, ed., *Debates*, 4:20.

24. Josiah Smith speech, Massachusetts Convention, January 25, 1788, in Elliot, ed., *Debates*, 2:102–3; see also Nathan Dane to Rufus King, August 17, 1786, Wetmore Family Papers (Yale University Library, New Haven).

25. Item dated October 6, 1787, *Pennsylvania Gazette*, October 12, cited in

James E. Brady, "Wyoming: A Study of John Franklin and the Connecticut Movement into Pennsylvania" (Ph.D. diss., Syracuse University, 1973), 257.

26. "Landholder" V, in Jensen, ed., *History of Ratification*, 3:482.

27. Wilson, speech in Pennsylvania Convention, December 11, 1787, in ibid., 2:574–85, at 577.

28. July 24, 1788, in Elliot, ed., *Debates*, 4:20.

29. Henry Lee to Madison, October 19, 1786, in *Madison Papers*, 9:144.

30. Cited in note 7, above.

31. Parsons to Henry Knox, November 6, 1786, Knox Papers (Massachusetts Historical Society, Boston), XIX.

32. Lincoln to Clinton, February 21, 1787, in *Bowdoin and Temple Papers*, 2 vols. (Boston, 1897–1906), 2:149–50.

33. Lee to Madison, October 25, 1786, in *Madison Papers*, 11:145.

34. Caleb Strong to Nathan Dane, March 7, 1787, Wetmore Papers; James Bowdoin to Rufus King and Dane, March 11, 1787, in *Bowdoin-Temple Papers*, 2:169–70.

35. Timothy Hosmer to John Paul Schott, February 2, 1787, in *Susquehannah Papers*, 9:21–22; Pickering to Clymer, November 1, 1787, in ibid., 9:255–60. See the discussion in Chapter 3, above.

36. On the ephemerality of state loyalties among frontier people, see Benjamin Franklin's speech, June 11, 1787, in *Madison's Notes*, 101, and the discussion in Chapter 2, above.

37. Edmund Randolph's speech, May 29, 1787, McHenry notes, in Max Farrand, ed., *The Records of the Federal Convention of 1787*, 4 vols. (New Haven, 1911–37), 1:26.

38. George Washington to Madison, November 5, 1786, in *Documentary History*, 5:33–35.

39. Noah Webster, *Examination into the Leading Principles*, 41. For a similar statement, see Hugh Henry Brackenridge speech, Pennsylvania Convention, September 28, 1787, in Jensen, ed., *History of Ratification*, 2:93.

40. "Aristides" (Alexander Contee Hanson), *Remarks on the Proposed Plan of a Federal Government* (Annapolis, January 1, 1788), 33. See also Edmund Randolph, *Letter on the Federal Constitution* (Richmond, October 10, 1787), reprinted in Paul Leicester Ford, ed., *Pamphlets on the Constitution of the United States* (Brooklyn, 1888), 259–76, at 264.

41. November 14, 1787, in Harold C. Syrett, ed., *The Papers of Alexander Hamilton*, 26 vols. (New York, 1961–79), 4:309–17, at 317. See also Madison's speech, June 29, 1787, in *Madison's Notes*, 214–15.

42. Randolph, speech in Virginia Convention, June 24, 1788, in Elliot, ed., *Debates*, 3:603.

43. John Jay, *An Address to the People of the State of New York* (New York, 1788), 16. Gunning Bedford warned that the small states "will find some foreign ally" if the large states dissolved the union, speech of June 30, 1787, in *Madison's Notes*, 230.

44. Ellsworth, speech in Connecticut Convention, January 4, 1788, in Jensen, ed., *History of Ratification*, 3:541–45.

45. "Landholder" (Ellsworth) X, *Connecticut Courant*, March 3, 1788.

46. Hamilton speech, New York Convention, June 20, 1788, in Elliot, ed., *Debates*, 2:232. See also Robert R. Livingston speech, New York Convention, June 19, 1788, in ibid., 212.

47. Gen. Charles C. Pinckney speech, South Carolina Convention, Janu-

ary 17, 1788, in ibid., 4:283–84. See also David Ramsay, *An Address to the Freemen of South Carolina* (Charleston, n.d.), reprinted in Ford, ed., *Pamphlets*, 371–80, at 373.

48. Maclaine, speech in North Carolina Convention, July 25, 1788, in Elliot, ed., *Debates*, 4:69.

49. "Aristides" (Hanson), *Remarks on the Plan*, 36.

50. "Landholder" (Ellsworth) X, *Connecticut Courant*, March 3, 1788.

51. Francis Dana speech, Massachusetts Convention, January 18, 1788, in Elliot, ed., *Debates*, 2:42–43.

52. Speech of July 5, 1787, in *Madison's Notes*, 241.

53. Speech of July 5, 1787, in ibid., 243.

54. "Landholder" IX, *Connecticut Courant*, December 31, 1787, in Jensen, ed., *History of Ratification*, 3:515. See also Knox to Washington, April 9, 1787, in *Documentary History*, 5:111–12.

55. Knox to Stephen Higginson, January 21, 1787, Knox Papers, XIX.

56. Extract of a letter from Halifax, October 10, 1786, *Carlisle Gazette* (Carlisle, Pennsylvania), November 15, 1786.

57. Ibid.; Elbridge Gerry to Rufus King, November 29, 1786, in Charles H. King, *The Life and Correspondence of Rufus King*, 6 vols. (New York, 1894–1900), 1:197; John Jay to Jefferson, December 14, 1786, in *Jefferson Papers*, 10:596. Vermonters denied the rumors (item dated Bennington, November 20, 1786, *Freeman's Journal* [Philadelphia], December 20, 1786).

58. John Campbell to Madison, February 21, 1787, in *Madison Papers*, 9:287–88. See also memoranda on Kentucky and Vermont, Sir Henry Clinton Papers (Clements Library, Ann Arbor), 228:48 and 232:11; and Madison's notes, February 19, 1787, in *Madison Papers*, 9:275–79. For the diplomatic context, see Charles R. Ritcheson, *Aftermath of Revolution: British Policy Toward the United States 1783–1795* (Dallas, 1969; paperback ed., New York, 1971).

59. Madison to Washington, March 18, 1787, in *Madison Papers*, 9:316.

60. Arthur Campbell to Madison, February 21, 1787, in ibid., 9:287–88.

61. William Grayson to Lt. Gov. Beverley Randolph, June 12, 1787, LMCC 8:609–10; Washington to Knox, January 10, 1788, in *Documentary History* 5:436–37.

62. Extract of a letter from a gentleman on the frontiers of Virginia, March 19, 1788, *Kentucky Gazette*, August 2, 1788. See Patricia Watlington, *The Partisan Spirit: Kentucky Politics, 1779–1792* (New York, 1972), 133–87.

63. Brown to James Breckinridge, August 5, 1788, Breckinridge Papers (University of Virginia Library, Charlottesville), no. 2752. I am indebted to Fredrika Teute for this citation.

64. Samuel Gordon to Nathan Denison, November 24, 1787, in *Susquehannah Papers*, 9:305. But for a denial of this rumor, see item signed by Zerah Beach, *Hudson Gazette* (Hudson, New York), November 8, 1787, in ibid., 9:260, 263.

65. *Massachusetts Centinel*, April 2, 1785, cited in Szatmary, *Shays' Rebellion*, 75; Gov. Alexander Martin's Manifesto, April 25, 1785, reprinted in Samuel C. Williams, *History of the Lost State of Franklin*, rev. ed. (New York, 1933), 67–71.

66. Carrington to Gov. Edmund Randolph, December 8, 1786, in William R. Palmer, ed., *Calendar of Virginia State Papers*, 11 vols. (Richmond, 1875–93), 4:199.

67. Knox to Gen. Samuel Parsons, November 19, 1786, Knox Papers, XIX.

68. Henry Lee to Washington, November 11, 1786, LMCC 8:505–6. See also Lee to Madison, October 19, 1786, in *Madison Papers*, 9:143–45.

69. William Hooker Smith to Pickering, May 5, 1787, in Oscar Jewell Harvey and Ernest Gray Smith, *A History of Wilkes-Barre*, 6 vols. (Wilkes-Barre, 1909–30), 3:1570.

70. The prediction was made in reference to the Wyoming Valley, item dated Philadelphia, June 19, 1786, *New York Daily Advertiser*, June 23, 1786. For a similar prediction regarding the state of Franklin, see Col. Anthony Bledsoe to Gov. Richard Caswell, March 26, 1787, in William L. Saunders, Walter Clark, and Stephen B. Weeks, eds., *Colonial and State Records of North Carolina*, 26 vols. (Raleigh, Winston, Goldsboro, and Charlotte, 1886–1914), 20:654–55.

71. E.g., see Jeremiah Wadsworth to Knox, September 23, 1787, in Jensen, ed., *History of Ratification*, 3:351.

72. Grayson to William Short, November 10, 1787, LMCC 8:679.

73. Higginson to Knox, November 25, 1787, Knox Papers, XIX.

74. According to William Shippen, Jr., in a letter to Thomas Lee Shippen, November 29, 1787, in Jensen, ed., *History of Ratification*, 2:424.

75. Carrington to Edmund Randolph, December 8, 1786, in *Virginia State Papers*, 4:195–96.

76. Knox to Washington, April 9, 1787, in *Documentary History*, 5:111–12.

77. "Letters from the Federal Farmer" I, October 8, 1787, reprinted in Ford, ed., *Pamphlets*, 279–88, at 280. See Gordon Wood, "The Authorship of the 'Letters from the Federal Farmer,'" *William and Mary Quarterly*, 3d ser., 21 (1974): 299–308.

78. Gov. John Sevier to Gov. George Mathews of Georgia, June 24, 1787, in J. G. M. Ramsey, *The Annals of Tennessee to the End of the Eighteenth Century* (Kingsport, Tenn., 1926), 390–91.

79. Hosmer to Schott, February 2, 1787, in *Susquehannah Papers*, 9:21–22.

80. Speech at Portland Convention, January 31, 1787, in Massachusetts Historical Society, *Collections*, ser. 1, 4 (1795): 33.

81. North to Knox, February 19, 1787, Knox Papers, XIX.

82. "Letter from New York," *Connecticut Journal*, October 24 and 31, 1787, in Jensen, ed., *History of Ratification*, 3:380–92, at 386.

83. Item dated Philadelphia, August 29, 1787, *Connecticut Courant*, September 10, 1787, in *Susquehannah Papers*, 9:188.

84. Pickering to Clymer, November 1, 1787, in ibid., 9:256–57.

85. Madison, speech in Virginia Convention, June 14, 1788, in Elliot, ed., *Debates*, 3:399.

86. "Landholder" II, *Connecticut Courant*, November 12, 1787, in Jensen, ed., *History of Ratification*, 3:401.

87. *Middlesex Gazette*, October 22, 1787, in ibid., 3:394–96 (emphasis mine).

88. King, Address to the Massachusetts House, October 11, 1786, LMCC 8:481.

89. Bowdoin, speech to General Court, February 1787, in *Bowdoin-Temple Papers*, 2:159–64, at 162.

CHAPTER 9: MAKING A "MIRACLE"

1. Samuel Parsons to William Cushing, January 11, 1788, in Merrill Jensen et al., eds., *The Documentary History of the Ratification of the Constitution*, 4 vols. to date (Madison, 1976–), 3:570.

2. Martin, speech of June 20, 1787, *Notes of Debates in the Federal Convention of 1787 Reported by James Madison*, intro. by Adrienne Koch (Athens, Ohio; reprint of C. C. Tansill, ed., Washington, D.C., 1927), 159.

3. See, e.g., John Lansing speech, New York Convention, July 23, 1788, in Jonathan Elliot, ed., *The Debates in the Several State Conventions on the Adoption of the Federal Constitution*, 5 vols. (Philadelphia, 1876), 2:272–73; (Samuel Bryan) "Centinel" I, *Independent Gazetteer* (Philadelphia), October 5, 1787, in Jensen, ed., *History of Ratification*, 2:158–67, at 165; William Findley speech, Pennsylvania Convention, December 5, 1787, in ibid., 2:503; and Joseph McDowell speech, North Carolina Convention, July 28, 1788, in Elliot, ed., *Debates*, 4:124.

4. Grayson, speech of June 24, 1788, in Elliot, ed., *Debates*, 3:615.

5. Bedford, speech of June 30, 1787, in *Madison's Notes*, 229.

6. The Dissent of the Minority of the Pennsylvania Convention, *Pennsylvania Packet*, December 18, 1787, in Jensen, ed., *History of Ratification*, 2:617–40, at 627.

7. William Grayson speech, Virginia Convention, June 12, 1788, in Elliot, ed., *Debates*, 3:287.

8. Tredwell, speech in New York Convention, July 2, 1788, in ibid., 2:403.

9. Dissent of Minority, December 18, 1787, in Jensen, ed., *History of Ratification*, 2:628.

10. Robert Whitehill speech, Pennsylvania Convention, November 28, 1787, in ibid., 2:393. See also Letters of Luther Martin, II, *Maryland Journal*, March 21, 1788, reprinted in Paul Leicester Ford, ed., *Essays on the Constitution of the United States* (Brooklyn, 1892), 360–71, at 366.

11. "Agrippa" (Winthrop) II and III, *Massachusetts Gazette*, November 27 and 30, 1787.

12. "John Dewitt" to the Free Citizens of Massachusetts, I, *American Herald* (Boston), October 22, 1787.

13. "A Plebeian" (Smith), *An Address to the People of the State of New-York* (New York, 1788), 7.

14. "An Officer of the Late Continental Army," *Independent Gazetteer*, November 6, 1787, in Jensen, ed., *History of Ratification*, 2:210–16, at 211. See also Luther Martin, *The Genuine Information, Delivered to the Legislature of Maryland . . .* (Annapolis, 1788), reprinted in Max Farrand, ed., *The Records of the Federal Convention of 1787*, 4 vols. (New Haven, 1911–37), 3:172–232.

15. Martin, speech of June 20, 1787, in *Madison's Notes*, 159. See also Martin's speech of June 27, 1787, in ibid., 201.

16. Samuel Parsons to William Cushing, January 11, 1788, in Jensen, ed., *History of Ratification*, 3:570.

17. King, speech in Massachusetts Convention, January 21, 1788, in Elliot, ed., *Debates*, 2:570.

18. Luther Martin speech, June 28, 1787, in *Madison's Notes*, 203–4.

19. According to Hugh Williamson in a letter to John Gray Blount, June 3, 1788, in Edmund Cody Burnett, ed., *Letters of the Members of the Continental Congress* (hereafter *LMCC*), 8 vols. (Washington, D.C., 1921–36), 8:747. See also Patrick Henry speech, Virginia Convention, June 9, 1788, in Elliot, ed., *Debates*, 3:154.

20. Madison to Edmund Randolph, January 10, 1788, in William T. Hutchinson et al., eds., *The Papers of James Madison*, 13 vols. to date (Chicago and Charlottesville, 1962–   ), 10:354–57; Edward Carrington to Thomas Jefferson, April 24,

1788, in Julian P. Boyd, ed., *The Papers of Thomas Jefferson*, 20 vols. to date (Princeton, 1950–   ), 13:100–103; Cyrus Griffin to Thomas FitzSimons, February 18, 1788, *LMCC* 8:699–700; John Blair Smith to Madison, June 12, 1788, in *Madison Papers*, 11:119–21.

21. Martin Letters, III, *Maryland Journal*, March 25, 1788, reprinted in Ford, ed., *Essays*, 372–77, at 375.

22. Gordon S. Wood, *The Creation of the American Republic, 1776–1787* (Chapel Hill, 1969), 483–99. But see Gordon S. Wood, ed., *The Confederation and the Constitution: The Critical Issues* (Boston, 1973), introduction; and the discussion in James H. Hutson, "Country, Court, and Constitution: Antifederalism and the Historians," *William and Mary Quarterly*, 3d ser., 38 (1981): 337–68, at 351–53.

23. McKean, speech in Pennsylvania Convention, November 28, 1787, in Jensen, ed., *History of Ratification*, 2:411–20, at 415.

24. Randolph, speech in Virginia Convention, June 21, 1788, in Elliot, ed., *Debates*, 3:570–71.

25. "Agrippa" (James Winthrop) XIII, *Massachusetts Gazette*, January 14, 1788.

26. George Thatcher to Pierse Long, April 23, 1788, *LMCC* 8:726–27.

27. Davie, speech in North Carolina Convention, July 29, 1788, in Elliot, ed., *Debates*, 4:159.

28. Pelatiah Webster, *The Weakness of Brutus Exposed* (Philadelphia, 1787), 6.

29. Robert R. Livingston speech, New York Convention, June 19, 1788, in Elliot, ed., *Debates*, 2:214–15. Though James Monroe opposed the Constitution, he conceded that the central government should have "the power of laying an impost" (speech in Virginia Convention, June 10, 1788, in ibid., 3:214–15).

30. Davie, speech in North Carolina Convention, July 29, 1788, in ibid., 4:158.

31. Smith, speech in New York Convention, June 25, 1788, in ibid., 2:313.

32. Hamilton, speech in New York Convention, June 20, 1788, in ibid., 2:231.

33. Madison, speech of July 14, 1787, in *Madison's Notes*, 294.

34. Hamilton, speech in New York Convention, June 20, 1788, in Elliot, ed., *Debates*, 2:233.

35. Ellsworth, speech in Connecticut Convention, January 7, 1788, in Jensen, ed., *History of Ratification*, 3:553–54.

36. *Middlesex Gazette*, October 22, 1787, in ibid., 3:395.

37. William Samuel Johnson speech, Connecticut Convention, January 4, 1788, in ibid., 3:546.

38. "An Officer," *Independent Gazetteer*, November 6, 1787, in ibid., 2:210–11.

39. Henry, speech in Virginia Convention, June 4, 1788, in Elliot, ed., *Debates*, 3:21–22. See also Joseph Taylor speech, North Carolina Convention, July 24, 1788, in ibid., 4:23–24.

40. Hamilton, speech of June 18, 1787, in *Madison's Notes*, 129; King notes, in Farrand, ed., *Records of the Convention*, 1:303.

41. See Bernard Bailyn, *The Ordeal of Thomas Hutchinson* (Cambridge, Mass., 1974), 91–92, 223ff.

42. Wilson, speech of June 1, 1787, King notes, in Farrand, ed., *Records of the Convention*, 1:71. For an analysis of Wilson's political thought, see Geoffrey Seed, *James Wilson* (Millwood, N.Y., 1978).

43. Monroe, speech in Virginia Convention, June 10, 1788, in Elliot, ed., *Debates*, 3:215.

44. "Agrippa" (Winthrop) IV, *Massachusetts Gazette*, December 3, 1787. See Paul M. Spurlin, *Montesquieu in America, 1760–1801* (Baton Rouge, 1940).

45. Gorham, speech of August 8, 1787, in *Madison's Notes*, 410. See also William Blount to John Gray Blount, July 19, 1787, LMCC 8:623–24.

46. "Agrippa" IV, *Massachusetts Gazette*, December 3, 1787.

47. "Agrippa" XII, ibid., January 11, 1788.

48. "Agrippa" XIII, ibid., January 14, 1788.

49. Yates and Lansing to Gov. George Clinton, [January 1788], in Farrand, ed., *Records of the Convention*, 3:246.

50. "Letters from the Federal Farmer" II, October 9, 1787, reprinted in Paul Leicester Ford, ed., *Pamphlets on the Constitution of the United States* (Brooklyn, 1888), 288–93, at 290.

51. Madison's speech of June 29, 1787, Yates notes, in Farrand, ed., *Records of the Convention*, 1:476; Charles Pinckney speech, July 2, 1787, in *Madison's Notes*, 232. The middle states were frequently referred to as a distinct section, particularly in the common prediction that three separate confederacies would emerge from the ruins of the union. Madison to Edmund Pendleton, February 24, 1787, in *Madison Papers*, 9:294–97. But many observers assumed that the middle states would be drawn into the vortex of one of the other two sections. See the discussion about Pennsylvania's future alignment, North Carolina Convention, July 29, 1788, in Elliot, ed., *Debates*, 4:185–87.

52. See, for northern examples, Samuel Nasson speech, Massachusetts Convention, January 17, 1788, and (?) Neal speech, January 25, 1788, in Elliot, ed., *Debates*, 2:39, 107; "Republican Federalist" V, *Massachusetts Centinel*, January 19, 1788, reprinted in Cecelia M. Kenyon, ed., *The Antifederalists* (Indianapolis, 1966), 123–29. For southern examples, see *The Objections of the Hon. George Mason* (broadside, ca. October 1787), reprinted in Ford, ed., *Pamphlets*, 327–32; William Grayson speech in Virginia Convention, June 11, 1788, and Patrick Henry speech, June 24, 1788, in Elliot, ed., *Debates*, 3:281–82, 589–90.

53. Paterson, notes for an undelivered speech, ca. June 30, 1787, in Farrand, ed., *Records of the Convention*, 1:505–6. For a discussion of Paterson's thought, see John E. O'Connor, *William Paterson, Lawyer and Statesman, 1745–1806* (New Brunswick, N.J., 1979), 131–44.

54. Paterson, speech of June 9, 1787, in *Madison's Notes*, 95–96.

55. Brearly, speech of June 9, 1787, in ibid., 94–95.

56. Wilson, speech of June 9, Yates notes, in Farrand, ed., *Records of the Convention*, 1:183; *Madison's Notes*, 97–98.

57. Gorham, speech of July 6, 1787, in *Madison's Notes*, 246; Madison speech, June 28, 1787, in ibid., 208.

58. Butler, speech of May 31, 1787, in ibid., 41.

59. Paterson, speech of June 9, 1787, Yates notes, in Farrand, ed., *Records of the Convention*, 1:183. See also the debate of June 25–27, 1787, on whether equalization should be achieved through a "division of the large States" or "junction of the small" (*Madison's Notes*, 181–203, quote [Luther Martin] at 203).

60. Emmerich de Vattel, *The Law of Nations, or the Principles of Natural Law Applied to the Conduct . . . of Nations* (trans. of 1758 ed., Washington, D.C., 1916), 251, 3:47–49.

61. Hamilton, speech of June 19, 1787, in *Madison's Notes*, 152. "As States, he thought they ought to be abolished."

62. Gorham, speech of June 29, 1787, Yates notes, in Farrand, ed., *Records of the Convention*, 1:470–71. See also his speech of June 25, 1787, in ibid., 1:413,

and the discussion in "Federalist" VII (Hamilton), in Harold C. Syrett, ed., *The Papers of Alexander Hamilton*, 26 vols. (New York, 1961–79), 4:319–26.

63. Gorham, speech of June 29, 1787, in *Madison's Notes*, 212.

64. *Genuine Information*, reprinted in Farrand, ed., *Records of the Convention*, 3:224–25.

65. Ellsworth, speech of June 25, 1787, in *Madison's Notes*, 189–90; Roger Sherman speech, June 6, 1787, in ibid., 74–75. But Sherman conceded that "States may indeed be too small," as the case of Rhode Island demonstrated.

66. Martin, speech of July 14, 1787, in ibid., 290.

67. Martin, speech of June 28, 1787, in ibid., 203–4. The arguments were reconciled by arguing that the "present" weakness of the large states would be transformed into preponderant power under the new union, thus making equalization of the states a necessary part of any constitutional reform.

68. Jefferson to Madison, December 16, 1786, in *Jefferson Papers*, 10:603.

69. Martin, speech of June 28, 1787, Yates notes, in Farrand, ed., *Records of the Convention*, 1:454.

70. Sherman, speech of July 7, 1787, in *Madison's Notes*, 253.

71. "Agrippa" V, *Massachusetts Gazette*, December 11, 1787.

72. "Cato" (George Clinton?), *New York Journal*, October 25, 1787.

73. Speech in Connecticut Convention, January 4, 1788, in Jensen, ed., *History of Ratification*, 3:542.

74. Pinckney, speech of June 16, 1787, in *Madison's Notes*, 127.

75. Rufus King, speech of June 30, 1787, in ibid., 228. See also Wilson speech, June 30, 1787, and Gouverneur Morris speech, July 7, 1787, in ibid., 220–22, 255.

76. Gerry, speech of July 6, 1787, in ibid., 246. For a discussion of Gerry's ideas about state sovereignty, see George Athan Billias, *Elbridge Gerry: Founding Father and Republican Statesman* (New York, 1976), 172–78.

77. Wilson, speech of August 30, 1787, in *Madison's Notes*, 555. On Wilson's "intellectual inconsistency" on this point—perhaps attributable to his speculative interest in western lands—see Seed, *Wilson*, 77–79.

78. Pendleton, speech in Virginia Convention, June 12, 1788, in Elliot, ed., *Debates*, 3:301. See also Fisher Ames speech, Massachusetts Convention, January 15, 1788, in ibid., 2:10.

79. The theme is extensively developed in "Letters from the Federal Farmer" I–V, reprinted in Ford, ed., *Pamphlets*, 277–325, and in the "Brutus" (Robert Yates?) Letters reprinted in Kenyon, ed., *Antifederalists*, 323–57.

80. Hamilton, speech of June 18, 1787, in *Madison's Notes*, 133.

81. Bedford, speech of June 30, 1787, in ibid., 229.

82. Stephen Higginson to Henry Knox, February 8, 1787, Knox Papers (Massachusetts Historical Society, Boston), XIX. See also "Harrington," *Carlisle Gazette*, July 4, 1787.

83. Rush to Timothy Pickering, August 30, 1787, in L. H. Butterfield, ed., *Letters of Benjamin Rush*, 2 vols. (Princeton, 1951), 1:439–40. See also Rush's speech in Pennsylvania Convention, December 3, 1787, in Jensen, ed., *History of Ratification*, 2:457–58.

84. Wilson, speech at Pennsylvania Convention, November 24, 1787, in Jensen, ed., *History of Ratification*, 2:335–36. See also James White to Gov. Richard Caswell, November 13, 1787, LMCC 8:681–82, and David Ramsay, *An Address to the Freemen of South Carolina* (Charleston, n.d.), reprinted in Ford, ed., *Pamphlets*, 371–80, at 373.

85. Preston, Connecticut, instructions, November 24, 1787, in Jensen, ed., *History of Ratification*, 3:439. See also "Plain Truth," *Independent Gazetteer*, November 10, 1787, in ibid., 2:218–19, for an argument, based on contract premises, that state sovereignty was incompatible with union.

86. Wilson, speech at Pennsylvania Convention, December 11, 1787, in ibid., 2:555. See the discussion in Wood, *Creation of the Republic*, 519–64, esp. 536–43.

87. *The Substance of a Speech Delivered by James Wilson* (Philadelphia, 1787), in Jensen, ed., *History of Ratification*, 2:340–50, at 348–49.

88. See Archibald Maclaine speech, North Carolina Convention, July 29, 1788, in Elliot, ed., *Debates*, 4:181: "what is the sovereignty, and who is Congress? . . . Do people fear the delegation of power to themselves—to their own representatives?"

89. "A Citizen of New Haven" (Roger Sherman), *Connecticut Courant*, January 7, 1788, in Jensen, ed., *History of Ratification*, 3:527. See also "Letter from New York," *Connecticut Journal*, October 24 and 31, 1787, in ibid., 3:387.

90. Item dated New York, April 23, 1787, *Carlisle Gazette* (Carlisle, Pa.), May 9, 1787.

91. Ellsworth, speech at Connecticut Convention, January 7, 1788, in Jensen, ed., *History of Ratification*, 3:553. See also Richard Dobbs Spaight to James Iredell, August 12, 1787, in Farrand, ed., *Records of the Convention*, 3:68, and George Thatcher speech, Massachusetts Convention, February 4, 1787, in Elliot, ed., *Debates*, 2:142–43. These comments usually referred to Rhode Island's supposed intransigence.

92. "Remarks on the New Plan of Government," *State Gazette of North Carolina*, (d.?), reprinted in Ford, ed., *Essays*, 393–406, at 403.

93. Wilson, speech of June 8, in *Madison's Notes*, 90–91.

94. Randolph, speech of June 6, 1788, Virginia Convention, in Elliot, ed., *Debates*, 3:82.

95. Washington to John Jay, August 1, 1786, in John C. Fitzpatrick, ed., *The Writings of George Washington*, 39 vols. (Washington, D.C., 1931–44), 28:502.

96. See the debates on new states, June 21 and July 5, 6, 9, 11, and 14, 1787, in *Madison's Notes*, passim.

97. See the discussion in Chapter 7, above.

98. Henry, speech at Virginia Convention, June 9, 1788, in Elliot, ed., *Debates*, 3:152.

99. See the discussion of union in "Agrippa" (Winthrop) VIII, *Massachusetts Gazette*, December 25, 1787. Antifederalists who recognized this contradiction and saw that the union would have to be reorganized were reduced to equivocation. See the call for "partial consolidation" in "Federal Farmer" I, October 8, 1787, reprinted in Ford, ed., *Pamphlets*, 279–88, at 287.

100. *Pennsylvania Gazette*, October 17, 1787, in Jensen, ed., *History of Ratification*, 2:190.

101. Webster, *Weakness of Brutus*, 7.

102. Robert R. Livingston speech, New York Convention, June 19, 1788, in Elliot, ed., *Debates*, 2:211; A "Jerseyman," To the Citizens of New Jersey, *Trenton Mercury*, November 6, 1787, in Jensen, ed., *History of Ratification*, 3:150; Randolph speech, Virginia Convention, June 7, 1788, in Elliot, ed., *Debates*, 3:123 (referring to Rhode Island).

103. Wilson, speech in Pennsylvania Convention, December 4, 1787, in Jen-

sen, ed., *History of Ratification*, 2:477.

104. Langdon, speech of August 23, 1787, in *Madison's Notes*, 514.

105. William Heath, speech at Massachusetts Convention, January 30, 1788, in Elliot, ed., *Debates*, 2:121.

106. "Social Compact," *New Haven Gazette*, October 4, 1787, in Jensen, ed., *History of Ratification*, 3:357. See James Innes's reference to "our *northern brethren*" in speech at Virginia Convention, June 25, 1788, in Elliot, ed., *Debates*, 3:633.

107. "A Federal Republican," *A Review of the Constitution . . .* (Philadelphia, 1787), in Jensen, ed., *History of Ratification*, 2:305 (excerpt). See also "Letters of Brutus" XII (part 1), reprinted in Kenyon, ed., *Antifederalists*, 342–47.

108. Hamilton, speech in New York Convention, June 25, 1788, in Elliot, ed., *Debates*, 2:319–20. See also Thomas McKean speech, Pennsylvania Convention, December 10, 1787, in Jensen, ed., *History of Ratification*, 2:543.

109. Wilson, speech of December 4, 1787, in Jensen, ed., *History of Ratification*, 2:496. See also John Dickinson speech, June 7, 1787, in *Madison's Notes*, 84–85.

110. Madison, speech of June 8, 1787, in *Madison's Notes*, 89. Madison was arguing for a federal veto of state laws.

111. States were frequently compared to stars and, of course, are symbolized by them in the American flag. See *Cumberland Gazette* (Portland, Massachusetts/Maine), April 6, 1787, for a reference to "the American constellation."

112. Wilson, speech of May 31, 1787, in *Madison's Notes*, 40.

113. Speech of December 11, 1787, in Jensen, ed., *History of Ratification*, 2:580.

114. George Lee Turberville to Madison, April 16, 1788, in *Madison Papers*, 11:24. See also Increase Sumner speech, Massachusetts Convention, January 22, 1788, in Elliot, ed., *Debates*, 2:64.

115. William Davie speech, North Carolina Convention, July 25, 1788, in Elliot, ed., *Debates*, 4:58.

116. Wolcott, speech in Connecticut Convention, January 9, 1788, in Jensen, ed., *History of Ratification*, 3:557.

117. Law, speech of January 9, 1788, in ibid., 3:559.

118. Page to Jefferson, March 7, 1788, in *Jefferson Papers*, 12:651. Jefferson's proposal for the new union was equally "complicated": "I wish to see our states made one as to all foreign, and several as to all domestic matters, a peaceable mode of compulsion over the states given to Congress, and the powers of this body divided. . . ." Letter to Joseph Jones, August 14, 1787, in ibid., 12:34.

119. John Dickinson, *The Letters of Fabius* (Wilmington, 1797), 63.

120. *Weakness of Brutus*, 9. See also Archibald Maclaine speech, North Carolina Convention, July 24, 1788, in Elliot, ed., *Debates*, 4:24–25.

121. *Carlisle Gazette*, November 14, 1787, in Jensen, ed., *History of Ratification*, 2:259.

122. Livingston, speech in New York Convention, June 19, 1788, in Elliot, ed., *Debates*, 2:210.

123. Speech of June 25, 1787, in *Madison's Notes*, 189–90.

124. Corbin, speech of June 7, 1788, in Elliot, ed., *Debates*, 3:107.

125. Gorham, speech of July 23, 1787, in *Madison's Notes*, 354.

126. "Aristides" (Hanson), *Remarks on the Proposed Plan* (Annapolis, January 1, 1788), 33.

127. Heath, speech of January 30, 1788, in Elliot, ed., *Debates*, 2:120.

128. Dickinson, *Letters of Fabius*, 62.

129. The best discussion of the peace plan tradition is in F. H. Hinsley, *Power and the Pursuit of Peace* (Cambridge, Eng., 1963). The most frequently cited plan was *The Great Design of Henry IV, from the Memoirs of the Duke of Sully*, ed. Edward Everett Hale, intro. by Edwin D. Mead (Boston, 1909). See also James Brown Scott, *The United States of America: A Study in International Organization* (New York, 1920).

130. Wilson, *Substance of a Speech*, in Jensen, ed., *History of Ratification*, 2:342.

131. Hanson, *Remarks on the Proposed Plan*, 33.

132. Nicholas, speech in Virginia Convention, June 13, 1788, in Elliot, ed., *Debates*, 3:358–59.

133. Dickinson, *Letters of Fabius*, 60. See the discussion on the origins of this line of reasoning in Chapter 7, above.

134. Smith, speech in New York Convention, July 1, 1788, in Elliot, ed., *Debates*, 2:382.

135. Clymer, speech in Pennsylvania House, September 28, 1787, in Jensen, ed., *History of Ratification*, 2:76.

136. Wilson, speech in Pennsylvania Convention, December 4, 1787, in ibid., 477.

137. George Nicholas, speech in Virginia Convention, June 6, 1788, in Elliot, ed., *Debates*, 3:102.

138. Wilson, speech in Pennsylvania Convention, December 4, 1787, in Jensen, ed., *History of Ratification*, 2:477.

139. Wilson speech in Pennsylvania Convention, December 11, 1787, in ibid., 2:560. Nathaniel Chipman later wrote (*Sketches of the Principles of Government* [Rutland, Vt., 1793], 278): "Solely an impression of the efficiency of the federal government, favored perhaps, by its national magnitude and importance, added, at the instant of organization, a degree of energy to the state governments, and put an end to those factions and turbulent commotions, which made some of them tremble for their political existence."

140. See Daniel J. Boorstin, *The Genius of American Politics* (Chicago, 1953); and Lance Banning, "Republican Ideology and the Triumph of the Constitution, 1789–1793," *William and Mary Quarterly*, 3d ser., 31 (1974): 167–88. For another discussion of the "Crisis of Legitimacy," with an emphasis on Washington's role as a "charismatic leader," see Seymour Martin Lipset, *The First New Nation: The United States in Historical and Comparative Perspective* (New York, 1963).

141. Pierce to St. George Tucker, September 28, 1787, in Farrand, ed., *Records of the Convention*, 3:100–101.

142. Madison to Philip Mazzei, October 8, 1788, in *Madison Papers*, 11:278–79.

143. Davie, speech in North Carolina Convention, July 24, 1788, in Elliot, ed., *Debates*, 4:22–23.

144. Pinckney, letter dated May 2, 1788, *State Gazette of South Carolina*, May 5, reprinted in Ford, ed., *Essays*, 411–13.

145. Madison to Jefferson, October 24, 1787, in *Madison Papers*, 10:205–20, at 208.

146. Washington to Lafayette, February 7, 1788, in Farrand, ed., *Records of the Convention*, 3:270.

147. Wilson, "Address to a Meeting," October 6, 1787, in ibid., 3:101–2.

148. "One of the People," *Pennsylvania Gazette*, October 17, 1787, in Jensen, ed., *History of Ratification*, 2:191.

149. "Aristides" (Hanson), *Remarks on the Proposed Plan*, 8.

150. Pinckney, letter in *State Gazette of South Carolina*, May 5, 1788, reprinted in Ford, ed., *Pamphlets*, 217–57, at 223–24, 255.

151. See the discussions in Garry Wills, *Explaining America: The Federalist* (Garden City, N.Y., 1981), esp. 185–92, and J. G. A. Pocock, *The Machiavellian Moment: Florentine Political Thought and the Atlantic Republican Tradition* (Princeton, 1975), 462ff.

Index

Adams, John: on imperial relationship, 26; on popular loyalty to union, 176; on role of Congress, 13–14; on Shays's Rebellion, 175; (*Thoughts on Government*), on central government, 12–13

Adams, Samuel, on Vermont independence, 115

Allen, Ethan: expedition against Yorkers, 143–44; on New York claims in Vermont, 132, 133; on Vermont and union, 136; on Vermont's neutrality, 135; on Vermont's use of force, 143; and Wyoming, 62, 69–70, 178

Allen, Ira, on procongressional feeling in Vermont, 136

American citizenship: Pennsylvania dissidents' claims to, 63, 72–73; separatists' claims to, 38, 157, 179; and state citizenship, 64–66; volitional idea of, 24

Antifederalists: on aristocracy, 189; on civil war, 176; conception of union, 187, 201, 208; on "critical period," 187–88; and disunion, 188, 206; fear of power, 207; on interstate conflict, 174, 186–89; prefer small states, 196; on size of United States, 192–94

Articles of Confederation: Article IX, 6, 19–20; Article IX and Vermont, 124; Article IX and Virginia, 90, 100 (*see also Connecticut* v. *Pennsylvania*); inadequacy of, 179 passim (*see also* "critical period"); and interstate conflict, 10–11, 17; and new states, 164, 165; ratification of, 3, 7, 12, 88, 91; and territorial guarantees, 14–15, 88, 130

Bailyn, Bernard, xiv

Bayley, Jacob: on collapse of state authority, 140; recommends use of force against Vermont, 138

Beard, Charles (*Economic Interpretation of the Constitution*), xiii

Beatty, John, introduces motion against guaranteeing Virginia claims, 100

Bedford, Gunning: advocates consolidation, 199; opposes Virginia Plan, 187

Benson, Egbert, reports divisions in New York on Vermont, 119

Berkhofer, Robert, Jr., on Territorial Government Ordinance (1784), 164

Bland, Theodorick: proposes Virginia cession compromise, 99; supports Vermont, 116

boundaries: importance of defining, 36, 131, 153, 154; and popular loyalties, 58; and state equality, 154, 194; and Territorial Government Ordinance (1784), 43–44, 163–65, 167. *See also* individual states

Bowdoin, James, on danger of civil war, 185

Bradley, Stephen R., predicts British victory, 136

Braxton, Carter (*Address to the Convention of Virginia*), on interstate conflict, 8

Brearly, David, on redrafting boundaries to achieve state equality, 194

British Constitution, American interpretation of, 25–26

British Empire, place of colonies in, 25–27. *See also* Great Britain